A CENTENNIAL BOOK

One hundred books
published between 1990 and 1995
bear this special imprint of
the University of California Press.
We have chosen each Centennial Book
as an example of the Press's finest
publishing and bookmaking traditions
as we celebrate the beginning of
our second century.

UNIVERSITY OF CALIFORNIA PRESS

Founded in 1893

DEAREST BELOVED

The New Historicism: Studies in Cultural Poetics
Stephen Greenblatt, General Editor

Dearest
Beloved

*The Hawthornes
and the Making
of the Middle-Class Family*

T. WALTER HERBERT

UNIVERSITY OF CALIFORNIA PRESS

Berkeley   Los Angeles   Oxford

University of California Press
Berkeley and Los Angeles, California

University of California Press, Ltd.
Oxford, England

Library of Congress Cataloging-in-Publication Data
Herbert, T. Walter (Thomas Walter), 1938–
     Dearest beloved: the Hawthornes and the making of the middle-class family /
T. Walter Herbert.
          p.   cm. — (The New historicism: 24)
     "A Centennial book"—p.
     Includes bibliographical references and index.
     ISBN 0-520-07587-0 (alk. paper)
     1. Hawthorne, Nathaniel, 1804–1864—Marriage.   2. Hawthorne,
Sophia Peabody, 1809–1871—Marriage.   3. Domestic fiction, American—
History and criticism.   4. Novelists, American—19th century
Biography.   5. Authors' wives—United States—Biography.
6. Psychoanalysis and literature.   7. Middle classes in literature.
8. Marriage in literature.   9. Family in literature.   10. Hawthorne
family.   I. Title.   II. Series.
PS1882.H47   1993
813'.3—dc20   92-6800
[B]

Printed in the United States of America
9 8 7 6 5 4 3 2 1

For my son, Tom

Contents

List of Illustrations

Note on Abbreviations

Hawthorne's works published in the Centenary Edition (ed. William Charvat, Roy Harvey Pearce, and Claude M. Simpson, 18 vols. to date [Columbus: Ohio State University Press, 1962–]) are cited parenthetically in the text by volume, as follows:

CE 1   *The Scarlet Letter*
CE 2   *The House of the Seven Gables*
CE 3   *The Blithedale Romance and Fanshawe*
CE 4   *The Marble Faun; or, the Romance of Monte Beni*
CE 6   *True Stories from History and Biography*
CE 7   *A Wonder Book and Tanglewood Tales*
CE 8   *The American Notebooks*
CE 10   *Mosses from an Old Manse*
CE 11   *The Snow Image and Uncollected Tales*
CE 12   *The American Claimant Manuscripts*
CE 13   *The Elixir of Life Manuscripts*
CE 14   *The French and Italian Notebooks*
CE 15   *The Letters, 1813–1843*
CE 16   *The Letters, 1843–1853*
CE 17   *The Letters, 1853–1856*
CE 18   *The Letters, 1857–1864*

For other works frequently cited in the text I have adopted the following abbreviations:

Cuba	Sophia Peabody [Hawthorne], *The Cuba Journal*
English	Nathaniel Hawthorne, *The English Notebooks*
Family Notebook	Journal kept jointly by Nathaniel and Sophia Hawthorne, with entries by the children, catalogued as Journal Dated 1842–1854, MA 569 and 580, Pierpont Morgan Library. Cited by date of entry
Italy	Sophia Hawthorne, six volumes of manuscript journals kept in Italy from 14 February to 21 October 1858. Berg Collection, New York Public Library. Cited by date of entry
NHW	Julian Hawthorne, *Nathaniel Hawthorne and His Wife,* 2 vols.

Shortened in-text citations of manuscript sources are explained in the notes for the chapters in which they occur.

Introduction

Nathaniel and Sophia began to keep a journal together as newlyweds at the Old Manse in Concord. They wrote about the joys and anguish of sex, about hikes and boating and reading, about Sophia cleaning wild berries and Nathaniel chopping wood. Over the next decade, from 1842 to 1852, they filled two substantial notebooks. As the children arrived—Una, Julian, and Rose—the couple took an absorbing interest in watching them grow up and play together and recorded success in schooling and discipline as well as recurring perplexities. They sought to "daguerreotype . . . the hours," as Sophia put it (Family Notebook, 7 September 1852): Una taking her first steps, Julian knocking over a house of blocks, Rose demanding her breakfast. The Hawthornes obeyed an impulse to capture and preserve the ordinary scenes of family life, an enterprise for which photography and home videos now provide a readier technology.

Nathaniel's contributions to this joint effort are published as sections 6 and 7 of *The American Notebooks,* with no trace remaining of Sophia's entries. The notebooks have become a record of her husband's singular genius, and their original shape and meaning have been obliterated. Yet Sophia herself made these excisions in the first instance, and she had good reasons for doing so.[1]

In accordance with the domestic ideal of family life that became dominant in the early nineteenth century, the Hawthornes' marriage took shape in private, their intimate sphere meant to remain secluded from public view. When the family was in Florence, years later, Nathaniel visited the home of Michelangelo, so as to gain a truer impression of this giant of Renaissance art by examining his "closest little personalities," his sword, his walking sticks, and his old slippers (CE 14:352). The personal substance of the Hawthornes' lives—and of the emerging domestic culture they exemplify— is likewise best revealed where the mess and tumult of daily life have left their mark.

Consider, for example, the Hawthorne children's scribbles and drawings, historical precursors of the free-form art that now decorates refrigerator doors and breakfast nooks across middle-class America (Fig. 1). Here are wild vigorous scrawlings in pencil and blotches of spilled ink through which move squiggles, on the scale of cursive writing, which occasionally become readable words: "dearest beloved I love thee best mamma" runs horizontally until it meets the edge of the page and then turns down. Elsewhere an intelligible fragment momentarily appears and then dissolves back into the chaos: "I am going to write to . . ."

Floating in this yeast of scribbles are large enigmatic figures, all looking tranquilly to the left. One seems to be a man, and another is certainly a woman; between them a figure like a court jester in a split cap appears to stand on the back of a cow. All three seem quietly intent on something that is off the page.

These ghostly figures symbolize an enigma that makes itself felt in the fluent sentences of mother and father. They invoke what is unwritable because it cannot become fully conscious, matters that lie beyond the scope of explicit speech because the reigning patterns of awareness exclude them.

We find here an image for the Hawthornes' story as a whole, as it will unfold in the following pages. Like other cultural formations, the domestic ideal of family life was established and sustained at a substantial cost, and it was accompanied by characteristic dilemmas and torments. For the Hawthornes as for other families, however, such chronic miseries inhabited a shadowy world of seeming unreality when they were visible at all. Nathaniel sharpened his "catlike faculty of seeing in the dark"—in Henry James's consummate phrase ("Hawthorne," 502)—even as he lived in the dark, together with Sophia and their children.

In exploring aspects of his family life that have remained in the shadows, we will encounter an unfamiliar Hawthorne, whom I have chosen to call "Nathaniel." Sophia referred to him as "Mr. Hawthorne" or "my lord." He was "Papa" to his children and "Hawthorne" to his friends. "Hawthorne"

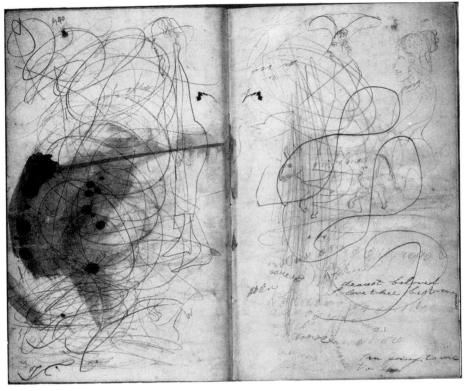

Fig. 1.   Hawthorne children's drawings and scribbles

is the name he gave himself, altering the "Hathorne" of his father's family, and "Hawthorne" is the name he made famous. It is a departure from established usage, then and now, to call him "Nathaniel," placing him on equal footing with "Sophia."

It has long been a truism that Hawthorne's fiction, with its dark preoccupations, contrasts with the character of the man known to friends and family. In a letter written shortly after the publication of *The Scarlet Letter,* his close friend George Hillard expressed the now familiar puzzlement: "How comes it that with so thoroughly healthy an organization as you have, you have such a taste for the morbid anatomy of the human heart, and such knowledge of it too?" (R. H. Lathrop, *Memories,* 121). The "thoroughly healthy" Hawthorne was massively documented in biographical studies published soon after his death, first by his son-in-law, George Parsons Lathrop, and then by his son, Julian. Hawthorne's daughter Rose followed with a biography summing up the family's vision of its life: the children considered their "beloved parents . . . absolutely perfect beings; and there was nothing that we ever perceived to make the supposition unreasonable" (305). Rose remembers her father standing at the glowing hearthside in the evening, surrounded by wife and children, enjoying "a picture of benevolent plea-sure" that offered relief from the struggles of his imaginative life. "Perhaps, for this moment, the soldier from the battlefields of the soul ceased to remember scenes of cruelty and agony" (216).

Hawthorne's notebooks, as edited for publication by Sophia, substan-tiated this picture of their home life in immense detail and led Henry James to conclude that Hawthorne "had lived primarily in his domestic affections, which were of the tenderest kind" ("Hawthorne," 565). Margaret Fuller was a firsthand witness and, like James, was a shrewd judge of human relation-ships. When she visited Nathaniel and Sophia at the Old Manse during the early years of their marriage, she described the baby, Una, as "the child of a holy and equal marriage. She will have a good chance for freedom and happiness in the quiet wisdom of her father, the obedient goodness of her mother" (Commonplace Book, 1844).[2]

The Hawthorne family vividly exemplified the domestic ideal of family relations that became dominant in the early nineteenth century; it provided a "vindication," Julian declared, of "true love and married happiness" (NHW 1:v–vi). Yet this union of perfect beings was simultaneously a battle-field of souls, marked at times with scenes of cruelty and agony; this ideal model of middle-class normality embraced fierce collisions of opposing psy-chic, social, and religious forces, and it produced a madwoman, a criminal, and a saint.

Nathaniel and Sophia absorbed the internal contradictions of the domes-tic ideal into a compelling display of spiritual coherence. They made a marriage in which the structures of the experienced world were peculiarly liable to stress-fracture, and in response they fashioned means of appearing invulnerable. The Hawthornes became shamans of domesticity: their con-temporaries felt that an aura of the sacred surrounded them, and their presence was felt to possess healing power.[3]

Hawthorne's writing explores the entanglement of misery and beatitude that was native to the domestic ideal—the morbidity intrinsic to its health, the sorrow inseparable from its joy, the disorder native to its harmonies. His imaginative creations took part in the cultural work of establishing and perpetuating this arrangement of family life, and they do so today.[4] If we are to appreciate the enduring force of Hawthorne's art, however, we must grasp its nineteenth-century origins, recognizing that the Hawthornes are denizens of their era, not ours, a family of psychosocial antiques.

In the introduction to *The Scarlet Letter,* Hawthorne indicates that his work gathered its momentous imaginative power from a transitory household scene. In the home he occupied at Salem, after his wife and children had gone to bed, he was left in the

> deserted parlor, lighted only by the glimmering coal-fire and the moon. . . . There is the little domestic scenery of the well-known apartment; the chairs, with each its separate individuality; the centre-table, sustaining a workbasket, a volume or two, and an extinguished lamp; the sofa; the book-case; the picture on the wall;—all these details, so completely seen, are so spiritualized by the unusual light, that they seem to lose their actual substance, and become things of intellect. Nothing is too small or too trifling to undergo this change, and acquire dignity thereby. A child's shoe; the doll, seated in her little wicker carriage. . . . Ghosts might enter here, without affrighting us. It would be too much in keeping with the scene to excite surprise, were we to look about us and discover a form, beloved, but gone hence, now sitting quietly in a streak of this magic moonshine.
>
> (CE 1:35)

In the half-darkness the furnishings and children's playthings cease to be "too small or too trifling" and are embued with the interplay of thought and feeling signified by the pale moonlight and the glow of the hearth. Yet the emotions stirred in Hawthorne by this domestic scene arose from his life within it: the spectral light allows him to see the "imaginary" that always pervades the "actual." Among the ghosts entering here was that of Hawthorne's mother, recently departed, and, more obscurely, that of his father, who had perished in Hawthorne's own Salem childhood. Hester Prynne's illegitimate child is modeled directly on the Hawthornes' daughter, who spent her days in this parlor.

The following chapters tell the Hawthornes' story in four parts, each focused on an epoch in the family's life and featuring a major romance. I begin near the end, when Nathaniel was entering what is now called a mid-life crisis. The family was soon to leave for Europe, and the conflict between Nathaniel and Sophia was particularly acute. In *The Blithedale Romance* Hawthorne explored doctrines of manhood and womanhood that claimed universal validity; but instead of finding an ideological resolution for his emerging distress, he articulated its uncanny persistence.

The intuitive cunning of Nathaniel's imagination—and of Sophia's—is strongly evident here, as is the claustrophobic intensity of the deadlock between them. Both are spelled out in their response to urgent contemporary issues. Events and persons that are now the province of historians were household words for the Hawthornes. They measured their own marriage against the feminist example of Margaret Fuller; and their treatment of ideological issues invokes the historic debate between Mary Wollstonecraft and Jean-Jacques Rousseau.

Part 2 returns to the beginning of the story, tracing the social origins of the Hawthornes' marital dilemmas by examining the circumstances in which Nathaniel and Sophia grew from childhood to maturity. Both were descendants of the pre-Revolutionary elite that was supplanted in Jacksonian America, and as they fell in love they saw each other as embodiments of the emerging democratic virtues. *The House of the Seven Gables* celebrates the union of a "democratic" man with a "true woman" against the background of a declining aristocratic order and indicates how this new model of family life worked to legitimate middle-class dominance.

The Hawthornes' immediate knowledge of the rising culture of the urban Northeast could hardly have been more abundant. Hawthorne himself became a key figure in mass-market publishing, as pioneered by his publisher Samuel Goodwyn Goodrich and later by the firm of Ticknor and Fields. His political life as a Democratic officeholder was aided by Sophia's well-connected sister Elizabeth Peabody, who interceded for him with George Bancroft, and by his college friends Horatio Bridge and Franklin Pierce. Elizabeth Peabody, like Sophia herself, deserves recognition as an early exponent of the transcendentalist movement; and when the Hawthornes settled in Concord, they enlarged their friendships with Ralph Waldo Emerson and Henry David Thoreau. They chose to live in domestic seclusion at the Old Manse only after Nathaniel's involvement in the communal experiment at Brook Farm, which was based on Charles Fourier's critique of the misery that results from living in "private" families.

Part 3 treats the psychic interior of the Hawthornes' domestic sphere, taking up psychological questions related to the ideological and social issues of the preceding sections. The intense spiritual communion of married love was embodied for Nathaniel and Sophia in their sexual relationship, as was generally true for exponents of domesticity. They spoke of sexual intercourse as "blissful interviews" (CE 16: 226, 241); yet they were all too familiar with the attendant anxiety, as articulated in the massive new literature of "purity," prominently including "male hygiene." Their confrontation with the resultant issues of child rearing took place in a particularly rich context: Sophia's sister Elizabeth was a pioneer in early childhood education, joining with Bronson Alcott to found the Temple School in Boston; and her sister Mary Mann wrote an important treatise, *The Moral Culture of Infancy.* The Hawthornes' stubborn commitment to home schooling formed a sharp contrast, as they were aware, to Horace Mann's leadership in the creation of public schools; yet the Hawthornes shared with the Manns a belief in disciplining children through nurturing love rather than applications of the rod. Hester Prynne's difficulty in rearing little Pearl is a study of how such discipline does and doesn't work.

Part 3 ends with *The Scarlet Letter* as an exploration of the joys and torments of domestic intimacy and brings the story of the family's life back to our point of departure.

Part 4 provides a conclusion. It takes up the severe convulsion that befell the Hawthornes in Rome, where Una suffered her first mental breakdown. The Hawthornes' Italian ordeal was personal, once again, but not private. Nathaniel and Sophia had absorbed a tradition of Anglo-American response to Italy dating from Madame de Staël's *Corinne; or, Italy* (1807), and they were caught up in the contemporary fascination at the legend of Beatrice Cenci, in which they saw an image of their own misery. They had been acquainted for a decade with Margaret Fuller's experiences in Italy, and now they tested their responses against those of the many American artists there: William Wetmore Story, Hiram Powers, Cephas Thompson, and Harriet Hosmer. The sculptor Louisa Lander became an intimate of the family and a role model for Una; and there followed an eruption of sexual conflicts that drove Sophia toward hysterical rigidity and overwhelmed Nathaniel with confusion and self-disgust. Hawthorne sought to find the meaning of his resultant distress by writing *The Marble Faun* as a compendium of his responses to Italy, with an abortive central narrative. Like many another man of middle-class achievement, Hawthorne was surprised and disabled by the inward torment that erupted in the midst of success.

Such a mutual reading of biography and art is not only a matter of locating revelatory incidents—a fictional circumstance that resonates with events in their lives—but of tracing a complex frontier along which the contours of Hawthorne's life and writing shape each other.

We seek through this interplay to answer questions we will not cease to ask: Is our interest in these psychosocial antiques merely antiquarian? In what does Hawthorne's literary power consist? What is the energy that envelops Hawthorne's readers and draws them into the fiction he produced? Is it the power of a disturbing clarification, the provision of a symbolic focus around which a familiar yet unwonted awareness can formulate itself? Or is it something more? The dilemmas of middle-class family life have not died away since Hawthorne's time but have taken new forms in becoming more explicit, and we are ourselves shaped and anguished by them.

Where Hawthorne's writing strikes us with full immediacy, we vibrate like a champagne glass when a singing voice calls forth its inherent harmonies. We too have resonance frequencies, a pattern of inward tensions against which great writing rings true. Touched by this foreign music, we are delivered into an otherwise unobtainable experience of ourselves.

PART ONE

Critical Vortex

CHAPTER ONE

Indices of a Problem

In September 1852 Hawthorne journeyed to Brunswick, Maine, at the invitation of Bowdoin College, his alma mater, which was celebrating its fiftieth anniversary. As a famous writer and a figure of national prominence in the Democratic party, he was among the most distinguished of Bowdoin's alumni. "My adventures thou shalt know when I return," Hawthorne wrote his wife, "and how I was celebrated by orators and poets—and how, by the grace of Divine Providence, I was not present, to be put to the blush. All my contemporaries have grown the funniest old men in the world. Am I a funny old man?" (CE 16:593).

This journey, extended to include a seaside vacation at the Isle of Shoals, gave Hawthorne an occasion to measure the distance he had traveled in the twenty-seven years since his graduation from Bowdoin. He had realized the dream of literary pre-eminence that had set him apart as a student and had led him through an arduous span of striving. Proud of his achievements and aware of his distinguished station in life, Hawthorne nonetheless had reason to feel an uneasy presentiment that his greatest work was behind him, that his remarkable personal adventure was ending, that what remained was to become one of the funny old men.[1]

Hawthorne was forty-eight years old, and his family was now complete. Una, the oldest daughter, was eight and Julian was six; they had a baby sister, Rose, just fifteen months. Hawthorne had recently moved this family into a

new home in Concord, which he renamed the Wayside with the air of a man
at long last settling down. "Since I was married, ten years ago," he wrote to
G. P. Putnam, "I have had no less than seven homes—the one to which I
am now going being the eighth" (CE 16:530). Hawthorne was mistaken in
expecting that the family would remain at the Wayside, but of the many
places he and Sophia had lived, this was the first he was able to purchase,
and he left it permanently only at the time of his death. "I am beginning to
take root here," he wrote to Longfellow, "and feel myself, for the first time
in my life, really at home" (CE 16:602).

Hawthorne's description of his journey to Bowdoin and the Isle of Shoals
evokes an ancient drama of masculine achievement: the hero undertakes an
odyssey into the great unknown, while his wife, like Penelope (or Clytemnes-
tra), waits by the hearth to celebrate and reward his adventures when he
returns. Hawthorne was living out a version of this drama that was becoming
typical of nineteenth-century America: a man's individual struggle to make
a name for himself. Sophia played the part allotted to women by a vision of
domesticity, also having ancient origins, that was now being consecrated as
a middle-class ideal.

On the day of Nathaniel's departure Sophia commenced a series of
journal entries that describe the household in his absence. Her first comments indicate how ardently she devoted herself to this sphere of womanly
fulfillment. She reports that Una and Julian pined for their father, and

> began to wonder how it would seem to Papa when he got back if they should never
> tease one another, never frown nor fret, always mind when first spoken to—if Papa
> would hear only lovely tones & see only pleasant faces—and all this joined to baby's
> angel talk & angel smiles, thought Una, would make Papa think he was in heaven with
> us—"or," said Julian, "not with *us* but with some other children"—"Yes," I replied,
> "with your spirits." "Oh," they exclaimed, "let us try & try & try & perhaps we can!"
> (Family Notebook, 30 August 1852)[2]

As Sophia's journal continues, however, this tableau of domestic felicity
is interrupted by gestures that parody and subvert the drama she and her
husband are playing out. The routine counterpoint of worldly manhood and
feminine nurture was echoed in the relation of crude and refined, earthy and
angelic, savage and civilized; and the Hawthornes' daughter Una had a knack
for uproarious burlesque that turned these antitheses all topsy-turvy.

> She took Julian's turtle & said to him, "Come, we are two boys—you are James
> Jones." So she went on about the turtle & perfectly amazed me with her talk. The
> voice & manner & phrases & pronunciations were of the most uncivilized barbarous
> clodhopper. Where she ever heard—how she ever knew—I cannot imagine. Julian

came near dying of laughter to see & hear her. Where was the grace, the softness, the humanity, the order of my little Una? Utterly gone. No changeling could have been a greater change. What an Elfish element there is in her! What a tract of untameable wilderness, whither she rushes to dens & morasses, to air herself, as it were. I never knew such a combination of the highest refinement & the rudest boorishness—one lies at the door of the other.

(5 September)

Sophia's uneasiness, like the turbulence in Una's conduct, reveals that the conventional gender categories were meant to enforce the maleness and femaleness that they pictured as inherent. To say that a girl is "boorish" when she acts like a boy is to carry forward a disciplinary program, against which Una evidently offered resistance.

Yet Sophia's disapproval of Una's boisterousness is mingled with latent appreciation, even encouragement. Sophia feels a certain exhilaration at Una's "wonderful power," and she likewise relishes Una's success in placing herself at the center of attention, reducing Julian to helpless spasms of laughter. "We had a very merry time after tea," Sophia wrote on another occasion, "for Una undertook to be comical & to imitate characters & she was irresistible. We nearly died of laughing & Julian exploded in a way that was alarming to hear!" (30 August).

Sophia's enjoyment of this unnerving laughter bespeaks her own divided mind. She felt an inward resistance to the proprieties she sought to impose and was aware of the sharp public controversy over the role designated for women. If Una's mock-masculinity expressed resistance to conventional womanhood, so also did the belligerence that Sophia found in her baby daughter, Rose. "She has scolded a great deal lately. I do not know what I shall do about it. She has an idea of woman's rights, I believe, & means to stand up for them in her own person." Sophia hastened to add that Rose also showed signs of feminine solicitude; she "has been very sweet too, going to kiss Julian when he cried, & trying to comfort him & displaying a thousand charming little ways" (5 September).

The domestic sphere Nathaniel left behind as he traveled to Bowdoin and the Isle of Shoals was teeming with covert sexual politics; it was alive with inward debates about the axioms of its own constitution. Gender conflict was also at work in Nathaniel's public endeavors, of which this journey was a triumphal celebration.

In the quarter century since his graduation from Bowdoin Hawthorne had pursued two careers—civil servant and writer—and in both had now attained remarkable success. The story of his literary triumph is famous: just three years before, he had been ejected from his post at the Salem Custom House and in the midst of severe financial straits had returned to writing. In seven months he produced *The Scarlet Letter;* as that work was winning international acclaim, he wrote *The House of the Seven Gables* and a book of children's stories entitled *A Wonder Book.* To take advantage of the status his publisher James T. Fields was laboring hard to secure for him, that of a "classic" American writer, Hawthorne then re-issued *Twice-Told Tales,* made a new collection of tales that was published as *The Snow Image,* and wrote *The Blithedale Romance.*[3]

Hawthorne had hardly moved into the Wayside when Franklin Pierce— his close friend and Bowdoin classmate—asked for a biography to aid him in running for the presidency of the United States. *The Life of Franklin Pierce* was printed soon after Hawthorne and Pierce met at the Bowdoin reunion. Pierce, once elected, rewarded Hawthorne with the consulship at Liverpool, the most lucrative office he controlled.

Hawthorne's two careers embraced a chronic interior tension. He had complained in boyhood, when his job at his uncle's office annoyed him, that "No Man can be a Poet & a Book-Keeper at the same time" (CE 15:132). But he likewise complained about the years of unobstructed artistic effort that produced *Twice-Told Tales,* because they seemed a departure from normal manliness. In his first civil service job, at the Boston Custom House, he took satisfaction in exercising qualities of manhood that his poetic endeavors had left idle. He described for Sophia his newly acquired "worldly wisdom" and the "stronger sense I have of power to act as a man among men" (CE 15:429). By the age of forty-eight he had demonstrated that in nineteenth-century America (as earlier in England for Chaucer, Spenser, Milton, Marvell, Swift, and Fielding) a man could discharge worldly responsibilities and exercise political authority and also become a writer of momentous imaginative power. Yet Hawthorne was persistently troubled by a sharp incongruity between these occupations. His poetic identity—centered on cultivating emotional sensitivities in seclusion from the world—was feminine. As a civil servant, he was a man among men.

The crowning success of both Hawthorne's careers released ambivalences that had been contained during the years of struggle, and as he looked around at the funny old men who were his classmates, the confidence born of his achievements threatened to seep away.

In writing *The Blithedale Romance* Hawthorne sought an ideological solution to gender conflicts that plagued him afresh during this season of triumphant consolidation and new misgiving. He explored alternative views of

"Nature" in the effort to grasp the essence of masculine and feminine identity, trying to locate a philosophical and religious Truth that could bring his own life into focus. Hawthorne's yearning for such an authority is evoked in a brief tableau that interrupts the inconclusive ponderings of *Blithedale*. It portrays a father's return home like the one his own children had imagined on the day of his departure for Bowdoin.

After a summer in a reformist commune, Hawthorne's narrator Miles Coverdale returns to "conventional" life, taking an apartment in the city from which he gazes across the alley at the back windows of a fashionable boarding house:

> Two children, prettily dressed, were looking out. By-and-by, a middle-aged gentleman came softly behind them, kissed the little girl, and playfully pulled the little boy's ear. It was a papa, no doubt, just come in from his counting-room or office; and anon appeared mamma, stealing as softly behind papa, as he had stolen behind the children, and laying her hand on his shoulder to surprise him. Then followed a kiss between papa and mamma, but a noiseless one; for the children did not turn their heads.
> (CE 3:150–151)

Like a father's departure from home, this is a key ceremonial moment of nineteenth-century American domesticity, when a man crosses the threshold that separates his domain of manly striving from woman's sphere. The children he greets so gently have been "prettily dressed" for the occasion, yet they inhabit an atmosphere not of formal constraint but of deeply ingrained mutual affection. They continue to look out the window as "mamma" appears to receive her delicate kiss. Mamma steals up on papa, just as he had stolen up on the children; the absence of surprise in their encounter implies that these figures have been spiritually present and attuned to one another even when apart. The "noiseless" kiss asserts that a spiritual logic—not physical desire—holds husband and wife together and connects them with their progeny.

"I bless God for these good folks!" Coverdale declares. "I have not seen a prettier piece of nature, in all my summer in the country, than they have shown me here in a rather stylish boarding-house" (CE 3:151).

Coverdale is susceptible to the "nature" symbolized by this moment because his experiences at Blithedale had stirred up severe ideological consternations. He fled to the city, he tells us, because "it was impossible, situated as we were, not to imbibe the idea that everything in nature and human existence was fluid, or fast becoming so; that the crust of the Earth, in many places, was broken, and its whole surface portentously upheaving; that it was a day of crisis, and we ourselves were in the critical vortex" (140).

These images of impermanence, chaotic violence, and directionless motion suggest a "nature" in which no moral order can be grounded, a nightmare that Coverdale dispels as he observes the family in the window. Not merely a reminder of conventional life, the little drama of papa's return is the emblem of a religious reality strong enough to rescue order from the threat of chaos.

The domestic ideal does not resolve the thematic conflicts that Hawthorne elaborates in *Blithedale,* nor does it describe life in the Hawthorne household. If Hawthorne on returning from Bowdoin should "hear only lovely tones & see only pleasant faces"—his children realized—he would imagine that he was not in this world at all, but in heaven, and "not with *us* but with some other children" (30 August). Sophia's vision of spiritual felicity and the parable that Hawthorne interpolated into his romance express an ideology that claimed to measure quotidian family life against an eternal order of Truth. Yet this system of ideas generated characteristic dilemmas; it produced confusions as well as resolving them, and a "day of crisis" descended when these endemic conflicts became acute. In this respect *The Blithedale Romance* and the Hawthorne household resemble and cast light on each other: both are wrenched in the critical vortex.

With *The Blithedale Romance* Hawthorne began to write fiction based explicitly on his personal experience. He had commented on his daily life in the introductions to *Mosses from an Old Manse* and *The Scarlet Letter,* but now his months at Brook Farm provide the setting of his tale, much as the family's stay in Italy is worked into *The Marble Faun.* This emerging biographical focus also appears in the narrative design of *Blithedale:* unique in Hawthorne's writing, the narrator is himself a writer, Miles Coverdale.

Coverdale tells us that Hollingsworth, Zenobia, and Priscilla—the three other leading characters—"were separated from the rest of the Community, to my imagination, and stood forth as the indices of a problem which it was my business to solve" (CE 3:69). All four figures embody issues that Hawthorne recurrently sought to puzzle out. Coverdale's pained and retiring temperament is like Arthur Dimmesdale's and like Clifford's in *The House of the Seven Gables;* Hollingsworth is the typical polar opposite, resembling the blunt and forceful blacksmith who matches the supersensitive watchmaker in "The Artist of the Beautiful." Passive and aggressive males are paired in *Blithedale* (Coverdale/Hollingsworth), *The House of the Seven Gables*

(Clifford/Judge Pyncheon), and the manuscripts Hawthorne left unfinished at the end of his life (Septimius Felton/Robert Hagburn).

The women in *Blithedale* are also native to Hawthorne's abiding perplexities. Zenobia is manifestly analogous to Hester Prynne and also to Hepzibah Pyncheon: all three have an air of aristocratic pride and are defiantly at odds with the world around them. The pairing of Zenobia with her docile half-sister, Priscilla, recapitulates a relation Hawthorne had developed in an early tale, "The White Old Maid," and pursued through Hilda and Miriam in *The Marble Faun*.[4]

The indices of Hawthorne's problem form a pattern in which male and female serve as defining opposites; and the axis of gender, so established, crosses an axis of power. Considered as a system of coordinates, the four figures define a world of sexual politics in which Hawthorne's imagination recurrently seeks its way. The question that now emerges is ideological; he asks whether the map of his abiding obsessions truthfully represents the contours of reality.

Hawthorne takes up a complex debate about the "natural" essence of gender that Sophia had invoked when she said that Rose—aged fifteen months—had an "idea of woman's rights" yet was also tenderly solicitous toward her brother.

The nineteenth-century claim to equal rights for women was grounded in the principle enunciated in the Declaration of Independence that such rights are created in human beings by nature's God. In drawing up the "Declaration of Sentiments" for the Seneca Falls Convention in 1848, Elizabeth Cady Stanton echoed this document to hammer the principle home: "We hold these truths to be self-evident: that all men and women are created equal" (Kraditor, 184). A conflicting tradition asserted that women are defined by the care they provide for others. In ascribing both forcefulness and solicitude to her infant daughter, Sophia suggests the appealing possibility that both these capacities are natural, so that a woman might care for a husband and children and exercise equal rights as a citizen. Yet Sophia did not believe, nor did Nathaniel, that nature had provided such an arrangement: the Hawthornes embraced a tradition that set the nurturing qualities of women at odds with the claim to political equality.

Women of the Revolutionary era were quick to observe that the egalitarian attack on monarchy and hereditary social privilege invoked natural rights that challenged the agelong subordination of women, and men were equally alert to ways in which democratic doctrine could justify male dominance. As natural equality became a sacred principle in America, the pressure to reconsider the place of women in the commonwealth grew ever stronger, and women found a language of moral authority in which to frame their discontents. Mary Wollstonecraft's *Vindication of the Rights of Woman* sounded familiar to Americans when it appeared in 1792 because it followed themes that had long been discussed informally.

This Enlightenment controversy was absorbed into the ideal of domesticity that arose in later decades, so that its key issues were still very much alive for the Hawthornes. Wollstonecraft's antagonist was Jean-Jacques Rousseau, who sought to justify the subordination of women by appealing to an equality of "natural" differences.

Rousseau focuses on differences in the way men and women pursue sexual satisfaction, from which "arises the first determinate difference between the moral relations of each. The one should be active and strong, the other passive and weak: it is necessary the one should have both the power and the will, and that the other should make little resistance" (Osborne, 108). Rousseau shies away from asserting that the relative muscular strength of males justifies domination and surrounds his declarations about sexuality with an elaborate discussion meant to deny such a claim. Rousseau likewise presents military force as a precondition of rule but not a title to it.[5]

Rousseau is fastidious on this point for good reason: to hold that male dominance is legitimate because nature awards physical strength to men is tantamount to claiming that might makes right—mere despotic power. Despite Rousseau's defensive maneuvers, Wollstonecraft grasped the central issue. She linked together his remarks about sexuality and male power in a famous accusation: "Tyrants and sensualists are in the right, when they endeavour to keep women in the dark, because the former only want slaves, and the latter a play-thing" (Wollstonecraft, 24).

Rousseauist attempts to justify male dominance by invoking biology were virtually guaranteed to backfire. Priscilla Mason seized the initiative in her valedictory oration at the Young Ladies Academy of Philadelphia in 1793, invoking male muscle to mount a forceful attack: "Being the stronger party . . . [men] seized the sceptre and the sword; with these they gave laws to society. . . . They doom'd the [female] sex to servile or frivolous employments, on purpose to degrade their minds. . . . The Church, the Bar, and the Senate are shut against us. Who shut them? *Man;* despotic man, first made us incapable of the duty, and then forbid us the exercise" (Lerner, 214).

If men usurp women's rightful power, Mason recognized, then the mental and psychological weaknesses of women are deformities produced by oppression, not innate properties revealing Nature's law. Elizabeth Cady Stanton reaffirmed this charge at mid-century, noting that male dominance worked "to destroy [woman's] confidence in her own powers, to lessen her self-respect, and to make her willing to lead a dependent and abject life" (Kraditor 186).

Hawthorne was intimately familiar with this array of feminist arguments, and flatly rejected the lot. Despite his ambivalent and androgynous sense of self and the sympathy he extends toward strong women in his works, he never retracted his early condemnation of "a false liberality, which mistakes the strong division-lines of Nature for mere arbitrary distinctions." The woman who feels compelled to seek a career at odds with her "natural" destiny must do so, he argued, "with sorrowing reluctance" because she is "relinquishing part of the loveliness of her sex" ("Mrs. Hutchinson," 168–169).

Hawthorne's mournful spectacle of a woman's forsaking her womanly nature conforms to a well-established feature of male resistance to feminism. Rather than exalting the exercise of muscular force, advocates of masculine privilege scorned distortions of natural womanhood. "Women of masculine minds," John Gardiner wrote in 1801, "have generally masculine manners," nowhere more dismayingly visible than in women who seek political power or in earlier ages actually possessed it. Queen Elizabeth "swore with the fluency of a sailor," Gardiner declared, "and boxed the ears of her courtiers." Womanly aggression was pictured as a misplaced manly trait, and quickly included sexual aggression. Timothy Dwight condemned Mary Wollstonecraft not only as a "hoyden" and a "non descript"—both terms suggesting a sexually anomalous makeup—but also as a "strumpet" (Kerber, 279–283).

This pattern of ideological combat, featuring reciprocal accusations of male despotism and female monstrosity, shapes a major debate in *Blithedale*. Zenobia condemns "the injustice which the world did to women . . . by not allowing them . . . their natural utterance in public," whereupon Hollingsworth replies that women who make such protests are "petticoated monstrosities" and threatens to "call upon my own sex to use its physical force, that unmistakeable evidence of sovereignty, to scourge them back within their proper bounds!" Coverdale accuses Hollingsworth of the male's reliance on violence, revealing "what he, and millions of despots like him, really felt." Priscilla, docile and timid, is alarmed by this quarrel. Unable to think for herself, she turns to Hollingsworth for guidance, whereupon Zenobia scoffs at her as "the type of womanhood, such as man has spent centuries in making it' " (CE 3:120, 122–123).

So is repeated the rhetorical scheme that asserts women's natural rights against male tyranny. The debate, however, does not resolve itself here; an enlarged and strengthened doctrine of male dominance is also at work. Hollingsworth declares that although men possess superior physical force, they need not use it to subdue women, since "the heart of true womanhood knows where its own sphere is, and never seeks to stray beyond it" (123).

Hawthorne dramatizes this claim by supplying Zenobia with just such a heart: instead of being outraged by Hollingsworth's assertion of masculine pre-eminence, she is "humbled" by it. Her angry defiance dissolves into weeping over her plight, now redefined as a deprivation of womanly fulfill-ment, not of natural rights. Zenobia's problem is that true womanhood can be realized only in subordination to true manhood, and a true man is hard to find. "Let man be but manly and godlike," she brokenly confesses to Hollingsworth, "and woman is only too ready to become to him what you say!" (CE 3:123–124). Zenobia's impulses are an adult version of those Sophia noted in baby Rose: equipped to speak up boldly for women's rights, she also has a loving heart. Yet these qualities are now put at odds: each capacity disqualifies her from exercising the other.

The feminist argument goes down to self-defeat in keeping with an ideological scheme that remains to be examined, the ideal of "true woman-hood" that became dominant in the 1830s and 1840s and transformed the debate concerning equal rights that had emerged in the Revolutionary pe-riod.

The emerging domestic ideal offered two rhetorical strategies in defense of male dominance: it enlarged on the "nature" women stood to lose if they demanded economic and political power; and it denied that masculine control of the public arena made women into playthings and slaves. As wives and mothers, women were said to possess a redemptive homemaking spiritu-ality that transcends the scramble for worldly advantage and provides them a fulfillment that obviates political discontent.[6] Zenobia's tearful submission doubly vindicates this ideological maneuver: she not only agrees that "true womanhood" can be realized only through marriage to a masterful man but also falls in love with Hollingsworth. Ceasing to seek fulfillment as a public figure, she sets her heart on marrying him.

Sophia Hawthorne explained how "true womanhood" cancels feminist protest in her response to Margaret Fuller's *Woman in the Nineteenth Century.* "If [Margaret] were married truly," Sophia wrote her mother, "she would no longer be puzzled about the rights of woman. . . . In perfect, high union there is no question of supremacy. Souls are equal in love and intelligent communion, and all things take their proper places as inevitably as the stars their orbits. Had there never been false and profane marriages, there would not only be no commotion about woman's rights, but it would be Heaven here at once" (*NHW* 1:257).

When *Blithedale* was published, Zenobia's resemblance to Margaret Fuller was instantly apparent.[7] Sophia and then Nathaniel had come to know Margaret in Boston before Nathaniel's stay at Brook Farm. She was closely associated with the reformers who sponsored the communal experiment and paid several visits there when Nathaniel was in residence. Zenobia's intention to speak out for women's liberty corresponds not only to *Woman in the Nineteenth Century* but also to the "Conversations" Margaret held for women in Boston, which Sophia attended. Zenobia's death by drowning in *Blithedale* alludes to Margaret's death in 1850 amid the wreckage of the ship bringing her home to America from Italy with her son and Angelo Ossoli, who had been first her lover in Italy and then her husband.[8]

When the Hawthornes married, they enjoyed a close friendship with Fuller, who twice visited them at the Old Manse in Concord, noting in her journals the long and searching conversations they carried on together. During the second visit, in the late summer of 1844, she was revising *Woman in the Nineteenth Century,* which appeared the following year. Margaret suffered violent headaches in this effort, and Sophia found a moving response to her friend's inward strife. "Sophia told me a truth for which I thank her," Margaret wrote in her journal: "Each Orpheus must to the depths descend."[9] Sophia and Margaret were following divergent paths toward a shared ambition, that of living out their womanly natures to the full. Sophia too had disabling headaches and believed that her spiritual mission as wife and mother required descents into the depths that gave her views an orphic authority as strong as Margaret's.

When *Woman in the Nineteenth Century* appeared, Sophia found herself in disagreement not only with Margaret but also with her own mother. Sophia voices the emerging domestic vision of womanly self-realization; Mrs. Peabody invokes the egalitarian rhetoric of the Revolutionary period and echoes Wollstonecraft's protest against male tyranny. "I could have written on the very same subjects," Peabody declared, "and set forth as strongly what rights yet belonged to woman which were not granted her. . . . [Man] has the physical power, as well as conventional, to treat her like a plaything or a slave" (*NHW* 1:258).

Peabody believed that "a consistent Christian woman will be exactly what Margaret would have woman to be; and a consistently religious man would readily award to her every rightful advantage"; but she did not anticipate an early correction of the injustices women suffer. Man will maintain his despotism, Peabody declared, "till his own soul is elevated to the standard set up by Him who spake as never man spoke." Peabody hopes Fuller's book "may do good" but remains doubtful because it makes scant reference to Christian teaching and in fact bears "the *look* of absolute irreligion" (*NHW* 1:258).

For Peabody, Christian faith provides the ultimate rationale for women's rights and is the only engine of social change capable of securing those rights. She locates this promised equality far in the future but emphatically declares that the elevation of masculine souls, once achieved, will remove all the barriers to equality for women against which Fuller protests.

Sophia claims, by contrast, that redemption takes place in the present, through a womanly nature attuned to private rather than public activities. Even before she was married, Sophia believed "that each woman could make her own sphere quietly," observing that "it was always a shock to me to have women mount the rostrum." Sophia does not see the home as a prison, but as "the great arena for women" where wives and mothers "can wield a power which no king or conqueror can cope with." Far from perpetuating degraded subservience, women who exercise this spiritual power set an example of moral pre-eminence. "I do not believe any man who ever knew one noble woman would ever speak as if she were an inferior in any sense: it is the fault of ignoble women that there is any such opinion in the world" (*NHW* 1:257).

This disagreement between mother and daughter illustrates the ideological translation of Enlightenment doctrines of gender equality into the gender complementarity of the domestic ideal in the early nineteenth century. Male force, symbolized by muscular bodies, remains a component of the domestic vision. "The greater physical strength of man," Thomas Dew explained, suits him for "the turmoil and bustle of an active, selfish world," where "he has to encounter innumerable difficulties, hardships and labors." Women must remain within the domestic sphere, "but out of that very weakness and dependance [*sic*] springs an irresistible power." Woman's power "is more emblematical of that of divinity," Dew observes: "it subdues without an effort" (Kraditor, 45–46). What Elizabeth Peabody had envisioned as a social apocalypse—when morally elevated men will voluntarily yield political rights to women—now describes the anatomy of a current social arrangement, in which the "kings and conquerors" of worldly strife are subdued by the godlike power of a noble woman.

Sophia may be accused of betraying the interests of women by espousing a doctrine that sprinkles holy water on patriarchal domination; and her remark that "ignoble women" have created the belief in women's inferiority leaps off the page as an instance of blaming the victim. Yet the womanly power enshrined by the domestic ideal had substance; it was grounded in an evangelical Christian vision of moral reality with notable consequences in nineteenth-century America.

The social power of *Uncle Tom's Cabin,* for example, was derived from its dramatization of the spiritual transformation brought about by women (as well as blacks and children) who lack means of physical or economic coercion and wield only suffering love.[10] Scenarios of triumphant victimization, long despised as sentimental trash, take on renewed energy when seen as invoking the religious warrant of domesticity. Evangelical Christianity promoted the story of "salvation through motherly love," a version of the Gospel story at whose center is the crucified Christ.

The evangelical experience of "conversion" restructured personal experience along the line of demarcation that Sophia's language invokes, separating a world of coercive public forces from the sacred privacy in which the sinful heart is transformed.[11] The domestic ideology installed this moral interaction at the heart of relations between men and women and in that respect incorporated a protest against male power into the definition of womanly subservience. The power of women lay in their appeal to the conscience of men, presumed to be a guilty conscience.

"If Christianity should be compelled to flee from . . . the throng of busy men," declared Joseph Stephens Buckminster, "we should find her last and purest retreat with woman at the fireside; her last altar would be the female heart." As Nancy Cott observed, Buckminster's pronouns identify Christianity itself as feminine, exiled from the sordid male world (Cott, *Bonds,* 129–130). In *Blithedale* Hawthorne presses this conception to its logical end; Coverdale affirms that the "ministry of souls" should be entirely given over to women. "God meant it for her. He has endowed her with the religious sentiment in its utmost depth and purity, refined from that gross, intellectual alloy, with which every masculine theologist . . . has been prone to mingle it." God's love can "stream upon the worshipper" without interference, Coverdale exclaims, "through the medium of a woman's tenderness" (CE 3:121–122).

Hollingsworth agrees that men are obliged to seek the reassurance of women because of generically masculine moral inadequacies. Unable to sustain a belief in his own virtue, a man requires the support of a "Sympathizer," an "unreserved, unquestioning Believer," lest he "should utterly lose faith in himself." Only through the pity of a woman's heart can a man receive "the Echo of God's own voice, pronouncing—'It is well done!' " (CE 3:122).

Middle-class mothers employed the power of suffering love in their rearing of children. Exponents of the rising domestic culture repudiated corporal punishment and sought to instill just such a guilty conscience as Hollingsworth describes, in which a woman's voice has become the voice of God. If a mother has secured "pre-eminence in the sanctuary of his mind," Lydia Sigourney declared, "her image will be as a tutelary seraph, not seeming to bear rule, yet spreading perpetually the wings of purity and peace over its beloved shrine, and keeping guard for God" (128).[12] Sophia Hawthorne had no ethical qualms about the emotional manipulation of this strategy; on the contrary, her conception of moral reality required it:

> Julian cried hard to go out at noon when it was red hot & I could not quiet him, till at last I said—"Here is a little boy who I believe pretends he loves his mother—" He interrupted me with "I don't *pretend.*"—"Well I think you do not & yet what love is this that gives his mother so much pain instead of happiness?—Because his mother will not let him get sick, if she can help it, he cries & complains so as to hurt her very much, especially as today she is not well. If I did not love you, I would say—'Go & play in the hot sun as much as you like—it is nothing to me.' " He stopped & was perfectly still & when I saw his face again, a smile was struggling out of his beautiful eyes.—I never saw a sweeter effort to prove real love and it lasted all the rest of the day.
>
> (1 September)

Sophia explains to her six-year-old son that it would be easier for her to let him go out and play but that for his sake she must refuse. The emotional dishonesty that requires correction, Sophia believes, is Julian's claim to love his mother while trying to punish her for her conscientious stand. The reality of love is demonstrated by the struggle to attain selflessness; and Sophia hoped to install such altruism in Julian's personality so it would work automatically.

Sophia did not believe that Nathaniel needed lessons in real love. She looked on him with reverent awe, as the creator of works of art embodying divine power. She describes reading "The Chimaera" to Julian: "Was ever any thing so divine as that story? Julian was powerfully affected. He had not heard it for a long time & he was thrilled & stirred by every sentence. . . . The color mounted up to his curls & his eyes softened & were suffused. . . . As for me, I could scarcely read, I was so moved" (12 September). Sophia did not subscribe to any of the avowedly Christian versions of romantic religion, believing instead that ultimate reality is conveyed through poetic imagination, supremely in men of genius.[13] Instead of invoking a religious standard that might be held over Nathaniel's head, she approaches him in the role of an "unreserved, unquestioning Believer."

In *The Blithedale Romance* Hawthorne portrays a comparable transformation of evangelical doctrine in the marital relationship between Priscilla and Hollingsworth. Priscilla's entire existence, we learn, is organized around the principle that Hollingsworth is morally faultless; in submitting herself to him with ardent and unquestioning devotion, she gains spiritual power. The key to Priscilla's power, however, is not her divine willingness to sacrifice herself but the blasphemous fury of Zenobia.

In the thematic structure of the Hawthornes' marriage, as of *The Blithedale Romance,* the romantic ontology of domestic relations has been recast in a form revealing the subversive tensions within it. The complementary "natures" of womanhood and manhood—selfless spirituality redeeming the exercise of worldly power—lose their authority in *Blithedale* as representations of a divine order, and the moral structure of the marital relation is correspondingly dislocated. The agent of this derangement is Zenobia's feminism, which asserts the "absolute irreligion" that Sophia's mother found in Margaret Fuller's book. Zenobia defies the authority of God Himself, as embodied in the loving relationship between a man who demands submission and a woman who gladly offers it.

CHAPTER TWO

Zenobia's Ghost

Hawthorne joins Hollingsworth and Priscilla as embodiments of "true manhood" and "true womanhood" and then uses their relation to advance a radical criticism of the domestic ideal. The power selfless women exercise to redeem the lives of worldly males dissolves into moral blackmail at whose heart is a disembodied and invisible womanly rage that provokes a disabling masculine guilt. This recasting exploits conflicts in the meaning of "natural" genders that Hawthorne pursues from the outset of the narrative.

Coverdale is sardonically aware that his journey from the city to the reformist commune at Blithedale has carried him across the familiar line dividing the artifice of social convention from the eternal realities of Nature. At first he makes fun of the "regenerated" existence his fellow Blithedalers anticipate, once they have removed themselves from the "system of society" (CE 3:12–13), and observes that his first encounter with Nature was a long exposure to harsh winter weather that made him ill. As he convalesces, however, Coverdale repents of his sarcasm, concluding that his illness has initiated him into a new life. "No otherwise could I have rid myself of a thousand follies, fripperies, prejudices, habits, and other such worldly dust" (61–62).

In his sickroom Coverdale also discovers that Nature speaks of gender in discordant voices. At certain moments manhood and womanhood appear to derive their character from the biological constitution of males and females,

18

in keeping with the Enlightenment view of Nature and Nature's God that was debated by Rousseau and Wollstonecraft. But this impression is contradicted by the qualities of gender that the cult of domesticity enshrined as God-given. The sickroom provides a theater in which Coverdale joins with the other indices of Hawthorne's problem in playing out the resultant ironies. Although both Hollingsworth and Zenobia appear as gender monsters, their aberrations do not invoke an authoritative pattern of the natural.

When Coverdale meets Zenobia, her sexual vitality strikes him as evidence of an authentic womanhood that has been "refined away out of the feminine system" by social convention: she evokes the naked splendor of "Eve, when she was just made, and her Creator brought her to Adam, saying—'Behold, here is a woman!'" (CE 3:17). Increasingly, however, Coverdale judges Zenobia by a hostile code. First he feels there is something indecent about gazing on "womanliness incarnated"; then he decides that the gorgeous flower in her hair was grown in a "hot-house" or in "fervid and spicy" tropical soil. Continuing to view the flower as an emblem of Zenobia's erotic vitality, Coverdale soon declares it "preternatural" (45).

Zenobia's overt sexuality—initially the emblem of her pristine womanhood—violates the domestic ideal. Coverdale becomes guiltily preoccupied wondering whether she has ever been married and blames himself for "a sin of wicked interpretation" (CE 3:47) because he suspects she is sexually experienced. Yet Coverdale's imaginings are "wicked" only because Zenobia arouses him. He is unsettled and annoyed by the erotic provocation she brings into his sickroom, and her cooking tastes like the handiwork of a witch.

Coverdale quickly comes to prefer the bed care provided by Hollingsworth, who shows him feminine solicitude that Zenobia cannot muster. In explaining this paradox, Coverdale observes that males likewise possess natural traits that are morally defective. Analogous to the Zenobia's sexual vigor is man's "natural indifference" toward the sufferings of the weak; men typically resemble "our brute brethren, who hunt the sick or disabled member of the herd from among them, as an enemy." Hollingsworth's tender nursing makes him an exception to this rule: "there was something of the woman moulded into [his] . . . great, stalwart frame" (CE 3:41–42).

These paradoxes play on a distinction central to the domestic ideal: true womanhood and manhood were divinely ordained spiritual essences, at odds with the animal instincts that males and females inherit biologically. Within this Neoplatonic Christian scheme men were understood to be more brutelike than women. Hawthorne tells us frankly that Hollingsworth's feminine qualities form the most admirable part of his character; and he sharpens the focus on this issue by introducing Professor Westervelt, a monster of hyper-masculinity.

Westervelt's unprincipled maleness illuminates the spiritual requirements of the domestic ideal by systematically violating them all. To him, the biological constitution of human beings represents a "nature" of blind amoral forces. His own "sceptical and sneering view" of life results from exactly such a wanton dispensation: "Nature thrusts some of us into the world miserably incomplete," Hawthorne explains, "with hardly any sensibilities except what pertain to us as animals" (CE 3:101, 103). Just as Zenobia's flower disconcertingly symbolizes her vagina, so Hawthorne's mock-modest circumlocutions conjure Westervelt's presence as an erect penis, displayed as an outrage against every form of refinement. "His countenance . . . had an indecorum in it, a kind of rudeness, a hard, coarse, forth-putting freedom of expression. . . . There was in his eyes . . . the naked exposure of something that ought not to be left prominent" (91–92).

Westervelt's entrance into the story sets in motion a contest between the "materialist" and "spiritual" visions of nature, which clash on a battleground offered by the innocent Priscilla, who is belatedly entering puberty. "We could see Nature shaping out a woman before our very eyes," Coverdale remarks "and yet had only a more reverential sense of the mystery of a woman's soul and frame" (CE 3:72–73). To Westervelt, by contrast, Priscilla is a perversion of natural female vitality, "one of those delicate, nervous young creatures, not uncommon in New England," whose constitution has been damaged by "the gradual refining away of the physical system." Westervelt scoffs at the philosophers who "glorify this habit of body by terming it spiritual" (95).

Hawthorne gives Priscilla the "selfless" quality of seeming to inhabit neither her own body nor her own mind. She readily enters states of dissociated consciousness in which "other" presences express themselves through her, and Hawthorne pitches the allegorical contest between spirituality and materialism on this trait. Does Priscilla's mental susceptibility merit reverence, as an especially pure expression of a "true woman's" nature? Westervelt decidedly thinks not. To him, Priscilla happens to be equipped with an unusual psychic knack, for which there exists a market on the lyceum circuit like that for mountebanks who trade in other puzzling illusions.

Hawthorne describes the exhibition Westervelt organizes as a perverted exercise in "mystic sensuality," in which sacred affections are secularized and presented as a commodity. "At the bidding of one of these wizards . . . a mother, with her babe's milk in her bosom, would thrust away her child. Human character was but soft wax in his hands; and guilt, or virtue, only the forms into which he should see fit to mould it. The religious sentiment was a flame which he could blow up with his breath, or a spark that he could utterly extinguish. . . . If these things were to be believed, the individual soul was virtually annihilated" (CE 3:198). Westervelt's materialism appears vindicated by the power he exercises over Priscilla in putting her through her mystical paces; yet just as the performance reaches its climax, Hollingsworth strides upon the stage and gazes at Priscilla "with a sad intentness that brought the whole power of his great, stern, yet tender soul, into his glance" (202–203).

Thus Hawthorne arranges an allegorical triumph of domestic spirituality that dramatizes the complementarity of gendered souls. Hollingsworth's manly force is spiritual here, not muscular: his soul is activated by the spectacle of Priscilla's innocent and helpless victimization. Priscilla displays the reciprocal impulses of true womanhood: "The true heart-throb of a woman's affection was too powerful for the jugglery that had hitherto environed her. She uttered a shriek and fled to Hollingsworth, like one escaping from her deadliest enemy, and was safe forever!" (CE 3:203). Male dominance here receives ideological ratification, selfless womanhood fleeing to the protection of male strength and bringing out in Hollingsworth a redeemed manhood he could not have attained on his own.

Hawthorne emphasizes that Priscilla's womanly magic operates only so long as she is entirely selfless and passive. Were she to "lift up her voice in public" like Zenobia, it would instantly become apparent that her spirituality has been tainted, just as Zenobia's political discontent is a consequence of her wretched marriage to Westervelt (or her affair with him). "When a woman wrecks herself on such a being," Hawthorne explains, "she ultimately finds that the real womanhood, within her, has no corresponding part in him." The result is a "moral deterioration" that leads to Zenobia's career of "eccentricity and defiance" and finally to her death (CE 3:103). Yet Zenobia's destruction negates the spiritual meanings imputed to the marriage of Priscilla and Hollingsworth.

At the first debate among the indices of Hawthorne's problem, Zenobia gave up her political ambitions and fell in love with Hollingsworth; but in trying to win his hand, she finds herself competing with Priscilla and be-

comes implicated in Westervelt's abuse of her spirituality. In the end
Zenobia is completely thwarted; her desire to lead a public life is forbidden
by the dictates of her womanly nature; yet when she seeks domestic fulfillment, she drives Hollingsworth into the arms of her angelically passive and
selfless rival.

Hawthorne arranges a second debate in which Zenobia's dilemma takes
the foreground immediately. The "selflessness" of true womanhood intrinsic
to Zenobia's character—but impossible for her to live out—implies that the
value of her life is determined by the "secret tribunals" of male opinion, and
Zenobia is compelled to judge herself accordingly: "this same secret tribunal
chances to be the only judgment-seat that a true woman stands in awe of,
and . . . any verdict short of acquittal is equivalent to a death-sentence" (CE
3:215).

Zenobia explodes in fury against Hollingsworth, denouncing him as "a
cold, heartless, self-beginning and self-ending piece of mechanism." She reels
off the offenses he has committed in pursuing his cherished prison-reform
project, which she condemns as a masquerade of altruism whose true motive
is nothing but "Self, self, self!" (CE 3: 218). Yet Zenobia still cannot reject
Hollingsworth as a spokesman for the "manhood" by which her "womanhood" is fitly to be judged, and she continues to accept his verdict against
her as the voice of God. "The whole universe," she exclaims to Coverdale,
"her own sex and yours, and Providence, or Destiny, to boot, make common
cause against the woman who swerves one hair's breadth out of the beaten
track" (223–224).

Zenobia's ultimate antagonist is the Supreme Patriarch whose ordering of
genders she had vainly sought to deny. Coverdale, gazing on Zenobia's rigid
corpse after her suicide by drowning, wonders whether she had reconciled
herself to God. Had her soul "given itself up to the Father, reconciled and
penitent"? Coverdale hopes so. "But her arms! They were bent before her,
as if she struggled against Providence in never-ending hostility. Her hands!
They were clenched in immitigable defiance" (CE 3: 235). This supernatural
rage does not die with Zenobia but acts as an invisible rogue force in the
spiritual economy of *Blithedale's* conclusion.

This happens because Zenobia's denunciation of Hollingsworth has a
correspondingly devastating effect on him. She hammers home the judgment
that his philanthropic project and indeed his moral being are monstrosities
of egotism. Hollingsworth is reduced to appealing for reassurance to Priscilla, calling out to her in "the abased and tremulous tone of a man, whose
faith in himself was shaken, and who sought, at last, to lean on an affection"

(CE 3:219). Zenobia and Coverdale hope that Priscilla will not supply the moral support Hollingsworth needs; but they are disappointed. Priscilla's "engrossing love made it all clear. Hollingsworth could have no fault. That was the one principle at the centre of the universe" (220–221).

Priscilla here wins out conclusively over Zenobia in the competition for Hollingsworth's affections. But the comfort she offers Hollingsworth is no stronger than his feelings of guilt. If he could set aside Zenobia's charges, he would not need the moral solace Priscilla gives him.

This moment of Priscilla's triumph establishes the psychological structure of the union between herself and her husband, and Coverdale discovers that with the passage of time Hollingsworth has become even more dependent on his wife. "I made a journey, some years since, for the sole purpose of catching a last glimpse at Hollingsworth, and judging for myself whether he were a happy man or no." It turns out that Hollingsworth and Priscilla now lead an exceedingly retired life, so that Coverdale must contrive to meet them on their daily walk. "As they approached me, I observed in Hollingsworth's face a depressed and melancholy look, that seemed habitual; the powerfully built man showed a self-distrustful weakness, and a childlike, or childish, tendency to press close, and closer still, to the side of the slender woman whose arm was within his. In Priscilla's manner, there was a protective and watchful quality, as if she felt herself the guardian of her companion, but, likewise, a deep, submissive, unquestioning reverence, and also a veiled happiness in her fair and quiet countenance" (CE 3:242).

Coverdale realizes, as he sizes up this complex tableau of psychic interdependence, that it includes a third party, namely the ghost of Zenobia. Hollingsworth reveals that he has abandoned his prison-reform project because he is obsessed with being a murderer himself, whereupon Coverdale recognizes that Zenobia's dying curse has taken effect. He recalls "the wild energy, the passionate shriek, with which Zenobia had spoken those words—'Tell him he has murdered me! Tell him that I'll haunt him!'—and I knew . . . whose vindictive shadow dogged the side where Priscilla was not" (CE 2:243).

Hollingsworth presents the paradoxical spectacle of a man so guilt-ridden that he has become childishly dependent on the company of a woman who treats him with unquestioning reverence. He languishes in moral paralysis while continuing to embrace the convictions that led him to his murderous condemnation of Zenobia in the first place, convictions that Priscilla's evidently selfless spirituality appears to vindicate.

Far from seeking to exorcise the demon that haunts her husband, Priscilla cannot even see it. She can remain the indirect beneficiary of Zenobia's doom only so long as Hollingsworth does not directly acknowledge the source of his guilt and seek to reclaim his self-respect by confronting the patriarchal axioms of his psychic constitution. Priscilla and Hollingsworth are held together in matrimony through their unconscious collusion in the destruction of Zenobia.

No scheme of eternal truth authorizes the moral anatomy with which Hawthorne accounts here for the domestic spirituality of Priscilla and Hollingsworth. Although womanly aggression is wholly absent from the character of Priscilla, in keeping with the altruistic readiness for martyrdom that is the keynote of "true womanhood," it remains alive in her relationship to her husband as a dissociated rage that psychologically overawes him.

Unlike the "Madwoman in the Attic," the ghost of Zenobia is not interior to womanhood formed in response to a monolith of male domination; it inhabits male consciousness, too. Zenobia's ghost is not locked away in the attic, able to make only occasional destructive forays into the household proper. She is a familiar spirit, present at bed and board, and at the sacred hearth of the middle-class home.

The conviction that divine power flows into human relations when hostile impulses are repressed was a central doctrine of life in the Hawthorne household, and Sophia was an astute observer of the key transaction:

> I believe Julian's sin today was impatience with baby, calling her "ugly thing" because she interfered with his cabinet when he was putting it in order, but this evening he told me that it was not he who called her ugly but the dragon—for he *never* thought her so.—I assured him that it was his fault for allowing the dragon to speak, for the least smile or sweet tone drove the dragon out of sight & made him dumb. His great dark wells of loving light shone like two stars as he answered "He shall not speak again."
>
> (Family Notebook, 31 August 1852)[1]

Observe how skillfully Sophia instructs Julian in the repression that produces the numinous glow in his eyes: when the child seeks to deny his anger by projecting it upon "the dragon," Sophia insists upon the next step, namely that the dragon should be driven out of sight and struck dumb.

The quashing of rage likewise defines Sophia's womanhood. There is a "Zenobia" of thwarted autonomy within the "Priscilla" of her worshipful solicitude toward her husband; and Sophia articulates her self-abnegation in terms that make the ghost of Zenobia strikingly visible: twisting currents of accusation complicate the flow of wifely adulation with which she tirelessly addresses Nathaniel. Her writing, like his, conveys a strong psychic turbulence that the writer tacitly disavows. She has a penetrating psychological insight that she appears not to recognize and becomes disconcerted and ashamed when circumstances threaten to confront her with what she knows.

Sophia's journal records her sharp awareness of the pleasures Nathaniel is enjoying on his trip, in contrast with her own discomfort. "Another red hot day—Oh how charming for my husband in mid-sea—I trust he is on the Isle of Shoals today. It was too hot to send to the village so I had to wait till night for the letter I was sure was there from my husband. We were quite uncomfortably hot sitting perfectly still, & finally were obliged to go into Papa's study (which I keep shut up generally) as the only cool spot" (8 September). Every phrase here is laced with accusation: Sophia and the children suffer severely from the heat, while Nathaniel has a "charming" day. His study is the only cool spot in the house, but she enters the sacred precinct reluctantly, only after she and the children try "sitting perfectly still" in the dreadful heat. She is likewise pained to forgo the letter from her husband, which she is "sure" has arrived at the village; in due course she learns no letter had come.

Even on more pleasant days, Sophia's commentary keeps up the refrain; her delight in Nathaniel's imagined joys is played against her own hardships. "The weather is superb. My husband has been most fortunate in this respect. He has had weather of the hottest & pleasant cool also. I trust there is nothing to mar his enjoyment & that he will stay a long, long time in that wide scene, without a care or a toil to fret his spirit & clog his wings. This morning the water proved too bad to drink or cook with—It has the most oppressive odor" (5 September). Sophia indicates that the children, too, have learned to think first of their father's pleasure, as when a rainy day prevents them from playing out of doors. "We all wished for rain & wind & all that would make a grand storm for Papa at the Isle of Shoals, because he wanted to see one there. It entirely reconciled the children to being imprisoned within doors to know that the rain was what Papa desired" (12 September).

Another form of Sophia's oppression was the labor of keeping the journal, which Nathaniel had requested:

> This journal takes all my time. . . . and after all it is a miserable disjointed journal, all hop, skip, & jump & nothing valuable told. But I write, because my husband

wished it so much—& what else do I desire but to do what he wishes? I only wish it were better done. . . . But I have not a moment all day & it is late at night before I can sit down to write & then I scrawl as fast as my pen can go & write nothing & that illegibly. My dear husband will be disappointed I am sure. It is now after ten & I know he would tell me to go to bed, so I will at least mind him.

(5, 7 September)

Sophia draws attention to her sufferings so as to amalgamate them into the postures of her self-abnegation. The circumstances that enrage her are transformed into burdens she bears gladly for his sake:

Another splendid day but red red hot. It is far the hottest day we have had this summer. I could not in conscience send the children to the Post Office this morning though I was very impatient to hear, because I began to have insane hopes of a letter from my husband. I was wholly prostrated & lay down on the sofa & put a newspaper over my head to keep off the terrible flies. . . . When I roused up, it was because I wanted to make a cushion for my husband's rocking chair. I do not think I could have done anything else or for any person else this hottest day and ill as I was.

(2 September)

The next day she continues making the cushion, after a misfortune reduces Julian to tears: "He mourned sadly for some time; but finally cleared up suddenly upon my assuring him that he was destroying me. I finished the cushion for my husband's rocking chair & when I was done, I found I had no more powers, & indeed could only have held up to do something for him, so down I lay on the carpet in the study with a severe headache" (3 September).

Sophia's emotional conflicts found expression in a lifelong physical disability, of which such headaches were a primary feature. Her chronic exhaustion and periods of virtual prostration were taken as evidences of an exceptionally "delicate" constitution and were accepted as a matter of routine in the household. The older children had been trained to obey the demands imposed by Sophia's torment, but this could hardly be expected of the fifteen-month-old Rose. The baby's mind-shattering bouts of weeping were provoked, Sophia records, by her father's absence:

Baby had a tragical time & therefore destroyed me for the day. . . . She had cried so much my head was broken all to pieces. Once she heard the gate swing & with an angelic smile, she exclaimed "Dere Papa"—I asked her if she wanted to see Papa & she stretched up her arms to be taken to him & cried bitterly because he was not to be found. The day was obliterated by this trouble of baby's & my head is so bruised that I cannot think of anything. Una & Julian have been very good. They feel a responsibility about me which is beautiful to see.

(31 August)

Within Sophia's anguish there were passions that made her ashamed. Sustaining her selfless spirituality required constant vigilance against impulses she hardly knew how to gauge, and external circumstances sometimes caught her off guard:

> I sent Julian to the Post Office . . . & he brought—Oh—he brought a letter from my husband! I was too happy to open it for some time—I had it—that was enough for the present. It seemed somewhat like the effect of his smile, his tone, his touch—awakening, resting, soothing, thrilling. . . . I retreated to the study. There I mused and wrote & wept bitterly till dinner time. . . . One would think that I must weep only for an offset to my blessedness in having such a husband & such children & it is probably something of this—but yet it is also because I am not better, more beautiful, more worthy to be his wife & to sun in his love. I should be a celestial angel to deserve him & I am not. I wish I were. But I will not write any more of this here.
> (4 September)

Sophia senses that she has not reached the true ground of her feelings, which included the sexual desire that produces her fantasy of Nathaniel's "awakening, resting, soothing, thrilling" touch. The Hawthornes had discontinued sexual intercourse after the birth of Rose, and she later ascribed this to his consideration for the "delicacy" of her constitution, three children being as much as she should be expected to bear. She was proud to be able to say, late in her life, that "Mr. Hawthorne's passions were under his feet" (Pearson, 276).[2] Yet her tears in part express grief at this restriction of their sexual lives. Nathaniel made a comment in his journal, some months later, that reflects on the dilemma they faced. "Caresses, expression of one sort or another, are necessary to the life of the affections, as leaves are to the life of a tree. If they are wholly restrained, love will die at the roots" (CE 8:551).

Sophia found a displaced sexual fulfillment, first in touching the letter and then in a climactic inward rush—an orgasm—of the turbulent conflicted passion that defined her relation to her husband. Like Zenobia's tears of grief and desire before Hollingsworth, Sophia's weeping expresses her upwelling spontaneous response to the presence of a man capable of stirring her in the deepest sources of her womanhood, except that here the man's presence is invoked altogether spiritually, through the metaphorical penis with which he writes to her. It is noteworthy that Sophia wants to relish her tears in private, as when a comparable spasm was touched off by reading one of Nathaniel's tales to Julian. "I wanted to be alone & shed delicious tears of wonder, admiration and awe. Oh my husband! Thy pen surely is inspired with the divinest fire" (12 September).[3]

At the heart of Sophia's description is the recognition that tears of bitterness and those of worshipful adulation are the same. Implicit in her weeping as an "offset to [her] blessedness" at having "such a husband & such children" is the womanly despair and rage built into such domestic blessedness itself. Her relationship to her husband and children is not a compensatory fulfillment, to be balanced against the miseries of her moral plight; it is central to those miseries and to the divine spirituality that forms the ideal by which she knows herself. Her love for her husband is the agony of a psychic conflict in which self-assertion and self-denial are so radically at odds that they unite in the rapture of being "destroyed."

Sophia attributed such awesome experiences to a pervasive universal energy, termed the "Od" by Charles von Reichenbach, that was active in mesmerism and spiritualist seances.[4] For Sophia, it was the "odic" energy locked up in Nathaniel's letters, not the distress endemic to her emotional constitution, that brought on the ecstatic voltage. She reports having been "beside myself for a letter" several days, and then giving up in despair. "The next thing I remember was . . . [the servant] rushing up to me after dinner as I lay extended on the floor with the letter I wanted in her hand. The revulsion of joy was so immense that my head almost burst asunder & all the rest of the day it ached so desperately that I had to hold it together, while my heart was dancing for joy." If Nathaniel had questioned her use of the term "revulsion," when he read the journal on his return from the Isle of Shoals, Sophia could reply that she meant only the "sudden onset" of her joy, in keeping with still-current usage, not that it made her want to throw up. Far from wishing to rid herself of this delicious agony, Sophia clung to it like a talisman. "I had worn the beloved letter all day in my bosom for consolation," she later says. "The odic power kept penetrating my heart from it" (10–13 September).

Sophia's groveling protestations of absolute devotion to her husband conceal an unvanquished will to power. The chronicle of the agonies she has suffered willingly for Nathaniel during his "charming" vacation asserts Sophia's claim to the entitlements of a martyr, which are as limitless as the martyr's self-abnegation and innocent pain. Yet this transaction cannot occur unless her husband feels answerable for her miseries, just as Priscilla's power depends upon Hollingsworth's being haunted by Zenobia's accusing ghost. Sophia's journal, taken as a whole, lays a prodigious claim on her husband's conscience, corresponding to the claim that prompted her children to feel a "responsibility about me which is beautiful to see" (31 August).

Although there is no reason to doubt that Hawthorne gave every appearance of meeting Sophia's expectations, he met her dissociated fury not only with acquiescent guilt but also with covert reciprocal rage. The concluding vision of Hollingsworth and Priscilla, living in a seclusion required by Hollingsworth's morbid preoccupations, bears evident resemblance to the life of retirement Nathaniel preferred to lead with Sophia. But this vision also suggests that a man's "self-distrustful weakness"—the need for moral reassurance that makes him emotionally dependent on his wife—might be terminated if he could silence the angry ghost that haunts his conscience.

Hollingsworth's chastened consciousness represents only a fraction of Hawthorne's; a larger fraction is embodied in Coverdale, who hungers like Priscilla for vicarious experience, with the difference that he is aware that this impulse serves a desire for psychic domination. He speaks of his impulse "to live in other lives, and to endeavor . . . by delicate intuitions . . . to learn the secret which was hidden even from themselves" (CE 3:160). The intimate communion of the Hawthornes' marriage engaged this shared subtlety of consciousness, which generated a wealth of psychic intercourse. Whatever subsequent readers have felt about *Blithedale,* Sophia can hardly have been startled, or felt tricked, when Coverdale reveals at the end of the work that he has been in love throughout with Priscilla.

Priscilla is strangely exempted from the unsparing moral criticism Hawthorne brings to bear on Hollingsworth, Zenobia, and even Coverdale. For a work so obsessed with the egotism hidden behind postures of selflessness, *Blithedale* is remarkable for never insinuating the slightest taint in Priscilla's altruism, even though she ends up inheriting a substantial fortune and marrying the man she wants, whom she dominates through submission. Nathaniel could not expunge the self-assertion from Sophia's adulation, nor could he fail to recognize that her selflessness was managed so as to place pressure on his conscience. She treated him like a god, as believers generally do, with a prostration that embodied her hatred of the all-too-godlike power he exercised over her, and also expressed her determination to extract as many compensatory benefits as possible. But he was her match in the "delicacy" of his perceptions and her spiritual kinsman in the simultaneous assertion and effacement of his rage, now expressed as the impulse to obliterate her worship altogether. "I burned heaps of old letters and other papers, a little while ago, preparatory to going to England," he records in his journal sometime after his return from the Isle of Shoals. "Among them were hundreds of Sophia's maiden letters—the world has no more such; and now they are all ashes. What a trustful guardian of secret matters fire is! What should we do without Fire and Death?" (CE 8:552).

It is easy to concoct an argument denying that this was a hostile act.

Hawthorne had every right, after all, to secure his privacy against intrusion, especially now that he was a famous writer and a public official. Better to destroy personal papers than to risk the embarrassment that might result if they fell into the wrong hands. Yet Hawthorne's meditation does not mention these practical concerns, which would not have been difficult to resolve had he preferred saving her letters to burning them. Hawthorne dwells instead on how unique the letters were, how many there were, how absolute a destruction he has visited upon them, and how comforting it is to have consigned them to the "trustful" guardianship of death by fire—not such a death as befell Zenobia, after which her spirit lived on, but an annihilation in which "secret matters" are obliterated.

The impulse to destroy and to cherish appear together in this peculiarly elegiacal bit of gloating, much as they appear together in Coverdale's remark on the retribution he imagines for Zenobia and Hollingsworth. After the dreadful punishment was completed, says Coverdale, "I would come, as if to gather up the white ashes of those who had perished at the stake, and to tell the world . . . how much had perished there, which it had never yet known how to praise" (CE 3:161). At least four maiden letters did escape destruction, providing an early glimpse of the worshipful adulation we find in Sophia's journal entries.[5] But Nathaniel is nonetheless right in saying that no one can now know what she wrote to him during their long courtship, as the marriage they made was taking its initial form. He occupies the role he gives to Coverdale, that of sole witness—uniquely entitled to describe, celebrate, and pronounce judgment on an uncontrollable mystery of love and loathing. Yet Hawthorne, like Coverdale, remains a witness whose testimony is riddled with self-doubt.

The ideological preoccupation that gripped Hawthorne in the writing of *Blithedale* was a version—so I have proposed—of the impulse that overtook Dante in the darksome wood, the desire to anchor his life in a vision of universal order as he passes from youthful striving, triumphantly concluded, into the shadow of death. Only twelve years of life now remained to Hawthorne; before he took his final departure from the Wayside in 1864, the seismic tensions within the family became uncontainable, erupting in a crisis at Rome that devastated his spirit and crystallized the alienation already visible between him and Sophia. The Hawthornes' marriage had seen happier days, and it was troubled now by dilemmas that were slow in emerging. Nathaniel and Sophia had arrived at their tenth year of wedlock by way of personal histories shaped by the social and psychological conditions of their earliest lives. To appreciate the broader meaning of their story, we must trace it from the beginnings.

PART TWO

Numinous Mates

Social hierarchy was being redefined in America when Nathaniel and Sophia were growing up: middle-class hegemony displaced the seaboard landholding gentry that had provided leadership in the Revolution and in the writing of the Constitution, and this shift brought about a transformation in the status system of American society. A new elite emerged as the old elite declined; what changed, however, was not merely the membership of a fixed upper class but the terms on which elite status could be claimed. Individual achievement supplanted family heritage as the keynote of social worth.[1]

In "The American Scholar" (1837) Ralph Waldo Emerson noted "the new importance given to the single person" (Whicher, 79) as a pre-eminent sign of the times and sought to provide a spiritual underpinning for the emerging ideal of individual autonomy. The story of self-reliant struggle from humble origins to high position became the ruling narrative of manly worth, supplanting that of the well-born lad demonstrating his superior breeding in the exercise of responsibilities that were his birthright. The ideal of the youthful aristocrat enacted by Alexander Hamilton and Thomas Jefferson gave way to that of the self-made man. This new model of manly worth was a creation of a bourgeois culture that sought to reconcile the egalitarianism of Revolutionary ideology with continuing social stratification, holding that men are equal at birth and that just inequalities develop as differences of talent and virtue reveal themselves in democratic competition.

Families, especially prominent, powerful families, have been considered sacred from the origins of Western civilization. In early nineteenth-century America, however, the family became a focal point of religious reality in a new way. Social faith in the differential sacredness of bloodlines gave way to a numinous authority newly invested in the domestic circle, with the nurturing presence of the middle-class wife and mother at the center of the sacred tableau.

Lineage through the male line certainly did not cease to count as a marker of identity and an indicator of status in nineteenth-century America, and marriages continued to be made so as to strengthen and perpetuate family wealth and position. Yet it became proverbial by mid-century that a young man could be crippled by distinguished origins, what Nathaniel Hawthorne called inheriting "a great misfortune" (CE 2:20).[2] As the culture of commercial capitalism became established, social arrangements arose to accommodate the "perennial gale of creative destruction" that Joseph Schumpeter marked as its central quality (84). With all fortunes now apparently at risk, the men who emerged winners in the competitive new society gave credit to wives who had assisted them by providing a space of retreat from the struggle and the vision of a loftier humanity that ennobled their financial success. The self-made man had his cultural counterpart in the domestic angel, the woman with whom he had formed a marriage based not on inherited property but on mutual affection and moral fitness.

These social issues are easily recognizable in the broad thematic structure of *The House of the Seven Gables:* the family as lineage is desacralized in the fall of the Pyncheons, and the emerging ideal of domesticity is celebrated in the relation of Holgrave and Phoebe. But the imaginative design of Hawthorne's novel is composed of elements through which Nathaniel and Sophia sought to make sense of themselves. If they had never met one another, they would nonetheless have formed narratives of their personal experience that deployed the emerging conceptions of family and gender and would have spelled out in their lives the warfare of meanings that characterized the social transformation then taking place. The middle-class home did not smoothly replace the dynastic household as a cultural ideal. As typical figures of the "new" arrangement, Nathaniel and Sophia were caught in the struggle to distinguish it from an "old" pattern that still entered strongly into their self-understanding.

Nathaniel and Sophia had already imagined one another before they met; on meeting, they found that their two narratives were already one. They lived out an ideal that asserted not merely "natural" manhood and "natural" womanhood coming into accord, but the perfection of an "individual" accord: their two stories appeared to be written for each other, the marriage made in heaven. This myth of a uniquely preordained interlocking of individual selves lay at the heart of the claim to elite status that such marriages embodied.

As their lives articulated social circumstance, so the Hawthornes became its local exemplars; and for a much larger public *The House of the Seven Gables* enacts a comparable drama, in which a cultural order is fashioned that both nourishes and consumes its offspring. The story of the Hawthornes as numinous mates does not offer a "source" of *The House of the Seven Gables,* as though it were raw material that was submitted to the transforming alembic of Hawthorne's creative imagination. Like the selfhoods that Nathaniel and Sophia brought to it, the relationship between them was an imaginative achievement in an especially strong sense.

When Sophia's older sister referred to their marriage as "the coming together of two self-sufficing worlds" (Pearson, 276), she meant more than a late marriage between persons who had become accustomed to living single. Both Nathaniel and Sophia projected a distinctive aura; neither was an easygoing person, smoothly accommodating the peculiarities of others. Julian Hawthorne frequently refers to the "enchanted circle" (*NHW* 1:48) his mother cast about her; and evidences are plentiful that Hawthorne projected a momentous "presence."

What is the relation between the spell cast by a work of literature and such personal charisma? How is the collective life of art related to the psychic energy that radiates from a man or woman so strongly as to compel the imagination? Is so urgent an aura the sign of social conflict within the self? Does an individual become a "self-sufficing world" because he or she has internalized unstable and shifting identities, so that the working coherence necessary to sanity becomes precarious? How do two such coherencies become one, as the imaginations of Nathaniel and Sophia postulate and then discover one another? And how do we ourselves, with our workaday self-hoods, find not only that we have imagined Hawthorne's writings before we read them but also that the shamanistic force contemporaries encountered when they dealt with him, or with Sophia, still reaches us?

CHAPTER THREE

The Queen of All She Surveys

Sophia Hawthorne is the most vilified wife in American literary history, after having been in her own time the most admired. Elizabeth Shaw Melville has been blamed for not having measured up to Fayaway, and although Lidian Emerson was eminently presentable, like her short-lived predecessor, Ellen Louisa Tucker, neither woman is credited with having a vital relation to her husband's imagination. Thoreau, Whitman, and James did not marry, and Henry Adams's wife, Clover Hooper, is omitted—a gasping silence—from the story of his education. Sophia Hawthorne, by contrast, was hailed as indispensable to the flowering of her husband's genius, a role that Hawthorne himself fervently celebrated and impressed upon his friends and his children. "Nothing seems less likely," Julian affirmed, "than that he would have accomplished his work in literature independently of her sympathy and companionship" (*NHW* 1:39).

Scholars in our own time have found Sophia a force to be reckoned with. When Randall Stewart discovered how extensively she had edited the English Notebooks, he noted "the Victorian ideal of decorum" that guided her and concluded that her interferences cannot fairly be judged against twentieth-century standards of editorial scholarship (*English,* xxi). Yet compared with Nathaniel's genius for undermining the decorums of Victorian life, Sophia's temperament seems an epitome of moralistic hypocrisy. Frederick Crews has noted the zealous minute care with which her revisions purify

Hawthorne's language, observing that many of her alterations draw attention to indecent meanings that would pass unnoticed if she had not marked them. Crews condemns this as "the work of a dirty mind" (12–14). Not only is Sophia peculiarly alert to what she considers nasty, but the whole course of her censoring impulse runs counter to the openness of Hawthorne's imagination. It has become hard to understand how the man who wrote Hawthorne's works could have married Sophia at all, to say nothing of pronouncing her an indispensable source of spiritual sympathy and support.

The commonly accepted picture of Sophia conceals her playful warmth, her intellectual fervor, and the fierce independence of her spirit. Sophia was a maker of manners; and she continues to stir involuntary loathing because she remains a powerful avatar of a perishing god. (It is not hard to show disinterested curiosity in a divinity one has never worshiped, by whose adherents one has never been injured or aided.) The domestic angel had a primal religious force in the nineteenth century that she no longer enjoys, yet something of the awesome old energy still haunts us.

The growing sadness of Sophia's life, like the growing shrillness of her moralism, results in good measure from a paradox at the heart of her achievement. She pioneered a convention of womanhood that obliged her to deploy her creative powers vicariously, through Nathaniel. Among women who have sought to fulfill themselves through the achievements of a man, few have succeeded better than Sophia. She chose a man bound for greatness, in whom her own ambitions could be realized and to whom she was truly indispensable. The ironies of that triumph and its fearful price will occupy us to the end of her story; and they are already evident at the outset, where the inner meanings of her illness took form.

The "female malady" that harassed and interrupted the lives of other Victorian women became for Sophia an embracing idiom of selfhood.[1] Her primary symptom was a disabling headache typically tripped off by unexpected noises, at times so slight as the clinking of silverware. Sophia found a spiritual portent in these agonizing experiences and persistently sought their meaning.

> All day yesterday my head raged, and I sat a passive subject for the various corkscrews, borers, pincers, daggers, squibs and bombs to effect their will upon it. Always I occupy myself with trying to penetrate the mystery of pain. Sceptics surely cannot disbelieve in one thing invisible, and that is *Pain*. Towards night my head was relieved, and I seemed let down from a weary height full of points into a quiet green valley, upon velvet turf. It was as if I had fought a fight all day and got through.[2]

A mythological haziness surrounds accounts of the onset of Sophia's problem, in which one nonetheless finds clear assertions of her having been
remarkably vigorous and healthy in girlhood (*Cuba,* xxx; Tharp, 24). At the
age of twenty-four Sophia spent a year in Cuba, hoping that relaxation and
the warm climate would cure her; she wrote home that "it would be utter
folly to expect a rooted pain of fifteen years or more to be expelled in 'one
little month' " (*Cuba,* 25). Taken as a key to chronology, this remark would
indicate that the illness began when Sophia was nine years old or younger;
but we are not dealing here with chronological time. This "rooted pain" was
deep in the self and thus is felt to be deep in the past. Julian traces the
trouble even closer to the sources of Sophia's identity; his version of the
family story blames her dentist father, who "incontinently" dosed her with
allopathic drugs when she was teething (*NHW* 1:47).

Louise Tharp's *Peabody Sisters of Salem* sketches a still earlier myth of
origins that suggests why it seemed plausible to blame her father's inepti-
tude. At the heart of Sophia's illness was an anti-patriarchal impulse that is
visible in the tradition of womanly character from which she sprang.

The Peabody family was among the most distinguished in New England
during Sophia's girlhood; but the Palmers—her mother's family—figured
largest in the claim to high status that the women of the family asserted.
Sophia's mother—Elizabeth Palmer Peabody—retained worshipful memories of a grandfather, General Palmer, who was a pre-Revolutionary aristocrat. He made his home at Friendship Hall, a splendid mansion set in the
midst of extensive landholdings, where Elizabeth in childhood stretched out
on the floor of the library to read Shakespeare and Spenser from leather-
bound volumes.

Sophia's crisis of health at her entry into adulthood replays that of
General Palmer's daughter Mary.[3] She too possessed unusual physical vigor
and was a crack shot and a fearless rider. So intrepid was she, in fact, that
her father consented to a test of nerve proposed by her fiancé, who crept up
on her while she was reading in the garden and fired a pistol close by her
head. Mary Palmer forthwith went into hysterics, broke the engagement, and
secluded herself in her bedroom as a nervous invalid unable to endure
sudden noises.

Alexis de Tocqueville observed that the transition from girlhood to womanhood in democratic America was a drastic change, and while he tried to
put an attractive face on it, his description makes clear it was a change for
the worse. "The independence of woman is irrecoverably lost in the bonds

of matrimony." She leaves her father's house, an "abode of freedom and of pleasure," to live "in the home of her husband as if it were a cloister" (2:201). This typical crisis may have become more pronounced in the 1830s, when Tocqueville came to America, than it was when young Miss Palmer took to her bed fifty years earlier. Yet the plight of a strong-minded young woman facing the limitations of marriage is a time-honored theme of family relations. It is a staple of Shakespeare's plays—as with Hermia, Portia, Juliet, and Cordelia—where the father's tyrannical command brings on the conflict.

The "joke" played on General Palmer's spirited daughter was a joint enterprise, carried out together by the two men, and it seems evident that her nervous ailment was a protest against the servitude that the gunshot announced, matrimony as a state of subjection to her husband, fully authorized by her father. General Palmer, it seems, yielded to his daughter's protest: he was stricken with remorse and gave orders that members of the household observe silence within earshot of her bedroom.

The rebellious spirit that goes into such a protest strongly characterized Sophia Peabody's foremothers. Her grandmother Betsey Hunt—also brought up in luxury—secretly taught herself to read because her father forbade instruction; and she eloped with young Joseph Palmer, the general's son, who had been willing to supply her with books.

Elizabeth Palmer Peabody, Sophia's mother, inherited a full share of this womanly valor; she struggled all her life to retain some purchase on the social prominence that was jeopardized following the loss of General Palmer's fortune. Having an "earnest wish to gain for herself a decent independence," Elizabeth accepted menial employments in her early twenties, but she also published poems in vigorous heroic couplets on political topics, prominently including the rights of women (Marshall, 45). For a time she set her hopes on her husband, Nathaniel Peabody, but his medical practice yielded only fitful success, and the family's circumstances did not markedly improve when he decided to try his hand as a dentist. Elizabeth developed a significant career of her own as a writer and an educator; her children grew up amid the bustle of the household schools that she established, for which she wrote class materials that were subsequently published as *Sabbath Lessons; or, an Abstract of Sacred History* and *Holiness; or, the Legend of St. George*. But this career did not bring financial security, so that her oldest daughter, Elizabeth, was encouraged to begin work as a schoolteacher at the earliest possible date, as was Mary, the next oldest.

Mrs. Peabody pursued these high-minded undertakings in a social situation that riddled them with contradictions. The vision of social eminence she derived from her memories of Friendship Hall was unrealizable in the turbulent economy of the early nineteenth century. The "unbought grace of life" that the colonial gentry transferred to America from the traditional aristocracy of Great Britain became impossible to sustain as the boom-and-bust cycles of an unregulated capitalism recurrently discomposed the status hierarchy. The New England gentry, responding to this threat by attempting to close ranks, asserted a new form of solidarity, centered on the possession and conservation of wealth as opposed to the maintenance of kin connections cutting across lines of economic difference. The separation of social groupings by levels of affluence meant that the prestige earlier attaching to names like Peabody and Palmer began to drain away (A. Rose, 5–12, 19–22).

For men, the freedom from mercenary struggle that earlier had marked social prominence was now replaced by the claim of having succeeded in that very struggle. Dramas of leisured cultivation were increasingly enacted by the wives of wealthy men, not by the men themselves. Instead of a manorial Friendship Hall presided over by a venerable old gentleman, the new emblems of status were the great McIntire mansions on the residential streets of Salem that were paid for by the profits of shipping ventures and managed by ladies of refinement.

Struggling to keep a school going and prodding her husband to greater efforts was unlike any such life. Because Mrs. Peabody was a married woman (unable to sign a contract, own property, or vote) there was no possibility that the life she led would one day be seen as a temporary encampment on the hard road to a splendid demesne. One of the lessons of Mrs. Peabody's adulthood was that a woman's self-reliant efforts, no matter how intelligent or vigorous, could not be rewarded with economic success.[4] Yet in her fierce commitment to education as a path to moral and cultural attainment, Mrs. Peabody explored alternative avenues to womanly triumph available in the rising middle-class order.

Sophia Peabody was proud to believe that the Peabodys were descended from Boudicca, the queen of the Britons, who led a bloody revolt against Roman overlordship (Tharp, 19). All three of Elizabeth Peabody's daughters—Elizabeth, Mary, and Sophia—were indomitable warriors; Sophia's distinctive armor was the identification of womanhood itself with an aristocratic spirituality, to be kept defiantly aloof from the squalor of mercenary preoccupations.

It seems that Mrs. Peabody assigned to Sophia the task of embodying what she herself had glimpsed in girlhood, the *otium cum dignitate* that was incompatible with the relentless striving of her adult years. On numerous occasions Mrs. Peabody declared that Sophia, because of her "delicate" nature, was unable to make a journey, or pay a visit, or take a job that Sophia herself was quite eager to accept. When Sophia was fourteen, her sisters were teaching in wealthy households in Maine, and Elizabeth wrote home in great excitement over meeting a woman who was personally acquainted with Madame de Staël. "Madame de Stael made no distinction between the sexes," she wrote to Sophia. "She treated men in the same manner as women. She knew that genius has no sex" (Tharp, 33). Mrs. Peabody would not allow Sophia to visit her sisters in Maine.

Splitting headaches are not the same thing as aristocratic leisure, and the feminine spirituality Sophia cultivated was a virtue enshrined by the rising American middle class, not by the landed gentry of the late eighteenth century; yet in Sophia's illness these divergent themes were fused, the symbolism of elite status being refashioned in a pattern that ascribed childlike innocence and purity to women while making them exemplars of unworldly cultivation. She lay abed, able to eat no foods except those of the purest white—white bread, white meat, and milk—and, like General Palmer's daughter, suffering dreadfully at the slightest noise. Yet she also deployed her extraordinary energy and ability in the study of literature, geography, science, European and American history, Latin, French (and later Greek, Hebrew, and German), and drawing.

The special treatment accorded Sophia did not set Mrs. Peabody at odds with the two older daughters, at least not overtly. Sophia's care, as well as her education and religious training, was a project in which both sisters cooperated, and in which her sister Elizabeth took a strong hand. The whole family worked together to treat Sophia as having a distinctive quality rightly demanding the utmost solicitude from those who cared about her and appreciated who she was. All her life Sophia expressed heartfelt gratitude for the selfless devotion that had been lavished on her.

The new democratic ethos offered strong incentives to women of gentry origins who carried high abilities and ambitions into the society of post-Revolutionary America. Even as the Constitution was being drafted, Abigail Adams, recognizing that the doctrine of equal rights should apply to herself, wrote the famous letter asking her husband to "remember the ladies." The grounding of human dignity in individual striving, especially where directed toward the public good, inspired women of talent and pride to dream of high achievement; and in the generation of Sophia's mother there was little contradiction between running schools and writing about education while being a wife and mother.

Trained to boldness and independence of mind, Sophia and her sisters expected to have "careers," lives of significant activity directed by their own choices.[5] Like men who are indoctrinated with this ideal, they faced the problem of making such lives their own, as distinct from obeying the precepts of their indoctrinators. How was Sophia to lead her own life, rather than live out a compensatory feature of her mother's? The Peabody sisters also faced additional dilemmas as the chasm deepened in their early years between a woman's domestic occupations and the world in which public achievement was possible. The undertakings that were united in their mother's life came under divergent pressures, so that the daughters were forced to choose: Elizabeth remained single as she pursued a public career; Sophia and Mary made marriages. But in the early nineteenth century these were not choices between clearly defined alternatives; each possibility was impregnated with the energies of its opposite. Like these rivalrous devoted sisters, the available possibilities were both united and at odds; and the tensions among them were at stake in the interior conflict that devastated and animated Sophia.

Sophia, whose interest in her inner life never waned, typically idealized her descriptions of formative experiences, celebrating the selfless maternal love that trained her in womanly spirituality. But when her own children were approaching maturity, she recalled a childhood experience that was "slightly bitter" and wrote it up for them in circumstances that indicate the attendant status anxieties.[6]

In March 1860, when the Hawthornes were preparing to return from England, the family made an expedition to Bath. On arriving at the railway station, they were directed to a hotel much finer than Sophia thought they could afford. A single night in such a place, Sophia wrote her sister, might consume a whole year's income. The family's sitting room was "hung with crimson," and the dining service featured the "finest cut crystal, and knives and forks with solid silver handles, and spoons too heavy to lift easily." Once they discovered that the expense was not prohibitive, the Hawthornes made the most of the occasion. Nathaniel and Sophia styled themselves "the Duke and Duchess of Maine" while Julian became "Lord Waldo," Una "Lady Raymond," and Rose "Lady Rose" (Hull, *Hawthorne,* 187), titles recalling the Hawthorne family legend of a vast manorial establishment near Raymond, Maine. Thus fortified with emblems of high place, Sophia drafted her story as told by "the Countess of Raymond" to "the Duchess Anna."

When Sophia was four or five years old, she was playing outdoors on a visit to her grandmother's house and picked up a fat puppy that squirmed too hard for her to manage, slipped from her grasp and dropped to the pavement with a loud squeal. Sophia's aunt rushed from the house, shook her violently by the arm, and gave her a severe scolding. The aunt was "tall, stately, and handsome," Sophia recalled, "and very terrible in her wrath. I felt like a criminal, and as it had never yet occurred to me that a grown person could do wrong, but that children only were naughty, I took the scolding, and the earthquake my aunt made of my little body, as a proper penalty for some fault which she saw, though I did not."

The victim of an injustice that she could not articulate, Sophia is sent off to her grandmother's upstairs bedroom and there, looking out the window, she beholds her nemesis:

> I saw a beggar girl, sitting on a doorstep directly opposite, and when she caught sight of me, she clenched her fist and uttered a sentence, which, though I did not in the least comprehend it, I never forgot. *"I'll maul you!"* said the beggar girl, with a scowling, spiteful face. I gazed at her in terror, feeling hardly safe, though within stone walls and half-way up to the sky, as it seemed to me. I was convinced she would have me at last, and that no power could prevent it, but I did not even appeal to my Grandmamma for aid, nor utter a word of my awful fate to anyone.

Sophia felt compelled to keep secret this terrifying image of her own fury. The beggar girl's wanton unprovoked rage is a perfect opposite to the speechless submission Sophia herself was then suffering, and a replication in small of the attack on her by her aunt. The threat of being "mauled" by the beggar girl could not be excluded by the bedroom walls, nor could Sophia's grandmother dispel it, and Sophia remained certain that this curse would pursue her until it was fulfilled.

It is possible that young Sophia associated the tyranny of her grandmother and her aunt with the minute supervisory attention lavished on her by her mother and sisters. But it is hardly likely that—in her little-girlhood—she connected the beggary of the urchin with the economic dependence of women and secretly sympathized with the beggar girl's defiant fury (and felt all the more threatened by it) because it symbolized a rebellion against the humiliating necessities that prompted her mother and sisters to treat her as they did. But we are not dealing here with a five-year-old's account. Sophia wrote this story after the years of puberty, in which the restriction of her life became fixed, and after seventeen years of marriage. An elaborate pattern of meaning had crystallized around the original incident, and Sophia describes an earlier encounter with the beggar girl that relates directly to her mother and includes broader themes of psychic and social subjugation.

Sophia reports that the advent of the beggar girl banished all thought of her aunt's anger; and as she gazed on the little hobgoblin, she realized they had met before. This had happened

when I had escaped out of the garden-gate at home, and was taking my first independent stroll. No maid nor footman was near me on that happy day. It was glorious. My steps were winged, and there seemed more room on every side than I had heretofore supposed the world contained. The sense of freedom from all shackles was intoxicating. I had on no hat, no walking dress, no gloves. What exquisite fun! I really think every child that is born ought to have the happiness of running away once in their lives at least,—it is so perfectly delightful. I went up a street that gradually ascended, till, at the summit, I believed I stood on the top of the earth. But alas! at that acme of success my joy ended, for there I confronted suddenly this beggar-girl,— the first ragged, begrimed human being I had ever seen.

The encounter with the urchin again takes place against the background of confinement, not at the hands of her wicked aunt, but in her beloved mother's home. The hat, gloves, and outdoor dress are paraphernalia of the genteel nurture that shackled Sophia, and her escape is an exercise of inner strength, the discovery of a larger space, the prospect of climbing to the top of the world. Yet her jubilant freedom leads straight to the encounter with a much more desperate enslavement.

What happened next was a grotesque parody of her lessons in genteel propriety: "She seized my hand, and said 'Make me a curtsey!' 'No!' I replied, '*I will not!*', the noble blood in my veins tingling with indignation. How I got away, and home again, I cannot tell; but as I did not obey the insolent command, I constantly expected revenge in some form, and yet never told mamma anything about it."

The story presents Sophia as having her choice of shackles, and choosing with great energy. Fearlessly defying the "insolent" girl, she retains the dignity of her class position as a young lady. But in fleeing home she is fleeing to a world of curtsies, not enforced with rough commands, but enforced nonetheless.

As she amalgamated the two incidents, Sophia became fascinated by the word *mauled*. "What was that? Something doubtless, unspeakably dreadful. The new, strange word cast an indefinite horror over the process to which I was to be subjected. Where could the creature have got the expression?" Not only does the beggar girl know about curtsies, but she has also acquired somewhere a relatively sophisticated vocabulary. As her years unfolded, Sophia had good reason to dread the prospect of collapsing, with all her education and sensibilities, into poverty. She knew she did not have family wealth by which to bankroll a life of genteel invalidism, and when the time came for her to scramble for her own living—by way of editing Hawthorne's notebooks after his death—she proved fit for the task. Other New England women of her class and generation did not fare so well and suffered the degradation of carrying their cultural attainments into circumstances of financial ruin and of watching their children grow up in squalor.[7]

The conventional recourse for a woman in Sophia's circumstances was to uphold the standard of womanly refinement whose imperatives were as harsh as those of the beggar girl but which served as the regalia of the emerging middle class. If a growing girl failed to attain the selfless delicacy of a "true woman," she risked falling into the working class, or beneath, where beggars and bullies lived out their desolate lives and sought occasions for taking futile vengeance on their social superiors, or on the working-class women who often served as vicarious targets. For a woman to unsex herself by asserting her aggressive impulses (to say nothing of her erotic impulses) was to invite consignment to this outer darkness, which was the sharpest social terror now assailing the old New England gentry, that of failing to negotiate the transition into the new elite and falling into laboring-class degradation.

Sophia's story is a parable of the cross-pressures inherent in the ideal of womanhood she sought to make her own. The beggar girl polices the genteel "feminine" order by reduplicating its commands with harsh clarity and by reminding the potential rebel of what lies outside. She is thus the object of the policing action she herself executes. The story invests the beggar girl with two opposed impulses, both of structural significance to the emerging gender arrangement as Sophia came to embody it: violence exploding in opposition to the standard of womanhood that was set before her as mandatory, and violence exerted to support the same standard.

The horror Sophia felt at the prospect of being "mauled" by this figure was generated by the psychosocial contradiction grinding away in her own personality. Her life was conditioned permanently by a psychic autoimmune reaction in which, spontaneously and with fierce dedication, she sought to rid herself of the very qualities of fierce spontaneity that were built into the reaction itself. A feedback loop of inner conflict was established that could be set in motion by a slight external irritation and would then, under its own self-driven dynamic, crescendo to a mind-splitting roar. The experience of being ripped apart, of being made into an "earthquake," of being "mauled," of being "destroyed": all these were imposed on her by the inherent contradictions of a social situation that both cultivated and repressed the direct exercise of her native force.

Sophia managed to place her conflicts—and the illness to which they led—in the service of her own initiative, wresting a degree of mastery from the conditions of her victimization. She became a careful student of her own condition, and as one doctor after another proved unable to "cure" her, she emerged as an authority on the treatment she required. "This morning I awoke very tired," she writes in her journal, "& as if I must take some exercise to change the nature of the fatigue—so although it snowed & Molly [her sister Mary] thought it 'absurd'—I took a drive with Mamma for half an hour & as I expected was relieved of the vital weariness, though I acquired physical." Noting that Mary considers her "wilfully & foolishly imprudent," Sophia insists that she is herself the only judge because the knowledge of her pain is incommunicable. "Heaven grant," she piously concludes, "that none may *through experience* understand the excruciating sensation I perpetually feel."[8]

Sophia found one avenue toward mastering her condition in the conviction that it offered spiritual insight. Having disposed of Mary's claim that the sleigh ride was "absurd," Sophia turns to comment on the opinion of a physician she admired: "Dr. Shattuck was right when he so decidedly declared I never should be relieved 'till I heard the music of the spheres'—in other words—till I had put off corruption." Sophia here is not anticipating her own death but referring to a mystical transaction in which her miseries are sublimated in a communion with the divine. The inner conflicts that threatened her with psychic disintegration also gave her experiences of transcendent harmony.

Sophia cherished throughout her life a girlhood dream that portrayed this process, recounting it to her children and to intimate friends as an emblem of her essential spirituality. The dream—as Julian described it—was "of a dark cloud, which suddenly arose in the west and obscured the celestial tints of a splendid sunset. But while she was deploring this eclipse, and the cloud spread wider and gloomier, all at once it underwent a glorious transformation; for it consisted of countless myriads of birds, which by one movement turned their rainbow-colored breasts to the sun, and burst into a rejoicing chorus of heavenly song" (*NHW* 1:49).[9]

This is not a dream about a silver lining, or about the sun bursting through a cloud, but of the whole cloud instantly transformed into a heavenly chorus. Sophia would certainly have agreed that the process depicted here is "sublimation," inverting the post-Freudian sense of the term, in which the earthy desires sublimated are considered to be real. Sophia's inward experience attested a central axiom of romantic Neoplatonism, that sublimation gives access to the sublime, the movement from earthly murk into radiant spiritual truth taking place at a single step. As her son declared, the transcendental ontology of Sophia's dream was "among the firmest articles of her faith" (NHW 1:49).

Sophia's experience of redemptive communion with the divine meant that her agonizing sensitivity counted as a moral litmus, unerringly reactive to earthly evils. Since freedom from nervous headaches required "putting off corruption," she acquired a command post within the consciences of all who knew and understood her. Her sister Elizabeth remarked on the voluntary acquiescence Sophia's needs inspired. "All these years mother was her devoted nurse,—watching in the entries that no door should be hard shut, etc. . . . I had a school of 40 scholars, and she became interested in them, and they would go into her room; and the necessity of keeping still in the house so as not to disturb her, was my means of governing my school: for they all spontaneously governed themselves" (Pearson, 272–273).

Elizabeth was one of the most forceful and accomplished American women of the century, accustomed at an early age to managing her own life and to setting plans for others to follow. After opening a school in Brookline in 1825, she became a friend and disciple of William Ellery Channing, with whose endorsement she enlarged her school and took on as partner a prominent teacher of elocution named William Russell. By 1828 the whole family had moved from Salem to Boston, and Elizabeth's long career of educational and cultural leadership in that city commenced. Elizabeth knew a struggle for dominance when she saw one, and she was frankly astonished at Sophia's successes. "I never knew any human creature who had such sovereign power over everybody—grown and child—that came into her sweet and gracious presence. Her brothers reverenced and idolized her" (Pearson, 273).

Sophia found it virtually impossible to act frankly in her own behalf because self-assertion invited a "nervous" attack. At age thirteen she discovered, for example, that she had an exceptional talent for drawing and painting, yet the first dawning of this realization brought on a bout of incapacity. "She was thrown into a sickness," her sister observed, "from which she never rose into the possibility of so much excitation again; and by a slight accident was disabled in the hand and could not draw" (Pearson, 272). When Sophia returned to drawing and painting several years later, she sought to resolve this dilemma by becoming a copyist instead of creating her own pictures.[10] She soon became so skillful that knowledgeable observers could scarcely distinguish her work from the originals, and her copies of pictures by Washington Allston, Chester Harding, and other leading painters were much in demand.

Sophia was both fascinated and repelled by Elizabeth's public enterprises. Sophia sent letters home from Cuba, which her sister circulated among friends in Boston, and before the year was out, Sophia's "Cuba Journal" had made a name for itself. Word got abroad that Sophia's "effusions" were "ravishing," so that Elizabeth was able to organize readings for invited guests that on some occasions ran as long as seven hours (*Cuba,* xxxviii). Sophia professed herself "aghast": "I do not like at all that my journal should be made such public property of—I think Betty is *VERY* naughty. . . . I assure you I am really provoked. I shall be ashamed to shew my face in the places that knew me—for it seems exactly as if I were in print—as if every body had got the key of my private cabinet & without leave of the owner—are appropriating whatever they please" (249, 470–471). Elizabeth in reply urged Sophia to publish in *The Atlantic Monthly,* which Sophia refused to do. Early in their courtship, however, she offered the journal to Nathaniel Hawthorne, who—doubtless pleased at being handed the key to her private cabinet—copied sections of it into his own notebook. From him she received a recognition suited to the sovereign aloofness she wished to maintain: he called her the "Queen of Journalizers" (xxxix, xli).

Elizabeth and Sophia present a contrast of spirits deeply alike. The pressure Elizabeth exerted against the conventions of domesticity in her public undertakings was felt by Sophia as an inner imperative, as was the pressure of those conventions themselves. Sophia's psychic struggle was an internalized version of the conflict Elizabeth waged outwardly, so that the drama and danger of Elizabeth's public career were recapitulated as a subjective experience by her younger sister.

Sophia describes her artistic endeavors in the winter of 1832 in language that indicates the blend of overpowering excitement and overpowering dread that accompanied the effort to put her talent to work. "Yesterday I began copying Mr. Allston's picture," she begins.

> It was intense enjoyment—almost intoxicating. It was an emotion altogether too intense for my physicals. A most refined torture did it work & has it worked today

upon my head—accompanied with a deathly sickness. After a ride yesterday the sickness passed away in a degree & left . . . [a] headache which seemed to exalt every faculty of my mind & everything of which I thought was tinged with a burning splendor which was almost terrible & I did not dare to let my imagination excurse.[11]

Observe the fusion of seemingly contradictory emotions. The ecstasy that she expresses in sustaining "a refined torture" is masochistic, yet at the heart of this ravishment is the purposeful exercise of her talent. To "excurse" is to play with fire, a daring and passionate adventure of the mind along the borders of insanity. "What do you think I have actually begun to do?" she writes to Elizabeth on another occasion. "Nothing less than *create* and do you wonder that I lay awake all last night after sketching my first picture. I actually thought my head would have made its final explosion. When once I began to excurse, I could not stop" (Tharp, 55).

Sophia's effort to comprehend her experience took the path marked out by her Neoplatonic faith. Instead of examining the concrete dilemmas of being a woman, and of being Sophia Peabody, she undertook a meditative exploration of transcendental realities. Here is a journal entry from her twentieth year:

A dubious morning. I felt rather as if a tempest had passed over & crushed my powers when I awoke—for such a violent pain—while it is on me, gives me a supernatural force—combined with an excessive excitement of all my tenderest nerves, which nearly drives me mad. Yesterday whenever a door slammed or a loud voice made me start throughout in my powerless state—I could not keep the tears—burning tears from pouring over my cheeks. . . . Oh how mysterious is this unseen mighty agent. There is evident reason why a murderous instrument should cause anguish—but how is this inward-invisible agony caused? It seems as if a revelation had passed in my head & that I can no more mingle with the noisy world.[12]

Sophia sustains a supernatural revelation that would not have seized her if she were free of her malady. On the journey to Cuba, undertaken in hopes of a cure, she commented on the spiritual loss entailed by getting well: "I believe I understand in a degree the very great blessing of sickness. . . . Coming years of 'Health' never can be so dear to me as the past years of suffering—I shall go back to them as I would enter the inner chamber of the tabernacle where the throne & the ark—were filled with the presence & commands of the Invisible GOD" (*Cuba,* 250).

Sophia's pain exalts her from the earthly to the divine by making her preternaturally aware of the intricacy of her psychic and physical organization, and thus of her own miraculous character as a creation of God. If she were merely a "nervous" woman, she affirms, her mind would have collapsed under the pressure; instead, she is a visionary prophet.

> We are indeed fearfully & wonderfully made, & no one can know *how* fearfully till they are sensitive in the nicest parts of this wonderful machinery—If I had been *nervous* in the common acceptation of the term, I think I should not only have been *mad*, but afraid to move or feel. . . . In the extremity of my suffering when I was conscious of a floating off of my senses—a resolute fixing of my mind upon immutable, never changing essence . . . has enabled me to regain my balance so entirely that I feel as if I had had direct revelation to my own mind of the existence of such a Being.
>
> (*Cuba*, 252–253)

This interior experience opened Sophia's mind to the Godhead spiritually immanent in the creation, not merely to the rational order that natural theologians like William Paley found in it. Sophia's romantic ecstasy testified directly to the great soul pervading nature, the local syntax of her ego dissolving into the universal discourse. "When the omnipresent beauty of the universe comes & touches the cells of Memory," she wrote home from Cuba, "& has an answer from all our individual experiences of the beautiful in thought & act during the Past—& blending with the Present—in symphonious oneness—carries us on to the future by the power of that trust or faith which is nobler because more disinterested than any other attitude of the mind, connecting all. . . . There is no need of logic to convince the hearkening spirit that there is a GOD—Knowledge by intuition is the unerring truth" (*Cuba*, 585).

If Elizabeth had succeeded in publishing the Cuba Journal in 1833, Sophia Peabody would be numbered among the earliest public exponents of transcendentalist spirituality. Both sisters were caught up in the ferment among young Unitarian clergymen who were inspired by Wordsworth, Coleridge, and Carlyle and who published articles in the *Christian Examiner* seeking to articulate the new consciousness.

Elizabeth had taken charge of her younger sister's education when Sophia was five years old and had inculcated Unitarian convictions regarding rational virtue and the perfectibility of human nature, scrupulously shielding her from the "terrible doctrines" of Calvinism (Pearson, 270). By the time Elizabeth moved the family to Boston in 1828, she was already attuned to the themes in William Ellery Channing's teaching that encouraged the development of transcendentalism and caused the leaders of the new movement to look on him as a spiritual father. Elizabeth is best known for the practical support she provided for transcendentalists, for her role in Alcott's Temple School, and for establishing the West Street Bookstore, where *The Dial* was published and Margaret Fuller held her conversations. But Elizabeth was intellectually active as well; she published a series of articles titled "The Spirit of the Hebrew Scriptures" in the *Christian Examiner* for 1834—grounded on her own reading of the Hebrew and of German criticism. Her ideas greatly alarmed Professor Andrews Norton of Harvard, a defender of Unitarianism against the new movement, so that he ordered the cancellation of Elizabeth's series after the third of her six articles had been published (A. Rose, 54). When Frederic Henry Hedge formed the Transcendental Club in 1836, Elizabeth Peabody (and Margaret Fuller) were invited to join (Miller, 106).

Sophia quickly accepted the transcendentalist doctrine most alarming to orthodox Unitarians, namely that spontaneous impulses of the soul could serve as a guide to truth, replacing the cold conclusions of reason. Unitarians were especially touchy on this point because their Calvinist opponents had claimed all along that liberal worship of reason would lead in the end to wanton irrationalism, and the transcendentalists appeared to fulfill this prophecy. Because it advanced the claims of religious intuition, an 1833 article on Coleridge by Frederic Henry Hedge was seen by proponents of transcendentalism as the *"first word"* uttered in public in behalf of the new spirituality (Miller, 67).

Sophia started reading Coleridge in 1830 and attempted a conclusion to the unfinished "Christabel."[13] On the journey to Cuba three years later she was ready to articulate the relationship between Coleridge's romantic ontology and her own aesthetic raptures. "A forest always seems to me to have intelligence—a soul—The trees seem a brotherhood—Especially when they are all motionless—It must be the 'intellectual breeze' of which Coleridge speaks, that wakes that feeling within us, in the presence of nature, or 'the intense Reply of hers to our Intelligence' & we are the 'harps diversely framed' " (*Cuba*, 480).

In reply, Elizabeth sounded a note of caution that echoes the Unitarian resistance to transcendental teaching and serves as yet another reminder of the way issues of the public controversy were also fought out within the partisans. "Sentiments about Beauty," Elizabeth declared, "do not constitute Religion" (*Cuba*, xxxiii).

Early in 1835 Sophia drafted a meditation in her personal notebook concerning Coleridge and Plato, exploring the union of self-knowledge with knowledge of the transcendent: "To study our own Life is to study all Life—since in this Life of ours are emblems and representations of every form and power and spirit of life. And this is Life—to apprehend . . . the IDEAL that images itself in our Being, wherein by self study & self representation, sustained and purified by the Actual not less than by the Speculative powers, we find the Absolute, All Representing One, and finding Him we know & in Him image ourselves."[14]

The purity of soul required for such knowledge, Sophia explained, was possible only for those unsullied by traffic with this world. Far from lamenting her lengthy postponement of conventional adult responsibilities, she celebrated childlikeness. "In the heart of Infancy do I hope for that Light & Life to spring that shall regenerate the Philosophy and Life of future Time, when Literature shall flourish in the greenness of youth . . . when Language shall become the transcript and representative of the unshadowed Life of Childhood."[15]

Sophia rejected the suspicion that her childlike consciousness was merely naive and that her convulsive recoil from the "earthly" might blind her to realities that deserve to be taken seriously. "My meditations turned upon my habit of viewing things through the 'coleur de rose' medium," she wrote, "when suddenly, like a night-blooming cereus, my mind opened, and I read in letters of paly golden green, words to this effect. The beautiful and good and true are the only real and abiding things, the only proper *use* of the soul and Nature. Evil and ugliness and falsehood are *abuses,* monstrous and transient. I do not see *what is not,* but what *is,* through the passing clouds."[16]

Sophia thus adopted an understanding of evil as nonbeing that found expression in the romantic religion diversely articulated in Massachusetts by Emerson and Mary Baker Eddy. To Sophia, as to Emerson and Eddy, the perception of evil is a defect of spiritual sight that leads people to mistake the transient clouds of earth for the eternal sunlight passing through them. But the essential quality of Sophia's mind is not in the conclusions she reached, but in the vigor with which she pursued her spiritual excitements. Well before Emerson issued to the Phi Beta Kappa society at Harvard College his dictum that "the one thing in the world, of value, is the active soul" (Whicher, 68), Sophia was living it out.

She was Woman Thinking, and she laid claim to the poetic power of vision according to which the ennobled spirit is able to refashion reality itself. Yet the plastic power of her eye and its expression in language were only subordinate modes—romantic doctrine equally affirmed—of her personal presence, which brought this creative force to bear on other souls (Fig. 2). "Natures apparently far sturdier and ruder than hers depended upon her, almost abjectly, for support," Julian declares. "She was a blessing and an

Fig. 2. Sophia Hawthorne as a young woman

illumination wherever she went; and no one ever knew her without receiving
from her far more than could be given in return. Her pure confidence
created what it trusted in" (*NHW* 1:48).

Sophia's piety retained a strongly social meaning. Like those throughout
New England who responded to transcendentalist doctrines, Sophia felt a
desire to buttress an elite identity that was increasingly threatened in the
rising commercial economy. Without inherited wealth to defend, transcendentalists asserted an aristocracy of intellect and virtue against whose lofty
standards of taste and moral cultivation the rude multitude could plausibly

be scorned or made targets of "improving" enterprises. In *Transcendentalism as a Social Movement* Anne Rose discusses the defensive consolidation of wealth that split the old elite class into affluent and penurious sectors, and she ably portrays the radical critique of contemporary social developments that the transcendentalists provided; but Rose does not notice the reactionary and defensive impulses arising from the transcendentalists' own elite identity, which they shared with doctrinal antagonists among the Unitarians and Calvinists, as against vulgarian Methodists, Baptists, and the Roman Catholic Irish.

Sophia was aware that the economic instability of American society was forcing a revision in the way elite status was marked. "In America," she wrote in her commonplace book, "greatness can never be predicated of a man on account of position—but only of character, because from the nature of our institutions, place changes like the figures of a kaleidoscope—and what is a man profitted because he *has been* a President—a Governor, or what not. This comes near to showing how factitious is all outward rank and show and especially American rank & show. In the old world birth, culture, permanence and habit give more prestige and Quality."[17] Sophia's yearning for the "Quality" conferred by Old World position carries over into the vocabulary she uses to describe the greatness of character that distinguishes superior persons in the New World: they are a nobility whose station is permanent because it is rooted in the eternal.

The transcendental ecstasy in which Sophia gazes out over the Cuban landscape vindicates her claim to aristocratic pre-eminence: "I felt like an eagle & like the Queen of all I surveyed." Sophia was well aware of speaking here for a community of moral sentiment. She articulates what Emerson and Thoreau were to establish as a commonplace of romantic revolt, namely that the true possession of property is enjoyed by those who respond to its inherent poetry, not those who hold the deeds to it. "We who enjoy it, not in proportion to the revenue of gold it yields to our coffers, but in the infinite proportion of unappropriating & immaterial pleasure it pours into our hearts. . . . We it is who possess the earth. It was mine that morning—I was the queen of it all" (*Cuba,* 566–567).

Sophia was painfully aware that she was not rich: her life of leisure on the Cuban coffee plantation was purchased through the efforts of her sister Mary, who worked in the household as a governess. Sophia realized that cultivated persons may be placed at the mercy of vulgar souls who have the money to hire and fire them. She writes home from Cuba sympathizing with the effort of a Mr. Gardiner to find a teaching job where his "disinterested, uncalculating, elevated soul" would be properly appreciated, and she lashes out at Salem, where the leaders of society are indifferent to Mr. Gardiner's value, because in Salem "the God Mammon decides all ranks & degrees." Sophia detested the formation of a new moneyed class from which she was excluded: "Oh mean & pitiful Aristocracy! even more despicable than the pride of noble blood & of bought titles!" (*Cuba,* 305).

Sophia thinks of herself as a queen set apart from the corrupt British aristocracy yet also distinct from the American high priesthood of Mammon. Her response to the troubles of yet another noble-souled teacher—Francis Graeter, who had been her drawing instructor—displays the humiliation and fury at stake in her claim to exalted status:

> When you speak of the treatment of our friend Mr. G by the purse-proud mean-souled aristocracy of Salem, my soul is just like a volcano spouting fire & flame. . . . I wonder when the day will come that man will consider money as nothing but a trust for the good of others—instead of making a throne of base metal to sit thereon & look down with disdain upon the far nobler, far more exalted crowd below, who have not the pitiful & dangerous advantage of dollars & cents—but nevertheless are the true & unacknowledged nobility of GOD's kingdom.
>
> (*Cuba,* 410)

Sophia envisions a nobility consisting of persons like herself, and she now had a system of religious ideas to account for her own experience and that of her spiritual kindred. The cruel fate of such exalted spirits is to live perforce in a materialistic self-seeking society. Their sufferings appeared to Sophia—like her own sufferings—to be evidence of exceptional stature. "I do not realize how coarse & rough the world is till I see the crushing & bruising of an exquisitely attuned nature under its trampling foot." The victims of this rude world should not give way to despair, she declares, but should remember that vindication is in the hands of God.

Francis Graeter's difficulty in making a living reminds Sophia of her own brother Nathaniel, who seemed unable to find a purpose in life. The idea strikes her "with *overwhelming* force" that Nathaniel is at heart an artist:

> I thought of his contemplative, gentle, uncalculating—solitary disposition—his love of being by himself—his abhorrence of bustle & noise—his fits of abstraction—his purity and singleness of mind—his difficulty in realizing that there could be cheating & falsehood in the world, & it struck me as with a flash of lightning that a great mistake had been made, that GOD designed him for an artist & that we had been pushing & urging him against his organization & natural gifts.
>
> (*Cuba,* 411–412)

Sophia imagines here a fit companion for herself, and her imagination races forward to picture their working together. "Nothing must be done rashly," she tells her mother,

> but I want to fly home, put the pencil into his hand, & see what he would do at once, giving him the idea that he could do any thing. . . . How delightful to think of having a bona fide brother artist—I could colour & he, with his exquisite truth of eye, could draw & we could be all to one another that each is wanting in. He could illustrate story books—& help me draw my men and women in my landscapes—& we should be as happy as a king and queen in fairy land with creating wands in their hands.
>
> (*Cuba*, 413–414)

It had long been understood that Sophia would never marry, principally because she looked on herself—so her sister Elizabeth remarked—"as a little girl" (Pearson, 267). Sophia's disabilities rendered her incapable of keeping house with her mother, and marriage would surely entail the added burdens of rearing children. The obstacles to marriage, however, were not only practical. What mate could be found for such an extraordinary being, deep within whose character there lay a violent conflict in which "submission" embraced a vehement self-assertive ambition? Her ambition, moreover, reached out to include projects that could be paid for only by a well-to-do husband.

Sophia envied an elderly Mrs. Kirkland in Salem, doubtless one of the aristocracy of Mammon, who had taken an exciting trip to the Near East. "Shall I ever stand upon the Imperial Palace of Persepolis? Who knows but when I am dried to an atomy like Mrs. Kirkland. . . . And when I go, perhaps my husband will not be a paralytic. Oh! I forget. I never intend to have a husband. Rather, I should say, I never intend any one shall have me for a wife" (*NHW* 1:185–186). Sophia puts her finger exactly where the central problem lay, not in "having a husband" but in being "had." Subordination to the authority of a man seemed inseparable from marriage, especially if the man—unlike her father—were capable of achieving worldly success sufficient to pay for a journey to the East. In erecting a transcendental philosophy on the sublimation of her inner torment, however, Sophia had opened a way to find a suitable kindred spirit.

The tenuousness of Sophia's membership in the "nobility of the Kingdom of God" comes through clearly in the manic excitement with which she claims it. Was it a nobility only of spiritual communion, or could it be perpetuated on this earth through a noble marriage? How many young men were available who had kept themselves in childlike innocence, unspoiled by the world, and could also manage to support a wife? These were urgent issues of Sophia's experience when she discovered in 1837 that just a few streets away, in her own home town of Salem, there had lived for years in quiet seclusion a man of unearthly beauty writing great works of literature.

Toward such a figure the yearnings of Sophia's royal soul could be directed: her desire for a life of heroic sacrifice, in which her achievements would be selfless because they were the achievements of another, and her wish to exercise her spiritual influence, strengthening the divine spirit in the artist as he struggled to keep his own supernal vision undimmed by earthly distractions. Here was a relation in which the deepest submission, the most reverent obedience, could lead to a spectacular triumph.

As they were just becoming acquainted, Sophia made the following remarks: "Mr. Hawthorne said he wished he could have intercourse with some beautiful children,—beautiful little girls; he did not care for boys. What a beautiful smile he has! . . . He said he had imagined a story, of which the principal incident is my cleaning that picture of Fernandez. To be the means, in any way, of calling forth one of his divine creations, is no small happiness, is it? . . . He has a celestial expression. It is a manifestation of the divine in the human."[18]

As her wedding approached, five years later, Sophia rejoiced that her membership in the nobility of the kingdom of God would soon be sealed for all eternity, by way of marriage to the King. "I marvel how I can be so blessed among mortals—how that the very king & poet of the world should be my eternal companion henceforth. . . . Time is so swallowed up in Eternity now that I have found my being in him, that life seems all one—now & the remotest hereafter are blended together. In the presence of majestic, serene Nature we shall stand transfigured with a noble complete happiness."[19]

CHAPTER FOUR

Portrait of the Artist as a Self-Made Man

Late in life Hawthorne explored his solitary personal anguish in terms that sketch an emerging commonplace of his time:

> If you know anything of me, you know how I sprang out of mystery, akin to none, a thing concocted out of the elements, without visible agency—how, all through my boyhood, I was alone; how I grew up without a root, yet continually longing for one—longing to be connected with somebody—and never feeling myself so. . . . I have tried to keep down this yearning, to stifle it, annihilate it, with making a position for myself, with being my own past, but I cannot overcome this natural horror of being a creature floating in the air, attached to nothing; nor this feeling that there is no reality in the life and fortunes, good or bad, of a being so unconnected.
>
> (CE 12:257–258)

This wrenching lament is spectacularly at odds with the story of Hawthorne's boyhood. Far from being alone, Hawthorne grew up in a welter of kinfolk. He was born in his Hathorne grandmother's house on Union Street in Salem, where his mother and older sister crowded in with Ruth and Eunice, his two unmarried Hathorne aunts. Here his father lived during the intervals between ocean voyages, and so did his uncle Daniel Hathorne, who was also a ship-captain.

When young Nathaniel was four years old, after the birth of his younger sister, word arrived in Salem that his father had died of yellow fever in Surinam. Nathaniel's mother then moved with him and his two sisters back

to the Manning family home where she had grown up, and where her parents
presided over a household that included her eight brothers and sisters. The
Manning house faced on Herbert Street but adjoined the Hathornes' by way
of a back lot on which the children played, so that young Nathaniel was
immediately surrounded in the early years by over a dozen close relations,
apart from his mother and sisters and not including his aunts Sarah Hathorne Crowninshield and Rachel Hathorne Forrester, to whom he refers
familiarly in early letters, who had homes of their own where he and his
sisters were welcome (CE 15:117–118, 126–127).

Yet in picturing himself as a lad without connections, burdened with
"making a position for myself," Hawthorne recapitulates a typical irony in
the social construction of the self-made man. Mary Ryan's *Cradle of the
Middle Class* studies the family histories of men in Utica, New York, who
embraced the gospel of self-help and were celebrated for having pulled
themselves up by their own bootstraps. Ryan describes a pattern to which
Hawthorne's early life corresponds, in which a collective family strategy is
put in motion to supply funds for advanced education and provide a place
for the young man to live inexpensively during the early years of adulthood
as he gets his career underway (166–169). To refashion such a story of
marked dependency into a myth of self-creation required attributing the
work of tangible exterior resources to an inward spiritual potency. The
denial of an indispensable support network and its absorption into the
self-creating self enacted in the careers of business and professional men were
also at the heart of Emerson's vision of the selfhood from which a uniquely
American intellectual and poetic achievement would spring.[1]

Sophia had invented Nathaniel before she met him, formulating her ideal
of the brother-artist as a nobleman in the kingdom of God. When Nathaniel
met Sophia, by contrast, he was struggling to invent himself and loved her
for her role in that enterprise. To say that Hawthorne's identity as a writer
is rooted in social circumstance is not to deny what was strikingly unusual
in his experience. Comparatively few boys lost their fathers in boyhood as
Hawthorne and Emerson did; this exceptional experience, however, placed
these men (as analogous circumstances placed Melville, Thoreau, and Whitman) in a situation that accentuated conflicts typical of the era: in male
relations both with fathers and with patriarchal authority in general. The
same is true of Hawthorne's relation to Sophia: it was markedly unusual, but
certain of its features make it typical of the social arrangements that gave rise
to the domestic ideal. The "cult of domesticity" envisions a self-made man
taking to wife an angel, a figure whose religious energies counteract the
unreality "of a being so unconnected" as himself.

Like Sophia, young Nathaniel Hawthorne found a "delicate" physical condition useful in managing the internal conflicts that were consolidated into his vocation as an artist. When he was nine years old, he spent more than a year recovering from an injury to his foot that occurred when he was playing with a bat and ball. A procession of local doctors, including Nathaniel Peabody, came through the household to give their opinions. It seemed the boy was unable to walk on the injured foot; then it seemed he simply refused to walk on it. As the months passed by, Nathaniel hopped about the yard or used a crutch to get around; he played with his kittens and read what he wanted to read. A teacher brought in to carry on with his schooling did not find him zealous to follow directions. On the contrary, the boy took the occasion to do just as he pleased. "He amuses himself with playing about the yard, and in Herbert St. nearly all day," his Aunt Priscilla Manning tartly observed.[2] The doctors warned that the foot would not improve without exercise and noted with alarm that it did not seem to be growing properly. Dr. Smith of Hanover, perhaps suspecting a psychic cause, determined that the lame foot would benefit from cold water poured over it every morning. This advice was followed religiously, and in the following January the family rejoiced at young Nathaniel's full recovery. A more severe illness soon after, however, made the family fear he would always be lame, if he survived.[3]

It's almost too perfect, this psychologically loaded incident from the boyhood of a man who had trouble learning to stand on his own two feet, the lad refusing to walk so long as there appeared no path before him that he could call his own. Yet the evidence is compelling. Hawthorne's boyhood illnesses "conspired," his sister Elizabeth recalled, "to unfit him for a life of business," and she noted that Hawthorne's lifelong "habit of constant reading" began during this seeming idleness. The suspension of his formal schooling marked his decisive entry into the world of books, which he would eventually command. Self-direction was essential to the development of Hawthorne's true nature, Elizabeth maintained: "intentional cultivation" would have spoiled his talents. If "his genius had not been thus shielded in childhood," she explained, Hawthorne would never have developed "the qualities that distinguished him in after life."[4] These fourteen months are a harbinger of Hawthorne's "long seclusion" in Salem after college, when he likewise cultivated his genius in his own way.

Studies of Hawthorne's development as an artist generally agree that he needed independence to provide for an innate imaginative power. Such a view is in keeping with the romantic conception of the artist's imagination as an ontological fountain, pouring forth beauty and truth from its own self-contained energies or by way of its contact with transcendental reality.

Nina Baym affirms that Hawthorne's career is given shape by a struggle between the claims of such an imagination and Hawthorne's effort to make his writing acceptable to a "skeptical, practical-minded audience" (Baym, *Career*, 8). Yet Baym discovers that this audience celebrated Hawthorne loudest when he took his stand—in *The Scarlet Letter*—on the artist "as an independent person responsible only to his art and to himself" (112). Hawthorne's ascent to fame, rather than confirming the power of a free-standing imaginative faculty acting in defiance of social expectations, recapitulates the ironical conventions of fulfillment that an "individual" perforce obeyed in a society of self-made men. Like many another aspirant to middle-class success, Hawthorne had misfired when he "dependently courted public approbation" only to be "rewarded for independence" (151).

Hawthorne's stance over against the familial community of his boyhood foreshadows the preference for solitude—and the anguish of solitude—that characterized his adult life. But this stance did not originate in his artistic vocation. On the contrary, his artistic vocation offered him one way of managing the psychosocial conflicts that led him to think of himself as a unique being, uniquely obligated (and uniquely entitled) to follow his own destiny. Young Nathaniel did not choose these generative conflicts, which, though intimate, were not private. The symbolic energies surrounding and penetrating the psychic space he claimed for himself were inherent in the large familial community in which he grew up and were linked in turn to the broad-scale social changes amid which self-making emerged as an ideal of male identity.

Hawthorne did not occupy alone the domain of independence that his foot injury provided; he shared it with his mother and sisters. The complicated community of Hathornes and Mannings in the two neighboring houses takes on a starkly contrastive design very early in Nathaniel's responses to it; both the Hathornes and the Mannings appear as aliens, menacing the fragile quartet of mother, daughters, and son.

Students of Hawthorne's life have given careful attention to the atmosphere of the Manning household—its bustling commercial spirit and the psychosexual crosscurrents running through it—and have demonstrated its lifelong impact on Hawthorne and his work.[5] Yet we would hardly be alerted to the Mannings' existence from what Hawthorne himself said in his voluminous journals and correspondence. His earliest letters express regret at his depending on them and at his mother's depending on them, and then the record goes silent. What little we learn from later years speaks of an icy estrangement and even of vengeance. He pointedly did not attend the funeral of his uncle Robert, who had borne most of his educational expenses. When his own political influence was at its zenith, after Pierce's election to the presidency, Hawthorne wrote a curt letter endorsing his uncle William Manning's effort to get a job as a janitor at the Salem Custom House (CE 16:682). In 1855 he instructed his publisher to make payments "to the extent of $100 (one hundred dollars) for the benefit of W. Manning, an old and poor relation of mine" (CE 17:422). The surviving record gives scant evidence that Hawthorne felt gratitude for the treatment he had received when he was himself the poor relation.

Spurning the Mannings did not mean embracing the available Hathornes. Although the biographical record here is even slimmer, it suggests a corresponding alienation. On a visit to New Haven in his twenties Hawthorne encountered a young man who knew Salem society and who remarked that he didn't "in the least resemble any of the Hawthorne family." To this Hawthorne replied "with considerable force and emphasis. 'I am glad to hear you say that, for I don't wish to look like any Hawthorne.' " (M. Hawthorne, 264–265).

Hawthorne did not make such gestures of repudiation to defend himself as an artist-in-the-making; they began before he entered on that venture and continued long after he had succeeded in it. They arise from a conviction of radical uniqueness that he, his sisters, and their mother cherished in their bereavement. The death of Hawthorne's father sharpened a chronic tension between the Hathorne and Manning households that would have been present even if no marriage had taken place between them, because of the uneasy relation between their social positions.

There were no pre-Revolutionary landed gentry among the Hathorne forebears. Such eminence as the family had enjoyed in Puritan times had declined by the middle of the eighteenth century. Paul Boyer and Stephen Nissenbaum's *Salem Possessed* demonstrates clearly that the Hathornes were on the wrong side of the witch controversy, economically as well as morally. Hawthorne was right in sensing—as he says in the introduction to *The Scarlet Letter*—that the deterioration of the family's fortunes was somehow linked with his ancestors' role in those old persecutions. The economic future in Salem lay with the shipping industry, not the farming community where the Hathornes had their stronghold. Hawthorne's great-grandfather was a farmer of modest means whose sons commanded ships they did not own. Hawthorne's father was a ship-captain, we've seen, who at the time of his death had not managed to move his wife and three children out of his mother's home; no one on the Hathorne side of the family stepped forward to support this small cluster of recent offspring.

Yet as the nineteenth century dawned in Salem, old family connections still counted for social rank, in a restive competition with new wealth. The Hathornes retained an air of social ascendancy, which made the Hathorne daughters attractive to men who had acquired fortunes in the burgeoning commercial economy and wanted to ally themselves with a distinguished name. Hawthorne's aunts Crowninshield and Forrester might be thought to have married "down" socially; they had certainly married "up" financially. Their husbands were among the new rich; and Hawthorne's father turned to them for employment. The Hathorne family experience suggests that among members of the declining pre-Revolutionary elite, women found better prospects through marriage than men did through careers; the social pretensions that disabled men from competitive enterprise made women suitable ornaments of hard-won success. Nathaniel Hathorne's marriage to Elizabeth Manning did not, however, match a woman of position to a man of means.

The most memorable story of the ancestral Mannings was a trial and conviction for incest that took place at Salem in 1680.[6] The Manning forebears were known for sexual misconduct, and the old Hathorne magistrates were famous for punishing it. By the early nineteenth century Elizabeth Manning's family was less wealthy than the Crowninshields and Forresters, but their prosperity considerably exceeded that of the Hathornes; and the Mannings' current affluence had been gained in the expanding commercial economy. Elizabeth's father had begun as a blacksmith and then made his fortune as owner of the Boston and Salem Stage Company.

Elizabeth Manning was two months pregnant when she married Nathaniel Hathorne, which suggests that the match between them arose from a mutual attraction exercised in defiance of family preferences.[7] Elizabeth's marriage stands out against the strong ethos of joint effort that bound together the multi-generational Manning household, aimed at keeping the family businesses thriving: none of Elizabeth's brothers or sisters married until fifteen years after her marriage to Nathaniel Hathorne. Since Hathorne was not capable of setting up a household, the marriage can hardly have appeared desirable to the Mannings, and it certainly created a financial liability when he died.

Elizabeth countered her family's disparagement with a marked commitment to her Hathorne identity, expressed most tellingly in the bosom of the Manning family after her husband's death.[8] The disputes about her grief for Nathaniel—what Elizabeth Peabody termed "her all but Hindoo self-devotion to the manes of her husband" (Pearson, 267)—began during the lifetimes of those immediately involved and has been continued in twentieth-century scholarship. Although the vision of Elizabeth and her children as paralyzed with sorrow has on occasion been overdrawn, the long-term effects of bereavement may run deep in the lives of people who are not markedly gloomy. Elizabeth's clinging to the memory of her husband redoubled the assertion she had made in marrying him; she formed a pattern of life that insisted on her refinement, at odds with the mercenary scramble of the Manning household.

Other widows of Elizabeth's time and place made second marriages; and while she certainly maintained affectionate ties within the Manning household, Elizabeth was also discernibly reclusive, holding herself apart and somewhat above them. She was referred to customarily as "Madame Hathorne," which if not exactly a taunt, still marked the family's awareness that she cherished an intangible distinction conferred by her marriage, a distinction they did not share. Gloria Erlich, observing that Elizabeth did not take a strong hand in family disagreements about how her children should be managed, interprets her aloofness as revealing a "lack of vitality and trust in her own competence," further demonstrated by frequent bouts of illness (38–40, 44, 51, 62–64). Yet it seems more likely that Elizabeth's sensitive nerves—like Sophia's delicacy—were her effort to impose a meaning she cherished on recalcitrant circumstances. Rather than bespeaking a feeble spirit, her remoteness was the passive-aggressive assertion of her own worth as a being of superior sensibilities in a crude world.

This does not imply a dreary temperament but one whose intelligence and force were most evident in settings where her fragile claim to gentility was acknowledged. The Essex Institute at Salem preserves an unsigned family document that vigorously disputes early biographers who claimed that Madame Hathorne lived in unbroken solitude under "a life-long grief." The writer points out that the Manning household entertained a great deal of company, because their large family traveled freely to and from Salem on the family-owned stagecoach line. Only later, after others had married and the household had been reduced in size, did Elizabeth begin to seclude herself, because she was "somewhat straitened pecuniarily" so that it was "not easy . . . to mingle in society."[9]

The bereavement had resulted not in a mood of depression, but in a pattern of living. Within the family, where she was known as she wished, Hawthorne's mother was sociable enough. But she did not have the money to keep up appearances beyond the household. Even in later years, Elizabeth Peabody observed the notable vivacity Mrs. Hathorne displayed when she was confident of being respected for a bygone gentility. "Widow Hawthorne always looked as if she had walked out of an old picture, with her ancient costume and a face of lovely sensibility, and great brightness" (Pearson, 267).

Nathaniel and his sisters took part in this drama as compelled by their own distinctive experience of grief. Children who suffer loss at an early age internalize an impression of the departed parent that becomes a model for their own selfhood; and the child has no further experience of the living adult against whom that early impression can be corrected. This happens with special intensity when the surviving parent sees her children as a link with the lost spouse, seeking to keep alive through them the marital relationship that death has broken. This process aided in forming the magic circle around Elizabeth Hathorne and her children, setting them not only *apart from* the Hathornes and Mannings but also *against* them. Hawthorne's sister Elizabeth refused in girlhood to soil her hands with housekeeping chores, much to the Mannings' disgust.[10]

The fierce pride behind Madame Hathorne's aloofness appears in the bellicose, lucid intelligence of this namesake and oldest child, nicknamed Ebe. Ebe was well recognized within the family for her aggressive and penetrating wit, with which she discussed political and literary affairs. But this identity found little welcome in the world beyond the home, where Elizabeth confronted a respectable society decreasingly prepared to admire aggressive women. After her mother's death Ebe left Salem for good, going to live in retirement with a farm family in Maine, where she occupied herself with reading, walking in the woods, and keeping up a correspondence with her kinfolk.

Ebe cherished Nathaniel's insistent sense of transcendent distinction, asserted in the cross fire of old names and new money in the family connection. She proudly told and retold the story of an occasion on which his uncle Simon Forrester offered him a ten-dollar bill, which the lad disdainfully refused on the ground that Forrester was not "nearly enough related to have a right to bestow it."[11] Both Elizabeth and Nathaniel were vividly aware that Simon Forrester—before he got rich, married their aunt, and gave their father a job—had come to America from Ireland as a cabin boy in a vessel commanded by their grandfather. Elizabeth treasured the story of the rejected money because it exposed and spurned Forrester's assumption that he could purchase social rank comparable to Nathaniel's own.[12] Simon Forrester was a prime exemplar of what Sophia Peabody scorned as the aristocracy of Mammon in Salem, against whom persons of inherited status were hard-pressed to define their own worth. The year before Hawthorne died, in fact, Nathaniel and Sophia reviewed the Forrester relationship—as well as the Forrester offspring—and asserted the orthodox hierarchy: "The only claim to position they had was from connection with the Hawthornes," Sophia affirmed. "They were no·descendants of Earls" (CE 18:532).

The complex legacy of Hawthorne's bereavement, whose ultimate consequences are visible in the circumstances of his own death, entered the formation of his artistic vocation and made him exceptionally responsive to pressures bearing generally on young men of his class in the early nineteenth century. Hawthorne accepted the Mannings' sending him to college, but he did not accept them as sponsors of his identity. By altering the spelling of his name to "Hawthorne," he signaled, likewise, that no psychic anchor could lodge securely in his father's family. Hawthorne's artistic self was in that respect self-made; it was formed over against the expectations of those who sought to assume the place of his father, and it engaged him in a professional domain with which they had virtually no experience.

Hawthorne's relation to his family of origin resembled that of many young men during this era who sought their fortunes in places and in occupations inaccessible to their fathers and who discovered that the father's economic position—even if inheritable—could not rival the opportunities that beckoned in the urban centers of mass-market commerce or in the West. Such young men faced manifold ironies arising from the cross-pressures between money making and claims of status grounded in family relation: how to despise a Simon Forrester while attempting to become one? The myth of the self-made man helped provide an answer to this question. Indeed, by the 1860s Hawthorne scorned the Forresters not merely because they were new rich but also because they were immoderately fond of whiskey, failing what the intervening years had established as a conventional test of manly self-discipline. Old Forrester "drank terribly through life," Hawthorne stated, "and transmitted the tendency, I believe, to all his sons, several of whom killed themselves by it" (CE 18:531).[13]

To stress the psychosocial dimensions of Hawthorne's artistic vocation is not to deny his talent, without which he would have had no prospect of becoming a writer. But the intimate circle of shared bereavement provided a matrix for creating a writer selfhood that would not have existed had his ship-captain father been alive to point the way toward a maritime career, or even to present Nathaniel with a tangible figure against whom to rebel. Early letters indicate young Nathaniel's growing awareness of his abilities: he speaks, for example, of verses coming profusely and unprompted into his mind (CE 15:114–115). But such letters are addressed to his mother and his sisters, with instructions to keep them secret from outsiders, namely the Mannings.

The earliest evidence of Hawthorne's literary aptitude survives in articulations of his loss. Before he was old enough to "speak quite plainly," Ebe recalled, "he used to repeat, with vehement emphasis and gesture, this line, which somebody had taught him, from Richard Third; 'My Lord, stand back and let the coffin pass.' " More tellingly, he enacted scenes that recapitulate his father's death, with the bereft son in the role of the departed. "He used to invent long stories, wild and fanciful, and to tell us where he was going when he grew up, and of wonderful adventures he was to meet with, always ending with 'and I'm never coming back again.' That, perhaps, he said that we might value him the more while he stayed with us."[14]

A principal source of such stories were logbooks of his father's voyages, over which Nathaniel dreamed for hours on end. The son's effort to ground his own identity in these traces of his father's life appears most poignantly in his profuse marginalia, often his father's words copied in elaborate script like his father's. Nathaniel wrote his own signature on the flyleaves, again and again and again. On the front fly of the *America* logbook, his father had written in graceful cursive "Nathaniel Hathorne's Book . . . 1795, Calcutta"; on the facing title page the son's heavy block capitals echo: "Nathaniel Hathorne's Book, 1820, Salem" (Fig. 3). Hawthorne's grief-stricken obsessive effort to work the textures of his selfhood around and through his dead namesake's writing continued from early boyhood at least until his college years (Luedtke, 5–7).

In the microworld inhabited by Madame Hathorne and her three children Hawthorne's identity as an artist took form; and although this setting empowered him, it also entailed conflict. What sort of life would be faithful

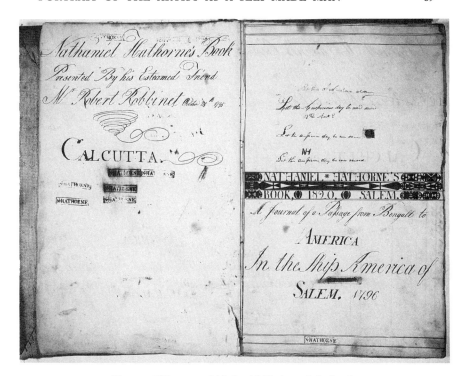

Fig. 3. Title page of Nathaniel Hathorne's logbook

to a true self visible only to the immediate family and in principle too mysterious and aloof to be appreciated by others? Having internalized an identity he was both required and forbidden to fulfill, Hawthorne recurrently sought to reproduce the incestuous self-enclosure of his boyhood home.[15] He could never negotiate confidently the turbulent passage into the world beyond and lamented the dismal and sordid existence that resulted. Hawthorne makes his most telling observations about his literary consciousness, we shall see in due course, when he tries to explain to Sophia why he cannot tell his mother and sisters that he plans to marry her.

Ebe deserves to be believed when she denies Hawthorne was notably reclusive in boyhood, asserting that "he began to withdraw into himself" only after his return to Salem after college, "when he felt as if he could not get away from there and yet was conscious of being utterly unlike every one else in the place" (Stewart, 325). As Hawthorne became acquainted with Elizabeth and Sophia Peabody during the 1830s, he described his torpid imprisonment in "Castle Dismal" and blamed the "morbid consciousness that paralyses my powers" (Pearson, 267) on an atmosphere of stale grief at home. But while the gloom of Castle Dismal had psychological origins in his father's death, the mood of depression did not date from his early boy-hood.[16] The paralysis and stagnation set in when he attempted to start a career that would keep inviolate an inward dignity as fragile as it was vehement.

Nathaniel was able to realize his cherished identity most fully when he lived with his mother and sisters in Raymond, Maine, for a summer in 1816, when he was twelve, and for a period of some eight months during his fourteenth year. In the course of the later stay an effort was made to send him to school in nearby Stroudwater, but after a month of homesickness and rebellion he was restored to the enchanted circle.

For all his fabled ambivalence, Hawthorne never expressed any second thoughts about regretting his departure from Raymond. "Here I ran quite wild," he later said, "and would, I doubt not, have willingly run wild till this time, fishing all day long, or shooting with an old fowling piece; but reading a good deal, too, on the rainy days, especially in Shakspeare and 'The Pilgrim's Progress,' and any poetry or light books within my reach" (*NHW* 1:95–96). After Nathaniel had been returned to Salem, his aunt Mary Manning thought he would soon reconcile himself to preparing for a career. He "sighs for the woods of Raymond," she wrote, "and yet he seems to be convinced of the necessity of prepairing to do something. I think after he gets engaged in business his views of things will be much altered" (CE 15:113).[17] But his letters during the next two years keep up his lamentation over the lost felicity. He dreams at night of running wild again, only to waken and find himself in the house on Herbert Street. He resists any plans for his sisters or his mother to return to Salem, seeking to keep intact the tableau within which he felt real. "Do you not regret the time when I was a little boy?" he writes his mother as his seventeenth birthday approached; "I do almost" (CE 15:137).

Hawthorne's sisters were under no obligation to prepare themselves for a career, whether they returned to Salem or not. But young Nathaniel confronted the necessity of establishing relations outside the enchanted circle. His abilities persuaded the Mannings that the best prospect lay with providing him a college education, especially since the economic recession of 1818 made business in Salem very slow. His aunt Mary urged the family to shoulder the expense that college would impose. "I am willing to put down for 100 Dollars perhaps it will be said thats but a drop. well but it's a great drop and if everyone of his Relations who are as near to him as I am would put down as much I think his buckett would be full" (CE 15:118). Nathaniel himself was not attracted by any of the professions to which college training would lead. "Shall you want me to be a Minister, Doctor or Lawyer?" he writes to his mother, "A Minister I will not be." What he really desired was to go back to Raymond, and as the months passed he complained more and more. "The happiest days of my life are gone. Why was I not a girl that I might have been pinned all my life to my Mother's apron" (CE 15:117).

There appeared no escape from a masculine destiny, yet accepting it put him at odds with his vision of transcendent distinction, of a sort to make his mother proud. These crosscurrents of aspiration and dismay shape his dream of becoming a writer. "Oh that I was rich enough to live without a profession," he writes to his mother. "What do you think of my becoming an Author, and relying for my support upon my pen. . . . How proud you would feel to see my works praised by the reviewers, as equal to proudest productions of the scribbling sons of John Bull. But Authors are always poor Devils, and therefore Satan may take them" (CE 15:139).

This sounds very remote from the ethos of manly striving that was taking form in the culture at large. Instead of welcoming the contest among democratic equals, young Hawthorne yearns for a seclusion that is both girlish and aristocratic. If he can't remain pinned to his mother's apron, then he wishes he were wealthy enough to be excused from the effort to support himself. The prospect of becoming a writer is tainted by the inevitable entanglement with the marketplace and the likelihood of poverty. Yet coupled with this squeamishness is a startling ambition, rising from an interior consciousness of his own capacities: he would create works of literature of the highest rank, equal to the best of the English. Thirty years later he would have at hand reviews of his work—notably Herman Melville's "Hawthorne and His Mosses"—meeting exactly this prediction.

No record survives of what Aunt Mary and the other Mannings had to say about Nathaniel's wasting the college education they had paid for, but he was known in Salem as an idler and hid in his mother's home in part because he preferred not to be dressed down for his idleness in public. His sister Elizabeth recalled an occasion when he left the house to look at a great fire, only to be accosted by an old woman who "scolded him in threatening terms . . . in her indignation 'at a strong young man's not going to work as other people did' " (Stewart, 322). Elizabeth Peabody seems likewise to have been aware of Hawthorne's reputation as a do-nothing. When she heard he had written "The Gentle Boy," she did not believe it and decided the author was his older sister, whose brilliance Elizabeth recalled from girlhood. She presented herself at the house on Herbert Street to offer her congratulations, only to be told by Louisa that Nathaniel had actually written the tale. "But if your brother can write like that," said Elizabeth Peabody, "he has no right to be idle" (Pearson, 263).

Hawthorne's "womanly" seclusion and mysterious aloofness were built into the literary career he fashioned. He crystallizes these themes in *Fanshawe,* whose solitary and sensitive hero treasures up a "dream of undying fame, which, dream as it is, is more powerful than a thousand realities" (CE 3:350). The young man harboring this dream is among the lords of nature. "There was a nobleness on his high forehead, which time would have deepened into majesty. . . . The expression of his countenance was not a melancholy one;—on the contrary, it was proud and high—perhaps triumphant—like one who was a ruler in a world of his own, and independent of the beings that surrounded him" (346). In "works of imagination," Hawthorne was later to say, "the author himself should be despotic and aristocratical" (CE 16:302), there being no appeal from his intuitive verdicts.

Paradoxically, what seems unmanly and undemocratic in this depiction of the romantic artist was inherent in democratic manhood. The ideal of the self-made man incorporated the "womanly" and "royal" qualities that it projected on actual women and kings. To be an individual, after all, is to assert one's absolute right to oneself, a right enshrined in social contract theory, which imagines a state of nature from which solitary individuals chose to enter collective relationships. The classic doctrines of American democracy hold that government exists to secure such rights—deemed inherent in the created nature of all men—and derives its just powers from the consent of the governed. Thus the political substance of kingship is transferred to ordinary men. Political authority in a republic derives from this substrate of intrinsic (or divine) entitlement, which is embodied not in a monarch but in every citizen. Ralph Waldo Emerson—now widely recognized as America's classic ideologue of individualism in poetry, politics, and economics[18]—hailed the emergence of an America promising "to insulate the individual,—to surround him with barriers of natural respect, so that each man shall feel the world is his, and man shall treat with man as a sovereign state with a sovereign state" (Whicher, 79).

Yet to enact this royal autonomy, men must become womanly. As the competitive struggle remodeled male-male relations to resemble international relations, it was discovered that each individual sovereignty needed a privy council. Survival in the public arena required the maintenance of an inward forum where policies could be evolved in the freedom of creative disarray and uncertainties could be entertained that must be hidden from view in public exchanges with other sovereignties. The self-made man in a society of citizen-kings retains a nurturing inward spirituality, whose broodings are never visible to his fellows but give shrewdness and force to the initiatives by which he makes himself known to others. In a community of poker players, to switch to a homelier metaphor of American entrepreneurship, it is not the cards you hold that measure your manhood, but the way you play them. A subtle, intuitive, and inscrutable interiority—the sacred essence of nineteenth-century "femininity"—lies at the heart of self-made manliness.

Andrew Jackson was celebrated, Amy Lang has shown, as "a male public figure whose greatness is directly associated with his reliance upon an intuitive, oracular, and feminine private self" (150). His eulogists affirmed that instead of merely upholding the law as president, Jackson broke laws so as to create them anew, acting at the behest of "warm and instinctive impulses" that are "more to be trusted than the cold inductions of the understanding" (151). After Hawthorne had secured his own literary standing, he praised Jackson's poetic gift: "The highest, or perhaps any high, administrative ability is intuitive, and precedes argument, and rises above it. It is a revelation of the very thing to be done; and its propriety and necessity are felt so strongly, that, ten to one, it cannot be talked about; if the doer can likewise talk, it is an additional and gratuitous faculty, as little to be expected as that a poet should be able to write an explanatory criticism on his own poem" (CE 14:367). During the years of his solitary struggle in his mother's house, Andrew Jackson had likewise served Hawthorne as a hero. His sister Elizabeth recalled that when the General visited Salem in 1833, Hawthorne "walked out to the boundaries of the town to meet him . . . and found only a few men and boys collected, not enough, without the assistance that he rendered, to welcome the General with a good cheer." Ebe found it hard to picture her brother "doing such a thing as shouting" (Stewart, 325), yet Jackson embodied for Hawthorne the heroic manhood that made sense of his secluded life.

CHAPTER FIVE

Subservient Angel

Studies of American Christianity in the early republic have not recognized the fundamental transformation that attended the sacralization of womanhood. The established historical account emphasizes the surge of evangelical Protestantism in cities and on the frontier and the rise of internal and foreign missions. These developments shaped denominational competition as well as the famous theological controversies that pitted orthodox Calvinism against more liberal teachings better adapted to spreading the gospel (Walker, 509–518; Ahlstrom, 387–614). While male religious leaders in America were maneuvering furiously for advantage on this complex landscape of battle, they were also engaged in making the domestic angel the most powerful Christian goddess since the medieval Virgin. Henry Adams's "Dynamo and the Virgin" was less a contrast of the nineteenth and thirteenth centuries than a description of nineteenth-century culture itself: as machinery became a primary symbol of social relationships among men, a symbolic counterforce came into being. Instead of the Virgin, however, Victorian males worshiped their wives.

Nathaniel's love letters to Sophia explore the emerging structure of male need that imparted a religious force to the domestic angel: he discovers her divine presence when he looks within himself:[1]

> I feel as if my being were dissolved, and the idea of you were diffused throughout it.
> . . . While I love you so dearly, and while I am so conscious of the deep embrace of

our spirits . . . still I have an awe of you that I never felt for anybody else. Awe is not the word, either; because it might imply something stern in you. . . . I suppose I should have pretty much the same feeling if an angel were to come from Heaven and be my dearest friend—only the angel could not have the tenderest of human natures too, the sense of which is mingled with this sentiment. . . . But I leave the mystery here. Sometime or other, it may be made plainer to me. But methinks it converts my love into religion. And then it is singular, too, that this awe (or whatever it be) does not prevent me from feeling that it is I who have the charge of you, and that my Dove is to follow my guidance and do my bidding.

(CE 15:316–317)

Hawthorne's broodings have led him to a paradox at the heart of the domestic ideal. He feels a religious awe for Sophia; yet it is different from the awe that springs immediately to his mind, the obedient dread aroused by the stern God of Calvinism, or indeed by more liberal versions of the divine Judge. Hawthorne's spirit bows in reverence before a friend who is to do his bidding.

The contradiction is so blatant as to seem downright silly, American husbands claiming the right to make decisions for their wives because they looked up to them. Yet nineteenth-century family correspondence reveals that husbands did attribute moral and spiritual superiority to their wives, even as they exercised masculine authority as head of the household (Degler, 26, 30). The sanctified woman gave her husband the power to take command of her, and his response was reverent gratitude.

Yet Hawthorne is not merely reciting a conventional litany; he actually finds that when his "being" is dissolved, the idea of his "Dove" is "diffused throughout it." This ontological reverie gives rise to a dream:

Since writing the above, I have been asleep; and I dreamed that I had been sleeping a whole year in the open air; and that while I slept, the grass grew around me. It seemed, in my dream, that the very bed-clothes which actually covered me were spread beneath me, and when I awoke (in my dream) I snatched them up, and the earth under them looked black, as if it had been burnt—one square place, exactly the size of the bed clothes. Yet there was grass and herbage scattered over this burnt space, looking as fresh, and bright, and dewy, as if the summer rain and the summer sun had been cherishing them all the time. Interpret this for me, my Dove—but do not draw any sombre omens from it. What is signified by my nap of a whole year? . . . and what was the fire that blasted the spot of earth which I occupied, while the grass flourished all around?—and what comfort am I to draw from the fresh herbage amid the burnt space?

(CE 15:317–318)

Represented here is Hawthorne's anxiety about the years of seclusion in Salem, when he felt trapped in suspended animation while everything around him continued to grow. Even though this period can be described as a triumph of Jacksonian self-making, Hawthorne never described it in such confident terms. The drama of his self-formation took place in his mother's home, if it took place anywhere, but it was a drama about whose meaning Hawthorne continued to feel acute uncertainties. Unable whole-heartedly to embrace the myth of self-creation, he traces out the cultural contradictions that the myth concealed and the critical role of the domestic angel.

At the height of his fame in 1853, Hawthorne explained that his reclusive quest for a literary career was at best semi-deliberate: "I sat myself down to consider what pursuit in life I was best fit for. . . . And year after year I kept on considering what I was fit for, and time and my destiny decided that I was to be the writer that I am" (NHW 1:95). Hawthorne firmly disavows making a deliberate choice, claiming the now obvious verdict of time and his destiny. But before that authorization was clear, Hawthorne had been haunted by fears of being fit for nothing or of betraying his potential fitness by continuing obsessively to read and scribble. His awareness that he lacked the power to act in his own behalf then took a more sinister form; it seemed he had fallen under an evil enchantment. Even after he received congratulations from Henry Wadsworth Longfellow in 1837 for Twice-Told Tales, his seclusion seemed a stale and dreary horror, which had not ended:

> By some witchcraft or other . . . I have been carried apart from the main current of life, and find it impossible to get back again. . . . For the last ten years, I have not lived, but only dreamed about living. It may be true that there have been some insubstantial pleasures here in the shade, which I should have missed in the sunshine; but you cannot conceive how utterly devoid of satisfaction all my retrospects are.
> (CE 15:251–252)

Sophia's role in this chronic malaise may be observed by comparing this description to the account he gives Sophia of his dream two years later. The emotional drama of the dream is sharply contrapuntal: he was both "blasted" by fire and "cherished" by sunlight and rain, and within the scorched rectangle there were flowers of dewy freshness. The impression he provides for Longfellow, by contrast, is bleakly monotonous. He concedes nothing more than "insubstantial pleasures," and indicates that he is still only half-alive.

His relationship to Sophia permitted Hawthorne to sustain the awareness of stark terrors and supernal hopes that had earlier been mingled together in a seemingly unreal experience. The puzzling shadows of that recollected landscape now resolve themselves into violent opposites of divine light and fiery demonic blackness, images that transpose a vague subjective nightmare into the collision of religious realities. Images of hellish darkness and redemptive light pervade both Hawthorne's work and his meditations on the significance he found in Sophia, but the issue here is how his "Dove"—diffused throughout his being—makes real for him an organization of consciousness in which that counterpoint becomes authoritative. Sophia as "Dove" invokes the Holy Spirit as the agent of primordial creation: the separation of the light from the darkness and their joint action at the place where he lay asleep.

Sophia's religious authority as the angel of Hawthorne's self-making is rooted in a culturally specific spiritual hunger: his own desperate need to reinforce the conviction that his selfhood as a man and artist had actually taken form during the years of solitary labor he had sustained before he met her. Sophia enabled him to give firmer credence to the dangerously frail belief that his identity was alive and real and not the delusion of a demon-haunted dreamer. She counteracted a self-mistrust that was inherent in the struggle by which Hawthorne's mature selfhood took form, and in so doing she enacted the spiritual role assigned to the domestic angel generally.

Hawthorne, more severely plagued by paralyzing self-doubts than most men of his time, became a subtle and exact student of distresses that remained unconscious in the lives of the healthy-minded. A self-made man in the making depends, as we have seen, on collective support; yet he is nonetheless compelled to "make" something that earlier had been provided to a young man by his father and the network of "fathers" who shepherded junior males into the roles available to them in a relatively stable hierarchical society. The deferential dependence of young men on established elders continued in the early decades of the republic, but such patriarchal social relationships ceased to predominate, and the confusions of this transitional circumstance harshened the anxieties of individualism. The role of the domestic angel was fashioned in the rearranged relations of men with men.

"In proportion as manners and laws become more democratic," Alexis de Tocqueville declared, "the relation of father and son becomes more intimate and more affectionate; rules and authority are less talked of, confidence and tenderness are often increased, and it would seem that the natural bond is drawn closer in proportion as the social bond is loosened." By the "social

bond" Tocqueville means the formal and ceremonious relations that prevail
between fathers and sons in aristocracies, where the father's power compels
fear and the son's affection is blurred into the habits of deference required
of inferiors in a social arrangement defining a man's "condition" by his
position in a hierarchy of rank. "The austere, the conventional, and the legal
part of parental authority vanishes and a species of equality prevails around
the domestic hearth," now that "the natural warmth of the heart" is allowed
to express itself without obstruction.

The "old conventional rules of society," Tocqueville conceded, had given
rise to certain conventional habits of feeling whose artificiality is demonstrated by the speed with which they wither away when the social arrangements supporting them are supplanted by democracy and democratic manners. "The remarks I have made on filial love," he asserts, "are applicable
to all the passions that emanate spontaneously from human nature itself.
. . . Democracy loosens social ties, but tightens natural ones" (2:195–197).

Hawthorne was passionately devoted to the democratic ideology that led
Tocqueville to misconstrue a social transformation as the yielding of social
reality itself to spontaneous and universal promptings of nature. Hawthorne's interior battle over whether he was "morbid"—which was taken up
by his family and by later students of his life—results largely from the guilt
he felt for his own preoccupation with the psychic conflicts this social
transformation brought about. Hawthorne probed the "foul cavern of the
human heart," as the source from which Tocqueville's "natural warmth"
emanated.

The psychosocial conflict that Tocqueville absorbed into the new ideology
of family relations becomes starkly visible, however, when he turns to the
relations of masters and servants. "While the transition from one social
condition to another is going on, there is almost always a time when men's
minds fluctuate between the aristocratic notion of subjection and the democratic notion of obedience." Male household servants in America are
haunted by "a confused and imperfect phantom of equality. . . . [They]
conceive that they ought] themselves to be masters, and they are inclined to
consider him who orders them as an unjust usurper of their own rights"
(2:184–185).

In a frankly hierarchical social system these rancorous uncertainties do not
arise, because a servant's individuality merges into that of his master. He
"detaches his notion of interest from his own person; he deserts himself as
it were, or rather he transports himself into the character of his master and
thus assumes an imaginary personality" (Tocqueville, 2:180). Hawthorne's

sense of being trapped in shadows is a mark of the transition from one form of manhood to another, when the identities of actual men stand empty, to be haunted by the ghosts that inhabit the two discrepant worlds. On the one side is the vicarious "imaginary personality" generated by habits of deference in an aristocracy; on the other side is the "phantom of equality" in democratic societies, whispering to every subordinated man that he is a sovereign.

Tocqueville glimpses, in fact, that this dilemma is not merely a psychic cost of the transition from one social arrangement to another but is endemic to democratic society itself, where an ideal of natural equality confronts the enduring reality of social stratification. "In democracies servants are not only equal among themselves, but . . . are, in some sort, the equals of their masters." That men who think themselves equal individual sovereigns feel a systemic unrest in the presence of social power and are strongly disposed to deny its reality is a major source of the famous paradox of the middle class, the class that denies the existence of class. "It is in vain that wealth and poverty, authority and obedience, accidentally interpose great distances between two men; public opinion, founded upon the usual order of things, draws them to a common level and creates a species of imaginary equality between them, in spite of the real inequality of their conditions" (2:181). The actual experience of rich and poor men, as of bosses and employees, renders evanescent the most sacred axiom of democratic manhood—that of natural equality; it too becomes a figment of the imagination.

These dilemmas of social transition and status conflict in a democratic society are redoubled in the relation of fathers and sons. The convergence of familial and historical issues on the question of "patriarchy" helps explain why the middle class is chronically described as "emerging," not only in the late Middle Ages but even in the epoch of its greatest power, before corporate capitalism in the later nineteenth century consolidated a relatively stable elite in America.

As Nancy Chodorow has argued, every man—whether a democratic individual or not—begins life as an infant, in a condition of total dependence on powerful superiors to whom he must look not only for physical support but also for his identity. Rather than merely "transporting himself" into the character of his father (or "fathers"), a growing boy receives his personality in large part by internalizing the possibilities of manhood presented to him. The boy comes to know himself as he is seen by his father and as he sees himself in his father. What Tocqueville dismissed as a "conventional" feature of aristocratic social relations has been identified as a psychological process intrinsic to becoming an adult.

Traditional societies harnessed this early filial bond in the service of a hierarchical social order, fully elaborated in doctrines of divinely ordained rank; and it is well known that the historical development of middle-class societies was marked by the formation of social institutions (like the free market, joint-stock corporations, or government by separated powers) that are not analogues of the patriarchal household. But democratic men have hierarchical childhoods: the man who has learned to think of himself as *in essence* an individual, on an equal footing with his fellows, has a primordial memory of total psychic and physical dependency and a more recent memory of his "emergence" as a individual. A glimpse of the psychic power that democratic men invest in domestic angels may be obtained by recalling that the earliest memories of any such man concern the sponsorship of his being not by a man but a woman.

Hawthorne explores these conflicts of manhood in "My Kinsman Major Molineux," taking advantage of the analogy between the psychic development of the "individual" and the historical emergence of middle-class society that makes social history a vehicle for psychological romance.

Robin Molineux enacts the quandary of a young man who carries the social habits of deferential hierarchy into the era of their overthrow. He comes to town to take up the promise of his kinsman, a prominent colonial official. Major Molineux and Robin's father were brothers' children, Hawthorne informs us. "The Major, having inherited riches, and acquired civil and military rank, had visited his cousin in great pomp a year or two before." Being childless, he had "thrown out hints respecting the future establishment of . . . [Robin] in life" (CE 11:224). Robin, as he enters town, does not expect a competition among democratic equals. His automatic responses are those native to deferential hierarchy, and he assumes that he himself is owed a measure of respect from his kinsman's social inferiors. When an innkeeper addresses him with overelaborate courtesy, Robin mistakenly concludes that "the rogue has guessed that I am related to the Major" and makes his reply, "with such an assumption of consequence, as befitted the Major's relative" (213–214).

The social world in Robin's head is sharply at odds with the actual situation, with the townspeople preparing to tar and feather Major Molineux because they resent the royal administration he serves. This "temporary inflammation of the popular mind" (CE 11:209) sets off a revolution in

Robin's psychic constitution; he is compelled to repudiate, as by an irresistible inborn force, the deferential social habits he brought with him.

The scene in which Robin confronts his ruined kinsman is managed by Hawthorne as an initiation in the emotional realities of self-made manhood. This patricidal ritual—where Robin joins in to shower ridicule on his shattered and degraded kinsman—is also filicidal, aimed at cauterizing the deferential affections of childhood that must be supplanted if sovereign individualism is to be formed in an adult man. His loyalty to his elderly kinsman now repudiated, Robin enters a new frame of mind that allows him to join easily in the cheerfully sardonic manner of his new mentor. "Thanks to you, and to my other friends," Robin says, "I have at last met my kinsman, and he will scarce desire to see my face again" (CE 11:231).

The mentor helps Robin understand the meaning of this wrenching initiation, acting temporarily in loco parentis without the emotional entanglements of kinship; he makes no pretence of arranging Robin's "establishment in life" or of providing him money or land. Instead, he offers Robin insight into his psychological condition, his social environment, and his prospects—in terms that make it clear the mentor assumes no responsibility for the outcome.

The mentor possesses an impersonal authority based on superior knowledge, which displaces the authority of patriarchal sponsorship. He emerges as a precursory embodiment of "the professional" that Burton Bledstein identifies as a central figure of middle-class culture (88–105, 126–127). In refusing to show Robin to the ferry, the old gentleman echoes the youth's sardonic use of the term "friend," but without the sarcasm, indicating an ad hoc affiliation serving Robin's self-interest. " 'No, my good friend Robin, not to-night, at least,' said the gentleman. 'Some few days hence, if you continue to wish it, I will speed you on your journey. Or, if you prefer to remain with us, perhaps, as you are a shrewd youth, you may rise in the world, without the help of your kinsman, Major Molineux' " (CE 11:231).

Hawthorne does not portray Robin as making a decisive entry into the ethos of self-help or a clean break with patriarchal dependency. His tale evokes instead the dilemmas of the self-made man-on-the-make, caught between the incompatible moral requirements of these two schemes of value: it is a study in obligatory guilt. Hawthorne celebrates the social changes heralding the advent of democracy, just as he acknowledges the moral dignity that follows from rising in the world on one's own enterprise. Yet he also recognizes the wrong done to Major Molineux. "On they went, like fiends that throng in mockery round some dead potentate, mighty no more, but majestic still in his agony. On they went, in counterfeited pomp, in senseless uproar, in frenzied merriment, trampling all on an old man's heart" (230).

The intensity of this language—as of the entire tale—results from the shift within it: the collision between aristocratic and democratic orders of meaning merges into a structural conflict within democracy that redoubles the assertion that patricide is both mandatory and prohibited. The mockery directed against the fraudulent authority of a "potentate," Major Molineux, asserts democratic principle; yet because of his lingering "majesty" Molineux embodies the same principle his humiliation exalts. Hawthorne's concluding phrases protest Molineux's degradation as an outrage, not on the prerogatives of the British throne and its colonial representative but on the royalty that democratic doctrine ascribed to all equally created human hearts, here that of an old man in torment. Centrally active here is a contradiction *within* the ethos of democratic self-sovereignty. The filial revolt required of the democratic individual may free him from the entanglements of deferential dependence, but it also strikes a blow against the source of his own identity: to trample on an old man's heart is to defile one's own. This interior dissonance supports Hawthorne's designation of the moment as unreal—as "counterfeited," "senseless," and "frenzied"—the state of consciousness that arises when experience becomes uninterpretable by reason of conflicts within the system of interpretation that is invoked to give it reality and sense. "My Kinsman, Major Molineux" articulates the interior contradictions of self-made manhood without invoking the domestic angel who holds out the prospect of redemption.

The ideal of manly selfhood that led Hawthorne to doubt his own reality—and to reverence his Dove for helping overcome that doubt—was linked to a correlative vision of "the world" that he likewise traces out in his letters to her. In 1840, the second year of their correspondence, Nathaniel was working at the Boston Custom House, and in October of that year he returned to Salem for a visit, where he drafted the best-known account of his writerly self-creation:

> Here sits thy husband in his old accustomed chamber, where he used to sit in years gone by, before his soul became acquainted with thine. Here I have written many tales—many that have been burned to ashes—many that doubtless deserved the same fate. This deserves to be called a haunted chamber; for thousands upon thousands of visions have appeared to me in it; and some few of them have become visible to the

world. If ever I should have a biographer, he ought to make great mention of this chamber in my memoirs, because so much of my lonely youth was wasted here; and here my mind and character were formed; and here I have been glad and hopeful, and here I have been despondent.

(CE 15:294)

The contrapuntal drama of Hawthorne's dream is fully elaborated in this description of the haunted chamber. It is a place of demonic fire, of tales written only to be consumed; yet it is a place of green plenitude as well, where uncountable visions have appeared. Here he "wasted" his youth, yet here his character was formed. Hawthorne now establishes a presence beyond these ambivalences, in the voice that conveys them. "Thy husband" can look on his former joys and despondence with equanimity, and he gestures with confidence toward prospective biographers. Spiritually reinforced by his Dove, Hawthorne's "I" is capable of standing firmly over against "the world": "And here I sat a long, long time, waiting patiently for the world to know me. . . . By and bye, the world found me out in my lonely chamber, and called me forth—not, indeed, with a loud roar of acclamation, but rather with a still, small voice; and forth I went, but found nothing in the world that I thought preferable to my own solitude, till at length a certain Dove was revealed to me" (CE 15:494–495).

"The world" had summoned Hawthorne when he published *Twice-Told Tales* three years before, and the circumstances surrounding that event reveal dilemmas that "the world" as a symbolic construction was adapted to manage. The characters in this comedy of misperceptions are Hawthorne, his wealthy college friend Horatio Bridge, and the successful publisher Samuel Goodwyn Goodrich, each of whom is constrained by a social environment that imposes conflicted standards of manly self-respect.

Goodrich had published several of Hawthorne's tales anonymously in *The Token,* gaining reputation as well as profit without any of the credit going to Hawthorne. But when Hawthorne approached him with the idea of bringing out a collection, Goodrich was uncooperative. Then Horatio Bridge approached Goodrich and offered a guarantee against losses. Bridge insisted that this offer be kept secret from Hawthorne, because he was fearful that Hawthorne—in his self-reliant pride—would be offended and would refuse to be the object of patronage. Goodrich's change of heart led Hawthorne to conclude that the publisher's personal interest in him had overcome his fear of losing money. Instead of being exasperated by this apparent act of patronage, Hawthorne was overwhelmed with gratitude and replied in kind. He proposed to dedicate the volume to Goodrich.

This dismayed Horatio Bridge, who had actually shown the generosity for which Goodrich now was to be rewarded; so Bridge set about dissuading Hawthorne from the proposed dedication, still without disclosing his own role. To compound the irony further, Bridge wrote to Hawthorne affirming that Goodrich's own selfish interests were well served by the deal, not because of Bridge's guarantee, but because Goodrich expected Hawthorne's writing would make money. "There is no doubt in my mind of his selfishness in regard to your work and yourself. I am perfectly aware that he has taken a good deal of interest in you, but when did he ever do anything for you without a *quid pro quo?* . . . *The Token* was saved by your writing" (Mellow, 76). Observe the crosscurrents set up here by opposing ideas of masculine worth: for Goodrich to have "taken a good deal of interest" in Hawthorne suggests the patriarchal relation; his readiness for a "quid pro quo," however, removes him from the role of Hawthorne's fatherly guide and protector and indicates respect for Hawthorne's unaided achievement. Bridge himself actually takes the role of patron, but covertly, so as to confirm an illusion of self-reliance that Hawthorne at once cherishes and is ready to cast aside.

Bridge knew well that Hawthorne's efforts to establish himself were severely hampered by his paralysis in the face of such consternations and scolded him in language that anticipates Ralph Waldo Emerson's famous assertion that self-trust is the prime requisite of the manly soul. "The bane of your life has been self-distrust. . . . I wish to God that I could impart to you a little of my own brass," Bridge declares. "You would dash into the contest of literary men, and do honor to yourself and your country in a short time. But you never will have confidence enough in yourself, though you will have fame" (*NHW* 2:147, 149).

The harsh tumult of competitive striving was no fantasy in the turbulent economy of early nineteenth-century America; but an unbreakable core of self-confidence was desirable not only because the external strife was intense but also because it aroused inner confusions. Young men were compelled (they are still compelled) to make their way toward middle-class success by securing the assistance of older, established, men, who themselves play out the same ambivalence, expecting gestures of deference while demanding that younger men make it on their own. A psychic maneuver to control such perplexity, as Emerson recognized, was that of setting a firm boundary between the "self" and the "not-self," and such transcendental teachings translated quickly into popular moral advice. "You must be a law to yourselves," David Magie proclaimed in 1853, "or you will soon make a shipwreck of faith and good conscience" (Halttunen, 25). Thus "the world" was invented as the domain of the not-self, an inhuman unpredictable ocean permanently threatening to drown a man's true inner reality.

To contend with the world, so conceived, was necessarily to endanger one's inner coherence, since worldly dealings mirrored and intensified psychic contradictions. For this reason Hawthorne is grateful that he had remained in seclusion before meeting Sophia: otherwise, "my heart would have become callous by rude encounters with the multitude. . . . But living in solitude till the fulness of time was come, I still kept the dew of my youth and the freshness of my heart, and had these to offer to my Dove" (CE 15:495).

This tribute makes Sophia the recipient of the character he had formed in the secluded chamber. She makes the world worth knowing, makes it preferable to his own solitude; and she confirms the identity that he has made for himself, "keeping my heart warm, and renewing my life with her own" (CE 15:495). But Sophia does more than sustain the completed self; she is an agent in its making:

> Thou only hast revealed me to myself; for without thy aid, my best knowledge of myself would have been merely to know my own shadow—to watch it flickering on the wall, and to mistake its fantasies for my own real actions. Indeed we are but shadows—we are not endowed with real life, and all that seems most real about us is but the thinnest substance of a dream—till the heart is touched. That touch creates us—then we begin to be—thereby we are beings of reality, and inheritors of eternity. Now, dearest, dost thou comprehend what thou hast done for me?
>
> (CE 15:495)

Here self-making reveals its ontological emptiness. How is a man to believe wholeheartedly in an identity he knows he has concocted? How can he deny being counterfeit when the person he puts in circulation carries only the backing of his own sovereignty? At the end of his life, when Hawthorne was internationally famous as a "classic" figure of American letters, he was still unable to overcome his "natural horror of being a creature floating in the air, attached to nothing," nor can he escape "this feeling that there is no reality in the life and fortunes, good or bad, of a being so unconnected" (CE 12:258). In his haunted chamber in Salem, before the social confirmation of his identity had taken place, Hawthorne observed the same dismaying correlation between the unreality of a man's own being and the unreality of his world. "Insincerity in a man's own heart makes all his enjoyments, all that concerns him, unreal; so that his whole life must seem like merely a dramatic representation" (*Hawthorne's Lost Notebook*, 38).

Unable to endow any version of his own possible selfhood with reality, the

miserable subject of such internal division is subject to thoughts and emotions, judgments and perceptions for which he has no stable location. The
pantomime of living then swallows the perceiver himself in experiences of
which he can make many kinds of sense or story, none of which he can take
to be genuine.

The religious power of the domestic angel redeems the self-made man-in-
the-making; she "believes in him" as he wishes to believe in himself. This
psychic assurance replaced the support for identity formation that males had
supplied one another before competitive individual relations supplanted
patriarchal folkways. "A man that knows himself," wrote an exponent of
traditional hierarchy, "will deliberately consider and attend to the particular
rank and station in life in which Providence hath placed him; and what is
the duty and decorum of that station. . . . For a man to assume a character,
or aim at a part that does not belong to him, is affectation" (Mason, 51). Yet
when Providence ceases assigning parts at birth in the hierarchical pageant,
all the players are lost in affectation and self-ignorance until a force appears
that can reveal the self to itself; and since psychic coherence depends on this
force, the moment in which it is apprehended stands forth as a revelation of
the divine Reality, in which one's private reality can be anchored.

Yet Sophia's power to make Hawthorne real does not mean that he told
her about his difficulties with Samuel Goodwyn Goodrich. Part of the reason
Sophia became his angel was that she came to know him after he published
Twice-Told Tales, when her sister Elizabeth found out he had written it and
introduced him to her. Sophia's first knowledge of "Nathaniel Hawthorne"
was knowledge of a literary reputation he had been excruciatingly anxious
not to mar by amateurish early efforts. He published his first novel, *Fanshawe*, at his own expense, quickly determined that he wanted to disown it,
and asked his friends to return the copies he had sent them. He never came
to regard this episode with indulgent humor, as a bout of youthful distress
long since superseded. On the contrary, the repudiation of *Fanshawe* was an
action essential to the lifelong strategy of his self-making; Sophia learned
about it only after his death and refused at first to believe such a book had
ever existed (CE 3:308–314).

The religious force of the domestic angel did not depend on her redemptive engagement with the world but on her isolation from it. Since "the
world" echoed and magnified the structural conflicts of the self-made man,
she must remain sequestered from it if she is to be truly at one with
"him"—that is, if she is to help him sustain the delusions innate to his
selfhood. This logic helps explain why middle-class men believed so urgently

in the "innocence" of their wives, meaning their freedom from the contaminations of worldly life. Hawthorne found in Sophia a presence capable of assuaging his deepest anxieties and relieving his morbid and guilt-stricken preoccupations by showing no awareness of them.

Nathaniel and Sophia discovered that the two of them were one as a remarkable calmness enveloped their relationship. "You could not have felt such quiet," Nathaniel remarked on one occasion, "unless I had felt it too—nor could I, unless you had. If either of our spirits had been troubled, they were then in such close communion that both must have felt the same grief and turmoil" (CE 15:299). The joint identity thus taking form corresponded—from Nathaniel's point of view, at least—to the legal doctrine of marital unity then in force, according to which a woman at marriage suffered "civil death."

Nathaniel and Sophia formed a single person, namely Nathaniel. The salutations of his letters echo and re-echo this fervent tribute: "Ownest Dove," "My Ownest," and inevitably "My own Self." Hawthorne expresses amazement and joy that his vision of her, so minutely adapted to his needs, is confirmed as their relationship unfolds. "My own Dove, I hardly know how it is, but nothing that you do or say ever surprises or disappoints me. . . . There exists latent within me a prophetic knowledge of all your vicissitudes of joy or sorrow; so that, though I cannot foretell them beforehand, yet I recognize them when they come. Nothing disturbs the preconceived idea of you in my mind" (CE 15:378–379).

CHAPTER SIX

Democratic Mythmaking
in *The House of the Seven Gables*

As the fall of 1834 gave way to winter, George Bancroft announced a political conversion: he aborted his promising career as a Whig politician and cast his lot with the Democrats. Bancroft's family background, his education at Harvard and Göttingen, and his extensive connections among Unitarian men of letters placed him naturally among the conservative Whigs, where he had swiftly found positions of public leadership. His change of parties was taken as a desertion of his class; it was denounced as apostasy, and gave him a reputation for deviousness and opportunism he was never to live down. The Democrats were quick to reward Bancroft for his services and especially for the tone of distinction he brought to the party of Andrew Jackson in Massachusetts, where—as Emerson observed—the Democrats had the best cause, while the Whigs had the best men (Fox, 439). By 1838 Bancroft had acquired a substantial patronage post as collector of the Port of Boston, in which capacity he appointed Nathaniel Hawthorne to his job as measurer.

Bancroft's decision to become a Democrat was rooted in his vision of America's historical mission to lead the upward march of civilization through stages of struggle in which the forces of liberty are pitted against tyranny and oppression. Bancroft asserted this stirring thesis in the first volume of his *History of the United States,* which enlarged his reputation for literary learning and established him as a pioneer of modern historical research. Bancroft's career as politician and writer makes a rough but telling parallel with Hawthorne's. Hawthorne's social origins aligned him with the old elite class (his sister Elizabeth was a Whig), yet he made an early, ardent commitment to the Jacksonians. Hawthorne likewise in due course became an anomaly, a poet and a cultivated gentleman in the party of the common man.

In announcing his apostasy, Bancroft took up Jackson's attack on the Bank of the United States, charging that it threatened democratic liberties because of "its tendency to promote extreme inequalities in point of fortune" (Schlesinger, 162). Jacksonians denounced the bank as the mainspring of a complex economic mechanism by which the "Whig moneyed aristocracy" retained a position of illicit power over the citizenry at large. Hatred for the "aristocracy of Mammon," such as drew Nathaniel and Sophia together, was given voice in Jacksonian rhetoric, and Jackson's cause was styled a resurgence of the love of liberty that had triumphed in the American Revolution. "Whiggish aristocracy" was now the enemy of the people's rights, as "Tory feudalism" had been a half-century earlier.

In *The Jacksonian Persuasion* Marvin Meyers finds a complex social meaning in this seemingly anachronistic temperament. The "real people" (18) at the heart of Jackson's rhetoric evoke a virtuous yeoman republic composed of individuals engaged in self-respecting toil for honest gains. Menacing them is a "moneyed aristocracy" that enjoys special privileges and controls the lives of ordinary folk by manipulating "the money power" (22). Meyers demonstrates how shrewdly this rhetoric addressed emergent features of American life. Rather than engaging in a belated confrontation with the pre-Revolutionary past, the Jacksonians struggled to come to terms with alarming features of the society taking form in their midst.

Jackson's war on the bank had the symbolic power of concentrating public anxieties that had been aroused by several interconnected new realities: the mysterious creation of credit during periods of economic boom and its equally mysterious destruction in panic and depression; the complex new politics, with its party apparatuses and national constituencies; the instability of status in a society where rapid changes of fortune were frequent; the scramble for wealth that cannot cease when wealth has been attained. Americans who followed Jackson in assailing aristocratic luxury and illicit power were making war, Meyers observes, on attitudes and conduct in which they were themselves enmeshed (Meyers, 121–141).

A comparable split vision characterizes Hawthorne's treatment of family relations in *The House of the Seven Gables*. Jaffrey Pyncheon is presented as the embodiment of anti-democratic evil. He is the descendant of a family that traces its origin to an autocratic Puritan magistrate by way of eighteenth-century ancestors who adopted the dress and manner of British aristocrats. Broadly envisioned, the narrative recounts the collapse of this aristocratic dynasty and its displacement by the domestic family, joining parties (Holgrave and Phoebe) who embody democratic virtues rather than corrupt aristocratic delusions. Yet behind this thematic structure stands another, in which the new family arrangement takes form in response to distinctively nineteenth-century social dilemmas. Like his fellow Jacksonians, Hawthorne deploys the rhetoric of egalitarian revolution in making sense of an expanding middle-class capitalist society. Hawthorne asserts fresh "democratic" energies against a corrupt "Past," but the ogre of the discredited old order represents emerging features of the American society.

The opening of Hepzibah Pyncheon's cent-shop celebrates the fresh breeze of democratic change: Hepzibah's transformation from a "patrician lady" into a "plebeian woman" dramatizes the welcome collapse of inherited hierarchy. "In this republican country, amid the fluctuating waves of our social life, somebody is always at the drowning point," Hawthorne observes (CE 2:38). Hepzibah's calamity is painful as well as ludicrous because she retains an aristocratic consciousness. "I was born a lady," she stiffly informs Holgrave, "and have always lived one—no matter in what narrowness of means, always a lady!" (45). Yet Holgrave assures her that being compelled to open the cent-shop is a piece of good fortune, since she will now join the "united struggle of mankind," will enjoy the moral benefits of that "healthy and natural effort," and will realize a true humanity that was obscured by the social arrangements in which she was reared. Holgrave is confident that Hepzibah's humiliation will lead her to discover that it is "better to be a true woman, than a lady" (44–45).

The founding father of the Pyncheon dynasty had built a "family-mansion . . . calculated to endure for many generations of his posterity" (CE 2:9) and had bequeathed landholdings "more extensive than many a dukedom" (18). Yet his nineteenth-century descendants find that their claim to exalted position not only cannot be validated but has lost its meaning. Like other wealthy families in the early national period, the Pyncheons lost out to lowly farming folk who cleared the land on which aristocratic status had been based.[1] Hawthorne taunts the Pyncheons for continuing to search for the deed to their dukedom after it was occupied by settlers. "These last," Hawthorne observes, "if they ever heard of the Pyncheon title, would have laughed at the idea of any man's asserting a right—on the strength of mouldy parchments, signed with the faded autographs of governors and legislators, long dead and forgotten—to the lands which they or their fathers had wrested from the wild hand of Nature" (18–19).

The actual Pyncheon legacy is "an absurd delusion of family importance" which breeds in some descendants a "liability to sluggishness and dependence" (CE 2:19) and also produces Jaffrey Pyncheon's ferocious determination to amass a large fortune, so as to impart a specious validity to his claim to aristocratic station. The true tradition of the family is this ancestral curse, the perpetuation of self-contradictory striving, as figured in the dissonant meanings of the term *blood*.

Persons are related to one another by blood if they are biologically akin: parents and children are thus related; husband and wife are not. Although this sense of blood relations (as opposed to in-law relations) is distinct among living contemporaries, it takes on an altered sense when projected on earlier generations. Then *blood* refers to a procession of males bearing the family name, so that a mother becomes merely the carrier of the blood relationship, not an agent in it. When blood, as a way of describing descent, takes on the patriarchal bearings inherent in patrilineage, it cuts across the significance that prevails in immediate domestic relations (Schneider, 23–25).

Holgrave asserts that the wretchedness of the Pyncheons—like that of other balked dynasts—results from their frantic entanglement in these contradictions. "To plant a family! This idea is at the bottom of most of the wrong and mischief which men do. The truth is, that, once in every half-century, at longest, a family should be merged into the great, obscure mass of humanity, and forget all about its ancestors. Human blood, in order to keep its freshness, should run in hidden streams" (CE 2:185).

The curse on the Pyncheons' self-confounded existence—"God will give you blood to drink!"—focuses these conflicts. Strangled on the meanings of the dynastic family whose illusion of permanence is embodied in a family mansion, the Pyncheons' collapse validates a new concept of family life, suited to "the future condition of society." Holgrave envisions a wholesale social renovation, in which "no man shall build his house for posterity. . . . If each generation were allowed and expected to build its own houses, that single change, comparatively unimportant in itself, would imply almost every reform which society is now suffering for" (CE 2:183–184).

In the end, to be sure, Holgrave abandons this view. It turns out that he has not forgotten about his Maule ancestry and has every intention of assigning that name to his wife and perpetuating it in his offspring. Yet

Holgrave's insistence that families be created anew in each generation is integral to Hawthorne's parable of the transition to a domestic family ideology: a family is grounded not in an ancestral establishment but in the mutual love between a self-sufficient man and a "true woman."[2]

Holgrave's story of Alice Pyncheon portrays the repression of such mutual affections in the aristocratic past, when an impassable boundary was fixed between persons of high and low station, so that the "natural" gender identities of men and women could not find healthy expression and took perverted forms. The denatured manhood fostered by this arrangement is symbolized by Alice's father Gervayse Pyncheon's effeminate dress: his flowered waistcoat, lace-embroidered blue velvet coat, and powdered wig. Matthew Maule, by contrast, is a manly man of blunt and direct address, wearing a woolen jacket and leather breeches, which include a long pocket for his phallic carpenter's ruler. Alice Pyncheon is delighted by "the remarkable comeliness, strength, and energy of Maule's figure" (CE 2:201), and Maule is himself correspondingly stirred. But the sexual spark that leaps between Alice and Matthew ignites a destructive blaze because of the wrongful social distance separating them. Presuming on her social advantage, Alice looks at Matthew as though he were a work of art or a handsome animal; Maule responds with bitter resentment. Alice, however, blinded by the prerogatives of her station, is unaware that she has given offense. She also does not realize that the social convention placing her "above" Matthew Maule cannot defend her against the greater strength he enjoys by nature, because he is a man. When Maule challenges her to submit to hypnotism, she foolishly agrees: "Alice put woman's might against man's might; a match not often equal, on the part of woman" (203).

As Alice is subjugated, her father's dignity is shattered, "natural" reality discomposing the regalia of aristocratic ascendancy. "How the man of conventionalities shook the powder out of his periwig," Hawthorne jeers (CE 2:205). Yet Maule is also degraded; his justifiable indignation finds no healthy expression, so that he enacts an odious exaggeration of his natural dominance over Alice, ordering her to perform shameful and pointless tasks. As Holgrave—Matthew's descendant—tells this story to Phoebe Pyncheon, she (like her equally suggestible and passive ancestor) falls into a hypnotic trance. Holgrave chooses not to bring her under his control, Hawthorne affirms, because of his "reverence" for her "individuality" (212). The eventual marriage of Holgrave and Phoebe is a sign that "the sin of long ago," with its sorry harvest of abortive relationships, is at long last to be abolished.

Hawthorne dramatizes this Jacksonian progressivism by describing a complex transitional situation, in which elements of the "past" and the "future" are jumbled together. The domestic ideal wins out at the end and asserts a "new" organization of social space in which "home" is set against "the world." Yet this triumph takes place in defiance of a patriarchal social arrangement that remains secretly alive, even as its demise is celebrated.

When the master of a preindustrial household looked beyond the boundaries of his own domain, he contemplated a social landscape of patriarchal units analogous to the one he headed. The church and institutions of government recapitulated the model set by the household, with "fatherhood" as a recurrent metaphor designating authority in multiple realms, including the ultimate authority of Godhead. As William Gouge explained in *Of Domesticall Duties,* the household was a training ground for positions of responsibility in any institution: "It is as a schoole wherein the first principles and grounds of government and subjection are learned: whereby men are fitted to greater matters in Church or commonwealth" (Demos, xix).

The early nineteenth century witnessed a rearrangement of community life as economic institutions emerged that the household metaphor could not embrace. The relation of master and apprentice in the shoemaker's household included the master's responsibility to provide the young man shelter and guidance and to aid him in finding his eventual place in the community. The "boss" at the shoe factory, by contrast, discharged his responsibility when he paid an employee. Newly estranged also were the relations between the owner of the shoe factory and those for whom the shoes were produced. Mass production required that a marketing and distribution system be created to reach the faceless denizens of a regional market, where earlier the local shoemaker had served neighbors whose lives he knew and who were likewise well versed in his peculiarities. The communal network of local relations was interrupted by a new pattern of social space; a "world" now emerged that transcended local knowledge, in which uncertain new forces were at work (Ryan, *Cradle,* 147–152).

In *The House of the Seven Gables* Hawthorne dramatizes this transitional situation. Hepzibah opens her cent-shop amid the small-scale communal life of an earlier era. Working men passing down the street swiftly fix the enterprise in a network of familiar information. "Well, well, this is a sight, to be sure. . . . In the old Pyncheon-house, and underneath the Pyncheonelm! Who would have thought it! Old Maid Pyncheon is setting up a cent-shop!" (CE 2:47). Hepzibah's shame and confusion result from the abasement of her aristocratic pride—soiling her hands with "trade"—not from any sense of violating a space sacred to domestic felicities. The notion that business belongs in the "world" and not in the "home" does not occur to her, or to the passing workmen. On the contrary, they observe that such household enterprises are so commonplace that Hepzibah can hardly expect to succeed.

This portrayal of the shop and its social context is sharply contrasted against a vision of urban commerce that comes uninvited into Hepzibah's mind. She sees a

> panorama, representing the great thoroughfare of a city, all astir with customers. So many and so magnificent shops as there were! Groceries, toy-shops, dry-goods stores, with their immense panes of plate-glass, their gorgeous fixtures, their vast and complete assortments of merchandize, in which fortunes had been invested; and those noble mirrors at the farther end of each establishment, doubling all this wealth by a brightly burnished vista of unrealities!
>
> (CE 2:48)

The elements of a transformed retail economy are present in this vision: the specialization of shops by products, the large capital outlay, the huge display windows and mirrors that catch the eyes of shoppers crowding an urban business district. Most telling is Hawthorne's disdainful sketch of the "perfumed and glossy salesmen, smirking, smiling, bowing" (49), whose function is identical to that of the shining glass. Their transactions with customers reach no deeper than the exchange of goods for cash, and their miming of friendship is meant to facilitate a brief anonymous encounter.

Hawthorne gives Hepzibah this vision in defiance of narrative logic. We are told she had lived in "strict seclusion" (CE 2:31) for over a quarter of a century, and nothing suggests she ever made a trip to the city where she might have seen such things. This incongruity in Hepzibah's knowledge marks an important feature of the transitional reality that embraces the action of *The House of the Seven Gables:* instances of the old order and the new are figured as discordant psychic structures even as they illustrate historical change.

Later in the narrative Clifford gazes through the arched window of the old Pyncheon house and is vividly aware of the "novelties" (CE 2:160) that have made their appearance in the street during his years in prison. He observes with distress the omnibus, the cabs, the street sprinkler, and the railroad cars—features of an urbanized transportation system that have supplanted the stagecoaches Clifford sorely misses. He takes comfort in what remains of "the antique fashions" of a still active local commerce: the butcher's cart, the fish cart, the baker's cart and the itinerant scissor-grinder (161). A major theme of this transition is given in Hawthorne's depiction of an organ-grinder bearing a show-box in which typical characters of village life are represented by figurines: "the cobbler, the blacksmith, the soldier, the lady with her fan, the toper with his bottle, the milk-maid sitting by her cow" (162–163). These seeming individualities are tied together by a single machinery, which is put in motion when the organ-grinder turns his crank. The ultimate reality that drives this pantomime is "Mammon," as represented by the organ-grinder's monkey, who goes about with "joyless eagerness" (164) collecting coins from the audience.

The new order of social relations is not merely juxtaposed against the old, as a butcher's cart might be parked beside the municipal street sprinkler. Hawthorne's organ-grinder symbolizes the capacity of the "money power" to penetrate the traditional patterns of social life and empty them of their apparent meaning. The life of the "new" circulates like a virus through the organs of a familiar social body, so that unhealthy new processes are found to be at work in what look like old virtues.

The ambiguities pervading the social landscape of *The House of the Seven Gables* are eventually resolved through Phoebe's spiritual force, her ontological power to establish the reality of "home" and to define its character as a redemptive form of the "new." Hawthorne fervently celebrates her numinous homemaking energy: "A wild hut of underbrush, tossed together by wayfarers through the primitive forest, would acquire the home-aspect by one night's lodging of such a woman, and would retain it, long after her quiet figure had disappeared into the surrounding shade" (CE 2:71–72). In Phoebe the democratic future is already accomplished, Hawthorne explains; she is an "example of feminine grace and availability combined, in a state of society, if there were any such, where ladies did not exist. There, it should be woman's office to move in the midst of practical affairs, and to gild them all—the very homeliest, were it even the scouring of pots and kettles—with an atmosphere of loveliness and joy" (80). The "spontaneous grace" with which Phoebe carries out her housekeeping chores forms a sharp contrast with the "squalid and ugly" character of worldly labor. "Angels do not toil," Hawthorne explains, "but let their good works grow out of them; and so did Phoebe" (82).[3]

In the Manning household, where Hawthorne was reared, careful accounts were kept assigning a money value to cooking and household maintenance as well as to "business" functions, so that "Madame Hathorne" and her children were charged for the efforts others put forward on their behalf (Erlich, 54–55). In this traditional pattern of household organization, little tension was felt between financial and familial relations. Phoebe herself is a shrewd negotiator and does a thriving trade in Hepzibah's cent-shop precisely because she is able to carry a cheerful home-like atmosphere with her wherever she goes. In this respect she resembles the salesmen in Hepzibah's envisioned department store; yet Hawthorne offers her as their opposite. She embodies the standard of spiritual authenticity against which the sordidness of worldly commerce is to be measured.[4]

Phoebe's religious power is genuine, Hawthorne asserts, because it is inherent to her being. She does not intend to bring others under her spell; it just happens. Men are drawn toward her because of a masculine anguish of which she herself is unaware:

> Phoebe's presence made a home about her—that very sphere which the outcast, the prisoner, the potentate, the wretch beneath mankind, the wretch aside from it, or the wretch above it, instinctively pines after—a home! She was real! Holding her hand, you felt something; a tender something; a substance, and a warm one; and so long as you should feel its grasp, soft as it was, you might be certain that your place was good in the whole sympathetic chain of human nature. The world was no longer a delusion.
> (CE 2:140–141)

It is worth noting that the "home" radiating from Phoebe's presence is not so much a refuge from "the world" as an avenue of access to it. She creates a domestic sphere that places a man in contact with "human nature" and makes the world real. Rather than drawing him into solitude, she delivers him from it. Active religious symbols embrace opposed meanings; they are telling paradoxes for those who live within the spell cast by the symbols and look like mere contradictions to those who do not. In Phoebe we find "labor" and "play" at odds and yet trading places, as do "home" and "world."

Hawthorne does not shrink from insisting on such fusions, and his climactic invocation of Phoebe's divinity multiplies them further:

> In her aspect, there was a familiar gladness, and a holiness that you could play with, and yet reverence it as much as ever. She was like a prayer, offered up in the homeliest beauty of one's mother-tongue. Fresh was Phoebe, moreover, and airy and sweet in her apparel; as if nothing she wore—neither her gown, nor her small straw bonnet, nor her little kerchief, any more than her snowy stockings—had ever been put on,

before; or, if worn, were all the fresher for it, and with a fragrance as if they had lain among the rosebuds.

(CE 2:168)

At the center of Phoebe's being is a body that is not a body, without sweat or menstrual discharges, a physical presence so intensely pure that it cleanses her garments from within. Phoebe is "a Religion in herself" (168), acting as an ontological laundry that washes away the corruptions Hawthorne designates as "old."

Jaffrey Pyncheon is repeatedly identified with the ancestral crime of the family and meets his death in the ancestral fashion, by strangling on his own blood. This embodiment of the "sin of long ago," however, also represents moral shortcomings of the new urban and industrial society, in particular the predicament arising from a new public anonymity. The rich context of personal knowledge supplied through communal networks of information exchange was absent in the competitive urban environment. Compelled to take each other at face value, men based their mutual knowledge on superficial and uncertain marks of character. In the growing cities they were strangers not merely to the unknown multitude but also to the men with whom they had regular dealings. By mid-century it was a commonplace that "men are not the natural confidants of men" (Rothman, 111); they were compelled, like Jaffrey Pyncheon, to know each other by way of "the external phenomena of life" (CE 2:229).

The ambivalence produced by this situation is reflected in a newly emerging mythic figure: the confidence man. In the 1830s and 1840s a massive advice literature was generated that featured young men entering the urban environment only to be ensnared by new acquaintances in whom they mistakenly put their trust.

A key to Pyncheon's success is thus his feigning of personal interest and personal accountability; he seems to approach others from a world that is no longer there. Yet the appearance of "benignity" that Pyncheon maintains is only one of the new arts of dominance in a social system where power has drained out of communal relations and become vested in impersonal, collective processes. The newly anonymous public order that created an unfamiliar context for personal relations also revolutionized the formation of political power.

One classic form of the confidence man is the demagogue, Karen Halttunen has shown, who takes advantage of the emerging politics. Local communities increasingly lost power to national systems of patronage and publicity that were aimed at mobilizing a mass electorate, securing voters' support for political leaders they could not know firsthand. As professional politicians learned to shape public opinion, Americans came to fear that elections had become a masquerade of republican governance, concealing the cynical manipulations of an all-powerful elite (Halttunen, 16).

On the evening of Pyncheon's death, he was scheduled to secure the governorship of Massachusetts at a private party, his dinner companions having the power to get him nominated and elected. "They are practised politicians, every man of them, and skilled to adjust those preliminary measures, which steal from the people, without its knowledge, the power of choosing its own rulers. The popular voice, at the next gubernatorial election, though loud as thunder, will be really but an echo of what these gentlemen shall speak, under their breath" (CE 2:274). Pyncheon, having worked his way to political power through large contributions, plans that very evening to make a donation better than twice what the party asked. He embodies that classic nemesis of Jacksonianism, the "money power" acting to corrupt republican virtue.

Pyncheon has amassed a fortune by exploiting those aspects of the American economy Jacksonians found most disturbing. He is a financial manipulator whose efforts produce nothing substantial but nonetheless lead to wealth. Hawthorne reviews his speculative investments: "his real estate in town and country, his railroad, bank, and insurance shares, his United States stock." Pyncheon enjoys an inner knowledge of the new financial systems that ordinary citizens cannot obtain; he makes it a custom to visit the "Insurance Office" so as to hear and appraise the current gossip, and to drop "some deeply designed chance-word, which will be certain to become the gossip of tomorrow" (CE 2:270). He is also well practiced in creating pseudonymous bank accounts, both foreign and domestic, and in using other arcane methods, "familiar enough to capitalists" (234), to conceal the extent of his holdings.

Jaffrey Pyncheon accordingly represents anti-democratic arrangements that are native to the new economic and political order. He is a figure of the irony according to which a presumptively republican America sponsored the formation of a capitalist elite.

A central emblem of Pyncheon's social character is the timepiece he holds in his hand as he sits dead in the ancestral chair, by which the narrator marks the hours that pass after his death. The watch—and the daily schedule it measures out—symbolize the improvisational freedom now available to an enterprising man. Far from suggesting confinement, or the dreariness of a "time-disciplined" proletarian life, Pyncheon's watch betokens his freedom to maneuver, ticking off an abstract scale against which he can manage a series of prearranged encounters.

Pyncheon's interviews stand against a social void; they are separate affairs, unconnected except as they serve his personal interests. One of the people on his schedule is a "decayed widow" who has appealed to him for help; he cancels the visit, aware that disappointing her will not injure his reputation for benevolence. The widow has no contact with the other people on his schedule, especially not with the persons among whom his reputation counts. Judge Pyncheon can go through his sequence of appointments without anyone else knowing what his whole day looks like.

The narrator's taunting of Pyncheon's dead body strips away the freedom he had found in anonymity. As the narrator takes us through Pyncheon's date book, the mask of pretended benevolence disintegrates and the judge's ruthless self-aggrandizement stands revealed. Hawthorne presents this exposure as a revelation of moral reality. The narrator's interior knowledge replaces the now defunct communal network in which members of a community were continuously known and appraised from multiple points of view and where the daily round of life routinely brought persons into contact with no need of scheduled appointments.

Yet it turns out that Pyncheon's true character has been known all along, in a "a hidden stream of private talk, such as it would have shocked all decency to speak loudly at the street-corners" (CE 2:310). The deceit inherent in living in public is counterbalanced by the revelations of intimate contact, to which women are by nature attuned. Moral reality is to be found in "the woman's, the private and domestic view, of a public man," Hawthorne informs us, "nor can anything be more curious than the vast discrepancy between portraits intended for engraving, and the pencil-sketches that pass from hand to hand, behind the original's back" (122). Phoebe's aversion to Judge Pyncheon shows her unerring spontaneous moral responses; without knowing his private story, she instinctively draws back from his gestures of affectionate kinship. In place of communal knowledge as a test of virtue we now find "true womanhood," credited with an intuitive awareness of a man's moral essence.

Jaffrey Pyncheon embodies the spiritual emptiness—and ultimately the metaphysical horror—of a man made of masks in an anonymous world.

Pyncheon is actuated throughout by a partly conscious self-disgust, so that outward rebuffs are echoed within him. In describing Pyncheon's smile, Hawthorne observes that it "was a good deal akin to the shine on his boots, and that each must have cost him and his boot-black, respectively, a good deal of hard labor to bring out and preserve" (CE 2:117). The toil of keeping up the smile does not counteract simple malice, which smiles without being prompted; the black smile hides displeasure and inward pain.

This blackness flows out of Pyncheon's being, "darkening forth" to fill his surroundings. Just as Phoebe symbolizes divine light, so Judge Pyncheon embodies the blackness of nonbeing, which is asserted as an ontological principle when his dead body is engulfed in midnight: "Has it yet vanished? No!—yes!—not quite! And there is still the swarthy whiteness . . . of Judge Pyncheon's face. The features are all gone; there is only the paleness of them left. And how looks it now? . . . There is no face! An infinite, inscrutable blackness has annihilated sight! Where is our universe?" (CE 2:276). The desperation that enters the narrator's voice at this juncture indicates that the "darkness visible" into which Pyncheon dissolves is contagious, and the figure most susceptible to infection is Holgrave, who watches obsessively as Pyncheon sits dead in his chair.

Hawthorne offers Holgrave as a representative of self-reliant manhood. Like "many compeers in his native land," he takes pride in having no advantages of inherited wealth and family position. His attitude toward his various lines of work marks him as a figure of the new social instability, in which a young man could not afford to tie his personal worth to the outcome of any given enterprise. Ralph Waldo Emerson describes the collapse of morale that could result: "If our young men miscarry in their first enterprises they lose all heart," he observed in 1840. "If the young merchant fails, men say he is *ruined.*" Emerson praises by contrast the lad "who in turn tries all the professions"; but instead of becoming a teamster, a farmer, a peddler, a schoolmaster, a clergyman, a newspaper editor, or even a Congressman, "he *teams it, farms it, peddles,* keeps a school, preaches, edits a newspaper, goes to Congress . . . and always like a cat falls on his feet" (Whicher, 161). Hawthorne similarly describes Holgrave's various ad hoc enterprises, explaining that "his present phase, as a Daguerreotypist, was of no more importance in his own view, nor likely to be more permanent, than any of the preceding ones." Hawthorne observes that in "putting off one exterior, and snatching up another, to be soon shifted for a third," Holgrave "had never violated the innermost man" (CE 2:177).

For all his vaunted autonomy, Holgrave is nonetheless unmanned when he enters the gloom that surrounds Judge Pyncheon's demise, because the demon-ridden non-selfhood of the judge and Holgrave's democratic self-reliance are fundamentally akin. The self-made individual is perforce a confidence man, who succeeds in "self-trust" insofar as he deceives himself, denying that his existence is determined by the vicissitudes of gender, class position, and economic happenstance. The theater of his self-creation is "the rude struggle of man with man" (CE 2:213), where no individual self-in-the-making can have distinctive value, since all are in that respect identical. To measure one's worth by the standards of value that prevail in the world of striving men is to submit oneself to the "great unrealities" of wealth and power from which the inner truth of the self is excluded. The quest for such worldly trophies cannot succeed without the cooperation of other men, and to secure that cooperation it is necessary to make a credible show of concern for their welfare. It follows that the arts of the confidence man and those of the self-reliant middle-class male are the same. One cannot influence people without knowing how to win friends.

Holgrave, shaken to his foundations when he confronts the judge's fate, turns urgently to Phoebe for solace. " 'Could you but know, Phoebe, how it was with me, the hour before you came!' exclaimed the artist. 'A dark, cold, miserable hour! The presence of yonder dead man threw a great black shadow over everything; he made the universe, so far as my perception could reach, a scene of guilt, and of retribution more dreadful than the guilt' " (CE 2:306). Why is not Holgrave jubilant, given the agelong injustice done against his family? Why should he be frightened or depressed at this triumphant vindication of the Maules? Pyncheon's death represents the nemesis peculiar to the confidence man and accordingly undermines Holgrave's self-trust. "My past life, so lonesome and dreary; my future, a shapeless gloom, which I must mould into gloomy shapes" (306). Holgrave recognizes that so long as his undertakings are self-ratified, they are spurious. Whatever shape he may give his future can only be formed of shadows.

The strange scene in which Holgrave and Phoebe profess their mutual love, while the day-old corpse sits in the next room, depicts the reorganization of social space in which the polarity of "world versus home" emerges against the background of the old communal order. Holgrave and Phoebe have markedly different visions of the society beyond the house. Phoebe urges him to " 'throw open the doors, and call all the neighborhood to see the truth.' . . . Yet the artist. . . . [was not] in haste, like her, to betake himself within the precincts of common life." Holgrave is not environed by "the neighborhood" or "the precincts of common life": he inhabits an "illimitable desert," whose desolation this moment with Phoebe magically counteracts. "He gathered a wild enjoyment—as it were, a flower of strange beauty, growing in a desolate spot" (CE 2:305).

Holgrave prolongs the moment because "it separated Phoebe and himself from the world, and bound them to each other. . . . [It] kept them within the circle of a spell, a solitude in the midst of men, a remoteness as entire as that of an island in mid-ocean" (CE 2:305). The two share a fragile new intimacy through which they move toward a new pattern of social experience. The "magnetic chain of humanity" that once ran at large through the community is now coiled within their private relation. The blackness that swallowed Jaffrey Pyncheon has now been counteracted by the reality-working power that Holgrave finds in Phoebe. "It was in this hour, so full of doubt and awe, that the one miracle was wrought, without which every human existence is a blank" (307). Holgrave can now face the neighbors, who have assembled outside the house, and is prepared to contend with the questions aroused by Pyncheon's death. The language in which he frames that readiness quietly underscores the social terrain the loving couple now inhabit. "Now let us," he says to Phoebe, "meet the world" (307).

Phoebe's profession of love for Holgrave redeems him from the masquerade of male selfhood even as it consummates his confidence game, whose prize is Judge Pyncheon's fortune, to be obtained by marrying Phoebe.[5]

Hawthorne does not indict Holgrave as a fortune hunter, but he assembles circumstances that frame such an indictment, and this implicit charge is central to the domestic ideology endorsed here. In the night-vigil scene, in which Hawthorne presented a procession of Pyncheon's deceased kinfolk, we learned that the judge's only son is dead, so that the great estate is to devolve on Hepzibah, Clifford, and "rustic little Phoebe" (CE 2:280). Does one read the anxious rhetoric of Holgrave's lovemaking without being subliminally aware that the judge's bank stock, insurance shares, railroad holdings, and extensive real estate are all riding on the outcome? Holgrave does not reveal the false pretenses under which he has courted Phoebe, nor does the redemptive bliss that makes "all things true, beautiful, and holy" prompt him to show his true colors. He reveals his identity only after it strikes Phoebe as odd that he knows where the old Pyncheon claim to Maine lands is hidden. Then Holgrave mentions—as though casually—that Phoebe will be assuming the name Maule when they marry. The cynical audacity of

Holgrave's game reaches a climax when he tells Phoebe he would have disclosed his identity sooner, "only that I was afraid of frightening you away" (316).[6]

What are we to make of this thematic pattern, in which Holgrave exploits Phoebe's trustful ignorance and prevents her from becoming economically independent? It would be possible to claim that the domestic ideology works to exclude such mercenary considerations, to mark them as "worldly" and thus irrelevant to the domestic relation. Yet the very reverse is true: the social meaning of this marriage between self-made man and domestic angel necessarily includes his assuming control of her property without her understanding what has taken place. The reader, too, is meant to accept this transaction without objection, tacitly consenting to the ideology that renders Holgrave's acquisition of Pyncheon's wealth legitimate. Staked here, at last, are the ratification of a democratic, middle-class elite supplanting the dynastic landed gentry and the relation of domesticity—that central emblem of middle-class status—to the terms on which that ratification is made to occur.

The House of the Seven Gables is pervasively occupied with the dilemmas of asserting high status in a democratic society. Hawthorne warns against blurring the distinction between the possession of power and its rightful possession:

> There is something so massive, stable, and almost irresistibly imposing, in the exterior presentment of established rank and great possessions, that their very existence seems to give them a right to exist; at least, so excellent a counterfeit of right, that few poor and humble men have moral force enough to question it, even in their secret minds. Such is the case now, after so many ancient prejudices have been overthrown; and it was far more so in ante-revolutionary days, when the aristocracy could venture to be proud, and the low were content to be abased.
>
> (CE 2:25)

Can any claim to social rank be sustained now that aristocratic prejudices have disappeared? When a nobleman falls into poverty, Hawthorne observes, he retains the dignity of the order to which his birth assigned him; when the citizen of a republic suffers economic ruin, his status is altogether destroyed. "With us, rank is the grosser substance of wealth and a splendid establishment, and has no spiritual existence after the death of these" (CE 2:38). It would seem to follow that high position and great wealth have no right to exist in a democracy but only acquire the "counterfeit of right" that their mere possession imposes on the imaginations of men who lack moral force.

Real social worth momentarily seems attainable through the self-help Holgrave recommends to Hepzibah as she opens her cent-shop. Yet commercial enterprise on a scale sufficient to produce wealth, or only to sustain a family in middle-class respectability, requires engagement in the world of "unrealities" that Hepzibah envisions when she measures her chances against the competition from large department stores in the city. Far from cultivating republican virtue, fighting out a battle in the newly developing urban marketplaces of Jacksonian America leads straight to the depravity of Jaffrey Pyncheon. So the dilemma takes form: elite status is contrary to democratic principle if it is inherited, but the self-reliant effort to gain it requires contaminating involvement in the power games of commerce and politics.

A classic response to this dilemma is marked out in Holgrave's way to wealth, which anticipates the pattern of the Horatio Alger narratives, where the likely lad is never compelled to dramatize his self-reliant diligence in economic competition. Despite Holgrave's enthusiasm for the united struggle of mankind, he is exempted from competing against Jaffrey Pyncheon and his ilk, and even from seeking their favor. He displays the virtue that establishes his right to a fortune only in his relation to the woman from whom he filches it, and her love for him cleanses away the stain of his having dispossessed her. At the moment when Holgrave and Phoebe declare their love, he gains his fortune, and her love for him validates his virtue—against his own doubts—as a man deserving a sunlit future. Hawthorne arranges the climax so that Phoebe's subordination to Holgrave and the transfer of her fortune into his hands testify to his social worth and mark his elite status.

Working-class misery is not portrayed at length in *The House of the Seven Gables,* but it surfaces on one occasion that underscores the role of the domestic angel in legitimating middle-class privilege. Shortly after Hepzibah opens the cent-shop, a man in a soiled blue cotton frock enters and buys a pipe, "filling the whole shop, meanwhile, with the hot odor of strong drink . . . oozing out of his entire system, like an inflammable gas." This "brutal" figure portrays the vices making it appear that the sufferings of working-class men are self-inflicted. His depravity is further marked by the wretchedness of his wife, "one of those women, naturally delicate, whom you at once recognize as worn to death by a brute—probably, a drunken brute—of a husband, and at least nine children" (CE 2:53).

The middle-class claim to elite status is covert; it translates social pre-eminence into ethical worth, and the gender system featured in the domestic ideal is at the heart of that translation. Holgrave is entitled to control the lives of men in dirty blue frocks because he is entitled to control a far superior being, his wife, who willingly submits to the superior force that nature has granted him. God has provided him with "man's might," meaning the capacity to beat her up and wear her to death with multiple unwelcome pregnancies; but unlike working-class drunkards, he is capable of respecting the natural "delicacy" of his woman. In fact, he worships her.

The mutual adaptation of the spiritualities of husband and wife in the domestic ideal is a sacred paradigm of legitimate subordination. Phoebe's "true womanhood" validates Holgrave's ascent to mastery, just as the abuse of the workingman's wife is an emblem of the disorder that would result if such a brute ever had real power. The spirituality of the domestic sphere is a test of public virtue that takes place in a domain mythically segregated from the conflicts of public life, a domain in which womanly dispossession and subordination are asserted as the ground on which manly virtue is established. Holgrave makes of Jaffrey Pyncheon's numerous economic victims a single victim, namely Phoebe, whose love for him authorizes his dominion over the rest. Thus the sacred radiance of domesticity that surrounds the moment in which they profess their mutual love must incorporate his making himself rich to perfect the legitimation of his rank on democratic terms.

Phoebe's intense purity launders Pyncheon's money as it is transferred to Holgrave. Dynastic pollutions, as well as pollutions arising from the "world," are washed away; they are amalgamated into a "Past" that is entirely transcended by the love that makes all things fresh and new. Because Hawthorne was uneasy with this solution, he gives Clifford a vision of an existence transcending the domestic ideal that will "do away with those stale ideas of home and fireside" (CE 2:259). Clifford pictures a future life in which the railroad and other technological innovations will allow a family to roam from one temporary encampment to the next. He looks forward to an endless landscape of free individual movement, in which the loving couple are the sole inhabitants, their felicity unmolested by even so much worldly constraint as is built into owning a house.

Yet the marital relation itself is implicated in Clifford's horror of fixed dwellings: "Morbid influences, in a thousand-fold variety, gather about hearths, and pollute the life of households" (CE 2:261). Clifford implies that corruptions arise in the domestic sphere itself that are likewise to be escaped by frequent changes of locale before they contaminate the building in which husband and wife lead their lives. The exploitation and oppression of the emerging middle-class order are made to vanish into the intense purity of Phoebe but remain there, hidden.

In the latter stages of composition, Hawthorne became troubled at his realization that the work "darkens damnably toward the close" and further troubled by the difficulties he encountered in trying "to pour some setting sunshine over it." As Michael Gilmore has noted, Hawthorne's effort to give the work a cheerful ending, and thus to make it more attractive in the literary marketplace, recapitulates Jaffrey Pyncheon's effort to spread a sunny and appealing smile over his avarice (CE 2:106–112). Yet the confidence game in which Hawthorne himself was engaged—as depicted in Holgrave as well as Pyncheon—is more insidious than a market strategy. It engages the substance of the domestic relation, whose "sunshine" is itself a deception. The morbid influences that pollute the life of households result in good measure because the domestic ideal renders invisible the link between social injustice and marital intimacy and denies the political and economic conflict that takes place within the domestic bond.

Hawthorne's conclusion may well leave us wondering how the newly constituted Maule household will lead its life. Will Phoebe continue to clean her clothes by wearing them? How will the fastidious Mr. Maule respond when he finds out that she doesn't? Will Phoebe continue to relieve her husband of the moral uneasiness that he feels when he deceives her? How will she, with her practical shrewdness and her gift for bargaining, reconcile herself to his lifelong control of the family's finances? What if they have a son who insists on living like Clifford? What if they have a daughter with the talents and temperament of Jaffrey Pyncheon? Now that the domestic sphere has been formed, how will they live in it?

As we return to the Hawthornes' family life, it will become apparent that they themselves were disconcerted by such questions. The sweaty toil of running a household and the surprises of child rearing could not be escaped, and they forced political and economic struggles that were supposed to remain in "the world." The courtship of Nathaniel and Sophia reveals how subtly their inner lives coalesced, forming the intimate union at the heart of middle-class marital bliss. Sophia rejoiced, we shall see, in the "miraculous interweaving of spirits" between herself and Nathaniel, and she likewise treasured a close spiritual communion with her children. These psychic bonds, however, were freighted with anxieties and conflicts that set family members at odds, even amid the tenderest affections.

PART THREE

Marital Politics

On a Sunday morning in June 1850 Sophia Hawthorne sat down to write her mother a letter; she continued well into the evening, because the writing was a joyful celebration of her fulfillment as wife and mother. The Hawthornes had at last moved away from Salem, where they had lived in close confinement with Nathaniel's mother and sisters, and now occupied the "little Red House," a snug home on a country road in Lenox, Massachusetts, commanding one of the finest prospects in the Berkshires. There were also two children for Sophia to be proud of: Una was six years old, and Julian had just reached his fourth birthday.

Sophia describes the interior of her household in loving, unhurried detail: "We seem to have such a large house! *inside,*" she tells her mother, "though outside, the little reddest thing looks like the smallest of ten feet houses." Sophia writes as though she were leading her mother on a tour, which begins in the garden where a stately double rose columbine grows in honor of her sisters, Elizabeth and Mary. It is a letter of womanly achievement, from daughter to mother, rich with personal symbolism:

On the right hand side of the hall is a door. Will you enter the drawing-room? Between the front windows stands the beautiful antique ottoman, the monument of Elizabeth's loving kindness, covered with woven flowers. In the corner on that side stands crosswise the fairy tea-table,—a Hawthorne heir-loom, & upon an embroidered mat upon it lies my pretty white greyhound. In the other corner on the same side stands Apollo, whose head I have tied on! Diagonally opposite Apollo, stands the ancient carved chair, with its tapestry of roses. Opposite the ottoman is the card-table, with the alabaster vase, & over the vase hangs Correggio's Madonna. Over the ottoman, Raphael's Transfiguration. Opposite the door you have entered stands the centre-table. On that are books, the beautiful India box, and *now* the superb India bowl & pitcher, which Mr. Hawthorne's father had made in India for himself. . . . In the corner aslant from the fairy-table stands the ancient Manning chair, with its worked cover. The scarlet stuffed chair wanders about the room. The black haircloth rocking chair was much abused in moving, & one of the rockers is off. It has not yet been mended. . . . Over the centre-table hangs Endymion, & over the fireplace, Leonardo da Vinci's Madonna au Bas relief. You cannot think how prettily the room looks, though with such a low stud that I have to get acclimated to it, and still fear to be crushed.

Opposite the ottoman is another door. Entrez, entrez, Madame ma mère, s'il vous plait. This is the dining room. . . ."[1]

So the description runs for several more paragraphs, a caressing inventory of treasures, each laden with meanings that connect the household with its sustaining contexts: the honored Hawthorne tradition with trophies of the merchant trade in exotic lands; Leonardo, Raphael, and Apollo the sun-god;

the more intimate contexts of family affection—the ottoman from Elizabeth, the Manning chair. Here also are emblems of household bustle and chores unaccomplished, the chair that rambles about and the rocker off its rocker. Her husband's genius is quietly mentioned by way of the carved chair with the roses, which Hawthorne had used as a device to tie together the children's stories in *Grandfather's Chair.* Sophia herself had painted the Endymion during the months at the Old Manse when she looked forward to Una's birth.

Writing this letter was a religious exercise, in which Sophia rehearsed her vision of a sacred space where art and the muses were present to cultivate the spirit of its human denizens. Hers was a divine household, and she was proud to claim that her husband made a spiritual contribution to its life. "He has perfect dominion over himself in every respect," she explained to her mother, "so that to do the highest, wisest, loveliest thing is not the least effort to him, any more than it is to Julian to be innocent. It is his spontaneous act & Julian is not more unconscious in his innocence than he in acting his best." Nathaniel's unerring childlike moral instinct was now receiving universal acclaim, Sophia believed, through the success of *The Scarlet Letter;* and she exulted at this vindication of her faith in his genius. "Such a person can never lose the prestige which commands & fascinates. I cannot possibly conceive of my happiness, but in a blissful kind of confusion, live on. . . . I am not deluded nor mistaken, as the angels know now, and as all my friends will know *in open vision!*"[2]

Sophia portrays the divine power that was transmitted to the household through such a father by describing a quarrel between Julian and Una:

> One day they asked me to read about Christ. Una got up out of her chair for something, & Julian took possession. Una complained very much. Her father said, "What did Christ say? If a man take your cloak, give him your coat also. Do you know what he meant?" Una responded with an inward voice, "Yes, I know." She soon rose & gave Julian the chair, which he received with a radiant smile, having caught light from the presence of the angel now descended—but immediately resigned again, feeling that he too must act well in such a presence. Do you think no glory was added to the sunshine by this scene, so trivial in appearance, but so universal in its influence?[3]

Hawthorne did not command his daughter to give up the chair, but allowed her to obey the scriptural injunction freely. The voluntary character of Una's compliance brings down the angel in whose aura mutual altruism takes the place of self-seeking. Sophia credits her husband with the qualities of spirit required to bring about this divine alchemy; but she also believes that promoting such transactions is a mother's special province.

On her own mother's birthday several months later, Sophia recalls how this view of motherhood had been instilled. "Some portions of my life I remember only in moments when, at some crisis of excitement or trouble, you said to me softly, 'My love.' The tone, the words used to pour balm & comfort over my whole being. . . . & I remember it when my own child is in the same kind of mood, & I also say to her 'my love'—& find the same effect follow. Alas for those who counsel sternness & severity instead of love toward these young children!"[4]

Sophia insists that "infinite patience" must be displayed in situations that might well provoke a mother to violence, because harsh measures invite reciprocal self-assertion in the child. If the mother's internal fury can be conquered, the child will learn to submit in a sweet and willing spirit. Instead of "the sharp rebuke" and "the cruel blow," Sophia recommends "a tender sorrow, a most sympathizing regret." "Naturally I have none of the pride of power toward my children," she explains. "When they disobey I am not personally aggrieved, & they see it, & find therefore that it is a disinterested desire that they should do right which induces me to insist."

The selflessness of mother and father in the Hawthorne household was sustained by the divine light that suffused their mutual love. Nathaniel alludes to this spiritual symbiosis in *The House of the Seven Gables,* which was written at the little Red House. "Phoebe" had long been a nickname for Sophia, invoking her kinship with Phoebus Apollo, and she likewise signaled their composite divine identity by referring to him as "Apollo." Yet the Hawthornes were in touch with an obverse domain, a torment of sexual politics lying beneath the joyful domestic surface and threatening continually to swallow it up. Sophia's strenuous tone betokens her engagement in this covert struggle, keeping the polluted darkness at bay.

Nathaniel's darker broodings are suggested by his remark—related by Sophia to her mother—that the little Red House "looks like the Scarlet Letter."[5] He meant by this, Sophia promptly makes clear, only that the house viewed externally was small and bright red; but for our purposes the comment has a larger import. The "hell-fired" story of Hester, Arthur, Chillingworth, and Pearl—that disjointed double family—is a meditation on the paradise of domesticity that Nathaniel and Sophia lived out; but it is likewise a commentary on the new convention of family relations of which "divine motherhood" was the central feature. Hawthorne's narrative of adultery is set in Puritan Boston, but the conflicts and psychic torment it portrays are native to the matrimonial convention under construction in the Hawthornes' time.

The domestic ideal gave adultery an enlarged significance. The honor of a dynastic family was menaced when the wife committed adultery, because she could introduce illegitimate heirs into the line; the husband's adultery, however offensive, was not a threat to the family's integrity. Within the domestic ideal, by contrast, adultery contaminated the relation from which the marriage itself took its meaning, poisoning the intimacy on which the sacredness of the home depended; and this was equally true for husband and wife.

The altered meaning of adultery was only one aspect of a new urgency given to intimacy in family life. It is easy to underestimate the sweeping power of the cultural change at stake here. The romantic movement in literature, like the accompanying movement in religious thought and practice during this period, is pervasively occupied with feeling, with gauging and evoking complex emotional states. Hawthorne's uncanny capacity to register and transcribe obscure psychological transactions—what Henry James called his "catlike faculty of seeing in the dark"—makes him one of the great romantic precursors of Freud, the psychoanalytic movement in our own time being an enlargement of the preoccupation with sexuality and private emotional experience that grew up in the early nineteenth century, with family life as its central focus. The zone of psychic experience identified as "interior" and "personal" was not invented in the nineteenth century; but it was mass-produced in volume sufficient to make it appear universally human.

Orthodox Freudian theory is individualist and ahistorical in a fashion unsuited to understanding the marital politics of the Hawthorne household. The psychological issues at stake in the Hawthornes' relationship are not merely the consequence of traits in Nathaniel and Sophia that arose separately in their personal development. Their relationship itself had an identity, of the sort that Jurg Willi describes as marital "collusion," in which an interactive correspondence between the two parties, partly conscious and partly unconscious, draws them together initially and informs the life they live together. The Hawthornes' marriage reveals such a metabolism of interior meanings, fashioned originally during their courtship and transformed under the pressures of married life and child rearing. *The Scarlet Letter* does not culminate this story of cultural creation so much as perpetuate it.

CHAPTER SEVEN

Inward and Eternal Union

On the eve of her wedding in the summer of 1842, Sophia informed her friend Mary Foote that she and Nathaniel were already married. "We long have been bound by heavenly ties. The ceremony is nothing. Our true marriage was three years ago."[1] The Hawthornes' extra-legal union was not merely a result of Nathaniel's incapacity to support a family or of Sophia's chronic nervous condition, practical problems that extended well beyond their wedding; on the contrary, the "true marriage" between Nathaniel and Sophia was a spiritual reality, of incomparably greater authority than the legal bond soon to be created. They both believed that their marriage consisted in their "heavenly" relation and that the public ceremony was a concession to "earthly" requirements.

Nathaniel celebrated the commencement of their marriage in a letter he had written just three years earlier, as Sophia accurately recalled. "Yes—we are married; and as God Himself has joined us, we may trust never to be separated, neither in Heaven nor on Earth. We will wait patiently and quietly, and He will lead us onward hand in hand . . . and will teach us when our union is to be revealed to the world. The world might, as yet, misjudge us; and therefore we will not speak to the world; but when I hold you in my arms, why should we not commune together about all our hopes of earthly and external, as well as our faith of inward and eternal union?" (CE 15:329–330). Nathaniel and Sophia were prompted by the inner logic of their experience to place religious and legal institutions in "the world," excluded from the holy privacy of marriage.

The Hawthornes were not alone in feeling—in the late 1830s—that the public apparatus defining marriage was at odds with its spiritual essence. John Humphrey Noyes's Oneida community aimed at restructuring sexual relations so that the exclusive connection of one man to one woman would be replaced by a "complex marriage" better attuned to individual and communal needs. "I know that the immortal union of the heart," Noyes affirmed, "which alone is worthy to be called marriage, can never be made by a ceremony."[2] Charles Fourier's argument that "isolated families" reinforce the evils of economic competition became available in translation in the early 1840s, including his advocacy of nonmarital sexual relations. Nathaniel and Sophia for a time considered setting up their household at Brook Farm, the communal experiment grounded on Fourierist ideas. The Brook Farmers did not adopt Fourier's recommendations concerning sexuality, but Sophia made a point of writing to her mother after she and Nathaniel were formally married, to say that she had at last read some of Fourier firsthand and was thoroughly disgusted and that Nathaniel had read more and was even more disgusted.[3]

Radical reformers found an audience during this period because of the growing public awareness that the legal structure regulating matrimonial relations was out-of-date. The common law doctrine of marital unity, in which a woman ceased to have a legal existence when she married, was in conflict with the newly enhanced role of wife and mother and was assailed successfully on a number of points.[4] Nathaniel and Sophia felt, accordingly, that their relationship did not discredit the institution of marriage but fulfilled its higher purposes: yet they considered this fulfillment altogether unique. "I could almost think," Nathaniel writes, "that the institution of marriage was ordained, first of all, for you and me, and for you and me alone; it seems so fresh and new—so unlike anything that the people around us enjoy or are acquainted with. Nobody ever had a wife but me—nobody a husband, save my Dove" (CE 15:334).

Nathaniel and Sophia were aware of moving onto tricky ground, where it might seem they were carrying on an illicit relationship or were in the grip of emotions whose true meaning and direction they did not understand. Since they claimed a marriage at odds with the law, and without analogue among their friends, it is not surprising they fended off doubts. "Let us make no question about our love, whether it be true and holy," Nathaniel wrote just a month after they pronounced themselves married. "Were it otherwise

. . . [angels] would have given you early and continued warning of the approach of Evil in my shape" (CE 15:338).

Their claim to an unexampled marriage rests on the "inward and eternal union" of their souls, a pre-existent joint identity that their acquaintance and deepening friendship had revealed. "We have met in Eternity," Hawthorne declared, "and there our intimacy was formed" (CE 15:299). The time they spend together does not fashion this bond, but only makes them aware of it, and provides evidences of its eternal presence.

Hawthorne confesses that he delayed speaking of this oneness for fear he might impair it. "I felt it long ago; and sometimes, when I was seeking for some fondest word, it has been on my lips to call you—'Wife'! I hardly know what restrained me from speaking it—unless a dread . . . of feeling you shrink back from my bosom, and thereby discovering that there was yet a deep place in your soul which did not know me" (CE 15:329). The notable fragility of this ostensibly eternal marriage follows in part from the definition of its essence that Hawthorne lays down here: there must not be any part of her soul that does not "know" him, in the sense of entering unrestrainedly into intimate communion.

Although Nathaniel and Sophia almost certainly did not consummate their relationship sexually before the wedding, their premarital marriage was not ascetic. On the contrary, Hawthorne's earliest love letters assert physical intimacy as a means of spiritual communion between them: their love is expressed in "holy kisses, which I do think have something supernatural in them." Amorous pleasure becomes a sacrament that makes the marriage between them real. "Any one of our innocent embraces—even when our lips did but touch for a moment, and then were withdrawn—dearest, was it not the symbol of a bond between our Souls, infinitely stronger than any external rite could twine around us?" (CE 15:295, 317, 329).

The Hawthornes' marital relation bears a striking analogy to the adultery portrayed in *The Scarlet Letter*. When Hester reminds Arthur that their sexual union "had a consecration of its own," she invokes a deep and self-validating love that sets at naught traditional religious and legal requirements and is livingly present in physical intimacy. The transcendental idiom of the Hawthornes' relationship contrasts sharply with the guilt-stricken urgency of the fictional lovers' declarations. But Nathaniel and Sophia invoked the ineffably otherworldly to convey earthy messages. Here, for example, Nathaniel looks forward to the consummation of their sexual relationship:

We have left expression—at least, such expression as can be achieved with pen and ink—far behind us. Even the spoken word has long been inadequate. Looks—pressures of the lips and hands, and the touch of bosom to bosom—these are a better language; but, bye-and-bye, our spirits will demand some more adequate expression even than these. And thus it will go on; until we shall be divested of these earthly forms, which are at once our medium of expression, and the impediments to full communion. Then we shall melt into another, and all be expressed, once and continually, without a word—without an effort.

(CE 15:606)

Thus "heavenly" melting invokes erotic bliss; yet the Neoplatonic rhetoric at work here puts the earthly and the divine at odds. Hawthorne is not alarmed, at least not yet, that their love might be contaminated through sexual intercourse; but he is anxiously alert to other forms of defilement. He insists on maintaining the holy secrecy of their love because he fears that it might be lost, or fatally compromised, if exposed to "worldly" circumstances.

Nathaniel's effort to prevent contaminating intrusions was spurred in good measure by impulses native to his relation with Sophia. This was the central paradox of their marital collusion: psychic forces capable of tearing the marriage apart were among the strongest of those holding it together. Nathaniel and Sophia joyously avowed a divine communion, but they were also bound together in a union they did not avow. Their "heavenly marriage" had an "earthly" counterpart, which they experienced as a violation of the marriage. They were uneasily aware of a relation that was adulterous, not by the standards of the "world" but by their own standards, a matrimonial adultery in which felicity and wretchedness were indissolubly united.

The language of transcendental love offers a way to understand these interior complexities; in it Nathaniel and Sophia negotiated issues they could not openly confront. Their tireless rejoicings over their premarital marriage reveal an intriguing play of double meanings as the hidden substance of their opposition and their union discloses itself. The Hawthornes carried on a lengthy and searching mutual reconnaissance; it was an "engagement," the conventional precursor of a companionate marriage, in which they worked out ways to manage their controversies within the terms of an intimacy they were planning to continue for life.

During his employment at the Boston Custom House, Nathaniel routinely declares that his "belovedest" preserves him from spiritual decay. He looks to her for rescue from the soul-withering circumstances of his worldly life. It is easy to see the rhetorical disadvantage that follows: in advance of any dispute, Nathaniel concedes that Sophia possesses divine truth while his own moral character is deteriorating. How could he question her judgment?

In November 1839 a disagreement arose (over issues now unknown) that makes visible the resultant rhetorical interplay. Sophia had wept with sorrow when Nathaniel implied that she had done (or thought) something morally wrong, and her tears placed the issue between them on her strongest ground, that of her exquisite moral sensitivity. This was an occasion of strategic significance in their unfolding marital combat, so that Nathaniel outlines at length the framework within which he will meet such occasions in the future:

> Little Dove, why did you shed tears the other day, when you supposed that your husband thought you to blame? . . . Dearest, I never think you to blame; for you positively have no faults. . . . But it is because you are too delicate and exquisitely wrought in heart, mind, and frame, to dwell in such a world—because, in short, you are fitter to be in Paradise than here. You needed, therefore, an interpreter between the world and yourself—one who should sometimes set you right, not in the abstract (for there you are never wrong) but relatively to human and earthly matters;—and such an interpreter is your husband, who can sympathise, though inadequately, with his wife's heavenly nature, and has likewise a portion of shrewd earthly sense, enough to guide us both through the labyrinth of time. Now, dearest, when I criticise any act, word, thought, or feeling of yours, you must not understand it as a reproof, or as imputing anything wrong, wherewith you are to burthen your conscience.
>
> (CE 15:375)

Now reaching the crux of his countering maneuver, Nathaniel blandly accepts the rhetorical contradiction into which Sophia's strategy had forced him—that of correcting her even as he acknowledges her moral superiority. He also repulses the emotional side of her appeal, by ordering her to obey him cheerfully. "Then do not grieve, nor grieve your husband's spirit, when he essays to do his office; but remember that he does it reverently, and in the devout belief that you are, in immortal reality, both wiser and better than himself. . . . Hear what I say, dearest, in a cheerful spirit, and act upon it with cheerful strength" (CE 15:375).

The "office" of the husband outlined here, arising from his traffic with a defiling world, is that of intimate and exhaustive domination. Nathaniel does not want an unquestioning robot-like obedience but invites her to express her disagreements openly so they can be removed. "Do not give an undue weight to my judgment," he continues, "nor imagine that there is no appeal from it, and that its decrees are not to be questioned. Rather, make it a rule always to question them and be satisfied of their correctness." Nathaniel pictures their relation as an extended tutorial in which Sophia will add worldly wisdom to her already complete knowledge of divine things, "and so shall my Dove be improved . . . till she become even *earthly-wiselier* than her sagacious husband" (CE 15:375–376).

As her tutor, Nathaniel will decide when his "little Dove" has acquired enough earthly wisdom to think for herself and to receive obedience from him. Meanwhile, she is to discontinue the practice of weeping at his decrees, since he worships her infallible judgment on the questions that really matter, questions of angelic truth. This maneuver strikes from Sophia's hands the weapons she had sought to forge from his avowals of her moral superiority, and it provides him a virtually limitless charter.

More than once Nathaniel declares his intention to exercise an authority that will reach exactly as far as he chooses. He observes, for example, that she cannot enjoy "an independent and separate right" in her mother's Salem household. Her true home is his apartment in Boston, because of his exclusive claim to it: "my dwelling, my castle, mine own place wherein to be, which I have bought, for the time being, with the profits of mine own labor. Then is it not our home?" (CE 15:385–386). A letter written the following week enlarges his fantasy of their living together, in terms that picture her independence as an expression of his mastery. "Now if my Dove were sitting in the easiest of our two easy chairs—(for sometimes I would choose to have her sit in a separate chair, in order to realize our individuality, as well as our unity)—then would the included space of these four walls, together with the little contiguous bed-room, seem indeed like home" (CE 15: 387). Sophia will realize her individuality when Nathaniel chooses to have her do so.

Another stratagem of control, grounded on the separation of Sophia's "angelic" domain from the workaday world, is Nathaniel's reluctance to give Sophia information about his daily life. He writes in dove-talk, which is hazy, fanciful, and strikingly uninformative. Concerning his work at the Custom House, he speaks of "durance" in the "darksome room," or about the "sons of toil" or of his labors in the "coal-pit," but only rarely does the name of a person come through or any concrete description of his duties, his boss, or his co-workers. Sophia is his "reality," and "nothing else is real for me, unless thou give it that golden quality by thy touch" (CE 15:486, 321, 511). Yet there are important matters he does not want her to touch, even when their plans are involved.

In March 1840, for example, Nathaniel wrote to John L. O'Sullivan about a clerkship he had been offered in Washington, D.C., raising a series of practical questions: Will he be at liberty between sessions of Congress? Will his salary continue during the intervals when his duties lapse? He points out that travel to Washington would be costly and living expenses high. In the end he asks O'Sullivan to hold the position open, if possible, so he will have time to consult with Franklin Pierce, who is currently out of town. On the same day, Nathaniel writes to Sophia about the opportunity:

> How would my Dove like to have her husband continually with her, twelve or fourteen months out of the next twenty? Would not that be real happiness?—in such long communion, should we not feel as if separation were a dream, something that never had been a reality, nor ever could be? Yes; but—for in all earthly happiness there is a but—but, during those twenty months, there would be two intervals of three months each, when thy husband would be five hundred miles away—as far away as Washington. That would be terrible. . . . Do not be frightened, dearest—nor rejoiced either—for the thing will not be. It might be, if I chose; but on multitudinous accounts, my present situation seems preferable.
>
> (CE 15:418–419, 421–422)

It is hardly momentous that Nathaniel tells Sophia he will not take the job while telling O'Sullivan to hold it open, because for all practical purposes he has told her nothing. The channel of his communication with Sophia ran deep into his personality but was nonetheless remarkably narrow. When the rhetoric of their divine union ceases to probe the urgent and complex psychic forces in which it is grounded, an oppressive decadence sets in. The relentless sweetness and vagueness and earnestness, and the iteration of "belovedest" and "ownest Dove," make a ludicrous fustian that itself became a theme of mawkish joking. "Will not my Dove confess that there is a little *nonsense* in this epistle? But be not wroth with me, darling wife." "Thy husband writes thee nonsense, as his custom is," Nathaniel later remarks. "I wonder how thou managest to retain any respect for him" (CE 15:352–353, 521).

Sophia wanted to know what Nathaniel's life was like, not only the mystical depths but his everyday pursuits. But he found himself unable to give her an account. "Thou wilt have a volume to tell me, when we meet, and wilt pour thy beloved voice into mine ears, in a stream of two hours' long. At length thou wilt pause, and say—'But what has *thy* life been?'—and then will thy stupid husband look back upon what he calls his life, for three or four days past, and behold a blank!" (CE 15:517). Nathaniel speaks here of a future conversation, and of the muteness that will then ensue. His life is not particularly uneventful at present, but his daily activities do not occupy the part of his mind that is open to his Dove.

The rhetoric of their relationship made it easy for Nathaniel to keep his practical dealings to himself. But when Sophia urged him to go hear the famous "sailor-preacher," Edward Taylor, Nathaniel's refusal required an elaborate defense. "Now, belovedest, it would not be an auspicious day for me to hear the aforesaid Son of Thunder. Thou knowest not how difficult is thy husband to be touched and moved, unless time, and circumstances, and his own inward state, be in a 'concatenation accordingly.' A dreadful thing would it be, were Father Taylor to fail in awakening a sympathy from my spirit to thine" (CE 15:420–421).

Nathaniel doesn't want to go hear the preacher, and he knows that if he does go he won't like it. But Father Taylor's eloquence is manifestly a spiritual issue, about which Sophia has infinite wisdom. Refusing to go would cast doubt on his professions of worship for her; but to attend the service would be worse. When Sophia asked for his response, he would be compelled to argue against her infallible knowledge of celestial truth.

If Sophia had looked forward to such a debate, she was to be disappointed. Nathaniel writes her two weeks later in terms that eliminate his problem. He promises that he will go, "at some auspicious hour, which I trust will soon arrive," but only if she also makes a promise. She must agree "not to be troubled, should thy husband be unable to appreciate the excellence of Father Taylor." He points out that "our souls are in happiest unison; but we must not disquiet ourselves if every tone be not re-echoed from one to the other—if every slightest shade be not reflected in the alternate mirror." They must agree to disagree, in short, before Father Taylor gets "an opportunity to make music with my soul" (CE 15:431).

Sophia must understand that while Nathaniel's spirit is minutely in tune with her own, he is not necessarily susceptible to what moves her. "Thou art not to suppose," he informs her, "because his spirit answers to every touch of thine, that therefore every breeze, or even every whirlwind, can upturn him from his depths." The spiritual sympathy between the two of them does not extend to third parties, or to anything that lies outside their relationship. She is the master of spiritual things, of all things divine, he ceaselessly repeats; but this mastery applies only to the sacred interior of their relationship and is real there only through his unprompted confession. He does not welcome any effort on her part to shape his sentiments or his conduct: "I forewarn thee, sweetest Dove, that thy husband is a most unmalleable man" (CE 15:431).

Nathaniel's elaboration of the union of souls between himself and Sophia thus arrives at a contradiction that points toward anxieties built into its structure. Nathaniel dreads disturbances of their sacred intimacy that threaten from multiplying sources. Their oneness must be protected from contact with such worldly business as Nathaniel's job offers and his current conditions of work; but purely spiritual matters are likewise to be sealed up in a separate compartment, where they cannot disturb the "inward and eternal union" binding Nathaniel and Sophia together. Nathaniel can have communion with his "Dove" only so long as that sweet bower is protected from connections to the life beyond it.

Nathaniel did not, in fact, prohibit Sophia from challenging his sentiments, but he strenuously resisted accepting any grounds on which such challenges might be decided. Looked at one way, this is patently a tactic of domination; yet Nathaniel's way asserting his dominion bespeaks an inward fear. He demands not only her compliance but also her heartfelt assent, and he strives to limit topics of potential discord because he dreads losing a communion so fragile that the slightest opposition could damage it. This anxiety prompts Nathaniel to insist on a system of shields, to shut out potential contaminants, and it also shapes the interior of their mystical autocosm.

Nathaniel saw two distinct personalities in Sophia. We have already met the "Dove"; the other he called "Sophie Hawthorne," a figure who emerges at the outset of their premarital marriage, bearing Sophia's "married" name. "Sophie" is associated with saucy smiles and playful kisses (as opposed to holy kisses), and with rebellion:

> My dearest, what a delightful scene was that between Sophie Hawthorne and my Dove, when the former rebelled so stoutly against Destiny, and the latter, with such meek mournfulness, submitted. Which do I love the best, I wonder—my Dove, or my little Wild-Flower? I love each best, and both equally; and my heart would inevitably wither, and dry up, and perish utterly, if either of them were torn away from it. Yet, truly, I have reason to apprehend more trouble with Sophie Hawthorne than with my Dove.
>
> (CE 15:359)

Sophia herself, a composite of "Sophie" and the "Dove," is thus given an androgynous character. Nathaniel, in ascribing assertiveness to "Sophie," shows his respect for her active and acute intelligence, and he looks forward to submitting his literary work to her criticism. "I have a high opinion of . . . [Sophie Hawthorne's] critical acumen, but a great dread of her severity—which, however, the Dove will not fail to temper with her sweetness."

This interplay of "masculine" and "feminine" qualities in Sophia corresponds to a counterpoint in Nathaniel's own nature: "I live through my Dove's heart," he observes, while living "an intellectual life in Sophie Hawthorne" (CE 15:364, 428–429).

The fusion of genders becomes even more striking, however, in Nathaniel's characterizations of Sophie herself. His earliest description states that her soul and intellect "breathe forth an influence like that of wildflowers," and images linking her to flowers, and the odor of flowers, frequently recur as he praises her (CE 15:343). Nathaniel employs in his fiction the convention linking flowers with the vagina, especially when erotic womanhood appears dangerous, as in Beatrice Rappacini and Zenobia.[5] This circuit of associations endows Sophie Hawthorne's headstrong intellectuality with a note of sensual provocation, so that her "masculine" assertiveness is tantamount to a stimulating yet unsettling womanly sexuality.

These gender blendings are compounded further by a phallic image equally typifying Sophie Hawthorne. With the half-deliberate condescending playfulness Nathaniel adopts when he treats questions that are both compelling and touchy, he persistently focuses attention on her nose, which becomes an emblem of her "defiance" (CE 15:372). He makes a teasing issue of his worshipful desire to kiss Sophie's nose, which she would saucily not permit. "I have even serious thoughts of giving up all further designs upon her nose," Nathaniel mock-mournfully relates, "since she hates so much to have it kissed. . . . I have a particular affection for that nose, insomuch that I intend, one of these days, to offer it an oblation of rich and delicate odours" (CE 15:379). Instead of receiving Nathaniel's attentions at his pleasure, Sophie Hawthorne, it appears, characteristically demands and then rejects them. Imperious sensuality is linked, accordingly, to sexually suggestive smells, further underscoring Hawthorne's intuition that Sophia's erotic energy is manlike but alluring nonetheless. She "breathes forth" the aroma of wildflowers and then becomes the organ by which the rich odors of Nathaniel's submission are to be relished.

Aggressive sexuality in women was branded as masculine by the ideological conventions Hawthorne invokes in depicting Zenobia, but here the reverse logic is at work: Nathaniel finds Sophia's manly traits sexually exciting. His imagery points toward a polymorphous engagement with both sides of an erotic interplay that he pictures taking place within Sophia, such that reverent kisses are offered by the Dove and resisted by "Sophie," Nathaniel taking a role that is both supervisory and beseeching. He appeals to "Sophie's" stubborn pride on behalf of the yearning and affectionate Dove:

Well-a-day! I have strolled thus far through my letter, without once making mention of naughty Sophie Hawthorne. Will she pardon the neglect? Present my profound respects to her beloved nose, and say that I still entreat her to allow my Dove to kiss her cheek. When she complies with this oft-repeated petition, I shall hope that her spirit is beginning to be tamed, and shall then meditate some other and more difficult trials of it. Nonsense! Do not believe me, dear little Sophie Hawthorne. I would not tame you for the whole Universe.

(CE 15:398–399)

Nathaniel's deeper yearnings and anxieties were aroused by an untamed spirit in Sophia that held forth the prospect of bisexual fulfillment. His obsessive baby talk holds his uneasiness in abeyance, even as it conveys the quality of Nathaniel's desire. A homoerotic impulse within his own sexuality is aroused by "naughty" Sophia's willful strength, yet that impulse is contained within the yearning for a wholly merged identity. "Are we singular or plural, dearest? Has not each of us a right to use the first person singular, when speaking in behalf of our united being? Does not 'I,' whether spoken by Sophie Hawthorne's lips or mine, express the one spirit of myself and that darlingest Sophie Hawthorne?" (CE 15:355). He speaks of her as a baby, but not from an adult point of view; he wants them to merge in a "darlingest" infancy together.

The domineering side of Nathaniel's relation to Sophia was rooted in a powerful contrary impulse, his desire not to govern but to submit. The androgynous character he discerns in Sophia, whereby her "womanly" submissiveness conveys and partly conceals a purposeful will, is analogous to his own inner paradox. He anticipates "trouble" with Sophie Hawthorne yet does not want her "tamed"; he expects to "have charge" of his Dove, yet offers her abject worship.

Nathaniel was addicted to passive enjoyment, as distinct from any intention to assume mature responsibilities. He felt obliged to assume a caring and conscientious manly posture in relation to Sophia, yet he also rebelled against that role for the sake of an infantile freedom that revels in polymorphous delight, leaving to others the initiation and guidance of events. Nathaniel playfully rejoices in this androgynous whimsical pleasure—feeling that the "deepest tenderness" takes place between them in moments that permit him to toy with a fusion of conquest and submission. "Most beloved, I am thinking at this moment of thy dearest nose! Thou canst not think how infinitely better I know and love Sophie Hawthorne, since, in moments of our deepest tenderness, she has yielded up that fortress. And, in requital, I yield my whole self up to her, and kiss her beloved foot, and acknowledge her for my queen and liege-lady forever more" (CE 15:621).

Collapsed polarities thus lie at the core of Nathaniel's love: the opposition of male and female sexual identity, and that of dominance and submission, are absorbed into an even more radical fusion in which the distinction between himself and her is erased. His fantasy of spending the night with Sophia pictures a spiritual ménage à trois in which he and Sophia and the Dove melt together into a blissful composite childlike selfhood. "And now if my Dove were here, she and that naughty Sophie Hawthorne, how happy we all three—two—one—(how many are there of us?)—how happy might we be! . . . Oh, beloved, if you were here now, I do not think I could possibly let you go till morning—my arms should imprison you—I would not be content, unless you nestled into my very heart, and there slept a sweet sleep with your own husband. My blessed Dove, how I long to hear your gentle breathing, as you lie asleep in my arms" (CE 15:357).

Much remains to be said concerning the psychic substance of Nathaniel's "inward and eternal" union with Sophia, but it is important to recognize here that such felicity places heavy demands on the person from whom it is obtained. Acting freely on his own impulses will necessarily result in giving offense, Nathaniel recognizes, and he begs her to indulge him. "Dearest, I beseech you grant me freedom to be careless and wayward—for I have had such freedom all my life. Oh, let me feel that I may even do you a little wrong without your avenging it (oh how cruelly) by being wounded" (CE 15:332).

Supplying Nathaniel with mystical bliss imposed psychological burdens on Sophia, but it also placed her in a position of strength. Granting him the "freedom to be careless and wayward" allowed her likewise to withhold that freedom or implicitly to place a price on it. The character of his attachment to her entailed a vulnerability answering to the menace it offered her. "What misery . . . would it be," he observes, "if, because we love one another better than all the Universe besides, our only gain thereby were a more exquisite sensibility to pain from the beloved hand, and a more terrible power of inflicting it" (CE 15:332). The fusion of dominance and submission that takes place in the magical solipsism of Nathaniel's yearnings thus has its counterpart in the practical politics of the relationship. By satisfying his demands, Sophia acquires a form of dominance; Nathaniel's submission is necessary if he is to get from her what he wants; and their sacred marriage is sealed by intimate reciprocal threats.

The "divine light" that results from the sublimation of selfish impulses—as celebrated in the joint identity of "Phoebe" and "Apollo"—was only the visible portion of a broader spectrum of psychic radiation. The intense atmosphere of holiness that pervaded Sophia and Nathaniel's relationship, giving it a self-consecrating interior glow, was generated by impulses of mutual antagonism. A union whose essence is the fusion of such antitheses— tenderness/vengeance, male/female, dominance/submission, self/other—depends for its meaning on the continuing energy of those oppositions, their continuing power to split the relationship apart. Like atoms of plutonium, the union of Nathaniel and Sophia was radioactive: the strong forces binding them together were barely capable of restraining the countervailing forces of disintegration: the uncanny divine light that bathed them was the result of nuclear instability.

Nathaniel insisted on maintaining an impermeable boundary between the sacred inwardness of this relationship and the "world" because he sensed that a stray particle from the outside might fatally disturb the uneasy balance of interior forces. In the normal course of living this was exceedingly difficult. Not only did the two of them have other friends and relationships, but they would also be obliged sooner or later to obey the requirements of the "world" by getting married, and in due course there would be children. To consider how Nathaniel and Sophia confronted such exigencies requires that we translate the metaphor of thermonuclear reactions back into their idiom of divine love.

CHAPTER EIGHT

Transplanting the Garden of Eden

Nathaniel pleads for reassurance throughout his love letters. "Dost thou love me?" he asks Sophia. "Dost thou love me at all?" "You love me dearly— don't you?"[1] He can't stop asking because he fears their love is unreal, that it will vanish as magically as it appeared. This distress arises most sharply when they see each other in the presence of other people.

He describes a social occasion in October 1839 as a chance "to meet in the wide desert of this world, and mingle our spirits in a conjugal embrace," and indicates that it would have troubled him to see her at all, if they'd not had a few moments in private. "It would have seemed all a vision then. . . . You looked like a vision, beautifullest wife, with the width of the room between us—so spiritual that my human heart wanted to be assured that you had an earthly vesture on, and your warm kisses gave me that assurance" (CE 15:350). They had an understandable desire for some time to themselves; but in Nathaniel the situation provoked an enduring anxiety.

Writing to Sophia about the event, he launches into an extended fantasy in which his "Dove" resumes the instincts of her animal counterpart and flies away. " 'Come back, naughty Dove!' " the bereft husband cries, " 'and fold your wings upon my heart again, or it will freeze!' " (CE 15:350). But the Dove refuses, insisting that her true home is in the air. "Then would the poor deserted husband do his best to fly in pursuit of the faithless Dove; and for that purpose would ascend to the top-mast of a salt-ship, and leap desperately into the air, and fall down head-foremost upon the deck, and break his neck. And there should be engraven on his tombstone—'Mate not thyself with a Dove, unless thou hast wings to fly'" (351). Seeing Sophia at the party had stirred a helpless suicidal desperation at the prospect of her deserting him.

Nathaniel disowns any serious meaning in "this foolish flight of fancy"; but the next day he appends a note, still vainly seeking to quiet his feelings. "I dreamed the queerest dreams last night, about being deserted, and all such nonsense—so you see how I was punished for that naughty romance of the Faithless Dove. . . . You have warmed my heart, mine own wife; and never again can I know what it is to be cold and desolate, save in dreams. You love me dearly—don't you?" (CE 15:351, 352).

In the course of any engagement one of the parties (or both) may become fearful the other will break it off. But Nathaniel's dread of being deserted was strong enough to persist through their wedding and the birth of two children; it showed up in a dream nine years after his fantasy of the Faithless Dove, when Sophia was visiting her sister Mary at West Newton:

> The other night, I dreamt that I was at Newton, in a room with thee, and with several other people; and thou tookst occasion to announce, that thou hadst now ceased to be my wife, and hadst taken another husband. Thou madest this intelligence known with such perfect composure and *sang froid*—not particularly addressing me, but the company generally—that it benumbed my thoughts and feelings, so that I had nothing to say. Thou wast perfectly decided, and I had only to submit without a word. But, hereupon, thy sister Elizabeth, who was likewise present, informed the company, that, in this state of affairs, having ceased to be thy husband, I of course became her's; and turning to me, very coolly inquired whether she or I should write to inform my mother of the new arrangement! How the children were to be divided, I know not. I only know that my heart suddenly broke loose, and I began to expostulate with thee in an infinite agony, in the midst of which I awoke; but the sense of unspeakable injury and outrage hung about me for a long time—and even yet it has not quite departed.
> (CE 16:228–229)

Nathaniel's terror is provoked by Sophia's membership in a community of women having the power to control his life. Sophia does not inform him in advance about having taken another husband, and, like her, the women to whom she announces it assume that Nathaniel will take no part in choosing his new wife. He frantically asserts a right to speak for himself amid the colloquy of women who are deciding his future; the dream indicates how infirm he felt that right to be.

Nathaniel was anxiously uncertain whether he could lay claim to his own life in resistance to the claims that others made, even so mildly as by their presence. Sophia had become indispensable to him, he goes on to explain, because she assuaged this abiding restiveness and the panic of self-alienation that lay behind it. "I was always more at ease alone than in any body's company, till I knew thee. And now I am only myself when thou art within my reach, and most myself when closest, closest to thee. Thou art an unspeakably beloved woman. How couldst thou inflict such frozen agony upon me, in that dream!" (CE 16:229).

A pattern of imagery linking these dreams is the warm embrace that counteracts a terrible disabling cold. Nathaniel's "frozen agony" echoes both the *sang froid* of Sophia's announcement and Elizabeth's "very coolly" inquiring whether she or Nathaniel should inform his mother. As in the earlier dream, the Dove "warms" his heart by keeping her wings folded and leaves him "cold and desolate" when she exercises her power to fly.

Nathaniel's panicky need to draw Sophia into seclusion created a problem when she paid a visit to Boston in May 1840. They had opportunities to get together, but he was aware that she was also seeing other people. Sophia's long-standing friend Connie Park invited Nathaniel to an evening party, but he went straight home to bed after work and spent a wakeful and restless night. Four days later, although he had seen Sophia privately in the interval, he was still in anguish. Far from acknowledging that he had shunned her company—as he certainly had done—he complains that she has abandoned him. "My spirit knows not whereabout to seek thee, and so it shivers as if there were no *Thou* at all—as if my Dove had been only a dream and a vision, and now had vanished into unlocality and nothingness" (CE 15:461).

Nathaniel's distress called for an explanation. Why should he feel as though her being in Boston, seeing other people as well as himself, abolished their mutual love? Why should he refuse to meet her in the company of her women friends? Sophia had noticed that he was perturbed throughout this visit and that he kept a gloomy silence even during the afternoon and evening they had spent together alone. But Nathaniel writes that he cannot talk about it: "Why didst thou look up in my face, as we walked, and ask why I was so grave? If I was grave, I know no cause for it, beloved. Lights and shadows are continually flitting across my inward sky, and I know neither whence they come nor whither they go; nor do I inquire too closely into them. It is dangerous to look too minutely at such phenomena. It is apt to create a substance, where at first there was a mere shadow" (CE 15:461–462). Nathaniel fears that exploring his unhappiness will provoke thoughts and feelings he could not bear to confront. So long as they remain mere shadows—flitting across the inward sky—he can avoid choosing words in which to articulate them and having to answer for those words to her.

What is one to make of this stunning contradiction? Nathaniel had tirelessly repeated that Sophia rescued him from an inward torment of "shadows" and "unrealities" and had celebrated their "full communion." But now she herself has slipped momentarily into his nightmare world of "unlocality and nothingness." Nathaniel vehemently insists that she is not to press him on this matter; nor is she to question *anything* that remains puzzling in their relationship. "If there should ever seem to be an expression unintelligible from one of our souls to another, we will not strive to interpret it into earthly language, but wait for the soul to make itself understood; and were we to wait a thousand years, we need deem it no more time than we can spare" (CE 15:462).

Nathaniel explains that the bond between himself and his Dove is best realized in the wordless and exclusive communion of physical embraces. Words are innately social; they carry specifiable implications and commitments that hugs and kisses do not. "It is not that I have any love for mystery," Nathaniel continues, "but because I abhor it—and because I have felt, a thousand times, that words may be a thick and darksome veil of mystery between the soul and the truth which it seeks. Wretched were we, indeed, if we had no better means of communicating ourselves, no fairer garb in which to array our essential selves, than these poor rags and tatters of Babel" (CE 15:462). Fallen humanity lives under a divine curse—Nathaniel knew the Calvinist doctrines well—of which a central feature was the corruption of language, setting people at odds even as they strive to understand themselves and others. A perfect communion is that of Adam and Eve, arrayed in the garb of Eden.

Even so, Nathaniel knew that he was presenting Sophia with a mystery that he abhorred. He says explicitly that he must himself obey the prohibition he declares upon Sophia's questions. He is forbidden to "inquire too closely" into the shadows of his own mind, maintaining a safe distance from issues that had troubled him from boyhood and would pursue him to the grave. Critical features of this abiding terror are suggested by a seemingly trivial boyhood prank the year his father died, when he filled a hollow bust of John Wesley with water and put it out on a winter night, in hopes the ice would rupture it (R. H. Lathrop, *Memories,* 453–454). Hawthorne dreaded a "frozen agony" that seized him when he felt deprived of maternal solicitude or subjected to matriarchal control. This inner coolness, however, when suitably moderated, also served to numb him against the torments arising directly from his grief. This agony was unfrozen, years later in Rome; it broke out of its icy stillness, and his creative identity was devastated by the resulting unsustainable torture.

The androgynous bliss of childlike tenderness that Nathaniel cherished in his relation to Sophia allayed the fear that his inward freezing would itself bring on psychic disintegration, bursting his fragile selfhood from within. Their sexuality—as he represents it—is not a passionate adventure but a source of compensatory repose in a world otherwise provoking psychological distress. He talks freely enough about embraces and about resting his head on Sophia's bosom. Yet these caresses have a notably bland and diffuse tenor: when he imagines spending the night with his Dove and "naughty" Sophia, he evokes the even breathing of a sound childlike sleep.

Nathaniel visualizes Sophia as a child in order to claim her as a mother. The "Dove" not only nestles in Nathaniel's heart but also takes him under her wing. We have already noted how his relationship to Sophia replays the emotional pattern established in response to his father's death. The charmed circle that bound Nathaniel to his mother and sisters bears a telling resemblance to his and Sophia's sacred oneness, which formed a similar bulwark against his exposure to an unendurable pain of abandonment.

His terror of Sophia's disappearing into "unlocality and nothingness" repeats the anguish he had expressed years before in trying to persuade his mother to remain at Raymond. "If you remove to Salem, I shall have no Mother to return to during the College Vacations. . . . If you remain where you are, think how delightfully the time will pass, with all your children round you, shut out from the world, and nothing to disturb us. It will be a second Garden of Eden" (CE 15:150). If his mother is caught up in the life of the Manning household, she and Eden will vanish. Yet when he met Sophia, Nathaniel represented his mother as the gloomy mistress of "Castle Dismal" where his young manhood had been wasted. To Elizabeth Peabody, and then to Sophia, Nathaniel represented his long seclusion in his mother's Salem household as "no life at all," which produced the "morbid consciousness that paralyses my powers" (Pearson, 266–267).

The myth of "Castle Dismal" forms the background against which Nathaniel celebrates Sophia's rescuing him; she brings blessed sunlight to scatter the shadows of unreality. This rhetorical maneuver was very flattering to Sophia, as it was meant to be; yet it also contained a double layer of denial. Nathaniel retained a strong attachment to his mother that is repeated, not eclipsed, in his relation to Sophia.[2] The courtship had already ripened into their premarital marriage when he sat for the glorious portrait by Charles

Fig. 4. Portrait of Nathaniel Hawthorne by Charles Osgood, 1840

Osgood (Fig. 4), which took its place in his mother's home to assuage the pain of his separation from her and from his sisters.³ Sophia was not to "save" him from his mother's household without replacing the solace and psychic support he had received there. He transferred to her the anxious demands that his mother and sisters had met, hoping to anchor more firmly the identity they had sponsored. As he did so, the "shadows" ostensibly confined to Castle Dismal began to infiltrate the union with his Dove.

Nathaniel maintained a "childlike" persona because his effort to become a "man" was complicated by the difficulties of crossing the gap between the maternal/marital sphere and the world beyond. To make a "worldly" career was to violate his deepest self, submitting to the desires of intrusive and uncaring aliens. To act independently in keeping with his true character was to remain within the solicitude of a powerful motherly figure who treasures him for who he is and guarantees his well-being. In Nathaniel's emotional world, submission to a loving woman's indulgent care is independence, whereas striving for manly self-sufficiency in contention with other males is servitude. Nathaniel's rebellion against the conventions of worldly manhood was intermingled with dread and resentment at lacking the strength to break these matriarchal bonds. Nathaniel's relationship with Sophia permitted him, as we shall see in due course, to exact vengeance for this intimate humiliation.

Long before he met Sophia, Nathaniel's mother and sisters indulged him in ridiculously high-handed demands. His sister Elizabeth related that Nathaniel was "particularly petted" in boyhood and that during the long seclusion his sisters were "almost . . . absurdly obedient to him." He required Elizabeth to bring him books from the Salem Athenaeum and also to choose them for him, since he would not soil his hands with looking through the catalogue. Nathaniel once observed that Elizabeth's ridicule was the only thing he had ever feared, and she indeed enjoyed a unique vantage from which to poke fun at the vulnerable self-importance she devoted herself to sustaining.[4] Louisa also joined in his game of imperial loftiness, taking the role of abject subservience to his whims. "I also send the bag of coins," he wrote her on one occasion. "I believe there is a silver threepence among them, which you must take out and bring home, as I cannot put myself to the trouble of looking for it at present" (CE 15:220).

Despite its element of playful humor, this hauteur was a persistent and deeply rooted trait, and it was well known to close friends. Nathaniel enjoyed a small circle of whist-playing companions in Salem during the late 1820s, in which each member was given a title: Harold Conolly was "The Cardinal"; others were "The Chancellor," "The Duchess," and "The Count." Nathaniel's title was "The Emperor."[5]

Nathaniel's grandiose self-importance flourished in his relation with Sophia. His mock-playful assertion that the institution of marriage had been invented solely for them was not meant to be taken "seriously"; yet Sophia subscribed to its inner meaning and considered herself uniquely fitted to cultivate his imperial pre-eminence. After paying him a visit at Brook Farm, she decided that his life there was unsuitable:

A sacred retreat thou shouldst have, of all men. Most other persons would not desire or like it, but notwithstanding thine exquisite courtesy & conformableness & geniality there, I could see very plainly that thou wast not leading thine ideal life. Never upon the face of any mortal was there such a divine expression of sweetness & kindliness as I saw upon thine during the various transactions & witticisms of the excellent fraternity. Yet it was also the expression of a witness & hearer rather than of comradeship. It seemed to me, that quite unconsciously on thy part, it was the assent & sympathy of a more celestial nature. Had I perceived a particle of even the highest kind of pride in thy manner, it would have spoiled the perfect beauty and fitness, but there was only thy inevitable superiority, which thy true & thorough loveliness could not entirely conceal. I do not wonder that they all worship thee, for nothing is so fascinating as the combination of intellectual greatness with angelic affections. Reverence & love, after struggling in vain for preeminence in those around thee, are finally obliged to sit down side by side on the same throne at thy feet & do thee homage with simultaneous movement. O King by divine right! no one can love & reverence thee as does thy wife. In her heart centers the world's admiration, & from its depths sparkles up, beside, the starry foam of her own separate & incomparable love.[6]

Did Nathaniel actually believe that the Brook Farmers were dazzled by his divine majesty? Did he believe that they offered him simultaneous love and reverence as an inevitable response to his celestial superiority? He would never openly subscribe to such ridiculous delusions, yet he drank in "the starry foam" of Sophia's adulation with the awareness that it nourished a vital inward self.

Nathaniel and Sophia were bound together by interlocking patterns of unconscious need, their two narcissisms becoming one.[7] Nathaniel's despotic self-assertions conceal a deep dependency, and Sophia's worship of his divine-right kingship bespeaks her equally repressed impulse to take charge of him. In this marriage of unavowed desire Nathaniel treasures a delicious wayward freedom in which the demands of "others" can be ignored, while Sophia hungers for the display of great intellectual and artistic powers and seeks worldly acclaim vicariously through him. Her worship of him, which was her fulfillment in him, entered the substance of his grandiose and fragile sense of self. Nathaniel's sister Elizabeth resented Sophia with increasing vehemence as the years passed and came to believe that she had enthralled Nathaniel by "the atmosphere of subtle flattery with which she surrounded him."[8]

As the date of their wedding approached, Sophia was distressed to realize that Nathaniel had not told his mother and sisters about their plans. She begged him to make the announcement on a visit he made to Salem in February 1842; instead, he wrote in a letter why he could not and indicated the link between his dependence on Sophia and the distinctive character of his art. "I cannot take my heart in my hand, and show it to them," he explains, "as if it would be as indecorous to do so, as to display to them the naked breast, on which God is well pleased that thou shouldst lay thy head" (CE 15:611–612).

The divine communion between them can only be wronged if put into words. "I doubt whether I ever have *really* spoken of thee, to any person. I have spoken the name of Sophia, it is true; but the idea in my mind was apart from thee—it embraced nothing of thy inner and essential self" (CE 15:612). Yet this "divine" unspeakableness, it now appears, is linked to the "strange reserve, in regard to matters of feeling," that prevails between himself and his mother and sisters. Nathaniel recognizes that "something wrong in our early intercourse" brought about "this incapacity of free communion," but his anguished protestations conceal the fact that he need not "gush out" his "deepest heart-concernments" in telling his mother and sisters of his plan to marry Sophia. Even if his mother and sisters asked to hear all about his relationship with Sophia, he could easily omit its sacred profundities (611–612).

Nathaniel's failure to disclose his marriage plans in a timely manner was a way of taking revenge all around.[9] What his silence conveyed, once the inevitable belated disclosure finally took place, was his impulse to let them know there were important matters in his own life about which he had told them nothing. Their intense attachment to him opened them to the blow that he strikes, and he likewise stealthily strikes out at Sophia, since she is inevitably implicated in the deception.

Nathaniel's sister Elizabeth, furious, sized up the dimensions of Nathaniel's affront exactly: "My brother has desired me to say only what was true," she wrote to Sophia,

> though I do not recognize his right so to speak of truth, after keeping us so long in ignorance of this affair. But I do believe him when he says that this was not in accordance with your wishes, for such concealment must naturally be unpleasant, and besides, what I know of your amiable disposition convinces me that you would not give us unnecessary pain. It was especially due to my mother that she should long ago have been made acquainted with the engagement of her only son; it is much more difficult to inform her of it at this late period.[10]

Nathaniel had not struck a "manly" blow but had given injury passively. Yet he was right to blame psychic forces he did not command. The moment drew him into a scenario of renewed grieving, stirred to life by his prospective departure from the incestuous solidarity with his mother and sisters, whom he now places in the position of knowing him as he had known his father, as one who had departed without warning and without explanation. Nathaniel had repeated in boyhood the fantasy that he was "going away to sea" and would "never come back again" (G. P. Lathrop, *A Study,* 64). He now confounds and grieves his intimate kin by his mysterious and agonizing remoteness.

Hawthorne seeks to establish a comparable relationship of tantalizing absence with the readers of his fiction. A central feature of his literary temperament is his provocation of troubled yearning. Psychic distress shocked Hawthorne into assuming a pose of transparent ease, even nonchalance, through which he lures the reader into a turbulent emotional engagement. Writing offered Nathaniel an ideal vehicle, since written language simply lies on the page, unaccompanied by a personal presence. Nathaniel's famous equivocations, even his "ambivalence," serve a paradoxical strategy of drawing attention to his remoteness, persistently reminding readers that he is inaccessible.[11] The conclusion of his letter to Sophia makes his strategy clear:

> I tell thee these things, in order that my Dove, into whose infinite depths the sunshine falls continually, may perceive what a cloudy veil stretches over the abyss of my nature. Thou wilt not think that it is caprice or stubbornness that has made me hitherto resist thy wishes. Neither, I think, is it a love of secrecy and darkness. I am glad to think that God sees through my heart; and if any angel has power to penetrate into it, he is welcome to know everything that is there. Yes; and so may any mortal, who is capable of full sympathy, and therefore worthy to come into my depths. But he must find his own way there. I can neither guide him nor enlighten him. It is this involuntary reserve, I suppose, that has given the objectivity to my writings. And when people think that I am pouring myself out in a tale or essay, I am merely telling what is common to human nature, not what is peculiar to myself. I sympathize with them—not they with me.
>
> (CE 15:612–613)

Sophia did not easily set aside her determination that no man would ever have her for a wife. Happy in her psychic union with Nathaniel, she shrank from the prospect of wedlock. Early in their courtship she proposed to be his "sister" and later suggested that "husband" and "wife" should continue in a spiritual relation, without actually getting married (CE 15:305, 452). As the wedding day drew near, her nervous disabilities grew more intense, and she asked Nathaniel for a postponement.

The womanly rebellion implicit in Sophia's headaches and prostrations drew her into an alternative communion. Through her beloved sisters she had made her way into a circle of Boston friends, women who frequented Elizabeth's West Street bookstore, and attended the readings that Margaret Fuller gave there.

The parties given by Mrs. Cornelia Hall Park that so alarmed Nathaniel were gatherings for this community of spirited women. Sophia's friendship with Connie Park reached back more than ten years, to a time before her marriage to Thomas Park in 1830. When Thomas departed in 1836 to seek his fortune in California, Connie supported herself alone in Boston, where Sophia (and Nathaniel) first met Margaret Fuller at one of her parties in 1839. Connie spent some time at Brook Farm in the early 1840s, resuming the name "Hall," since she had heard nothing in the intervening years from Mr. Park. When the Hawthornes were married in 1842, she was well on her way to obtaining a divorce (CE 15:383, 560).

Nathaniel did not approve of Sophia's friendships with cultivated and independent-minded women and warned against their parties as harmful worldly distractions. "Why do not people know better what is requisite for a Dove, than thus to keep her wings fluttering all day long, never allowing her a moment to fold them in peace and quietness? I am anxious for thee, mine ownest wife. When I have the sole charge of thee, these things shall not be" (CE 15:459).

The imposition of "peace and quietness" on a woman of nervous temperament corresponds to well-attested contemporary medical doctrine. Kathryn Sklar's biography of Catharine Beecher discusses the health spas for women that offered opportunities for just such a respite, and for strengthened womanly communion as well. But Nathaniel wants to eliminate Sophia's associations with other women; he wants her to "glide away from all the world" into her husband's control. Charlotte Perkins Gilman in "The Yellow Wallpaper" describes a comparable course of domestic seclusion, in which the husband insists that solitary rest is the cure that his wife requires, with the result that she goes altogether mad.

Sophia received "magnetic" treatments at the hands of Connie Park that helped to quiet her anxieties. She had been treated in Salem by Dr. Joseph E. Fiske, whose successes contributed to the wave of publicity mesmerism received during the 1830s (Stoehr, 41–42). Sophia's sister Elizabeth was enthusiastic about the spiritual insight and healing mesmerism provided and apparently tried to treat Sophia after the family moved to Boston. But Sophia found no help until she discovered that Connie Park had the touch.

Nathaniel was horrified by the proposed new treatments because they would give Connie access to Sophia's soul. "There would be an intrusion into thy holy of holies—and the intruder would not be thy husband! Canst thou think, without a shrinking of thy soul, of any human being coming into closer communion with thee than I may?" (CE 15:588). The rhetoric of his oneness with Sophia leads Nathaniel to the bizarre conclusion that Connie will penetrate Sophia sexually in their seances, as only he should do, and that in consequence an adulterous connection will be established between Connie and him. "I really do not like the idea of being brought, through thy medium, into such an intimate relation with Mrs. Park" (CE 15:588).

Sophia did not obey Nathaniel's commands, however, and as their wedding date drew near, she continued to avail herself of Park's treatments. The borderline states of consciousness into which Connie led her, and the womanly solidarity Sophia found there, seem to have assuaged her unconscious conflicts and moderated their physical consequences. Nathaniel's tone meanwhile shifted from the imperious to the pathetic: "My pillow was haunted with ghastly dreams . . . about thy being magnetized. God save me from any more such! I awoke in an absolute quake" (CE 15:634).

Although they claimed that "the ceremony is nothing," Nathaniel and Sophia knew they were approaching a great divide. The ethereal union they expressed in hugs and kisses would now sustain the full force of real sexual intimacy and the rhetoric of childhood would come into contact with actual children. Nathaniel was confident, however, that Sophia's nervous ailments would subside once he had taken control. "Oh, my poor little Dove," he wrote in response to her last fit of illness before their wedding, "thou dost need a husband with a strong will to take care of thee; and when I have the charge of thee, thou wilt find thyself under much stricter discipline than ever before" (CE 15:633).

CHAPTER NINE

Androgynous Paradise Lost

"I seem to be translated out of that former Sophia Peabody's body-corporate entirely," Sophia rejoiced as the newlyweds settled into the Old Manse, "& now inhabit the fair, round, dancing, rosy, elastic form of Mistress Sophie Hawthorne. Nothing can be farther from my purposes than to be upon a sickbed."[1] Living with Nathaniel fostered her saucy independence, what he had called the "Sophie Hawthorne" side of her character. She describes romping across a field that was waiting to be harvested; in the round of affectionate teasing that follows, she flaunts her "naughtiness" against his mock-serious authority:

> He told me I had transgressed the law of right in trampling down the unmown grass & he tried to induce me to come back, that he might not have to violate his conscience by doing the same thing. And I was very naughty & would not obey & therefore he punished me by staying behind. This I did not like very well, & I climbed the hill alone. We penetrated the pleasant gloom & sat down upon the carpet of dried pine leaves. Then I clasped him in my arms in the lovely shade & we lay down a few moments on the bosom of dear Mother Earth. Oh how sweet it was! And I told him I would not be so naughty again, & there was a very slight diamond shower without any thunder or lightning & we were happiest. . . . There was no wind & the stillness was profound. There seemed no movement in the world but that of our pulses.[2]

Their communion of souls was now consummated sexually, and Sophia's narrative—culminating in the thunderless diamond shower—traces the

138

emotional pattern of their lovemaking when it flowered as harmless play. Sophia takes the initiative, leading the way to the hilltop bower and clasps her man in her arms. The paradoxes of dominance and submission now appear in a complex minuet: Sophia's impudent assumption of leadership is framed so as to court her husband's need to yield himself up to her; yet the scene overtly acknowledges his authority, which is defied, asserted, and relaxed only in fun. These psychic complexities imparted a mysterious wealth to the newlyweds' intimacy. "We spend hours," Sophia writes, "in miraculous interweavings of spirit which confound my understanding. We find both that we did not imagine, with all our vivid imaginings, what wonderful happiness it is to dwell together, and interchange life every moment" (15 August 1842).

In keeping with the sexual conventions of the domestic ideal, the Hawthornes found that erotic pleasure was the medium of spiritual union, what Sarah Grimke termed "that yearning for *mutual absorption into each other, which alone gives vitality to every true marriage*" (Degler, 266).[3] The Hawthornes themselves referred to sexual relations as "blissful interviews," a mutual communication for which "intercourse" came to be the accepted name.[4] The famous prudery that policed the boundaries of the middle-class household and the repressive strategies at work within it take part in constituting Victorian sexual relations as a supremely meaning-intensive experience. The work of Michel Foucault and Peter Gay describes this Victorian paradox of repressed and proliferating sexuality, and the Hawthornes' experience amply illustrates its central element,[5] the role of sex as a sensuous language.

As Sophia's headstrong spirit becomes a theme of sexual pleasure, so also does Nathaniel's imperial pre-eminence. She made him a purple robe, clearly designed as royal regalia, to adorn and accentuate his breath-catching physical beauty. "Nathaniel wore it out once to walk with me," she tells his sister Louisa, and "he looks very imperial in it. I wish you could see him. He does not need any garnishing to make him splendid, but splendid attire becomes him very much. Miss Burley, you know, thinks he ought to dress in velvet, & sit in a sumptuous chair & write & muse" (CE 16:5). Hawthorne himself joined in the spirit of this occasion by adding the following peremptory notice to his sister: "I want you to send those pearl buttons—they being all that is wanting to the perfection of the imperial robe. Hereof fail not" (7–8).

Sophia was happy to play up to Nathaniel's role as "Emperor." "My dancing days have returned," she informs her mother. "I dance before him to the music of the musical box & of my own thoughts & he said once that

I deserve John the Baptist's head. I know I danced very well once. Now I can better" (5 August 1842). Thus Sophia announces her pleasure in figuring as a latter-day Salome, inflaming the desire of King Herod. The seduction of Nathaniel—as lustful oriental potentate—replays the paradox in which a worshiping Sophia stoops to conquer. Sophia danced to the tune of a music box that the Hawthornes called "our domestic harmony," but the music of the box was only a meager token of the ecstasy they found when erotic playfulness brought on orchestral thunder. "My husband & I do not need it now," Sophia declared after they lent the box to Thoreau. "All Beethoven is within us now, all the Symphonies ever composed & all that lay slumbering in his mighty soul that never found utterance" (2 October 1842).

Mrs. Peabody was hardly delighted by the implication that Sophia had joined herself in marriage to a voluptuary tyrant; she had long feared that her daughter's romantic impetuousness would lead to "ruin," and Sophia's oblique reference to Herod was a taunt, aimed unerringly at this maternal anxiety. Sophia's description of her dancing specifically invokes a conflict that arose during her voyage to Cuba, where she had become enamored of James Burroughs, whose bad reputation was quickly brought to the attention of her mother and sisters. When it was reported in Boston that Burroughs was reading Sophia's love letters aloud for the entertainment of his companions in a New Orleans boardinghouse, the ensuing moral panic prompted Mrs. Peabody to forbid dancing—at the parties Sophia attended in Cuba— on the ground that such excitement was bad for Sophia's health.[6] Now Sophia saucily reports that her husband is pleased by her return to the languorous and impulsive freedom of the tropics: "I sleep as I did in Cuba & can at any time take a good nap. Then I wake all dewy fresh & am ready to walk miles, or dance the Cachucha, Cracovienne or whatever jig. I was lazy exactly so in Cuba" (11 August 1842).

King Herod figured as a commonplace warning, in the imagery of republican manhood, against the failure of moral self-command that would doom the American experiment in democracy, ensuring its collapse into despotism. Slaves of passion, so the convention taught, would become slaves in fact, or slavemasters. In her running debate with her mother about Nathaniel's character, Sophia defiantly insists that his taste for oriental luxury was a mark of his perfect independence and self-government, not of despotic license. "Mr. Hawthorne said this morning that he should like to have a study with a soft, thick Turkey carpet upon the floor," Sophia wrote after eight years of marriage, "& hung round with full crimson curtains, so as to hide all rectangles." But Mr. Hawthorne would never accept such a voluptuous tabernacle, so long as it "would demand the slightest extravagance, because he is as severe as a stoic . . . & never in his life allowed himself a luxury. . . . It is both wonderful & admirable to see how his taste for splendor and perfection is not the slightest temptation to him; how wholly independent he is of what he would like" (29 September 1850).

Sophia also defended her husband against the related charge of womanish weakness, which rested on the conventional belief that erotic feeling "unlocks every manly power of the soul" so that "the body become effeminated."[7] The Peabodys were offended by Nathaniel's aversion to visiting in their homes, and his addiction to solitude appeared to them suspiciously feminine. Sophia concedes that it is often "a real torture to him to enter the room" when they have guests but insists that "he always faced that occasion like a man" (9–10 October 1842).

Her family fails to recognize, Sophia declares, that Nathaniel possesses a divine poetic manhood, into which feminine qualities are incorporated. He is not "a social visitor & chatting companion" but "a poet of the highest grade—who must stand apart and observe." Nathaniel's "extremely fine & harp-like organization" makes it difficult for him to meet people; and he simply cannot bandy words about in casual talk. To him words are "worlds—suns and systems—& cannot move easily and rapidly. The light of them radiates from his well-like eyes" (3 September 1843).

To comprehend Nathaniel's androgynous character as an "Apollo" of divine light, the Peabodys must understand that he tenderly absorbs his experience into a nurturing inward space. He allows his creative work to gestate, so that his own intentions are not rudely imposed but "clothed upon with language after their own will & pleasure" (9 January 1844). Sophia demands that her family cease to judge Nathaniel by a commonplace standard of manhood, pointedly observing that "Mr Emerson who is ever searching after a *man,* used always to call him 'The Man.' " As for Sophia's sister Mary, who had complained about his shyness, "she had not the smallest notion of him. What she regards as weakness in [him] is but *a very strong resolution*" (3 September 1843).

Reinforcing Sophia's faith was Margaret Fuller, who had praised Nathaniel's androgyny when she learned that he and Sophia were to marry. "I think there will be great happiness," she declared, "for if ever I saw a man who combined delicate tenderness to understand the heart of a woman, with quiet depth and manliness enough to satisfy her, it is Mr. Hawthorne."[8] Fuller visited the Hawthornes at the Old Manse a month after they were married and again when she was working on *Woman in the Nineteenth*

Century, where she declared that "there is no wholly masculine man, no purely feminine woman" and that "all men of genius" share "the feminine development." Fuller's remark that "man partakes of the feminine in the Apollo" may well echo Sophia's nickname for Nathaniel (113, 116).

Sophia staunchly defended her husband's androgynous character, and the "miraculous interweavings" of their intimacy, against her family's suspicions and disapproval. As in their courtship, they found a fulfillment in their life together that satisfied yearnings of their inmost souls. The complexity of their interdependence created misery enough, in due course, but it also meant they were suited to each other, and they clung to their precious union amid the sexual anxieties that now assailed them. For middle-class Americans in the early nineteenth century erotic experience became a language of sacred intimacy, as noted; it was also an arena of meanings in collision. The cultural arrangement that made sex a fountain of bliss simultaneously rendered it a morass of loathing and dread.

Companionate marriage provided a locale in which a man could make tangible his own reality, a haven from the dehumanizing forces of a competitive capitalist economy. Yet the manhood required for surviving worldly turmoil was not laid aside when the man escaped his disconcerting relations with other men and came home to his wife. On the contrary, his domestic existence was arranged so as to reinforce the necessary worldly virtues of stoical severity and self-reliance, not least because the failure to exercise these virtues at home could destroy the family's prospect of entering the middle class or remaining in it. Middle-class couples perforce became "prudent procreators," in Mary Ryan's memorable phrase, because having too many children could overwhelm a family's finances.[9] Erotic life was given its paradoxical character by the effort to make sex wholly voluntary, to fashion a sign of consummate self-control from an experience that has stubbornly involuntary features.

The emerging middle-class obsession with maintaining self-control in the face of sexual desire was expressed in the theories of John Humphrey Noyes, who proposed an alternative to monogamous marriage to preserve the spiritual communion enshrined as its essence. Although Noyes was denounced as a threat to public morals, his radical stance illuminates central themes of the sexual code becoming established as conventional. In the "free love" commune he founded at Oneida, New York, Noyes drew a sharp line between "amative" sexuality, which remained within voluntary control, and "propagative" sexuality, in which orgasm took place. In "amative" union, a couple engaged in mutual caresses, including penetration, so as to realize the exalted fusion of souls that is the God-given function of the penis and the vagina. These Noyes considered to be "organs of union," quite distinct from the testicles and the uterus, which were "organs of propagation." "Sexual Intercourse," Noyes explained, "is the conjunction of the organs of union, and the interchange of magnetic influences, or conversation of spirits, through the medium of that conjunction." The discharge of semen is no more necessary to sexual intercourse than the discharge of urine, Noyes taught, and must take place only when the couple has obtained specific authorization from the community to conceive a child.[10] It is doubtful that sexual continence has ever been put in practice more heroically, but the self-restraint enshrined at Oneida makes explicit a criterion of moral adequacy whose demands were felt in every middle-class home.

The ideal of self-sovereign middle-class manhood produced an autophobic sexuality, such that erotic arousal was chronically attended by dread and was experienced as disgust and guilt when it was felt to stray beyond the boundaries of self-control. Male terror and loathing in the presence of female sexual power were not invented in the nineteenth century; evidence of them is abundant at the mythological fountainheads of Western culture, in the image of Medusa, for example, and in the solitary Hebrew god Yahweh, who is notable among the divinities of the ancient Near East for lacking a consort. But the element of male self-loathing in this ancient scheme of responses was accentuated in the nineteenth century as men sought to hold themselves to a standard of inward self-sovereignty.

As the studies of G. J. Barker-Benfield and Stephen Nissenbaum have illustrated at length, middle-class males found involuntary sexual excitement a markedly disagreeable and frightening experience. An extensive advice literature appeared, promoting "male purity" and vividly portrayed the miseries of sexual "pollution." Sylvester Graham's program of diet and hygiene acquired many adherents, who hoped to escape the dreaded consequences of "excessive lasciviousness" within marriage as well as without. This literature of masculine panic referred to orgasm—when involuntary processes take control altogether—as a "paroxysm"; and Graham himself likened orgasm to the convulsions of acute cholera, epilepsy, and heart attack (Nissenbaum, Sex, 109–110). The relaxation that follows orgasm was felt as a penalty for the overmastering desire that precedes it and was termed "debilitation," a feverish state of erotic preoccupation that leads to additional failures of sexual self-command, lust once unbridled having a nasty self-propulsion that keeps running until exhaustion and self-disgust are complete. "Diseased prurience," "nervous melancholy," and "polluted lassitude" were terms for this all-too-familiar condition (Nissenbaum, *Sex,* 106–108).

Nathaniel projects images of such contaminated masculine sexuality into the Concord River, which ran close by the Old Manse, where he spent many hours fishing and gathering flowers for Sophia. "I can find nothing more fit to compare it with, than one of the half torpid earthworms, which I dig up for the purpose of bait. The worm is sluggish, and so is the river—the river is muddy, and so is the worm—you hardly know whether either of them is alive or dead." From his first fishing expedition Nathaniel brought home only "an enormous eel"—which he and Sophia ate—"and truly he had the taste of the whole river in his flesh, with a very prominent flavor of mud" (CE 8:320). Even when his luck at fishing improves, Nathaniel's vision of the river as a domain of sexual filth remains strong. "It seems as if we could catch nothing but frogs and mud-turtles, or reptiles akin to them; and even when a fish of reputable aspect is drawn out, you feel a shyness about touching him. As to our river, my little wife expressed its character admirably, last night; she said 'it was too lazy to keep itself clean' " (345). The voluptuous Cuban laziness Sophia had flaunted before her mother now reappears as the torpor of Nathaniel's sexual exhaustion, his penis after orgasm symbolized by the flabby muddy slime of worms and eels.

Nathaniel had long been devoted to a pattern of life—cultivating his own fancies in a compulsive bookish solitude—well recognized as conducive to prurient lassitude, and in particular to masturbation, a practice especially beset by the anxieties of self-made manhood. "Allow me to lift up a loud voice against those rovings of the imagination," the prominent anti-masturbationist Reverend John Todd cried out, "by which the mind is at once enfeebled, and the heart and feelings debased and polluted. It is almost inseparable from the habit of revery" (Barker-Benfield 173). Editing Hawthorne's notebooks for publication, Sophia discovered that her husband had written—about his long seclusion in Salem—that he had won fame "in this dismal and squalid chamber"; she promptly canceled the term "squalid" to remove the implication of sexual pollution.[11]

Nathaniel's custom, well established during the Salem years, was to counteract his own languor in the way recommended by the literature of sexual hygiene, by taking various forms of vigorous exercise, especially swimming.[12] But his conscientious efforts to keep himself clean by swimming in the Concord River only involve him further in its eerie defiling power. "I bathe once, and often twice a day, in our river; but one dip into the salt-sea would be worth more than a whole week's soaking in such a lifeless tide. I have read of a river somewhere . . . which seemed to dissolve and steal away the vigor of those who bathed in it. Perhaps our stream will be found to have this property" (CE 8:319). Nathaniel now had to contend not merely with his own reveries but with the round, dancing, rosy, elastic body of his wife, and his preoccupation with the sluggish, filthy river reflects the anxiety that he felt at her power to arouse him, bring him to "paroxysm," and leave him exhausted.

The ideal of feminine "purity"—that indispensable virtue of the domestic angel—recruited women to the task of allaying male sexual anxiety. Mrs. Peabody's distress about Sophia's reputation and her prohibition of dancing during the Cuban sojourn illustrate a familiar matronly role, that of policing conduct in relation to this code. But no matter how prominently women figured as enforcers, the politics of purity was rooted ultimately in male needs.

A pure woman aided men in retaining self-control by transmuting masculine lust into reverent admiration. Prompting her man to pay her adoring attentions that would not get her pregnant, this wifely virtue was a form of psychic birth control, necessary to limit family size and thus maintain middle-class status. Because the domestic angel did not seek her own pleasure, she did not become the target of her husband's self-disgust, which was projected upon such "impure" women as might illicitly arouse him.

Hawthorne was fascinated all his life by the male psychodynamics of feminine purity and treats them in such early tales as "Young Goodman Brown" and "The Minister's Black Veil." As Nina Baym observes, however, the vein of hostility against women deepens in the works he produced following his marriage, so that "The Birthmark" and "Rappacini's Daughter" depict a male imagination for which sexual attraction is virtually indistinguishable from revulsion.[13]

Reverence for the purity of woman is associated with chronic sexual guilt and convulsive misogynist loathing in Nathaniel's description of gathering flowers for his wife to arrange, a favorite ritual of their early married life. Nathaniel discovers that the filth of the river produces two sorts of lilies, of which the "pond lily" becomes a symbol of Sophia's purity. "It is a marvel whence it derives its loveliness and perfume, sprouting as it does from the black mud over which the river sleeps, and from which, likewise, the yellow lily draws its unclean life and noisome perfume." Hawthorne likens the yellow lily to persons who soak up and embody the evil of the world, whereas the "spotless and fragrant pond-lily" transforms the evil into loveliness. "I possess such a human and heavenly lily, and wear it in my bosom. Heaven grant that I myself may not be symbolized by its yellow companion" (CE 8:318–319).

Since the purity of the domestic angel inspires her husband to sublimate the sexual filth that stains his life, his worship conceals an inner liability to panic and disgust. Sophia plays her role in the Hawthornes' floral drama by arranging the flowers that Nathaniel brings in by the armful. Yet as he observes that she has a natural gift for putting all this erotic imagery in order, his language veers compulsively into loathing. "She has, in perfection, the love and taste for flowers," Nathaniel affirms, "without which a woman is a monster" (CE 8:319).

This invocation of womanly monstrosity serves notice that the bodily capacities expressing the Hawthornes' marital communion also had the power to drive them apart. Once sexual experience moved beyond the playful and the "naughty" and the full force of passionate desire entered their relationship, the imperial aloofness through which Nathaniel shored up his self-possession threatened to give way, and the underlying dread was stirred into fitful expression. Nathaniel's allusion to Herod and Salome, so jauntily reported by Sophia to her mother, arises through a reference to John the Baptist's head on a platter, a hideous image of unmanning. In saying that Sophia "deserves" such an offering, Nathaniel repeats the psychic strategy by which he sought to manage his fears, that of casting himself as a voluptuary emperor, and Sophia sustained this strategy by playing a spirited Salome. But Sophia had also internalized with special intensity the conventional wifely role: she was superangelic. She embodied an immaculate purity that shielded Nathaniel against the terrors of self-loss, the nightmare that erupts in his momentary hallucinations of monster women and the prophet's severed head.

The erotics of middle-class purity were inherently precarious, and for the Hawthornes the characteristic tensions were unusually strong, so that Sophia envisions sexuality as an all-but-forbidden fruit of wonderful deliciousness that is available only when the purity of the sexual partners is absolute:[14]

> It is the inward thought alone that renders the body either material or angelical. . . . Before our marriage I knew nothing of its capacities & the truly married alone can know what a wondrous instrument it is for the purposes of the heart. . . . The unholiness of union on any other ground than *entire* oneness of spirit, immediately & eternally causes the sword of the flaming Cherubim to wave before this tree of life. The prophane never can taste the joy of Elysium, because it is a spiritual joy & they cannot perceive it.
>
> (Family Notebook, undated entry)

The bliss of sex is perfect so long as it meets the demands of self-possession, remaining an "instrument" for expressing the *"entire* oneness" that makes up a true marriage. The two hearts must have exactly the same purposes if the couple is not to be cast forever out of Paradise.

This doctrine had practical consequences apart from the Hawthornes' sexual relations. To maintain "oneness," the couple must agree on decisions about the ordinary business of living. Mrs. Peabody was dismayed at Sophia's worship of Nathaniel, but soon after the newlyweds' arrival at the Old Manse, Sophia explains that his divine perfection gives her freedom. "Do not fear that I shall be too subject to my Adam," she writes to her mother.

> He loves power as little [as] any mortal I ever knew & it is never a question of private will between us, but of absolute right. His conscience is too fine & high toned to permit him to be arbitrary. His will is strong, but not to govern others. Our love is so wide & deep & equal that there could not be much difference of opinion between us upon any moral point. He is such a simple transcript of the angelic nature . . . that even should he will me to do, I should find my highest instinct correspond with his will. I never knew such etherial delicacy of nature.
>
> (30 August–4 September 1842)

This hardly looks like a charter of womanly power; yet it clearly asserts Sophia's right to pronounce on the quality of Nathaniel's character. The ideal of feminine purity provided grounds from which women could resist oppression, since "pure" women enjoyed a markedly enhanced moral authority, including the right to refuse sexual advances and to demand that men adhere to a new standard of moral rectitude. As sexual morality took on a heightened significance during the Victorian period, women emerged as arbiters of male virtue both in the home and beyond it.[15]

The ideal of purity plays this dual role in the Hawthorne household. Sophia looks on Nathaniel as a god but asserts her right to declare him one. Who better than Sophia could identify "etherial delicacy of nature"? As to Nathaniel's sexuality, Sophia claimed it was perfectly adjusted to the requirements of her own nature, even when these requirements became more complex as the months of marriage passed and her early physical exuberance gave way to returning spells of nervous distress. Rather than intruding his own demands, Nathaniel's body responded like a barometer to the fluctuating pressures of her delicate psychic organization. "He has no brute force; but every part of his frame seems in perfect diapason, as a bird's. I should be afraid of him if he were in ferocious health, unable to conceive of delicate bodies or untuned nerves. But he is as comprehensive of every imaginable state I could be in as if his own physique were my barometer . . . & as if the same plectrum struck both our chords together. This I call heavenly health" (21–22 January 1844).

Sophia believed Nathaniel as pure as she herself, having a communion like her own with absolute right, which canceled merely private will. This language of joint purity modifies their earlier rhetoric of "inward and eternal union" and forms the code within which they managed the new stresses of married life. Nathaniel's insistence on Sophia's absolute pond-lily purity aided him in overcoming his dread of sexual pollution through her; and her insistence on his "heavenly health" allayed her own sharp misgiving at the threat of subordination to him, including sexual subordination. But sexuality was not the only source of opposition they sought to master through a reassertion of their *entire* oneness; such reassertions become obsessive, in fact, as their marriage chronically set them at odds.

Both Nathaniel and Sophia were psychically dependent on their mothers and sought to perpetuate infantile satisfactions in their life together. "I wish I could be a wife & daughter at the same time," Sophia wrote to Mrs. Peabody within a month of her wedding (5 August 1842). After a visit in March 1843 she wrote, "Goodbye dear Mamma. . . . I shall sit in your corner with you a great deal & see the world from under your wing. Your happy child Sophiechen."[16] To Nathaniel their life in paradise secured an exemption from "the fight with the world—the struggle of a man among men—the agony of the universal effort to wrench the means of life from a host of greedy competitors." He leads, instead, a life of "boyish thoughtlessness" (CE 8:332).

Nathaniel demanded exclusive mothering attention from Sophia, and his desire to cut her off from other relationships could now be enforced. Within a week of the wedding, Nathaniel forbade her to write to her mother: "My noble lord has been so anxious lest I should do too much," Sophia explains, "that he has prevented my sending you another greeting" (15 July 1842). Sophia never overtly complains about such treatment, but after three years of marriage she writes a description of Nathaniel's petty tyranny in which her own gesture of adoring submission is all but frankly sarcastic. He "never lets me get tired. The intuitions of his heart are so unerring that he arrests me the moment before I do too much, & he is then immitigable, & I cannot obtain grace to sew even an inch more, even if an inch more would finish my work. I have such rich experience of his wisdom in these things, that whatever may be the inconvenience, I gratefully submit" (6 March 1846).

Sophia likewise professed herself blissfully happy with their isolation at the Old Manse. Nathaniel noted that she "has come to me from the midst of many friends, and a large circle of acquaintance; yet she lives from day-to-day in this solitude, seeing nobody but myself and our Molly [Mary O'Brien, the maid], while the snow of our avenue is untrodden for weeks by any footstep save mine; yet she is always cheerful, and far more than cheerful" (CE 8:367). Sophia enthusiastically agreed that satisfying Nathaniel's desire for "sole intercourse" was all the life she needed: "Not at balls & routs should I care to walk in silk attire, but in the profound shelter of this home, I would put on daily a velvet robe . . . to gratify my husband's taste. . . . Behold a true wife's world! It is her husband only."[17]

A journal Sophia kept during December 1843, however, recorded her misery at being kept within "a true wife's world," together with the hysterical outbursts that provide an outlet for her torment and allow her to place some modest demands on her husband. She describes a suffocating routine of sewing and reading, and reading with Nathaniel, and teaching the maid to read. When Nathaniel goes to the village, she waits anxiously for him to return and notes that "he brought no letters nor news" ("A Sophia Hawthorne Journal," 4). Only three times during the month does she go to the village herself. She takes walks in the lane, sometimes, but more frequently Nathaniel requires her to walk indoors, in the "gallery." When Mary O'Brien becomes ill, Sophia tires herself providing care but states that she was chiefly "wearied by the excessive anxiety of my beloved husband, who thought I should be injured" (11). Sophia rejoices when Nathaniel permits her the felicity of sitting silently in his company while he reads or writes. She herself struggles recurrently to paint, despite a besetting nervousness and drowsiness. More than once she cannot help interrupting her husband, without his permission, because she was "terribly homesick down stairs without him" (18).

Noting that the effort to paint distresses her, Nathaniel advises her to refrain, and for a time she acquiesces. On her next attempt she is "possessed with an obstinate fiend" that drives her to seek her husband's company, only to find she has again interrupted his writing, and, "conscience stricken," she goes back downstairs. "I felt desolate & nervous & as if I wanted to weep a river. I had to return to the study, it was so cold & comfortless below, & the wind all the while confusing my brain." The wind continued to blow and to haunt her dreadfully through the rest of the day, and into the following night, when she "dreamed of women in fits, & many horrors" ("A Sophia Hawthorne Journal," 19–20).

Sophia's frantic inner distress rose to the surface when Nathaniel accidentally knocked over a bust of Ceres, "who came tumbling down, scattering her remains over me & the room with an astounding crash." At first Sophia felt "very quiet"; then she "began to feel nervous & shocked & as if I must have a thunder gust of tears to relieve myself"; finally, she gave way to shattering sobs ("A Sophia Hawthorne Journal," 18). She is thankful for the kindness of "the best husband in the world," who soothes her "with his divine caresses & seraph tones" and comforts her in the night with stories of his boyhood paradise at Raymond (10, 18). As her chronicle of boredom, restlessness, hysteria, and terrifying nightmares comes to a close, Sophia invokes the uncanny union between herself and her husband as an all-sufficient solace. She records painting happily and well one day: "Every thing went right & I succeeded quite to my mind. I felt sure my husband above me must also be having a propitious morning with his muse, or I could not feel so altogether content. When he came to dinner, I asked him, & he said he did not know as he ever felt so much like writing on any one day. We seemed to respond to one another exactly, as if particularly united & I think it was so. Were we two persons?" (22).

Nathaniel's determination to keep Sophia within a regimen of rest and quiet was particularly resolute during this period because she was entering the last months of her second pregnancy, her first having ended in a miscarriage in February 1843. The Hawthornes eagerly looked forward to the birth of a child, and after the miscarriage Hawthorne consoled himself with the thought that the baby's coming had only been delayed. "The longer we live together—the deeper we penetrate into one another, and become mutually interfused—the happier we are. God will surely crown our union with children, because it fulfils the highest conditions of marriage" (CE 8:366).

For the children of Eden, to contemplate having a baby brought unacknowledged conflicts to a new pitch of intensity. Not only would the newcomer increase the burden of household expense, but it would also challenge Nathaniel's claim to Sophia's exclusive care and place unwonted burdens on Sophia. Hawthorne was distressed by the miscarriage, yet it appears that the temporary loss of Sophia's attention troubled him as much as losing the baby. "It was the first time I had been taken from him," Sophia explained to her mother, "& the world seemed standing on its head to him, boulversing himself with it. One can hardly estimate, except me, what an entire change of life it was to him. It seems now as if some invisible James Clarke had married us again" (February 1843; misdated 1844).

The Hawthornes met the anxieties of parenthood through a massive deployment of their characteristic strategy, sublimating discord into an exaltation of their union. The resultant emotional pattern defined the child's nurture in a system already taking form when her parents agreed on a name. "Many months before she was born," Sophia remarked, "we anticipated a daughter, & named her Una" (Family Notebook, 7 April 1844).

In choosing this name the Hawthornes asserted their "oneness" and declared its quality, invoking the nineteenth-century convention that had transformed Spenser's maiden of holiness into an icon of Victorian purity. Mrs. Peabody had herself produced a prose version—in contemporary English—of the first book of *The Faerie Queene* and focuses on the incident that became central to the Victorian meaning of Una's character, when the maiden's radiant beauty so overawes a charging lion that instead of devouring her, he becomes her willing slave and protector. "Una is more than Eve," Mrs. Peabody explained. "Innocence and truth melt into one, to form ideal woman, before whom bow the Lionhearted, in the service that elevates the very quality of their nature" (*Holiness; or, the Legend of St. George,* 177).

Sophia was quick to assert, however, that the name did not celebrate feminine virtue at her husband's expense. Nathaniel himself displays this sublime purity, and she hopes the baby will live up to the standard that he sets. "If she be like her father, as well in mind as face, she will be rightly named—of most delicate spirit, impatient of wrong & ugliness—demanding beauty of all things & persons & like the 'heavenly Una' of Spenser" (Family Notebook, 7 April 1844). This adulatory remark has a troubling sound and strikes a note that becomes more and more insistent in Sophia's responses to the child. She pointedly avoids intimating that she dotes on her baby any more than on Nathaniel: "Every morning when I wake & find the darling lying there" is "an additional felicity to my previously sufficient bliss" (5 April 1844).

The baby administered a powerful shock to the Hawthornes' relationship, as revealed by Sophia's abrupt announcement that Nathaniel is sending her home to her mother. "He feels a great desire that baby & I should change air & that I should change scene, & he wants me to stay a fortnight!! Was ever heard such a thing?" Unwilling to let this explanation stand, Nathaniel required Sophia to add a postscript about her "malady": "a congestion of blood in my head. . . . [which] feels as if it had had a blow . . . & my nose has bled three or four times" (May 1844).[18]

Sophia mentions several causes: "One is the heat I am in while washing & dressing baby in the morning for I must have a little fire, or she shivers— another is the stretch of mind I have had because I want to accomplish so many things & have time to do none—another is rocking while I hold baby sometimes. . . . My head not only feels as if it had had a blow, but once in a while I seem to have a new knock upon it. . . . It troubles my husband so much that I should like something to cure it if possible *directly*" (May 1844).

Both Sophia and Nathaniel were temporarily confounded, and each ascribed the collapse of their oneness to the other. Nathaniel had confidently expected that Sophia's nervous condition would clear up once he had removed her into the "natural" relations of marriage. Sophia herself had boasted, in the early weeks of marriage, that a physical metamorphosis had taken place; and later, when her headaches and hysterical weeping returned, she found the seraphic caresses of her husband an all-sufficient remedy. But in the midst of washing and dressing and rocking the baby she had received a blow to the head that Nathaniel's attentiveness could not cure; and Nathaniel was likewise severely disconcerted.

His letters to Sophia during her absence indicate how acutely he desired a restoration of the exclusive relation he had enjoyed before the child was born, when there was no third party to spoil his Eden. "Ah, why canst not thou be with me here—and no Mary—no nobody else!" As he acknowledges that Una's birth has now made this impossible, his language takes on a sinister ambiguity: "But our little Una! Should not she be of the party? Yes; we have linked a third spirit forever to our own; and there is no existing without her" (CE 16:39). Hawthorne conveys both love and loathing here; that "there is no existing without her" celebrates their fulfillment and expresses his bitter regret.

The fusion of contraries that was present in the union of Sophia and Nathaniel was thus focused on their newborn child. Una is made to represent the central tension of her parents' relationship, in which mutually divergent energies are sublimated into an Edenic childlike purity. As we shall see, Sophia found it relatively easy to project this supernatural energy into the child's character, to see her as a maiden of holiness in fact. Nathaniel, meanwhile, struggled with a hostility he could not openly express, trying to acknowledge his divided response in terms that would insist on the inviolacy of his union with Sophia. His first letter during Sophia's stay in Boston seems to find a solution. "How does our belovedest little Una?—whom I love more than I ever told thee, though not more than thou knowest—for is she not thine and mine, the symbol of the one true union in the world, and of our love in Paradise" (CE 16:37).

Una's birth sharpened Nathaniel's need to make money. Despite its claim on his emotional makeup, his escape into Eden from the scramble of "greedy competitors" had never been complete. He had married knowing that Sophia's delicacy forbade her to keep house, so that a maid would have to be provided, and he quickly resumed the effort to find a dependable source of income. Within six weeks of moving to the Old Manse, he hopes for an editorship with the *Boston Miscellany;* four months later he fails to land a job at the Salem Post Office and hopes another government position will show up soon. By March 1843 he cannot pay his bills; he himself had not been paid by his publishers and is enraged at being forced to break his word.[19]

Hawthorne thus confronted a bitter irony: the paradise in which he cultivated his art exposed him to the uncertainties of commerce in a way that holding a regular job would not. Fluctuations in the national economy, as well as the hazards of maintaining any particular magazine, struck directly at his pocketbook. So long as he depended on literary endeavors for a livelihood, the mercenary scrimmage bore in on him with added force.

Once Una was born, this dilemma grew more acute. He tells Hillard that the birth of a child "ought not to come too early in a man's life—not till he has fully enjoyed his youth—for methinks the spirit never can be thoroughly gay and careless again, after this great event. . . . It will never do for me to continue merely a writer of stories for the magazines—the most unprofitable business in the world." Earlier he had cherished a fantasy that the earth (with its "system of credit") might be smashed to pieces by a comet. Now he declares he would rather starve than be a writer for bread, but the baby makes this unthinkable. "In that case, poor little Una would have to take refuge in the alms-house—which, here in Concord, is a most gloomy old mansion. Her 'angel face' would hardly make a sunshine there" (CE 16:22–23).

After Sophia's return from Boston in June 1844, the Hawthornes dismissed their maid and vainly sought a replacement they could afford. By August Nathaniel had assumed a major share of the housekeeping. "My Hyperion is cook & maid," Sophia reports. "It is no poetry to cook and wash dishes. . . . But as the only way we can make money now seems to be *to save* it & as he declares we can manage till September, we will remain alone till then" (19–20 August 1844). Nathaniel's housework extended at least until Thanksgiving, however, when Sophia writes that "he will consent to cease to be kitchen-maid" since the Democrat James K. Polk has been elected president, and prospects for a government job have improved. A plan is now in motion for Sophia's sister Elizabeth to make an appeal on Nathaniel's behalf, as she had done before, and Sophia insists that Lizzie must not settle for a "moderate" income. "The greater the amount of thousands, the sooner can there be Otium cum dignitate—when works divine can be elaborated with an uncarefull mind" (20 November 1844).

Yet Hawthorne had just completed the greatest work of the Manse period, in the midst of cooking and housekeeping. It was not *otium cum dignitate* now or later that prompted his most powerful creations but circumstances forcing him into his internal torment. "Rappacini's Daughter" explores the fusion of celestial love with sexual loathing in an Eden of poisonous flowers (CE 16:66).

At the heart of the narrative is the interactive relationship between the "nature" of Beatrice Rappacini and the way she is viewed by her lover, Giovanni, an interaction that probes the dread of womanly sexuality that was hidden within the ideal of purity. Giovanni perceives that lethal toxins pervade Beatrice's body, yet she also strikes him as "worthiest to be worshipped" because endowed "with all gentle and feminine qualities" (CE 10:114). As he basks in "the Oriental sunshine of her beauty," Giovanni soon finds himself powerless to resist the "fierce and subtle poison" he conceives her to have instilled in him (110). He feels a "lurid intermixture" of contradictory emotions that make a "continual warfare in his breast": the poison within him is a "wild offspring of both love and horror" that "burned like one and shivered like the other" (105).

Giovanni's passions, like the "nature" of Beatrice, are contained within a larger framework of male contention, the rivalry between Giovanni's friend, Professor Baglioni, and Beatrice's father. Baglioni condemns Rappacini for pursuing a theory that restates the fusion of opposites Hawthorne pursues in the tale itself, that "all medicinal virtues are comprised within those substances which we term vegetable poisons" (CE 10:100). Rappacini cultivates his toxic garden for the sake of advancing this theory. "Was this garden, then, the Eden of the present world?" Giovanni asks; "and this man . . . was he the Adam?" (96). Rather than providing an innocent retreat from worldly competition, the garden is a laboratory where Rappacini carries out the ruthless experiments on which his fame is grounded, of which the most horrible is embuing Beatrice herself with the poison that is virtue.

Hawthorne's tale is fiercely engaged with the buried issues of his life at the Old Manse. It portrays an Edenic retreat where worldly striving is intensified, where male sexual horror is innate to the worship of feminine purity. Hawthorne's intimate struggles are at work here: his professional dilemma (where paradise was a cauldron of competitive stress) and his sexual confusion (where the pond lily of perfection was rooted in muck). Yet his personal anguish was a sharper version of male experience in the culture at large, where torments were objectified and controlled in the proliferating array of oppositions (home versus world, innocence versus corruption, woman versus man) that sustained the domestic ideal. "Rappacini's Daughter" dismantles the definition of moral reality, in particular womanly reality, that helped men conceal their helplessness and frailty behind the necessary facade of self-possession. The terms defining the "goodness" or "evil" of Beatrice are themselves put in question by the narrative. Yet those very terms were the accepted language of the Hawthornes' life together. When Nathaniel read the partly finished tale to Sophia, she asked whether Beatrice would turn out to be a demon or an angel, and he could only say that he had no idea (*NHW* 1:360).

Hawthorne's intuition of the bedrock stresses of his family life is also displayed in the uncanny accuracy with which Beatrice's death foretells the fate of Una Hawthorne. Rappacini claims to have made his daughter poisonous so she will be invulnerable to the evils of the world. Yet this fatherly precaution causes Beatrice to self-destruct when she falls in love with Giovanni, that is, when she attempts to find a life beyond her father's garden. As the Hawthornes drew Una into the emotional economy of the household as the exemplar of its absolute purity, her life was correspondingly poisoned. She acquired a character that forbade her to find fulfillment outside the sacred inwardness of her parents' relationship.

Sophia found new happiness in her life at the Old Manse after she returned from the stay with her mother in Boston. "It is beyond words enchanting to be alone as we are," she declares. "It seems much more Paradise than ever. But the floor wants washing & I must sew a little, & it will not do to have so much of my husband's time taken up with housewifery; for I assure you his office is no sinecure. He actually *does* everything & I sit up stairs & out of doors with baby, more of a queen than ever, for I have a king to my servitor" (19–20 August 1844). Sophia's royal condition was especially fulfilling because she had found a spiritual mission in motherhood. Hawthorne felt his child-self displaced by the coming of Una, but Sophia found her own to be redoubled; in communion with her baby, she could advance her own spiritual development, earlier pursued through meditative study and art.

Sophia had extensive connections in the network of educational reformers and theorists of child rearing who relied on the premise that infants are not infected by original sin but bring a primal innocence into the world to be preserved and cultivated. Sophia's sister Mary—author of *The Moral Culture of Infancy*—was a major figure in this network, as was her husband, Horace Mann. Sophia's sister Elizabeth and Bronson Alcott founded the Temple School, where children were encouraged to respond freely to moral and biblical questions; and Elizabeth drafted *Conversations with Children on the Gospels*, which presented the resultant discussions as "a natural history of the undepraved spirit" (xiii). Elizabeth had also encouraged Nathaniel to join in the "great moral enterprise" of "creating a new literature for the young" (CE 6:290), and in due course Hawthorne produced several volumes of children's stories in response to the emerging new market. Transforming the morally "hideous" Greek legends for retelling to children turns out to be surprisingly easy, he explains in *A Wonder Book*, "the instant he puts his imagination in sympathy with the innocent little circle, whose wide-open eyes are fixed so eagerly upon him" (CE 7:179).

During her stay in Boston, Sophia at last had an unobstructed opportunity to visit with the women friends who gathered at the West Street bookstore and at Connie Park's parties. Their responses to her baby testified to the greatness of soul she herself saw in the child. "When she was in Boston," Sophia explains in a letter to Louisa, "she had constant levees of all the great & good, & the testimony from all was the same as to her peerlessness. She was called 'a piece of statuary'—'a Picture'—'an Ideal child'—'a Queen,' 'a born-lady' 'a Princess'—'Morning glory'—'Morning star,' 'a Dove' & more sweet names than I can account" (CE 16:57).

Sophia also noted that Una was a remarkable "discerner of spirits" who was able to see into the souls of visiting adults with the unerring eye of perfect innocence and was even able to encompass the profound mystery of Margaret Fuller:

> At Margaret she gazed with earnest & ever frowning brow for a long time without recognizing her. Here she found a complex being, rich & magnificent but difficult to comprehend & of a peculiar kind, perhaps unique. But when Margaret next took her, after another examination she smiled approvingly & from that moment distinguished her by the gladdest welcome whenever she appeared, & sat in her arms with full content by the hour. She detected at last her greatness & real sweetness & love & trusted her wholly.
>
> (Family Notebook, 24 September 1844)

Just as Sophia found a vicarious life in Nathaniel, so she made a psychic counterpart of Una, with whom she could also enjoy a childlike communion.

Soon after the baby was born, Sophia initiated the practice of writing letters in the child's name. "You will consider that I am fresh from Paradise," writes Sophia/Una, "& have not learned the ways of the old world yet & therefore express my thoughts & the truth with angelic simplicity. Babies cannot be vain. They are truth itself."[20]

Sophia's impulse to merge her identity in Una's was to have unwelcome consequences. Her maternal attentiveness, however, joins her to the nineteenth-century social movement that first explored the rich mental and emotional life of babies. When Margaret Fuller visited the Old Manse in the summer of 1844, she too was fascinated by Una. "She acted like a little wild thing toward me," Margaret observed on their first encounter; and like Sophia, Margaret sought to establish spiritual communion. "Her prettiest and most marked way with me is to lean her forehead upon mine. As she does this she looks into my eyes, & I into hers. This act gives me singular pleasure. . . . It indicates I think great purity of relation."[21]

Sophia was riveted by inborn qualities of the infant that she took as revelations of the divine nature. "She listens to me . . . with comprehending attention," Sophia remarked just before Una's first birthday, "once in a while responding with that upward inflection of tone which evidently means 'Yes' & her eyes full of the deepest thought, as if her little mind was very busy. I never imagined any thing so enchanting as her rapid developments. I find I never really knew anything about an unfolding intelligence before. In heaven or earth there can be nothing more interesting & marvelous" (26 January 1845). Although Sophia found she had to suspend her former intellectual and aesthetic pursuits, her absorption in Una's life provided an equally satisfying spiritual diet. "I have no time to read anything excepting my little daughter," she wrote, "with which belle literature I am quite content" (6 March 1845).

Sophia was thrilled by Una's aggressive independence of spirit, which she likewise perceived as an innate quality. Before the child could walk, Sophia reports, she would "take a small chair & travel all about the room. When she comes hard up against an obstacle, she pushes with force enough to go through the side of the house, her cheeks deepening in color, till finally she shouts 'Make way' as loud as her lungs will let her" (12 January 1845; misdated 1844). When Una could manage without the chair, Sophia wrote a letter of celebration that begins with extra-large calligraphic capitals: "UNA WALKS ALONE! . . . Her whole being, body & soul, is wholly occupied with steering through the infinitude of space on her own responsibility. Her father calls it 'putting out to sea.' . . . It is very pretty to see her when she is undressed because then we see the action of her limbs, all in a quiver with eagerness and newly discovered power" (16 February 1845).

Una's unspoiled nature, radiant in the energy of her naked body, appeared to Sophia the harbinger of navigating on her own in adulthood. Just as the child was learning to walk, Margaret Fuller published *Woman in the Nineteenth Century,* with its demand that barriers to womanly self-development be removed, so that women could become ship-captains, if their native endowments were suited. Sophia finds just such a spirit of self-sufficient command in her daughter: "She is all awake inwardly & outwardly & so strong that her father calls her Samsona. My barricades of chairs round forbidden places such as [the] stove . . . are now of not much use. She pulls aside those great heavy oaken chairs . . . and walks off with entire independence" (16 February 1845).

Yet if Una was robust, she was also divinely pure. "Did you ever hear of a five months' baby keeping herself in perfect order so as not to be wet from morning till night—& from night till morning?" Sophia wrote to Louisa, "She sits on a funny little chair which I found up garret, & is exemplary in her proceedings thereon" (CE 16:61). Sophia asked her mother for medicine "to prevent baby from having foul breath" on those rare occasions when she ceased to smell "like clover and violets" (4 April 1844). To Sophia, Una's body is purity made flesh. Not only is her breath and bottom (mostly) sweet, but "she is in herself a perfect rose & lily of fragrance, & people who take her in their arms say they never held so *sweet* a baby. Her breath is like the perfume of a pond lily" (CE 16:61).

As Una was displaying her purity and sailor-like boldness, Nathaniel struggled unavailingly to support the family. He had written enough new tales to make up another collection, to be issued as *Mosses from an Old Manse,* and he submitted to the "humbug" of a new edition of *Twice-Told Tales.* He received a fee of $125 for editing his friend Horatio Bridge's *Journal of an African Cruiser* and was due a percentage of the profits. He also regularly turned to Bridge for loans.[22] His efforts to find a government post were incessant, especially by way of John L. O'Sullivan, the editor of the *Democratic Review* who represented Hawthorne as "dying of starvation" in the effort to obtain him an appointment at the Chelsea Hospital (CE 16:93).

Nathaniel was humiliated by gossip circulating in Salem, "the most pitiable stories about our poverty and misery; so as almost to make it appear that we were suffering for food. Everybody . . . seems tacitly to take it for granted that we are in a very desperate condition, and that a government office is the only alternative of the alms-house" (CE 16:70–71). Nathaniel did in fact lose flesh during what he called "our long Lent" (67) and feared that an extended absence from Concord would lead his creditors to believe he had run away from them (73). By late June 1845 there were creditors aplenty, as indicated in a note to an autograph seeker who surmised that Nathaniel Hawthorne was a pseudonym. "That it is my real name," Nathaniel replies, can be proved by reference not only to his own books but also to those of "the butcher, the baker, the tailor, the doctor, and the tax-gatherer, all of whom are likely to hold it in everlasting remembrance" (104).

The creditor who administered the final humiliation was the owner of the Old Manse, the Reverend Samuel Ripley. In March 1845 he informed the Hawthornes that he wanted to occupy the place himself the following spring, giving them better than a year to find a new situation. When the Hawthornes failed to pay their rent in the ensuing months (CE 16:99), Ripley proposed that they accept Caroline Sturgis as a "boarder," since she could provide some payment to the Ripleys, perhaps by way of doing the chores for which the Hawthornes were now paying their new servant, Mary Pray. Nathaniel himself was absolutely opposed to having a boarder, and when Mary Pray departed in early June he was less able than ever to afford a replacement, to say nothing of paying Ripley.

The Ripleys got rid of the Hawthornes by means of a familiar ruse. They informed Mr. Hawthorne that their plans had changed, and that they wanted the Manse early in the fall rather than the following spring. Sophia's sister Mary understood what this meant, passing along a "rumour" that Ripley did not really intend such an early move (CE 16:117). When Ripley requested on 1 September that the Hawthornes depart immediately, Nathaniel responded that he would need a month to make other arrangements, and on 2 October he and his family moved out. Ralph Waldo Emerson, who knew the Ripleys' side of the story, commented tersely that "Mr Hawthorne leaves Concord today. Mr Ripley comes not till spring" (117). Nathaniel himself summed it up in terms that underscore his powerless shame: "Our landlord has driven us out of our Paradise at Concord" (126).

In the fall of 1845, just as the expulsion was taking place, Nathaniel and Sophia conceived another child, and, given the circumstances, it is hard to believe they intended to. Rather than fulfilling the masculine ideal of economic self-sufficiency and prudent procreation, Nathaniel had quite visibly failed. During the ensuing year, as the family took lodgings with relatives in

Salem and Boston, and as Nathaniel kept hoping that an official position would come his way, he was compelled to acknowledge that he could not provide an adequate living for his wife and first child and that a second child would only make things worse. Although Nathaniel was now living at "Castle Dismal," he did not tell his mother and sisters of the pregnancy; it was Sophia—staying with her sister Mary Mann in Boston—who broke the news in a letter to Nathaniel's mother from "Una." "I read Una's note," Nathaniel wrote back, "then sealed it up and threw it down stairs. Doubtless, they find it a most interesting communication; and I feel a little shamefaced about meeting them. They will certainly rejoice at the prospect of another baby, and only temper their joy with the serious consideration of how the new-comer is to be provided for" (CE 16:129–130).

No name had been prepared for this child, and at least eight months elapsed—after his birth in June 1846—before he was given one. Sophia was partial to "Theodore" and then to "Gerald," but Nathaniel resisted both, and it may have been a full year before they were able to agree (See CE 16:201–202). Meanwhile Nathaniel called his son "Bundlebreech."

It is the opposite of "Una." Instead of sublimating the child's sexual and excretory capacities into a vision of transcendent purity, the name all too insistently calls attention to them, emphasizing the bulk of his diapers and the bundle of male genitals within them. As compared to the anxieties constraining Una, "Bundlebreech" has a refreshing air of candor. Yet behind its anti-genteel male bravado lies a deep qualm. Nathaniel had the physical capacity to father children, but could he sustain them? Did he have the moral and psychological equipment necessary for "putting out to sea," like his ship-captain father? Or would he leave his dependents to the charity of in-laws, as his father had done?

These conflicted issues had been deferred during his long solitude after college, and through his bachelor years; they were deferred again in the androgynous bliss of life at the Old Manse. During this long moratorium Nathaniel had sought to cultivate an artistic identity with intrinsic "feminine" capacities, passive and voluptuous susceptibilities that Sophia treasured in her divine "Apollo." But that identity required material support. Nathaniel gave his son a name only when he was securely established in his Custom House job and could seek a house for his wife and children that could also accommodate his mother and sisters.[23]

CHAPTER TEN

Soul-System in Salem

In his paradise at Concord Hawthorne made no money of consequence; during his service at the Salem Custom House he did little imaginative writing.[1] Hawthorne had sought to hold in abeyance the problems of gaining a livelihood while he cultivated his poetic identity; and the same root dilemma pursued him no less relentlessly now that he was bringing home regular pay. The demands of worldly manhood and those of his creative inwardness still seemed incompatible. In the late summer of 1849 the interlinked dilemmas of gender and vocation came to a head in the twofold crisis of his removal from the Custom House job and the death of his mother. These events have been taken singly as significant to the writing of *The Scarlet Letter;* befalling Hawthorne together, however, they formed a forcing-house of bitter confrontation, in which his poetic capacities were crossbred with worldly competence.

Hawthorne's battle to keep his job fused the two sides of his dual selfhood despite his effort to keep them distinct. In "The Custom House," Hawthorne pretends that he welcomed his removal from the post of surveyor because it had interfered with his true vocation as a poet, but not because the work coarsened his feminine sensibilities. On the contrary, Hawthorne claims that the monotonous security of government service had endangered his "manly character," sapping "its sturdy force, its courage and constancy, its truth, its self-reliance" and leading him to wonder whether he could stay in office much longer "and yet go forth a man" (CE 1:39–40).

Yet Hawthorne fought an intense public battle to keep the job, invoking his sacred calling to claim immunity from the squalid turmoil of spoils-system politics. He speaks scornfully of "common political brawlers" who understand nothing higher than their own dreary scrimmages (CE 16:270), but he knew that he had himself stirred up the brawl by refusing to give up the office without a fight after the Democratic party lost to the Whigs in the national elections of 1848. Charles W. Upham, a leader among his Whig opponents, was quick to point out that Hawthorne's being fired under these circumstances was "a liability to which all political office-holders are subject, and to which men of Mr. Hawthorne's true manliness of character have learned to submit with dignity and in silence" (Nissenbaum, "The Firing," 74). Hawthorne is "too old a soldier," wrote another enemy, "to whine at the fortunes of war" (67).

To acquit oneself as a man in the competitive worldly struggle is to accept the terms of the conflict, not to snivel at the misfortunes of the battlefield. But Hawthorne sought to make his presumptive exemption from the rules of combat into a fortress and to use his poetic capacities as a weapon. His rage at the "violation" of his sacred identity by his political opponents was harshened by his awareness that he had himself compromised it. Writing to Longfellow, he indulges an extended fantasy of worldly revenge, to be carried out by literary means. If his enemies prevail, Hawthorne "may perhaps select a victim"—most probably he was thinking of Charles Upham—

> and let fall one little drop of venom on his heart, that shall make him writhe before the grin of the multitude for a considerable time to come. This I will do, not as an act of individual vengeance, but in your behalf as well as mine, because he will have violated the sanctity of the priesthood to which we both, in our different degrees, belong. I do not claim to be a poet; and yet I cannot but feel that some of the sacredness of that character adheres to me, and ought to be respected in me, unless I step out of its immunities.
>
> (CE 16:270)

The interior contradictions of this outburst arise straight from the conflicts in which Hawthorne's poetic calling was now enmeshed. He claims membership in the "priesthood" so as to battle his greedy political competitors, who would not be so quick to challenge him if they realized that even in defeat he can damage their reputations by exercising his priestly powers.

Hawthorne's claim to have kept himself untainted by the squalor of politics was a readily demonstrable falsehood. He had authorized the assignment of overtime work to inspectors who were members of the local Democratic party, with half of their additional wages being paid back into the party treasury. When certain party members refused to pay the kickbacks, Hawthorne gave them letters suspending them temporarily from their jobs. His chances of keeping the surveyorship were destroyed when his enemies made public his role in this routine of political graft and extortion. But even had he never acted as an enforcer of party discipline, Hawthorne's sacred poetic identity would have been politicized. The Salem Democrats did not need Hawthorne's administrative skills to make the political machine work. His political value consisted in his name, his reputation as a man distinguished for achievements "above" the political tumult. Publishing literary reviews in the local Democratic newspaper was a political act; and the party featured him as a member of the Democratic Town Committee and a delegate to the state party convention, though he took no part in either (Nissenbaum, "The Firing," 80).

Hawthorne retained the traditional conception of literary endeavor as a gentleman's diversion, the avocation of a man whose social and economic advantages were secure. He sought to retain such an identity in an era of unprecedented commercialization, in which book publishing became an industry serving a mass market. Hawthorne shared the difficulty that Mary Kelley describes as plaguing the women who made a profession of writing, that of becoming public figures who market an identity that retains a distinctive quality of the private. The "classic" male writers of this period negotiated the paradox of the public and private, not because it was considered unsuitable for a man to have a public role but because their sense of the writer's true identity featured the stewardship of an inward flame of inspiration, antithetical to the sordid traffic of the marketplace. As women writers were struggling with the prohibition against "masculine" undertakings, male writers were forced—like clergymen—to confront the feminization of their social role. Even after he was celebrated as the choicest ornament of American letters, Hawthorne knew that several women had attained far more economic success as writers than he, and his humiliation prompted the famous outburst to his publisher, that the public taste was taken up by a "d——d mob of scribbling women."[2]

For now, however, a major effect of the Custom House fiasco was to harden his sense of the literary profession as a competitive enterprise. Writing to Evert Duyckinck in despair over being ejected from his paradise at the Old Manse, Hawthorne had recognized that the demands of the marketplace forbade his continuing as a writer of tales and sketches. It was necessary now to attempt a book-length work and to court the public. His letter to James T. Fields about publishing *The Scarlet Letter* amply demonstrates the resentment Hawthorne brought to this task. He considers whether the narrative of Hester Prynne might not be published together with several shorter tales, envisioning the public as quarry to be slain. "A hunter loads his gun with a bullet and several buck-shot; and, following his sagacious example, it was my purpose to conjoin the one long story with half a dozen shorter ones." Hawthorne stifled genteel qualms about the sexual titillation of his subject matter and considered whether "The Judgment Letter," would make a better title than anything "Scarlet." But as he thinks this over, an additional marketing idea comes to him, which the publisher adopted: "If 'The Scarlet Letter' is to be the title, would it not be well to print it on the title-page in red ink? I am not quite sure about the good taste of so doing; but it would certainly be piquant and appropriate—and, I think, attractive to the great gull whom we are endeavoring to circumvent" (CE 16:307–308).

In soliciting buyers by devices of questionable taste, Hawthorne bottled up an inward distress whose dimensions the novel itself explores, the dilemmas of a gender system requiring men to form and maintain a public identity, while women cultivate in retirement a sensitivity to the moral mysteries of the human heart. Since these definitions make Hester Prynne a manly woman and Arthur Dimmesdale a womanly man, their relationship richly elaborates these issues, but the disposition with which Hawthorne took them up was strongly conditioned by his strenuous determination to assume a "manly" posture.

Hawthorne's harsh inner turmoil is suggested by a daguerreotype image that survives from this period (Fig. 5). His mouth is drawn tight beneath coldly glaring eyes, and his arms are locked behind him, making the shoulders rigid. In telling contrast against the beautiful Osgood painting he gave his mother (see Fig. 4), this Hawthorne is wary, hostile, and tightly controlled. Whether requested by Fields or by John L. O'Sullivan, the picture seems to have been made in an effort to put Hawthorne before the public, "manufacturing you thus into a Personage," as O'Sullivan termed it. It appears that Sophia vigorously disliked the picture, not surprisingly, and would not allow it to be published.[3]

As news of the Hawthornes' return to poverty spread, George Hillard took up a collection for them. Hawthorne did not shrink from confessing that Hillard's generosity had moved him to tears. "I read your letter in the entry of the Post-Office; and it drew—what my troubles never have—the water to my eyes; so that I was glad of the sharply cold west wind that blew

Fig. 5.   Daguerreotype of Nathaniel Hawthorne, 1848

into them as I came homeward, and gave them an excuse for being red and bleared." The gift had driven home—so Hawthorne relates—a hard lesson concerning the maintenance of manly self-respect. "Ill-success in life is really and justly a matter of shame. I am ashamed of it, and I ought to be. The fault of a failure is attributable—in a great degree, at least—to the man who fails. I should apply this truth in judging of other men; and it behoves me not to shun its point or edge in taking it home to my own heart. Nobody has a right to live in this world, unless he be strong and able, and applies his ability to good purpose" (CE 16:309).

Four years later—after *The Scarlet Letter* had been followed in quick succession by *The House of the Seven Gables, A Wonder Book, The Snow Image, The Blithedale Romance,* the campaign biography of Franklin Pierce, and the appointment as consul at Liverpool—Hawthorne was able to repay the sum with interest. These years of relentless effort, Hawthorne explains, were driven by his determination to remove the shame of accepting it. "I have always hoped to . . . [repay], from the first moment when I made up my mind to accept the money. It would not have been right to speak of this purpose, before it was in my power to accomplish it; but it has never been out of my mind for a single day, nor hardly, I think, for a single waking hour" (CE 17: 154–155).

Hillard had offered the sum as imperfectly covering "the debt we owe you for what you have done for American literature."[4] But Hawthorne insists on treating it as a business proposition—an unsecured loan at interest, rather than a grant—since it brought him the supreme moral benefit: "making me sensible of the necessity of sterner efforts than my former ones, in order to establish a right for myself to live and be comfortable. For it is my creed (and was so, even at that wretched time) that a man has no claim upon his fellow creatures, beyond bread and water, and a grave, unless he can win it by his own strength and skill" (CE 17: 154–155).

In the androgynous paradise of Concord, Hawthorne had sought to live by the opposite creed. There, an exemption from the harsh struggle seemed necessary to the poetic nature he was cultivating. Even the trouble of putting in a vegetable garden grated on his sensibilities: "There is . . . an abominable quantity of labor to be done, or which ought to be done," he had complained. "I hate all labor, but less that of the hands than of the head" (CE 8:386). Sophia knew well how to coddle such proclivities and gloried in the divine creativenesss they expressed. "Dearest husband, thou shouldst not have to labour . . . & thou hatest it rightfully. Thou art a seraph come to observe Nature & men in still repose. . . . The Flower of Time should only unfold. It should be put to no Use. I wish I could be Midas long enough to turn into sufficient gold for thy life's sustenance & embellishment whatever I touch. But woe's me! I can do nothing but love thee" (Family Notebook, 9 May 1843).

Yet Sophia's worship also expresses an ambition she could not satisfy as the wife of a surveyor of custom, no matter how stable might be the resultant income. She had chafed at the interruption of her husband's literary endeavors, and was "overjoyed"—so the family legend runs—when he came home to say he had been fired. " 'Oh,' said his wife, gayly, 'now you can write your Romance!' " When he asked her how the family was to be fed, she produced a substantial sum of money, and to his astonished question how she had obtained it, she replied, "You earned it."[5]

Nathaniel knew nothing, it appears, about the way Sophia managed the household budget. He had simply turned his paychecks over to her and applied to her when he wanted cash for his own needs. He had no idea she had been laying money aside. This parable of wifely solicitude illustrates a major paradox in the cultural construction of domesticity at large, the close economic connections between the "woman's sphere" of home and the ostensibly separate outward world. As much as the gift/loan from Hillard, Sophia's sacrificial management of the domestic economy put Hawthorne on his manly mettle. His "ownest," "belovedest," "own self," in whom he had sought a psychic anchor for his unworldly poetic identity, had displayed more worldly shrewdness and foresight than he concerning the sponsorship of time for writing. During the months in which he composed *The Scarlet Letter,* she continued to bring in money by decorating cambric lampshades for sale (G. P. Lathrop, "Biographical Sketch," 497).

Nathaniel's mental life was shaken to its foundations by his mother's death. His literary identity, with its fragile aura of sacred privilege, was grounded in a prior selfhood that still bound him to her. "In taking to myself a wife," he had written home after their wedding, "I have neither given up my own relatives, nor adopted others" (CE 15:639). The issues underlying his maternal fixation were never to be resolved, nor was the anguish it entailed. But as his mother lay dying, Nathaniel sensed that the "involuntary reserve" that shielded him from unmanageable emotion was threatening to give way:

> I love my mother; but there has been, ever since my boyhood, a sort of coldness of
> intercourse between us, such as is apt to come between persons of strong feelings, if

they are not managed rightly. I did not expect to be much moved at the time—that is to say, not to feel any overpowering emotion struggling, just then—though I knew that I should deeply remember and regret her. Mrs. Dike was in the chamber. Louisa pointed to a chair near the bed; but I was moved to kneel down close by my mother, and take her hand. She knew me, but could only murmur a few indistinct words—among which I understood an injunction to take care of my sisters. Mrs. Dike left the chamber, and then I found the tears slowly gathering in my eyes. I tried to keep them down; but it would not be—I kept filling up, till, for a few moments, I shook with sobs. For a long time, I knelt there, holding her hand; and surely it is the darkest hour I ever lived.

(CE 8:429)

The woman Nathaniel refers to as "Mrs. Dike" was his aunt Priscilla, who had known him intimately since he was four. She had joined in the Mannings' effort to bring him up properly, insisting that he prepare himself for a constructive adult life instead of "playing about the yard" all day (Erlich 38, 44). "Madame Hathorne," by contrast, had indulged her children's waywardness; yet she had found no way to secure young Nathaniel's future other than to put him through the course of schooling that the Mannings planned out and paid for. A source of the "coldness" between Hawthorne and his mother may well lie in his confused resentment at having been encouraged to defy necessities to which he would eventually be required to submit. Only so long as he was a child within her protection could he indulge his own whims, and when he was forced to shoulder manly responsibilities, he suffered the liability of feeling that they wronged his nature.

The beautiful cherished boy was now forty-six years old. He had succeeded in proving that writing tales would not support a family, while his efforts to secure a regular income had yielded two short-lived civil service jobs. Hawthorne could not be certain what his mother was trying to say, though he knew she was speaking to him, and he hears an expression of well-founded anxiety: "an injunction to take care of my sisters." Although Elizabeth and Louisa had a little income, they looked to Nathaniel for help. More than once during the years at the Old Manse he had apologized for his inability to send money.[6] Now that the Custom House position was all but lost, they faced again the prospect of desolate penury.

What "Mrs. Dike" made of all this is not knowable directly. But it is hardly likely she viewed the wretchedness of Mrs. Hathorne's death, the financial incompetence of her expensively educated son, and the threatened destitution of his sisters as a poignant stage in the development of Hawthorne's godlike genius. Nor is it likely that Priscilla looked on her dying sister as a creature of tragic beauty who, with uncanny faithfulness to her son's promise, had promoted the conditions in which—albeit belatedly—he would rise to the first rank of living writers for a masterwork of ravishing beauty and truth. The only person attending the death of Mrs. Hathorne who could have embraced such rapturous conceptions, so obviously delusionary and so soon to be fulfilled, was Sophia; and Sophia's testimony suggests that Aunt Priscilla took a very cold view. "Mrs. Dike has been like some marble-souled fiend. But of that I cannot speak now, or perhaps ever. I hope God will forgive her, but I do not see how He can!" For Nathaniel the psychic agony was virtually unendurable; after this hour with his mother, Sophia relates, he came near suffering a "brain fever."[7]

His mother's death stirred up a deep and compounded grief; the loss of his father and the resultant stunting of his mother's life had bequeathed him a virtually unlivable existence. After his sobbing ended, Hawthorne stood at the window, "and now, through the crevice of the curtain, I saw my little Una of the golden locks, looking very beautiful; and so full of spirit and life, that she was life itself. And then I looked at my poor dying mother; and seemed to see the whole of human existence at once, standing in the dusty midst of it. Oh what a mockery, if what I saw were all,—let the interval between extreme youth and dying age be filled up with what happiness it might!" (CE 8:429). The lifespan reaching from Una's childhood to his mother's deathbed makes human life appear a woman's doom in which innate promise is wrongfully thwarted and human dignity intolerably affronted.

Nathaniel looks to Una for assurance that personal existence does not end at the grave. If there were "nothing beyond," he declares "it would have been a fiend that created us, . . . and not God. It would be something beyond wrong—it would be insult—to be thrust out of life into annihilation in this miserable way." Yet the child does not provide comfort. "Little Una's voice came up, very clear and distinct, into the chamber—'Yes;—she is going to die.' I wish she had said 'going to God'—which is her idea and usual expression of death; it would have been so hopeful and comforting, uttered in that bright young voice" (CE 8:429–430).

Looking to Una for divine consolation, Nathaniel is startled by glimmers of the fiendlike. Not only does the child speak bluntly of death, but she is also fascinated by the slow failure of his mother's body. Nathaniel is appalled by this specter of annihilation, while Una "takes a strong and strange interest in poor mother's condition, and can hardly be kept out of the chamber— endeavoring to thrust herself into the door, whenever it is opened" (CE 8:430). On the day following Nathaniel's paroxysm of sobbing, Una playacts the deathbed scene in hypnotic detail: "She groans, and speaks with difficulty, and moves herself feebly and wearisomely—then lies perfectly still, as if in an insensible state. Then rouses herself, and calls for wine. Then lies down on her back, with clasped hands—then puts them to her head." As Nathaniel witnesses this performance, he is startled to realize that the child appears to take pleasure in torturing him. "It recalls the scene of yesterday to me," Hawthorne writes, "with a frightful distinctness; and out of the midst of it, little Una looks at me with a smile of glee" (431).[8]

Returning Nathaniel to the darkest hour he ever lived, Una appeared to him an unaccountable compound of the divine and the demonic. "I now and then catch an aspect of her," he muses, "in which I cannot believe her to be my own human child, but a spirit strangely mingled with good and evil, haunting the house where I dwell" (CE 8:430–431). Hawthorne was intuitively aware that the enigma in Una's nature was somehow linked to the dilemmas of gender and vocation that were carried forward into the writing of *The Scarlet Letter,* during "the period of hardly accomplished revolution and still seething turmoil in which the story shaped itself" (CE 1:43). There seemed to him an uncanny communion between his own severest torments and the strange soul of this child.

In modeling the character of Pearl on Una, Hawthorne sought to make sense of the enigma he saw in her. His experience of domestic intimacy, since its inauguration at the Old Manse, now moved him to envision "the symbol of the one true union in the world, and of our love in paradise" as "the scarlet letter endowed with life." Yet this transformation did not occur exclusively in Hawthorne's imagination, as though it were an autonomous center of creative alchemy. The "hell-fire" in which the book was written had cast its glow on the hearthside of his Salem household.

Sophia wrote to Horatio Bridge in December 1846 to congratulate him on his marriage. "Human beings are wretched Arabs, until they find central points in other human beings around which all their highest & richest sentiments shall revolve. Every true & happy family is a soul-system that outshines all the solar-systems in space & time" (CE 16:193–194). The systemic character of family relations is stronger than Sophia asserts; rather than being solitary until they form families, persons exist communally from the outset.[9] Hawthorne was torn at his mother's deathbed by conflicts instilled in him when he was a child; Una's personality was likewise receiving an imprint that would never be effaced. Erik Erikson once remarked that insofar as psychic illness is the consequence of trouble in one's family of origin, it gains a cosmic forgivableness; yet since it produces mental agony in one's children, it seems equally unforgivable. In *The Scarlet Letter*, Hawthorne made his own the harsh side of this observation, blaming himself for his daughter's misery; but that gesture also took place within the soul-system.

The outward pattern of the Hawthornes' life changed dramatically after their departure from Concord in October 1845. Their precious seclusion gave way completely for eleven chaotic months: Nathaniel and Sophia lived for a while in Salem at Castle Dismal; then Nathaniel stayed on with his mother and sisters while Sophia and Una moved to Boston; then they all returned briefly to Castle Dismal before moving again to Boston, where Bundlebreech was born and Nathaniel commuted to his job at the Custom House. In August 1846 they all finally settled in Salem, in a small house on Chestnut Street. But a new arrangement was established: their daily lives conformed to the division between "man's world" and "woman's sphere." At the Old Manse Nathaniel had read his tales to Sophia, sometimes while they were still taking form; and before Una was born, Sophia had struggled with her painting while he labored over his stories. Now Nathaniel left the household every morning to go to his job, in a realm wholly alien from Sophia's. Her letter to Bridge offers a bit of news about his work at the Custom House, to which Nathaniel appends a contemptuous postscript: "My wife knows no more about these matters than I do about baby-linen" (CE 16:194).

Sophia responded to her exclusion from Nathaniel's working life by assuming control of her "babydom," exercising the authority that was celebrated by heralds of the domestic ideal. "You have gained an increase of power," Lydia Sigourney informed new mothers. "How entire and perfect is this dominion, over the unformed character of your infant. Write what you will, upon that printless tablet, with your wand of love" (10). Yet Sophia did not see an unformed soul in Una; on the contrary, the child evidently possessed the same boldness and independence of spirit with which she herself had been endowed. "Una's force is immense," Sophia declared.

> I am glad to see such will since there is also a fund of loveliness. No one, I think, has the right to break the will of a child, but God; and if the child is taught to submit to Him through love, all other submission will follow with heavenly effect upon the character. God never drives even the most desperate sinner, but only invites or suggests through the events of His providence. I remember my own wilfulness, and how I used to think, when quite a child, that God was gentle and never frowned upon me, and that I would try more and more to be gentle to everybody in gratitude to Him.

(NHW 1:306-307)

The work of loving motherhood does not include breaking a child's will; the mother establishes an intimate bond with her child that elicits an ethical consciousness the child will recognize as God's voice. Sophia's sister Mary Mann, in *The Moral Culture of Infancy,* insisted that mothers should make children aware that God has "given everybody a conscience which was sometimes called 'the voice of God within us'" (147). Sophia faithfully recorded that "for many months Una has liked very much to hold certain conversations after going to bed . . . of behaviour & goodness—GOD and Christ. . . . [This evening] she was very full of thought. 'I am sorry for all who do wrong'—said she—'very very sorry. I pity all, but I think that those who have had kind mothers to tell them what is right & yet choose the wrong, are the most wicked'" (Family Notebook, 9 February 1850).

Sophia's success at conscience-building was demonstrated in a crisis that arose while the Hawthornes were sharing the house with Nathaniel's mother and sisters. Una formed the custom of paying her aunt Elizabeth a daily visit. "On one occasion, however, when her mother was about sending her up as usual, Una said, 'I don't want to go to Aunt Ebe any more!' 'Why not?' her mother inquired. 'Because,' Una replied, 'Aunt Ebe makes me naughty. She gives me candy; and when I tell her you don't let me have candy, she says, "Oh, never mind; your mother will never know!"'" (*NHW* 1:328). A confrontation followed, Una's visits ceased, and Aunt Ebe became an "invisible entity" in the household.

Yet a lifelong friendship formed between Una and her aunt Elizabeth, at whose heart was a protest against Sophia's suffocating moral tyranny. "She always said that her Mother would be utterly astounded," Elizabeth observed, "at the things she was in the habit of saying to me." Una had been imprisoned during childhood in Sophia's mind, Elizabeth believed, pointing out that the child was not taught to read until she was seven years old, "and then she was forbidden to practice it. Her mother wished to keep her children in complete mental dependence upon herself. She would read to them in such books as suited herself." To be sure, Elizabeth hardly provides unbiased testimony; she bitterly hated Sophia and remarked what a "comfort" it was to "ascribe every infelicity and every short-coming to her."[10]

Sophia's obsessive involvement with her children's lives, however, was noted even by persons who dearly loved her. Mrs. Peabody urged her to develop social relationships in Salem that would give her a break from child-care; Sophia refused. "I have not been to church since Una was born, nor spent an evening away from home. I should like very much [to go to church]. . . . but I must wait till the children are old enough to go with me.

I shall never leave them with hired people for any reason whatever—And it is no cross to me to be confined to them. I consider it to be the highest privilege to be able to be their sole attendant" (30 August 1846). Nathaniel likewise noted Sophia's absorption. "Thou must not fear to leave Una occasionally," he wrote when the child was three months old. "I shall not love her, if she imprisons thee when thy health requires thee to be abroad" (CE 16:47). But Sophia insisted on keeping her child within reach. After Julian's birth three years later, Sophia decided that Aunt Louisa might be able to watch *one* of them, but only so that she herself can take the other for a walk. Sophia concedes that "it is barely possible that I may take a real walk with my husband again while in the body, and leave both children at home with an easy mind" (NHW 1:314).

Caring properly for Una was impossible, it seemed to Sophia, when other children were about. In March 1846 her sister Mary Mann invited her to take a house on Carver Street in Boston that the Manns were soon to vacate, but Sophia refused to come until they had actually moved out. "Keeping peace between Una and Mary's two children would be hard," Sophia explains. "It would worry my soul every minute to have the children together. . . . I cannot bear to have her loving ways repelled, nor her opposition excited by constant rebuff." Describing the "conversations & dramas" that Una ceaselessly devises with her dolls, Sophia proudly observes that they are "original," since "she has never seen nor heard children play" (22 March 1846).

"Una has had a day of infinite ennui," Sophia noted when the child was three, "like a bird with wings tied to its side. 'I'm tired.' 'I am *tired!*' was her cry all day. Finally she sighed out 'I am so tired I wish I could slip into GOD!' I read her Miss Barbauld's Hymns & her eyes looked vast & deep as she listened—at last she did not want to hear—she said she was tired of lying down, & of sitting up & of reading & of all sings" (Family Notebook, 20 June 1847). Nathaniel recorded Una's litany of tedium on the same day, and probed toward its sources in the family's life. " 'I'm tired of all sings, and want to slip into God. I'm tired of little Una Hawsorne.' 'Are you tired of Mamma?' 'No.' 'But you are tired of Papa?' 'No.' 'I am tired of Dora [the maid], and tired of little Julian, and tired of little Una Hawsorne.' " Two years later Nathaniel observed that "it would be an excellent thing to send her to school" because "we should see no more of this premature ennui," and Una would "have a much happier childhood than . . . we can secure to her by a home-education." Yet he concedes "there are reasons of greater weight on the other side," in language that clearly echoes Sophia's view: "Unless an angel should come down from Heaven for the purpose, I should hardly be willing to trust her to any schoolmistress" (CE 8:398, 422).

In *The Moral Culture of Infancy*, Mary Mann warned against the "home influence" becoming "too exclusive and oppressive" (186). Because families cannot offer a sufficient "variety of views," the minds of children "cannot easily expand, still less choose the best of several good ways. I have seen the victims of private education perpetuate family faults, and in later life left standing alone in the world, knowing little of its interests, and having no sympathy from without. I have seen morbid sensibility thus nourished into insanity itself" (190).[11]

Nathaniel and Sophia of course possessed notably divergent impulses and views. Sophia became obsessed with governing her "babydom" in part because there she could assert herself against his imperial domination; and his subsurface hostility toward the children resulted from his resentment at their having displaced him as the object of Sophia's mothering attention. But this opposition did not provide Una with psychic options; all potential conflicts were absorbed into the solid front of marital unity that husband and wife sustained for each other, and for which they had named her. Their "oneness" was rife with conflict that could not be acknowledged, so that Una was denied psychological room to maneuver and to find her own distinct reality. She could not do otherwise than subscribe to their strenuous claims of felicity.

"How I love thee!—how I love our children! Can it be that we are really parents!—that two beautiful lives have gushed out of our life!" So Nathaniel rhapsodized in the summer of 1847, when Sophia kept the children at her parents' home in Boston. Nathaniel wishes she could "now and then stand apart from thy lot, in the same manner, and behold how fair it is. I think we are very happy—a truth that is not always so evident to me, until I step aside from our daily life" (CE 16: 212). Sophia in reply tacitly scolds his dissatisfaction.

> *I* do not need to stand apart from our daily life to see how fair & blest is our lot, because it is the mother's vocation to be in the midst of little cares & great blisses & the little cares make no account by the side of the great blisses. . . . This I tell thee all the time, but thou canst not believe it. . . . In the very center of simultaneous screams from both darling little throats, I am quite as sensible of my happiness as when the most dulcet sounds are issuing thence. The screams are transient & superficial. The beauty & lovliness & nobleness & grace which possess me in the shape of these fairest children which enchant all peoples—these lay hold on the basis of being—these are permanent & immortal. . . . Above all, beyond them is thyself—who art my everlasting satisfaction—my ever present felicity—my pride & glory & sup-

port—my sufficiency. . . . I am the happiest of women. Thou, beloved, oughtst not to be obliged to undergo the wear & tear of the nursery. It is contrary to thy nature and to thy mood. Thou wast born to muse & to be silent & through undisturbed dreams, to enlighten the world. I have suffered only for thee in my babydom. When I can once shut thee away in thy study & shew thee our jewels only when they are shining—then it will be unalloyed delight day by day."[12]

This letter is a monument to repressed motherly and matrimonial fury. Sophia at times wanted to slit the darling little screaming throats, and Nathaniel's throat as well. She accordingly found a degree of satisfaction in Una's increasing disobedience and tantrums. Mrs. Peabody, alarmed at Una's misbehavior, urged Sophia to exercise firmer discipline; but Sophia reasserted her faith in the child's independent and defiant soul:

> Una is a superb child & I do not feel troubled at all about her pranks, because they are all innocent as regards herself, and only troublesome & inconvenient to others. . . . She is all nobleness and sweetness, & her crack-of-doom *NO* which always raises the roof of the house, will serve her a good turn in maturer life, & so will her independent choice in action. She will never be made an automaton of while the breath of life is in her—I do not care for her not obeying in every point, because she does not disobey from sullenness, nor obstinacy, nor want of love—but because she chooses another way. . . . I have no pride of authority which I desire her to gratify. She is much more satisfactory to me than if she were very docile & less trouble & in consequence what people call "good."
>
> (8–9 August 1846)

A major source of the distress underlying Una's explosive rages—as well as her ennui—was the advent of her little brother. Sophia stoutly affirmed that Una "has never once, in the smallest thing or greatest, shown the least shadow of jealousy, though I was always her sole companion & nurse for so long a time" (30 August 1846). Considering Sophia's knack for identifying hostility in the act of denying its existence, this remark might be accepted as sufficient evidence of sibling rivalry. Yet the birth of Julian did more than present a competitor for the adoring attention Una already had to share with her father; it also imposed with redoubled force the requirements of "feminine" conduct.

Conceived as a being fresh from the shores of paradise, Julian brought with him seemingly innate masculine qualities that threw into relief the divine femininity Sophia now saw in his sister. His parents gave him nicknames—in addition to Bundlebreech—that accentuated his manly force: they called him "the Black Prince" and "the infant Hercules." They had called Una "Samsona" when she was a toddler, but now her robust aggression is found to make way for selfless solicitude, a character both tender and fragile. She "looks like 'Fairy Gold-hair' beside him," Sophia relates; "she is opaline in lustre and delicacy, & she loves him most dearly" (12 November 1846).

Sophia explains that Una recognizes her brother's essential goodness in spite of his infuriating conduct. "If he seizes her hair with his titan-grasp so as to hurt a good deal, she disengages herself as gently as possible & succeeds in smiling instead of crying, because she knows he has no design of hurting her & she likes to have him do anything whatever to her, because it is he" (12 November 1846).

Sophia foresees "the most charming relation" between her daughter and her son. "She will I think repose securely in his large, genial, generous heart, & feel protected by his brave mind," while "her exquisite delicacy & loveliness of soul will touch with beauty every point of his character" (12 November 1846). Una will show her brother sweet forbearance, not in compliance with social convention, but because of her inner nature. Una faced a relentless pressure to deny her own impulses when they crossed the divinely innocent hair-pulling impulses of her brother; and this yielded an increasingly pronounced remoteness in Una's character that was subsumed into her presumptively divine endowment of feminine delicacy.

"She looks more like a seraph than ever by the side of his sturdiness," Sophia writes.

> She develops more & more that exquisite delicacy of soul which transcends all culture & never *can* be taught. At what makes most children shout and laugh—she bursts into tears—I mean anything grotesque or unseemly. . . . On account of her deepest sentiment, so deep & genuine, she cannot bear any vehement expression of it in others. She seems to wish to veil & to have veiled all profound emotion. She makes me think [of] Mozart sometimes from the fineness of [her] organization both physical & mental.
>
> (18–20 September 1846)

The misery of this little girl thus becomes a parable of the psychic entrapment of women. The torment imposed on her by the domestic ideal acts to endow that ideal with the uncanny glow of transcendent truth. Sophia finds in her daughter the same "exquisite delicacy of soul" she cherished in herself, the essence of her own childlike womanhood. Sophia describes Una taking "the character of a housewife" on the occasion of her eagerly volunteering to wash the dishes and focuses attention on the "opaline" quality of Una's inward changefulness, all the more divinely mysterious because it is hidden behind a veil. As Una stands on a chair to reach the washbasin on the kitchen table, Sophia gazes with fascination at "her bright hair half veiling her sweet little face." It looks to her like "a pearl glancing through sunbeams" (18–20 September 1846).

It was not solely through her relation to Sophia, however, that Una came to resemble a pearl.

Nathaniel's entries in the family journal during this period describe the children's behavior in remarkable detail. He himself participates in several of the scenes and on occasion writes as the events take place before him. The entries resemble home videos, in which the person operating the camera is acknowledged to be at work by the people being taped and from time to time turns the camera on himself.

The domestic ideal obscured the father's role in child rearing; in keeping with the convention, Nathaniel defers to Sophia's judgments about managing the children. Yet nothing could forestall his enormous power to shape the children's lives, especially since it was household doctrine that he was a model of moral perfection. Nathaniel and Sophia shared a secret admiration for womanly strength, and both covertly encouraged Una's independence of spirit; both checked her, however, when she responded to that encouragement openly. But Nathaniel's gestures of prohibition were not merely dutiful, as were Sophia's; they were laden with anxiety, and at times with malice and disgust.

Nathaniel was delighted when Una submitted to Julian's aggression. "Una is in her sweetest mood," Nathaniel once noted, "and bears with [Julian's] unreasonableness like a little saint. Just now, when she was doing her best to amuse him, he struck her; whereupon she looked up so martyrlike that it was most touching to behold;—not with that sort of martyrdom, either, that is more provoking than the utmost malice and impatience" (CE 8:408).

Like Sophia, Nathaniel observes the "opaline" beauty produced by Una's effort to contain her inward confusions, and he tries to see it as a revelation of her soul, but with imperfect success. "Her beauty is the most flitting, transitory, most uncertain and unaccountable affair, that ever had a real existence," he observes.

> It beams out when nobody expects it; it has mysteriously passed away, when you think yourself sure of it;—if you glance sideways at her, you perhaps think it is illuminating

her face, but, turning full round to enjoy it, it is gone again. Her mother sees it much oftener than I do; yet, neither is the revelation always withheld from me. When really visible, it is rare and precious as the vision of an angel; it is a transfiguration—a grace, delicacy, an ethereal fineness, which, at once, in my secret soul, makes me give up all severe opinions that I may have begun to form respecting her. It is but fair to conclude, that, on these occasions, we see her real soul; when she seems less lovely, we merely see something external. But, in truth, one manifestation belongs to her as much as another; for, before the establishment of principles, what is character but the series and succession of moods?

(CE 8:413)

The Hawthornes sought to establish principles that would confirm Una's ethereal fineness. "It is a very good discipline for Una to carry a book on her head," Nathaniel later observes,

> not merely physical discipliné, but moral as well; for it implies a restraint upon her usual giddy, impetuous . . . demeanor. She soon, however, begins to move with great strides, and sudden jerks, and to tumble about in extravagant postures;—a very unfortunate tendency that she has; for she is never graceful or beautiful, except when perfectly quiet. Violence—exhibitions of passion—strong expression of any kind— destroy her beauty. Her voice, face, gestures—every manifestation, in short—becomes disagreeable.

(CE 8:420)

Hawthorne found Una's irregular conduct particularly alarming because it appeared to arise from a disordered nature. He begins to form "severe opinions," not about Una's behavior, but about the child herself. Julian's misbehavior seems basically good-hearted; he "is a little outlaw or pirate— fonder, I think, of mischief than Una, and yet, more easily kept within rules. Now he has stolen the book I was reading, and refuses to give it up. . . . All this in perfect good humor." Una disobeys less frequently than Julian, but her disobedience is never playful. Nathaniel observes the note of defiance that Sophia treasured as a mark of her independent spirit, but he finds it sinister. "When Una is mischievous—which is not often—there seems to me a little spice of ill-nature in it, though I suppose her mother will not agree to this" (CE 8:407).

It was a household custom in Salem for the children to romp about naked before they were put to bed, and Nathaniel's description of Julian strikes again the note of boyish good humor. It delights him to look upon the animal vitality of his son: his appetite, his pleasure, and his mischievous little penis. "Enter mamma with the milk. He sits on his mother's knee, gulping the milk with grunts and sighs of satisfaction—nor ceases till the cup is exhausted, once, and again, and again—and even then asks for more. On being undressed, he is taking an air-bath—he enjoys the felicity of utter nakedness—running away . . . with cries of remonstrance, when she wishes to put on his night-gown. Now ensues a terrible catastrophe—not to be mentioned in our seemly history" (CE 8:402).

When Una was learning to walk, Sophia had been delighted by her naked vitality, and Nathaniel certainly takes notice of her body during the Salem years. But he does not celebrate Una's earthy force: on the contrary, his admiring comments illustrate the decorum that was swiftly becoming conventional in the discourse of respectable Victorian families, whereby repression draws pointed attention to erotically loaded circumstances. "Una is dressed in a dark, shaded, mousselin de laine morning gown, which her mother thinks unbecoming to her complexion; she being fair. But I think she never looked more comely in anything, perhaps owing to its cut—it not descending so far to conceal her very praiseworthy legs, below the knee" (CE 8:399). Nathaniel conveys his pleasure in the child's body by fastidiously obscuring it. His eye is taken not by the color of the gown, but by its cut, how it draws a line between what lies innocently below the knee, and what lies above. The term "very praiseworthy" participates in the same anxiety: to describe concretely what pleases him would convey an excitement Nathaniel considered impure. He found his daughter's thighs and buttocks sexually appealing, and as she romped about the house, she revealed what he wanted—yet did not want—to see. "Una is performing gymnastics by tumbling over a chair, thereby discovering much length of leg, which—to give them their due—are the only handsome legs that I ever knew a child to have" (CE 8:415).

Nathaniel could not celebrate Una's "felicity of utter nakedness" when she took her air-bath. Her exuberant prancing aroused a strong conscientious impulse to bring her (and thus himself) under control.

> Little Una . . . has an air-bath for a moment or two. Then complaining of cold, father wraps her in a blanket;—she resists—father insists—there is a terrible struggle—and she gets into almost a frenzy; which is now gradually subsiding and sobbing itself away, in her mother's arms. Meantime, Julian sits on father's knee, and sees him write—making remarks in some unknown tongue. He gets down and goes to Mamma, saying 'Nona'—(Una)—not knowing what to make of the scene that has just passed.
>   (CE 8:405–406)

This struggle carried Una beyond her own control, yet Nathaniel predicts that she will be angelic once the convulsive rage is out of her system. "Una is now quiet—having expended all her forces—and will probably be sweet and gentle in her next manifestations. And so it proves—she comes out of the trouble like the moon out of a cloud—with no shadow of sulkiness hanging about her. Or rather, perhaps, like a rose-bud out of a thunder-shower; for there is a sort of dewy softness remaining, although there is the brightness of sunshine in her smile" (CE 8:406).

The tantrum had the effect of a spiritual purification, and the emotional atmosphere has returned to normal, or to a state of dewy brightness even better than normal. But the inward filth that has been purged away—the dark thermodynamics that produced the thunder and lightning—are inherent in not only the relation between Hawthorne and Una but also the divided self that Una is forming. The irony could hardly be more terrible: Una now finds within herself the uncanny mutability of a Duessa.[13] Spenser's great monster—a classic imaginative achievement of anxious male power denigrating female sexuality—becomes an active agent in this five-year-old girl's mental life.

The reciprocal interplay of Nathaniel's fascinated repugnance and Una's inner tumult is sharpened as the entries continue. One evening Nathaniel leaves for a walk during the tense period before bedtime, but not before forming a clear mental picture of the conduct that disgusts him. Una is "running about the room in her chemise, which does not come down far enough to serve the purpose of a fig-leaf; never were seen such contortions and attitudinizing—prostrating herself on all fours, and thrusting up her little bum as a spectacle to men and angels, being among the least grotesque" (CE 8:417). Do Una's giddy antics reveal an inward awareness of doing something "bad"? Does she thrust up her anus as a gesture of defiance? Or does she simply want to catch her father's attention before he goes out the door? To ask such questions is to realize that Una had no choice but to respond to her father's disgust, and on this occasion he reacts as though she is "attitudinizing," aggressively seeking to provoke him.

At times it appears to Nathaniel that an alien presence has invaded Una's body, becoming most active when she gives herself up to strenuous play. He watches Una and Julian romp until they are exhausted, whereupon Una makes what strikes him as a sexually suggestive gesture. "Una, heated by the violence with which she plays, sits down on the floor, and complains grievously of warmth—opens her breast. This is the physical manifestation of the evil spirit that struggles for the mastery of her; he is not a spirit at all, but an earthy monster, who lays his grasp on her spinal marrow, her brain, and other parts of her body that lie in closest contiguity to her soul; so that the soul has the discredit of these evil deeds" (CE 8:420–421). That the child's pulling open her shirt should seem monstrous shows how deeply the conventions of feminine purity and filth structured Nathaniel's responses to her. It is significant that the "monster" that has laid hold of Una's spinal marrow is a "he." The vision of monstrosity that overwhelms Nathaniel's imagination is of a male spirit—passionate, violent, and aggressive—living within his little girl.

Nathaniel was especially troubled when Una's masculine spirit exploited her little brother's vulnerabilities. He observes that Julian has "more imagination" than Una, so that when their games involve playacting, Julian becomes emotionally identified with the drama in a way that Una does not. "The idea seems to enter deeply into him, and take possession of him. With her, it is merely intellectual." The result was that Una could torment him when the game placed his feelings at her disposal. "She has just blacked her face with ink, and calls herself an old coal-man; and Julian screams with positive terror—which she greatly enjoys. He possesses one masculine attribute, however—a disposition to make use of weapons—to brandish a stick, and use it against an adversary; and this, I believe, is the only way in which he is ever terrible to Una. She is sufficiently sensitive to the reality of hard knocks" (CE 8:434–435).

Una's power over Hawthorne's imagination may be read back through virtually all the situations in which Hawthorne's gender conflicts are projected, where Una delights, revolts, battles, or frightens him. Her mimicking his mother's death had arrested his attention, as had her thrusting up her buttocks. The fight over the air-bath was an occasion in which issues of sexuality and power running deep into Hawthorne's character were profusely engaged, so that little Julian was not the only person present who did not know what to make of the scene. Nathaniel's unstable vision of Una's "ethereal" delicacy, and of her victimization by an "earthy monster," likewise bespeak the hypnotic fascination that her personality exerted over him.

The profoundest level of Nathaniel's uneasiness toward Una was not erotic; he was haunted, rather, by the awareness that she was seeing things in himself, and in his ideal relation to Sophia, that were invisible to him. Both Nathaniel and Sophia were unnerved by Una's seeming intuitive penetration. "Una fixes her eyes on mamma's face, with such stedfastness that mamma beseeches her not to look so directly into her soul. She has often abashed me in the same way—not, however, by the depth of her insight, but because there seems to be a want of delicacy in dwelling upon any one's face so remorselessly" (CE 8:414).

Nathaniel was commonsensical enough to reject the idea that Una could make an articulate analysis of his inner life; he objects to her probing gaze

as indelicate, such aggression being a masculine prerogative. But his concluding remark indicates how deeply it unsettled him; "it seems to embarrass the
springs of spiritual life and the movement of the soul" (CE 8:414). Una
made Hawthorne aware that young children may register emotional realities
that their parents cannot recognize in themselves, or—more troublesome
yet—they may take an absorbing interest in emotional issues toward which
their parents have a confused and guilty response.

Nathaniel's uneasiness was augmented because the features of Una's
conduct that repelled and disgusted him, and the strain of "ill-nature" in her
psychic constitution, cast him into doubts about himself. The doctrine of
childhood innocence made it impossible to conclude that such evils were
inborn or that they belonged innately to a child's soul. Sophia's resolute
denial of Una's malicious conduct and mental torment was rooted in her
conviction that such defects simply could not exist in her angel-child; and
Nathaniel likewise ascribed to an "earthy monster" the moral defects for
which Una's soul wrongly gets the blame. Yet if such evils were not inborn,
where did they come from? Mary Mann observed in *The Moral Culture of
Infancy* that a bad child "seems an anomaly in nature" (156–157) and must
be produced by the malign influence of bad parents. Yet the subject of
"parents not having the right views of their parental duties," Mary observes,
"would take me still farther back, to the subject of being married on the right
principles" (185). Both Nathaniel and Sophia had exulted in Una as the
consummate expression of their relationship, the "symbol of the one true
union in the world." Now Nathaniel was compelled to wonder whether
there was something deeply amiss in that union.

An intimate and tormented communion between Nathaniel and Una was
interwoven with Hawthorne's experience of domestic life as it had unfolded
from the Eden-like days at the Old Manse to the current crisis. The anguish
with which he recalls his androgynous paradise is fused with his alarm at his
daughter's anomalous nature, yet his feelings toward her are tinged with
hostility, now as before. "The infant was worthy to have been brought forth
in Eden," Hawthorne writes of Pearl in *The Scarlet Letter,* and "worthy to
have been left there, to be the plaything of the angels, after the world's first
parents were driven out" (CE 1:90).

Hawthorne's masterwork embodies his brooding on the interior of the
domestic "sphere," not as a place of refuge from the conflicts of a selfish
world, but as a scene in which psychic and sexual intimacy brings on
emotional torments as severe as anything the world beyond might inflict. He
now bitterly reconsiders the androgynous joys of his paradise at Concord and

projects his own unwelcome transformation into worries about what will befall his son:

> Julian has too much tenderness, love, and sensibility in his nature; he needs to be hardened and tempered. I would not take a particle of the love out of him; but methinks it is highly desirable that some sterner quality should be interfused throughout the softness of his heart; else, in course of time, the hard intercourse of the world, and the many knocks and bruises he will receive, will cause a morbid crust of callousness to grow over his heart; so that, for at least a portion of his life, he will have less sympathy and love for his fellow-beings than those who began life with a much smaller portion. After a lapse of years, indeed, if he have native vigor enough, there may be a second growth of love and benevolence; but the first crop, with its wild luxuriance, stands a good chance of being blighted.
>
> (CE 8:424–425)

Two months after writing these words Hawthorne was prodigiously at work on a romance in which the "wild luxuriance" of a guilty androgynous passion produces a strange inhuman little girl.

CHAPTER ELEVEN

Double Marriage, Double Adultery

At the conclusion of *The Scarlet Letter* Hester Prynne returns to her lonely seaside cottage and becomes a counselor to persons suffering "the continually recurring trials of wounded, wasted, wronged, misplaced, or erring and sinful passion": women, in particular, come to her asking "why they were so wretched, and what the remedy." Hester shares her faith that the miseries accompanying intimate relationships will someday be corrected at their source. "At some brighter period . . . a new truth would be revealed, in order to establish the whole relation between man and woman on a surer ground of mutual happiness." Hester foretells that "the angel and apostle of the coming revelation must be a woman" and recognizes that the "destined prophetess" must be "lofty, pure, and beautiful; and wise, moreover, not through dusky grief, but the ethereal medium of joy; and showing how sacred love should make us happy, by the truest test of a life successful to such an end" (CE 1:263). Thus Hawthorne's narrative conclusion hails the advent of the domestic ideal, with the domestic angel as the embodiment of its sacred truth.

This passage culminates a rhetorical framework that quietly governs *The Scarlet Letter* from the outset, in which the anguish of the principal characters results from the inopportune social arrangements in which they are fated to live. Yet what Hawthorne proposes as the future remedy for these dilemmas is actually their source: the domestic ideal produces the "mighty trouble"

184

that Hester's story depicts. The details of Hawthorne's setting—and such ancillary figures as the Reverend Wilson, Governor Bellingham, and Mistress Hibbins—provide elaborate linkages with seventeenth-century Puritan Boston. But Hester, Arthur, Roger, and Pearl have no counterparts in the colonial record, and the torments they suffer are characteristic of nineteenth-century family life.[1]

In the opening scaffold scene Hawthorne includes a young wife holding her child by the hand, who serves as a harbinger of the coming revelation. In contrast to the "manlike" Puritan women who demand a harsher penalty, so that a proper lesson will be enforced upon the public, the young mother focuses sympathizing attention on Hester's inner pain. The view of punishment she represents is that of Sophia's child-rearing practices as well as that deployed in response to violations of the law: Victorian criminal "corrections" sought to rehabilitate criminals through an inward discipline, rather than use their bodies as instruments of public instruction enforced by terror. "Is there no virtue in woman," protests a witness to Hester's public shame, "save what springs from a wholesome fear of the gallows?" (CE 1:52). As the "iron-visaged" matrons loudly debate what additional sufferings Hester should undergo—a public flogging, or perhaps death—the young mother pleads with them: "Do not let her hear you! Not a stitch in that embroidered letter, but she has felt it in her heart" (54).[2]

Hawthorne himself denounces the public pillory as an "outrage" against "our common nature" because it makes a public spectacle of the suffering conscience and forbids the culprit "to hide his face for shame." In Hester's case the outrage is redoubled since the initial wrongdoing has an intimate character, involving "the taint of deepest sin in the most sacred quality of human life" (CE 1:55–56).

Placed on the scaffold by Puritan law, Hester is compelled to express her essential womanly nature by engaging in conduct that violates it, that is, by taking a public stand. She has "fantastically embroidered and illuminated" the letter so as to turn the tables on her accusers, reversing the meaning of the sentence they imposed. "Why, gossips," says one of the vindictive crones, "what is it but to laugh in the faces of our godly magistrates, and make a pride out of what they, worthy gentlemen, meant for a punishment?" (CE 1:53–54). Hester's public defiance, which paradoxically asserts the sacred privacy of intimate relations, culminates in her refusal to divulge her lover's name. Dimmesdale makes explicit the underlying principle, albeit for reasons of his own, in affirming "that it were wronging the very nature of woman to force her to lay open her heart's secrets in such broad daylight, and in presence of so great a multitude" (65). Hester's quandary—the necessity of asserting her nature by wronging it—introduces the dilemma that pervades *The Scarlet Letter*. Such vexations will not be typical of the future dispensation, once the "new truth" has been revealed. Or so Hawthorne's rhetorical schema implies.

This thematic system was not Hawthorne's invention; it was a conventional feature of the argument by which the domestic ideal became established. George B. Loring's early review of *The Scarlet Letter* observed that in former ages marriage was merely a legal obligation, the "bulwark of hereditary rights, and a bond for a deed of conveyance." But there is now a true form of marriage, Loring declared, founded on obligations "more sacred and binding than any which have been born of the statute-book" (Crowley, 170). Harriet Martineau's demand that marriage should be separated from "its impious alliance with worldly interest" replays these issues. "Designed to protect the sanctity of the love of one man for one woman," marriage "has become the very means of obstructing such love, and destroying the sanctity of it." Adultery is the inevitable result: "Is anyone irrational enough to expect fidelity in marriages thus made in markets?" (Martineau, n.p.).

Hester Prynne has two husbands, in keeping with these divergent conceptions of marriage. Roger is her husband at law; and Hester frankly declares that when she married him, she "felt no love, nor feigned any" (CE 1:74). Between Hester and Arthur, by contrast, there exists a bond of sacred love. The adultery they committed against Roger was the consummation of their soul-marriage, which they passionately reassert after years of punishment. "What we did had a consecration of its own," Hester cries out. "We felt it so! We said so to each other!" (195). Hawthorne unobtrusively yet firmly endorses this self-consecrating marriage by speaking routinely of Roger as Hester's "former husband" (167).[3]

In light of her soul-marriage to Arthur, Hester comes to realize that her sexual relationship to Roger was a defiling and degrading experience. She recalls with convulsive loathing the scenes of their life together and "deemed it her crime most to be repented of, that she had ever endured, and reciprocated, the lukewarm grasp of his hand, and had suffered the smile of her lips and eyes to mingle and melt into his own. And it seemed a fouler offence committed by Roger Chillingworth, than any which had since been done him, that, in the time when her heart knew no better, he had persuaded her to fancy herself happy by his side." In short, her relation to Roger was adulterous: "He betrayed me!" Hester concludes bitterly, "He has done me worse wrong than I did him" (CE 1:176).

Inherent in Hester's double marriage is a double adultery. The legal and public bond of matrimony establishes a requirement of sexual fidelity that the narrative questions but never discards. Yet marriage as a communion of souls is equally hedged about with sacred obligations, against which Roger offended when he took Hester to his lukewarm bed. He is the victim of the adultery between Hester and Arthur; yet his relation to Hester is revealed as a betrayal when judged by the sacred bond joining her to Arthur. The Puritan community is thus guilty of enforcing a wrongful standard: Hester's youthful mistake could be corrected in a healthier social arrangement, where she could obtain a divorce from Roger and proceed to formalize at law the true marriage of her heart; the development of matrimonial legislation since the early nineteenth century bears witness to the social force of this rhetoric.[4]

Yet the conflict between "worldly" requirements and the claims of the "heart" was sharpened, not moderated, by the emergence of the domestic ideal. The ostensible progress from a former to a future social condition bespeaks a tension within domesticity itself. Colonial life was not free of marital distress; and the same is true of its European antecedents. Indeed, the Hebrew and Greek literatures at the origins of Western culture portray the manifold tragic dilemmas inherent in family relations. But *The Scarlet Letter* depicts the quandaries of its own age and sets forth the heraldic emblem of middle-class marriage in its final sentence: "ON A FIELD, SABLE, THE LETTER A, GULES" (CE 1:26). Hester is enmeshed in a matrimonial adultery generic to the domestic ideal; her two marriages dramatize a conflict in the terms of its constitution.

Students of domesticity have described the troubles produced by the sharp division between "home" and "world." The expectation of deepened emotional satisfactions within marriage appeared simultaneously with the separation of the "spheres," so that husbands and wives were driven apart by their occupations—and by the temperaments suited to those occupations—even as they sought increased marital intimacy. As John Mack Faragher observes, this "marriage-defining conflict" was complicated by the difference in social power between men and women; like slaves attending to the personal needs of their owners, women formed intimate relationships on terms set by men. It follows that the definition of "woman's sphere" is itself a male creation and serves male needs, however much countervailing power it may afford the subordinated sex (1–3).[5]

Hester's difficulties arise, accordingly, from a problem deeper than the conflict between legal obligations and heart's desire. Her discrepant marriages subject her to an internally divided masculinity, to Roger and Arthur as fragments of a divided manhood. These reciprocal cuckolds spend more time with each other than either spends with Hester, and they are more intimately involved in each other's lives than in hers. Hawthorne tells us that they took "long walks on the sea-shore, or in the forest" (CE 1:123). "They discussed every topic of ethics and religion, of public affairs, and private character; they talked much, on both sides, of matters that seemed personal to themselves," so that a "kind of intimacy" (125) grew up between them, from which Hester was excluded. They decide to live together, and in the end they die together. Hester's two husbands are inseparable opposites; they are figures of the split manhood that sustained the domestic ideal, and Hester cannot have one without the other.

Hester demonstrates her continuing love for Arthur in her refusal to name him before the community and in the revival of their passion that takes place in the forest, where they agree to make a new life for themselves elsewhere. Hawthorne does not fail to observe that this faithfulness renews her adultery against Roger. Yet Hester also keeps faith with Roger, in response to a matrimonial claim that invokes not merely law but the intimacy of the domestic bond. Roger demands what Hester had given Arthur, namely her promise to keep secret their marital relation, and he includes Arthur within that sacred privacy. "Elsewhere a wanderer, and isolated from human interests, I find here a woman, a man, a child, amongst whom and myself there exist the closest ligaments. No matter whether of love or hate; no matter whether of right or wrong! Thou and thine, Hester Prynne, belong to me. My home is where thou art, and where he is." Roger blackmails Hester into keeping their secret by threatening a public revenge against Arthur, whose identity he appears to have discerned from the outset: "His fame, his position, his life, will be in my hands. Beware!" (CE 1:76). This deadly interior menace deepens and complicates the three-way bond of "home" that links Hester, Arthur, and Roger, a tormented and inwardly conflicted intimacy in which faithfulness and adultery are interfused.

While she was living at the Old Manse, Sophia quarreled with the view—put forward by her sister Elizabeth—that her relation to Nathaniel was a union of "self-sufficing worlds." Elizabeth had derived this marital ideal from Ralph Waldo Emerson, and she thought it applicable to several marriages; to Sophia, however, it was a flat contradiction in terms. "No one who has ever become one with another being, as true husband & wife must

become if really united, will ever, can ever, say that each is wholly independent of the other, except intellectually. Heart & spirit are forever indissolubly one." If a husband and wife "be indeed twin souls, if they belong
together, they are no longer each 'self-sufficing.' Waldo Emerson knows not
much of love. He has never yet said any thing to show that he does. He is
an isolation—He has never yet known what union meant with any soul."[6]
Sophia's jab at Emerson is not only personal; it goes to the marital dilemmas
generated by the ideal of self-made manhood, of which Emerson was a classic
exemplar.

Sophia is saying in effect that the Emersons have an adulterous legal
marriage, like that of Hester and Roger; and in bringing this charge, Sophia
echoes a domestic anguish that Waldo and Lidian did not conceal. Margaret
Fuller visited the Emersons in 1842 and noted Lidian's pain: her "hope that
Waldo's character will alter, and that he will be capable of an intimate
union." Waldo himself feigned no such capacity; he stated frankly that "the
soul knows nothing of marriage in the sense of permanent union between
two personal existences"; and this view was in keeping with his broader
doctrines of the self-sufficient soul (Myerson, 330–332). "Live no longer to
the expectation of these deceived and deceiving people with whom we
converse," he had proclaimed in "Self-Reliance." "Say to them, 'O father,
O mother, O wife . . . I have lived with you after appearances hitherto.
Henceforward I am the truth's.' " The self-reliant man agrees to remain "the
chaste husband of one wife," Emerson concedes, but his soul belongs to
himself alone (Whicher, 160).

Emerson enshrined psychic self-sovereignty as the essential manly virtue
and set his face against any impulse or duty that threatened it. "Nothing is
at last sacred," he declared "but the integrity of your own mind" (Whicher,
149). Yet maintaining this self-directed inward coherence is incompatible
with the union of souls that true marriage demands and sexual intercourse
within true marriage enacts.

The dread of sexuality—including marital sexuality—as a threat to masculine self-sovereignty was not invented in America, nor is it solely a product
of the rising middle class. But this concern was sharply accentuated in the
early national period, and it became a middle-class obsession as the culture
of individual competition became dominant. John Adams proposed that the
national seal of the United States should be engraved with a scene depicting
the Choice of Hercules, the hero's decision to pursue mighty endeavors
rather than the "Effeminacy" of amorous dalliance. In Adams's recurrent
discussions, sexual desire became an inclusive metaphor for activities menac-

ing the self-disciplined pursuit of manly distinction: "let no Girl, no Gun, no Cards, no flutes, no Violins, no Dress, no Tobacco, no Laziness, decoy you from your books," he sternly counseled himself. Adams condemned wasting time and spirit in "unmanly Pleasures," which he obsessively details: "a softening, enervating, dissipating series of hustling, pratling, Poetry, Love, Courtship, Marriage." Adams's anxiety is projected into fretting over his children's future: "I sometimes tremble when I hear the syren songs of sloth, least they should be captivated with her bewitching Charms, and her soft, insinuating Musick" (Greven, 246).

The discourse of self-sufficient manhood is a duet, more richly realized in Adams than in Emerson; yet the two voices are audible in both. The division in Adams's mind appears in the caressing eloquence with which he lists the allurements he seeks to repudiate; he is enormously attracted to poetry, love, courtship, and marriage, as well as to laziness and his gun, and he implicitly acknowledges the psychic wealth they offer. Emerson, by contrast, reduces such distractions to the "deceived and deceiving" presences that he dismisses in the act of summoning them up: "O father, O mother, O wife." Like Odysseus himself among the "syren songs," Emerson does not allow himself to hear the "soft, insinuating Musick."

This anxious dialectic, in which manly self-control speaks against a disconcerting yet alluring prospect of self-loss, is dramatized in Hawthorne's presentation of Roger and Arthur. The split between law and the heart, as between the spheres of world and home, now appears in the polarization of male selfhood. Hester's "worldly" marriage to Roger, with its legal authorization, joins her to a figure of notable self-possession; Arthur languishes, almost overwhelmed by his emotional impulses, taking a voluptuous pleasure even in his spasms of guilt. Yet neither marriage is visible to the public; both are contained within the sacred compacts that Hester keeps secret. She is an antitype of the domestic angel, in whom the moral anatomy of that role becomes visible, the queen and victim of a domestic intimacy given structure by the interior contradictions of self-sovereign manhood.

The Scarlet Letter drastically heightens the psychosexual drama of manhood split by desire; it portrays an intense inward battle along lines drawn up in a literature excluded from the canonical precincts inhabited by Adams and Emerson: the literature of masturbation phobia that burgeoned in the 1830s and 1840s. Masturbation sharply focused the interior contradictions of manly self-reliance; instead of setting men against violins and tobacco and wives, it put them at war with their own bodies.[7]

Masturbation is both a failure and a triumph of sexual self-command. Like sexual activity generally, it involves yielding to impulses that are not under voluntary control, which express themselves in erotic dreams and nocturnal emissions if orgasm is successfully avoided during waking hours. Masturbation is also a form of sexual self-sufficiency; it requires no entangling liaisons or commitments and no financial cost. The effort to realize oneself as a self-made man is ultimately self-liquidating because it embraces contradictory requirements that become inescapable in the presence of desire.[8] Masturbation thus came to possess contaminating power for men who sought to incarnate self-sovereign self-control.

As the ideal of self-sufficient manliness began to develop historically, masturbation was flagged early as a critical issue; in 1724 *Onania* appeared, with a subtitle that gave the deed its definitive new name: *Self-Pollution*. *Onania* presents the two voices that carry on a tireless dialogue throughout the succeeding tradition, the voice of the author and that of the self-polluted self. *Onania* includes letters, presented as the work of afflicted readers, with the author's replies appended, so that the work has an epistolary form, which remained standard in this literature well into the nineteenth century.[9] Brief pamphlets of admonition as well as learned treatises present the characteristic duet.

The voice of the author is self-contained and authoritative, probing the disgusting morass of self-pity, self-loathing, and dissolving ethical fiber from which the other voice speaks. Here is a nineteenth-century instance of the counterpoint: "My constitution . . . is broken down, and my mind, as well as body, completely enervated. I am haunted day and night with lascivious thoughts and dreams; suspicious of my friends and disgusted with myself. My memory has lost its power—unable to fix my attentions—my mind is filled with terrible forebodings—fear of insanity, and at times it has cost me a continual effort to retain my reason." In such squalor the author finds evidence of a stern and inflexible order: "We cannot, with impunity, violate the laws of our being. This organic law of our formation, is imperative and abiding—no abuse of it will go unpunished—suffering will follow, if it be not scrupulously obeyed" (Woodward, 8, 10).

Hawthorne's Chillingworth likewise pursues scientific knowledge with cold composure and comes to focus that pursuit obsessively on Dimmesdale's soul while Dimmesdale is ravaged and enervated by the conviction that his existence is "utterly a pollution and a lie" (CE 1:143). These dichotomous psychic constellations define a world of male erotic experience: Roger's self-possession and Arthur's self-loathing are both forms of masculine sexuality.

Roger's emotional containment is itself compulsive, as appears in the opening scene. He sees his wife on the scaffold, with another man's child in her arms; this spectacle triggers an involuntary effort at self-control. "A writhing horror twisted itself across his features, like a snake gliding swiftly over them, and making one little pause, with all its wreathed intervolutions in open sight. His face darkened with some powerful emotion, which, nevertheless, he so instantaneously controlled by an effort of his will, that, save at a single moment, its expression might have passed for calmness. After a brief space, the convulsion grew almost imperceptible, and finally subsided into the depths of his nature" (CE 1:61). Roger masters this passion by exercising his "will," but so "instantaneously" that the effort itself is marked as automatic. Momentarily visible is a snake-like writhing, which intimates the erotic energy invested both in the hidden feelings and in the compulsion to keep them concealed. The "keen and penetrative" glance that precedes this "convulsion" likewise bespeaks the sexual passion Chillingworth has incorporated into his commitment to a ruthless self-possessed rationality. As Frederick Crews aptly remarked, Roger's *libido sciendi* is heavily charged with libido (126).

From the outset of his researches into the identity of Hester's beloved, Roger looks forward to the crescendo of sexual excitement that will mark his progress. "There is a sympathy that will make me conscious of him. I shall see him tremble. I shall feel myself shudder, suddenly and unawares. Sooner or later, he must needs be mine!" (CE 1:75). His desire for such moments of delicious tremor is Roger's chief motive in pursuing Arthur. Hawthorne describes nothing in the way of a real investigation: no other suspects are even considered, and Roger makes no effort to dig up tangible evidence. He satisfies himself, instead, by torturing Arthur into bursts of unguarded feeling. "It is as well to have made this step" Roger gloats, after his questions drive Arthur into a rage. "See, now, how passion takes hold upon this man, and hurrieth him out of himself! As with one passion, so with another! He hath done a wild thing ere now, this pious Master Dimmesdale, in the hot passion of his heart!" (137).

Hawthorne repeatedly draws attention to the unconscious compulsion that takes control of Roger's seemingly self-regulated life. "He had begun an investigation, as he imagined, with the severe and equal integrity of a judge, desirous only of truth, even as if the question involved no more than the air-drawn lines and figures of a geometrical problem. . . . But, as he proceeded, a terrible fascination, a kind of fierce, though still calm, necessity seized the old man within its gripe, and never set him free again, until he had done all its bidding" (CE 1:129). Yet the covert eroticism of Roger's investigation bespeaks the autophobic sexuality that had marked his earlier life. Roger's compulsive self-containment—his inability to yield himself to Hester—lies at the heart of his failure to consummate a passionate union with her. "Let men tremble," Hawthorne warns "to win the hand of woman, unless they win along with it the utmost passion of her heart! Else it may be their miserable fortune, as it was Roger Chillingworth's, when some mightier touch than their own may have awakened all her sensibilities, to be reproached even for the calm content, the marble image of happiness, which they will have imposed upon her as the warm reality" (176–177).

As sexual anxiety governs Roger's craving, so it generates the emotional provender that Arthur serves up. As the clergyman writhes in the torture of a self-abused selfhood, Roger implicitly recognizes his own prospective plight, as does the community at large. Arthur provides his congregation, indeed, a diluted form of the gratification Roger derives from observing him, offering the public a chance to participate vicariously in the torment of his inner life. Arthur's sermons are powerful because of the emotional burden in his "tremulously sweet, rich, deep, and broken" voice (CE 1:67). His listeners are attuned to a "cry of pain" that softens their hearts, no matter what his ostensible topic may be (243).

Arthur's clerical selfhood is an anguished hymn of erotic submission, tacitly acknowledging that passion compels him to violate the principles of male virtue. The manliness he has polluted through yielding is the same as Chillingworth has demonized through unconscious denial and the quest for vicarious fulfillment. This specific form of pollution—the vice correlative to just such a manliness—gives Arthur "sympathies so intimate with the sinful brotherhood of mankind; so that his heart vibrated in unison with theirs" (CE 1:142).

Arthur knows, moreover, that he nurses and cultivates his desire in the act of repenting it, so that his displays of righteous self-abuse are themselves masturbatory and strongly solicit an erotic response. "The virgins of his church grew pale around him, victims of a passion so embued with religious sentiment that they imagined it to be all religion, and brought it openly, in their white bosoms, as their most acceptable sacrifice before the altar" (CE 1:142).

I do not propose Roger and Arthur as neurotics in the conventional
Freudian sense, as though their professions of scientific curiosity and of
moral suffering cover up an autonomous sexuality that they could learn to
enjoy if only they had the courage to face their true feelings. They represent
sexualities produced by the cultural formation that self-made men perforce
inhabited, in which erotic sentiment was experienced in the forms of anguish
Hawthorne depicts here.

The literary power of Hawthorne's portrayal results in part from the
density of such local resonances. The pair dramatize an all-ramifying seman-
tic interplay whose logic reaches across the boundaries separating distinct
zones of social experience. Roger and Arthur display this reverberant cen-
trality in relation to the split voices of Adams and Emerson and the intrapsy-
chic hothouse of masturbation phobia. But their interaction also engages the
public order of male endeavors, as figured in the emerging relation of the
clergy and the medical profession.

Hawthorne's description of the living quarters of the two men underscores their rival eruditions. Arthur

> piled up his library, rich with parchment-bound folios of the Fathers, and the lore of
> Rabbis, and monkish erudition, of which the Protestant divines, even while they
> vilified and decried that class of writers, were yet constrained often to avail themselves.
> On the other side of the house, old Roger Chillingworth arranged his study and
> laboratory; not such as a modern man of science would reckon even tolerably com-
> plete, but provided with a distilling apparatus, and the means of compounding drugs
> and chemicals.
>
> (CE 1:126)

Each learned man occupied "his own domain"; in Hawthorne's time the
relation of the two domains was changing.

The disestablishment of religion in the United States involved more than
the removal of the ordained ministry from the list of tax-supported institutions. The intellectual authority of the clergyman's professional stock-in-
trade was critically damaged by the interminable theological disputes to
which Hawthorne obliquely refers; and the emerging secular order of business and politics presented a host of issues that the knowledge of things
divine could do little to explain. In the reshaping of the social landscape that
separated the home from the world, the pastor found his professional place
shifting into the domain of women.[10]

During his stay at the Old Manse, Hawthorne encountered a Reverend
Mr. Frost, who seemed blissfully unaware of occupying an effeminated role.
"We certainly do need a new revelation," Hawthorne remarked, "for there

seems to be no life in the old one. Mr. Frost, however, is probably one of the best and most useful of his class; because no suspicion of the necessity of his profession . . . has hitherto disturbed him; and therefore he labors with faith and confidence, as ministers did a hundred years ago, when they had really something to do in the world" (CE 8:352). Dimmesdale's professional station, by contrast, offered a direct pathway to public authority. "Even political power," Hawthorne states, "was within the grasp of a successful priest" (CE 1:238). Dimmesdale, more akin to Mr. Frost than to his Puritan forebears, possesses the skills through which nineteenth-century ministers attained social power by exploiting the womanly domain to which they found themselves consigned.

Tender womanhood being exalted as the true expression of Christian love, pastors cultivated a sensitive life of sympathetic emotion that male denizens of the cold cruel world found it difficult to maintain. As women became leaders in the politics of local churches and in the proliferating system of volunteer organizations that churches sponsored, the preacher's ability to arouse the enthusiasm of women parishioners became essential to his professional success. The sexual conflicts of middle-class culture came to focus on the relationship between women and ministers, and when the spiritual, political, and erotic connections between shepherd and sheep were strongly mutual, they were likely to become explicit. The love affair of Henry Ward Beecher and his parishioner Elizabeth Tilton attained notoriety when it was revealed in 1872 because it dramatized issues concerning the meaning of "true" marriage and the sexually ambiguous character of the clergyman's role—precisely those Hawthorne had explored two decades earlier.

Victoria Woodhull, the advocate of sexual freedom who revealed the Beecher-Tilton affair to the public, extolled "the coming together of these two loving natures in the most intimate embrace" (Cott, *Root*, 260). Woodhull asserted that Beecher's deepest convictions were identical to her own but that he could not muster the courage to break with the "social slavery" he secretly despised. Woodhull's stand invokes the cultural logic at work in Sophia's assessment of Waldo and Lidian. In each case true marriage exists where loving natures are at one, and sexual intercourse is the outward and visible sign of that inward and spiritual union. Hawthorne's portrayal of the minister as a sex symbol strikes a chord that is still vibrating in American religious life.

The paradox in which anguished confessions of sin become incitements to sexual pleasure produced a related set of dilemmas for clergymen. The Reverend John Todd, who wrote voluminously about "manhood"—which always already means sexual self-control—was quick to warn his readers against books that pollute the mind; and he was particularly alarmed about writing whose pornographic effect is covert or springs on readers before they can prepare themselves. He complains that gifted but perverted writers "adorn and conceal a path which is full of holes, through which you may drop into the chambers of death" (Barker-Benfield, 171). Yet Todd could not help realizing that his own treatises might inspire the depravities they condemn; and when he wrote directly about the "secret vice," he did so in Latin (169–170).

The Reverend Arthur Cleveland Coxe, in reviewing *The Scarlet Letter,* finds that Hawthorne exploits the opportunities for pornographic euphemism provided by the erotics of pious guilt. Coxe declines to convict Hawthorne as a "literary pimp," because his work is not "coarse in its details, or indecent in its phraseology." But Hawthorne's very fastidiousness, Coxe finds, advances the work of corruption, as the blunt language of the Bible does not: "Damsels who shrink at the reading of the Decalogue, would probably luxuriate in bathing their imagination in the crystal of . . . [*The Scarlet Letter*'s] delicate sensuality" (Kesterson, 44). Coxe goes on to describe his encounter with a group of schoolgirls who were polluting themselves with Hawthorne's "delicately immoral" story by sharing their enthusiasm for it. The girls agreed it was about "a very fascinating young preacher," and a "hateful creature named Chillingworth, who persecuted the said preacher" (44–45).[11] My point here is not (or not only) that Hawthorne was scolded by the champions of prudery, and not that he refashioned the erotic conventions of his time into an autonomous work of art, but that his work fiercely intensifies the ambivalent sexual rhetoric that informed the responses both of the Reverend Mr. Coxe and of the schoolgirls.

The sexual anxieties that express themselves in the dilemmas of middle-class clergyman are also at work in the emerging science of sexuality, which became a province of the medical profession.

Chillingworth's professional character reflects the displacement of the minister as a counselor to sick souls and the acquisition of that role by physicians. John and Robin Haller observe that the medical doctor "had more opportunity than any other person outside the family circle to enter it on terms of intimacy," becoming "a party to family secrets in the natural course of his duties" (*The Physician and Sexuality,* x). The physician also enjoyed authority as the possessor of scientific truth, which increased in power and scope as the credibility of theological knowledge deteriorated. The psychoanalytic movement, now so multifarious, had its origins in Sigmund Freud's insistence that he had created a verifiable "science of the unconscious," to be based on conversations between doctors and persons suffering mental distress. In *The Scarlet Letter* Hawthorne indicates that the physician's power to gain knowledge of spiritual matters was well advanced by mid-century, especially if he was skilled in exploiting the confessional qualities of the diagnostic interview:

> A man burdened with a secret should especially avoid the intimacy of his physician. If the latter possess native sagacity, and a nameless something more,—let us call it intuition; if he show no intrusive egotism, nor disagreeably prominent characteristics of his own; if he have the power, which must be born with him, to bring his mind into such affinity with his patient's, that this last shall unawares have spoken what he imagines himself only to have thought; if such revelations be received without tumult, and acknowledged not so often by an uttered sympathy, as by silence, an inarticulate breath, and here and there a word, to indicate that all is understood; if, to these qualifications of a confidant be joined the advantages afforded by his recognized character as a physician;—then, at some inevitable moment, will the soul of the sufferer be dissolved, and flow forth in a dark, but transparent stream, bringing all its mysteries into the daylight.
>
> (CE 1:124)

For all its claim to objective scientific authority, however, medical litera-ture retained the language of sexual disgust. "A Brief and Intelligible View of the Nature, Origin and Cure of Tubercular Disease,"—a title dispassion-ate in tone—finds the source of such a disease in masturbation, which is characterized as a "polluting stream" that befouls the most genteel. Even those "who have been surrounded by every thing that could inspire the heart with sentiments of virtue and purity, have desecrated the scene . . . by indulgence in a vice, in view of which angels . . . weep, and creation sighs" (Rosenberg, 136). Like Roger Chillingworth, presumptively disinterested investigators of this "disease" found themselves enmeshed in a loathing fascination, and prescriptions for cure were often sadistic.

Leopold Deslandes advised that the masturbator should be placed in a straitjacket, with his feet tied apart, in such a way that his penis would not be tickled by his thighs. Deslandes also recommended the use of a "genital cage," which secured the penis and scrotum within a metal truss, to be held in place by springs (Haller and Haller, 207–208). Other practitioners em-ployed bloodletting and applied leeches and heated pneumatic cups to the genitals, so as to draw forth "congestion." Inserting a metal ring in a hole punched through the foreskin was another form of treatment, as was cutting the foreskin apart with jagged scissors. Red iron, tartar emetic ointment, and Spanish fly-blister were applied to make the genitals painful to the touch, so that straying hands would not seek them out. "It is better . . . to endure any physical discomfort," wrote Henry Guernsey, M.D., in his *Plain Talks on Avoided Subjects,* "than to sacrifice one's chastity" (Haller and Haller, 208–209).[12]

The erotics of cruelty illustrated by such medical counsel answers to the clerical erotics of guilt. The root identity of these seemingly opposite psychic formations is evoked by Hawthorne's suggestion that the pain in Arthur's chest—and the wound presumably visible there—may have arisen equally from Arthur's self-torture and the poison vengefully administered by Roger.

Roger's sadistic gratification reaches its climax in the famous moment of his observing Arthur's naked breast. Like the "convulsion" Roger momentarily experienced when he first saw Hester on the scaffold and the "shudder" he expected to feel when he drew close to his quarry, this is a spasm in which involuntary responses take command. "What a wild look of wonder, joy, and horror! With what a ghastly rapture, as it were, too mighty to be expressed only by the eye and features, and therefore bursting forth through the whole ugliness of his figure, and making itself even riotously manifest by the extravagant gestures with which he threw up his arms towards the ceiling, and stamped his foot upon the floor!" (CE 1:138).

Figures of a manhood that is self-alienated under the pressure of sexual passion, Arthur and Roger live together and die together, leaving Hester to live on alone. In describing Roger's death, Hawthorne proposes that the hatred the two men bore each other testifies to a bond as deep as love. He wonders, indeed, "whether hatred and love be not the same thing at bottom. Each, in its utmost development, supposes a high degree of intimacy and heart-knowledge; each renders one individual dependent for the food of his affections and spiritual life upon another; each leaves the passionate lover, or the no less passionate hater, forlorn and desolate by the withdrawal of his object" (CE 1:260). The factor linking hatred and love is the interdependence of the parties in question: both are "passions" of the sort that menace the self-containment of self-made men. Hawthorne's concluding remark emerges accordingly as a hope that this internal split in the male psyche might someday be healed. "In the spiritual world, the old physician and the minister—mutual victims as they have been—may, unawares, have found their earthly stock of hatred and antipathy transmuted into golden love" (260–261).

In the meanwhile, however, Hester's two marriages join her to inseparable figures who are convulsively at war; they dramatize a torment endemic to the sexual intimacy of middle-class marriage, the lurid balefire of matrimonial adultery.

CHAPTER TWELVE

Domesticity as Redemption

As a woman "stained" with sin, Hester represents the classic opposite of domestic purity. Instead of sublimating male desire into worship, her nature has "a rich, voluptuous, Oriental characteristic" (CE 1:83). Roger's addiction to voyeuristic cruelty and Arthur's addiction to exhibitionist guilt are correlative transformations of the passion she stirs up. Yet even as Hester plays her part in this system of interlocking emotional contradictions, Hawthorne gives her qualities of the "true womanhood" that promises to place the relation of the sexes on a new footing. Like the brief description of the young woman at the scaffold, her story is a harbinger of the redemption she foretells in her old age but will not live to see. Hawthorne seeks, that is, to contain his material within the rhetoric of the domestic ideal, even as he lays open the dilemmas intrinsic to that ideal. This pervading metabolism of meanings—in which domesticity is established in the act of being subverted—strongly contributes to the cultural power *The Scarlet Letter* has been found to possess.

The narrative intimates that Roger and Arthur are indissolubly united, yet it manifestly presents them as two different men between whom Hester may choose. Hester eventually decides, not surprisingly, to keep faith with Arthur, breaking the promise she had given Roger to keep their "former" marriage a secret. She confirms her commitment, that is, to marriage as a sacred communion of souls, and her relationship to Arthur is a parable of redemptive spiritual intercourse. Hester's love rescues Arthur from his debilitated effeminacy, and in displaying such love Hester transcends the "manlike" qualities in herself. Yet she does not become a "true woman" until Arthur likewise asserts a self-sufficient "manhood." The reciprocal creation of these ideal gender identities has a further redemptive effect: it delivers Pearl from her unreal existence.

Hester bitterly resents the thwarted life her society has compelled her to accept and sees her plight as bearing on "the whole race of womanhood. Was existence worth accepting, even to the happiest among them?" She is appalled at the social changes that are necessary to remove the injustices women suffer:

> As a first step, the whole system of society is to be torn down, and built up anew. Then, the very nature of the opposite sex, or its long hereditary habit, which has become like nature, is to be essentially modified, before woman can be allowed to assume what seems a fair and suitable position. Finally, all other difficulties being obviated, woman cannot take advantage of these preliminary reforms, until she herself shall have undergone a still mightier change; in which, perhaps, the ethereal essence, wherein she has her truest life, will be found to have evaporated.
>
> (CE 1:165–166)

Thus manhood and womanhood are affirmed as gender identities ordained by nature and nature's God, universal essences at once biological and ethereal. Yet this affirmation is surrounded by the chronic ambivalences. Is it the "nature" of the male sex that must be changed, or merely its "long hereditary habit?" Is it *necessary* for the "truest life" of a woman to be sacrificed, or is that only a danger? Is the psychosocial revolution Hester contemplates a perversion, or is it simply very difficult?

Hester's pursuit of such speculations is itself presented as an "exercise of thought" at odds with her feminine nature. In taking up this baffling intellectual quest, she has forsaken woman's natural engagement with concerns of the heart. "There seemed to be no longer any thing in Hester's face for Love to dwell upon; . . . nothing in Hester's bosom, to make it ever again the pillow of Affection. Some attribute had departed from her, the permanence of which had been essential to keep her a woman" (CE 1:163). Hester's lost femininity is not irretrievable, however. Looking forward to her meeting with Dimmesdale in the forest, Hawthorne observes that she "might at any moment become a woman again, if there were only the magic touch to effect the transfiguration" (164).

Well before that transfiguring moment, however, Hester gives evidence of innate womanhood prevailing still amid the oppressive social circumstances that tempt her to replace it with an unnatural masculinity. She is preserved from the wilder excesses of rebellion by the devotion she pours into the rearing of Pearl; and in her relation to the community at large she displays compassionate self-sacrifice. Hawthorne speaks of her uncomplaining submission to the abuse she received from the public and celebrates the "blameless purity" of her life. Sickbed and deathbed scenes best reveal her distinctive feminine virtue; there "Hester's nature showed itself warm and rich; a well-spring of human tenderness, unfailing to every real demand, and inexhaustible by the largest" (CE 1:161). The townsfolk begin to tell each other that the scarlet A "meant Able; so strong was Hester Prynne, with a woman's strength" (161).

The reciprocal magic touch, in which Hester recovers her womanhood and, in the consummate exercise of her woman's strength, makes a "man" out of Arthur Dimmesdale, is enacted in the forest. As Hester sees Arthur approaching, she observes his "nerveless despondency" (CE 1:188); and the ensuing scene reveals that he has lost the ascribed masculine qualities of public initiative and self-possession, of rational judgment and resolute will. When Dimmesdale learns that Roger "was" Hester's husband, he collapses altogether and turns to Hester for guidance. "Think for me, Hester! Thou art strong. Resolve for me!" (196). Hester has already contrived the plan that she now persuades Arthur to adopt. She wants them to leave the colony for a better life elsewhere; in the course of pursuing this objective, she asserts her psychological dominion over him. " 'Is the world then so narrow?' exclaimed Hester Prynne, fixing her deep eyes on the minister's, and instinctively exercising a magnetic power over a spirit so shattered and subdued, that it could hardly hold itself erect" (197).

This encounter does not bring Arthur under her power for long, however. Instead of complying with her plan, he conceives and executes a plan of his own to extend and, indeed, to culminate his public responsibilities. Hester is startled and dismayed, after the Election Day sermon, when Arthur approaches the scaffold to proclaim his guilt. Yet something within her compels her to acquiesce: "slowly, as if impelled by inevitable fate, and against her strongest will" (CE 1:252), Hester joins him. Innate womanly submission undermines the long-practiced assertion of her will now that Arthur assumes command. She has rendered him capable of fulfilling his manhood, which includes taking charge of her, and he continues to depend on her "woman's strength," now subordinated to the purpose he has chosen without consulting her. As they mount the scaffold together, they form a tableau in which the domestic vision of natural genders is triumphant:

essential manhood and essential womanhood have been mutually re-created and are reciprocally confirmed. "Come hither now, and twine thy strength about me! Thy strength, Hester; but let it be guided by the will which God hath granted me!" (253).

Pearl's redemption occurs at this moment of confession and expiation and fulfillment. The child has inherited Hester's defiance and seems to anticipate that she too will eventually be at odds with the world. Instead of playing with the children of the town, Pearl invents imaginary playmates, whom she regards with vehement hostility: "She never created a friend, but seemed always to be sowing broadcast the dragon's teeth, whence sprung a harvest of armed enemies, against whom she rushed to battle. It was inexpressibly sad—then what depth of sorrow to a mother, who felt in her own heart the cause!—to observe, in one so young, this constant recognition of an adverse world, and so fierce a training of the energies that were to make good her cause, in the contest that must ensue" (CE 1:95–96).

Just as Hester's rebellion puts her at odds with her own "womanly" nature, so Pearl's character is a battleground. She is an agent of Hester's punishment, upholding the validity of the order Hester violates: her preoccupation with the scarlet letter, her persistent allusions to it, and her eerily apt questions to Hester about Arthur fill out her character as an enforcer of the lawful order of society. Yet she herself "could not be made amenable to rules" (CE 1:91).

This contradictory situation comes to a head in the forest after Hester has removed the scarlet letter from her breast and the severe cap from her head, so that her dark hair flows voluptuously down over her shoulders, stirring Arthur to a resumption of his manhood. Having agreed to flee the colony, they call the child to join them, but instead of responding with sympathy, Pearl throws a tantrum that is at once commanding and uncontrolled. "Assuming a singular air of authority, Pearl stretched out her hand, with the small forefinger extended, and pointing evidently towards her mother's breast," and then "stamped her foot with a yet more imperious look and gesture." When Hester sternly repeats her demand, Pearl "suddenly burst into a fit of passion, gesticulating violently, and throwing her small figure into the most extravagant contortions. She accompanied this wild outbreak with piercing shrieks" (CE 1:209–210), whereupon Hester gives in and restores the letter.

Pearl's peremptory force, here as elsewhere, recalls what Hawthorne saw in Una; his notebook entries complain that she was often "exceedingly ungracious in her mode of asking, or rather demanding favors. For instance, wishing to have a story read to her, she has just said, 'Now I'm going to have some reading'; and she always seems to adopt the imperative mood, in this manner. She uses it to me, I think, more than to her mother, and, from what I observe of some of her collateral predecessors, I believe it to be an hereditary trait to assume the government of her father" (CE 8:414).

Pearl gains control of others by losing control of herself, a stratagem Una found successful with her father. Hawthorne's journal returns again and again to the "tempestuous" protests that erupt when Una's will is crossed (CE 8:411); and he preferred not to contend with "little Tornada in one of her tantrums" (CE 16:231). When Hawthorne was overawed by Una's fury, as on the evening of the air-bath fight, he looked to Sophia to calm her, and Arthur Dimmesdale is likewise intimidated by Pearl. "I know nothing that I would not sooner encounter than this passion in a child," he says to Hester. "In Pearl's young beauty, as in the wrinkled witch, it has a preternatural effect. Pacify her, if thou lovest me" (CE 1:210).

Pearl's hysterical insistence on maintaining decorum carries the note of inward desperation that was audible in Una's outbursts. Sophia once read aloud a story titled "The Bear and the Skrattel," and her imitation of the Skrattel's unearthly shrill voice set Una off. "Little Una cries 'No; no!' with a kind of dread," Hawthorne noted, and he then specifies with an unnerving serenity the chronic distress of which this outcry gave evidence. "It is rather singular that she should so strongly oppose herself to whatever is unbeautiful or even unusual, while she is continually doing unbeautiful things in her own person. I think, if she were to see a little girl who behaved in all respects like herself, it would be a continual horror and misery to her, and would ultimately drive her mad" (CE 8:419).

Hawthorne uncannily predicts the psychic breakdowns that befell Una in later years, yet he could see that the child's mental torment was already severe. It could hardly have escaped him that she was doomed to her own company. More startling than Hawthorne's insight, however, is the tone of detached inquiry in which he pursues the "rather singular" puzzle of Una's inward war. Just as Dimmesdale's terror at Pearl's rage bespeaks Una's power to disconcert her father, so this cold diagnosis—with a vengeful impulse lurking beneath its objective surface—discloses Hawthorne's kinship with Chillingworth.

In Pearl these contradictions are resolved as Hester helps Arthur mount the scaffold: "The great scene of grief, in which the wild infant bore a part, had developed all her sympathies; and as her tears fell upon her father's cheek, they were the pledge that she would grow up amid human joy and sorrow, nor for ever do battle with the world, but be a woman in it" (CE 1:256). The child's "manlike" imperiousness gives way to tears of sympathy, and the "elflike" impersonal remoteness gives way to warm human relations. Like Pinocchio, Pearl is transformed from an unnatural creature, endowed with life but not truly human, into a "real little girl." Hawthorne expresses the confidence, as the narrative closes, that "her wild, rich nature had been softened and subdued, and made capable of a woman's gentle happiness" (262).

As many critics have observed, however, Pearl's prospective domestic felicity is not located in the United States or in any other clearly definable place. It is supported by a fabulous inheritance, which makes her "the richest heiress of her day," and Hawthorne is careful to point out that the seals on her letters have "bearings unknown to English heraldry" (CE 1:261–262). Hawthorne's conclusion exempts Pearl from the dilemmas that the book portrays but does not resolve them.

Even the concluding scaffold scene, where Pearl's redemption takes place, testifies to the interior disharmonies of the domestic ideal. The completed family group obeys Pearl's demand that Dimmesdale acknowledge her and her mother before the community. Yet that tableau also includes Chillingworth, "as one intimately connected with the drama of guilt and sorrow in which they had all been actors" (CE 1:253). While Chillingworth concedes that Dimmesdale has finally escaped his vengeance, his claim on Dimmesdale's conscience is vindicated—not dismissed—by the clergyman's final confession. The self-divided manhood represented by Arthur and Roger is not healed at the final scaffold scene; it comes to a crisis that neither man survives.

Hawthorne establishes a special relation between Pearl and Chillingworth that probes issues beyond the dilemmas of split manhood and of "true womanhood," namely the responsibilities of child rearing. The sin of Hester and Arthur is not only their defiance of Roger's legal claim; their soul-marriage fails to provide adequate nurture for Pearl. Hester refuses the injunction to break the child's will by a "frequent application of the rod" and instead "sought to impose a tender, but strict, control over the infant immortality that was committed to her charge" (CE 1:91–92). Yet Pearl's stubborn waywardness makes a mockery of sentimental blandishments. She is an incorrigible, like the slave child Topsy, in *Uncle Tom's Cabin,* who becomes tractable only when little Eva's death brings tears to her eyes, like those Pearl sheds over the expiring Arthur. Hester "grew acquainted with a certain peculiar look, that warned her when it would be labor thrown away to insist, persuade, or plead. It was a look so intelligent, yet inexplicable, so perverse, sometimes so malicious, . . . that Hester could not help questioning . . . whether Pearl was a human child" (92). Unlike Topsy, who has been beaten into hardness of heart, Pearl is demonically rebellious because her father does not acknowledge her.

Hawthorne repeatedly asserts the connection between Roger's claim and Pearl's need. As Hester refuses to name her lover, Roger calls from the crowd, "Speak, woman! . . . Speak; and give your child a father" (CE 1:68). In the midnight scaffold scene, when Hester and Pearl join hand in hand with Arthur, Pearl gestures toward Roger standing alone in the shadows, and includes him in the family group. Roger bequeaths his fortune to Pearl, a circumstance all the more striking in view of Arthur's failure to make provision for his child's support at any point in the narrative.

It never dawns on Arthur, despite his orgy of guilt over falling into sin, that he has any moral or material responsibility for his child. When the magistrates propose to remove Pearl from Hester's care, Arthur defends Hester's "indefeasible rights" by invoking "a quality of awful sacredness in the relation between this mother and this child" (CE 1:113–114). Yet the Reverend Wilson underscores the material responsibility that Arthur ignores, the need for "a father's kindness towards the poor, deserted babe." (116). As David Leverenz rightly noted, the relation of Pearl and Arthur presents a sharply intensified version of domesticity, in which the mother is overpresent and the father is absent, busy attaining distinction in the world (274).

As Dimmesdale marches toward the Election Day ceremony where he will consummate his career, Hester becomes miserably aware of the gulf that stands between them: Dimmesdale seems "so unattainable in his worldly position, and still more so in that far vista of his unsympathizing thoughts" (CE 1:239). Dimmesdale's prospective worldly triumph will be fueled by the emotional energies awakened by his conversation with Hester in the forest. Yet to Hester, that renewal of their self-consecrating love evaporates. "Her spirit sank with the idea that all must have been a delusion, and that . . . there could be no real bond betwixt the clergyman and herself" (239–240).

This moment dramatizes a paradox that has existed from the outset of the narrative, in which Hester and Dimmesdale are bound by a compelling intimate tie yet live solitary and apart. The daily experience of their communion of souls is, for the most part, an alien proximity in which each keeps a pained and guilty silence. Hester "could scarcely forgive him" Hawthorne tells us, "for being able so completely to withdraw himself from their mutual world; while she groped darkly, and stretched forth her cold hands, and found him not" (240).

This marriage-defining wretchedness besieges them even at the fullest dramatization of their marital bond. In the forest scene where Hester and Arthur re-enact their self-consecration, Hawthorne presents a collision between the claims of their relationship and the obligations represented by Pearl. Instead of staging a triumph of "natural" genders over social convention, this conflict pits nature against nature.

The renewal of marital communion begins as Arthur "put forth his hand, chill as death, and touched the chill hand of Hester Prynne." The two engage in commonplace small talk, which opens "the doors of intercourse," so that they could move onward, "step by step, into the themes that were brooding deepest in their hearts" (CE 1:190). Their spiritual and sexual bond comes slowly back to life, until at length Hester removes the letter from her bosom and throws it away, whereupon "there played around her mouth, and beamed out of her eyes, a radiant and tender smile, that seemed gushing from the very heart of womanhood" (202). As we have seen, the "womanhood" expressed here is not submissive and angelic domesticity, but the triumph of Hester's purposeful intelligence, releasing the full wealth of her sexual power. She has persuaded Arthur to begin a new life in a new place and has promised to sustain him with her strength and courage.

This moment of androgynous consummation is blessed by a flood of sunshine. "Such was the sympathy of Nature—that wild, heathen Nature of the forest, never subjugated by human law, nor illumined by higher truth—with the bliss of these two spirits! Love, whether newly born, or aroused from a deathlike slumber, must always create a sunshine, filling the heart so full of radiance, that it overflows upon the outward world" (CE 1:203). Yet this validation of their mutual world is soon crosscut by Pearl's refusal to accept it, and Hawthorne specifies this refusal as equally blessed by Nature.

During her parents' conversation, Pearl enters a prelapsarian communion with creatures of the forest: a partridge, a pigeon, a squirrel, and a fox. Even a wolf lets her pat its head. "The mother-forest, and these wild things which it nourished, all recognized a kindred wildness in the human child" (CE

1:204–205). Decking herself out with flowers and greenery, Pearl becomes "a nymph-child, or an infant dryad, or whatever else was in closest sympathy with the antique wood" (205). So adorned, Pearl fulfills her parents' sacred union. "It was with a feeling which neither of them had ever before experienced, that they sat and watched Pearl's slow advance. In her was visible the tie that united them. She had been offered to the world, these seven years past, as the living hieroglyphic, in which was revealed the secret they so darkly sought to hide,—all written in this symbol. . . . Pearl was the oneness of their being" (206–207).

Yet the child of nature is excluded from the relationship whose nature she embodies. "Another inmate had been admitted within the circle of the mother's feelings, and so modified the aspect of them all, that Pearl, the returning wanderer, could not find her wonted place, and hardly knew where she was" (CE 1:208). Pearl accordingly demands that the letter, with its "withering spell" be restored. Hester loses her power to animate Arthur's natural manhood as "the warmth and richness of her womanhood departed, like fading sunshine; and a gray shadow seemed to fall across her" (211). The soul-marriage of Arthur and Hester is again marked as adulterous, not by outmoded marital legislation or the self-division of self-made men, but by a logic that asserts itself when sexual intercourse is made a sacrament of the marital bond. The spiritual communion of the two souls is checked by the offspring that its enactment produces.

Running through the forest episode is an emblem of this native dissonance, a little brook that almost never flows clear in the sunlight because it is obstructed by fallen branches, boulders, and the roots of great trees. These obstacles, as natural as the stream itself, "choked up the current, and compelled it to form eddies and black depths" (CE 1:186). The stream has a wordless voice, like Dimmesdale's sorrowful and haunting undertone; it "still kept telling its unintelligible secret of some very mournful mystery that had happened—or making a prophetic lamentation about something that was yet to happen—within the verge of the dismal forest" (187). At the conclusion of the episode, after the communion of souls has been revived and self-stifled, Hawthorne tells us that "the melancholy brook would add this other tale to the mystery with which its little heart was already overburdened, and whereof it still kept up a murmuring babble, with not a whit more cheerfulness of tone than for ages heretofore" (213).

This device will serve as an emblem of Hawthorne's literary power, by which the miseries attendant on a specific form of marital intimacy are made to appear the blight that man was born for. The brook ceaselessly intimates a sorrow arising from the nature of nature and offers a mild and rueful comfort more compelling than Arthur's triumphant confession or Hester's messianic vision of a future day. The voice of the brook will not cancel the torments intrinsic to the domestic ideal but will keep saying them forever: "kind, quiet, soothing, but melancholy, like the voice of a young child that was spending its infancy without playfulness, and knew not how to be merry among sad acquaintance and events of sombre hue" (CE 1:186). The allusion here to Una's psychic disorder and early sorrow marks the paradox of Hawthorne's greatest art. The most luminous passages, whose wave fronts seem to travel across the relativities of history at an absolute speed and to create a radiance independent of any local reference, are entangled with the painful contingencies amid which they originate.

Hawthorne's masterwork occasioned a communion between Nathaniel and Sophia from which the rhetoric of domestic bliss was notably absent. Nathaniel later recalled "my emotions when I read the last scene of the Scarlet Letter to my wife, just after writing it—tried to read it, rather, for my voice swelled and heaved, as if I were tossed up and down on an ocean, as it subsided after a storm. But I was in a very nervous state, then, having gone through a great diversity and severity of emotion, for many months past. I think I have never overcome my own adamant in any other instance" (*English*, 225). That Nathaniel should consummate the months of creative torment in the image of an ocean storm is uncannily suited to its sources in himself, recalling his lost ship-captain father and the unresolvable grief that lay at the root of his lifelong struggle with the meaning of manliness. The "adamant" that allowed him to hold this suffering at bay, and thus to maintain the working coherence of his own mind, was relaxed for a moment here, so that it was almost impossible for him to read his own words. Yet the image also implies that the struggle had reached a pause; what Nathaniel feels is the subsiding.

Sophia was likewise filled with distress. "It broke her heart," her husband wrote the following day, "and sent her to bed with a grievous headache." His adamant now restored, Nathaniel considered Sophia's anguish "a triumphant success" (CE 16:311). When Sophia likewise regained her composure, she sent a letter to her sister Mary: "I do not know what you will think of the Romance," she wrote. "It is most powerful, & contains a moral as terrific & stunning as a thunder bolt. It shows that the Law cannot be broken" (313).

Sophia and Nathaniel were brought together and set apart by the same text, which each felt to be overpowering. Sophia contains her celebration in an assertion of unbreakable moral law, as though anyone reading it would receive the same thunderbolt of truth. Yet in admitting she has no idea what her sister will think, Sophia indicates her awareness of having passed through a distinctively personal and intimate experience. She was herself prospectively designated by Hawthorne's description—which he read to her that night—of the "angel" of the coming revelation who will show "how sacred love should make us happy, by the truest test of a life successful to such an end." Yet her headache was hardly caused by this compliment, even if she took it ironically. The thunderbolt lay in Hawthorne's compelling depiction of the burdens that were entailed on women by this ideal, the burdens borne by Hester Prynne.

It has long been customary to propose Hester as an opposite of Sophia, as a figure of erotic vitality and womanly defiance in contrast to Sophia's pasteboard propriety. Yet Sophia, too, had a "rich, Oriental characteristic," visible as she danced like Salome for her husband at the Old Manse. She was also a woman of resolute will, jealous of her independence. She met efforts to subdue her, including Nathaniel's efforts, with stubborn resistance; and her worshipful obedience and delicacy of soul were mobilized as stratagems of defiance. Sophia's headache indicates that she shared the experience her husband described in the Custom House Introduction, when he placed Hester's letter against his own breast and felt a burning heat. Sophia knew the demonic energy as her own, having long sought to quash it through the transcendant power of art, including her husband's art. When her sister Elizabeth proposed that Nathaniel had "purified himself by casting out a legion of devils" in *The Scarlet Letter,* Sophia denied it with her customary vehemence: "It was a work of the imagination wholly & no personal experience, as you know well."[1]

A critical separation was now taking place, however, because the book was ready to lead an independent life. It was just beginning a career of literary power that has run on for nearly a century and a half, while the Hawthornes continued their daily lives in the allotted span. Nathaniel lived another fourteen years, until 1864; Sophia died seven years later. They had sustained difficulties during the years of struggle that were to be augmented in the wake of success and were sharply visible in the scenes with which we began, at the Wayside in Concord.

The domestic ideal best served the needs of self-made men-in-the-making, recruiting women and children into subordinate roles. Yet once manly self-making is complete, the ideal loses its imperative urgency and its power to hold conflicts in abeyance. A woman who bolsters her husband's self-trust finds her importance diminished as he gains recognition beyond the home. A man who marries "my own self" will be disconcerted to confront her distinctive ambitions. Once their alliance attains its goals, the accustomed comradeship decays and symptoms of alienation mark the ordinary business of the household. At the Old Manse, as later in Salem, Sophia shared her husband's work before it went to the publishers. She was stung when word arrived at the Wayside that Nathaniel's biography of Pierce was in print. "It is rather too bad," she snapped, "that all the world should read it before I do" (Family Notebook, 8 September 1852).

If worldly triumph is spectacular, as it was for Hawthorne after the publication of *The Scarlet Letter,* both husband and wife will contend with the adulation of strangers and the jealousy of former friends, now of lower status. Yet the wife may have grounds for jealousy as well and may reflect bitterly on what she has suffered for the sake of her husband's victory. Such gestures of gratitude as she receives (and Sophia received many) are necessarily qualified, since the ethos of self-making portrays her husband as the unaided author of his own success. Did Sophia notice that she is never mentioned in the introduction to *Mosses from an Old Manse,* where Nathaniel creates the impression that he is an autonomous genius, working alone?[2]

The self-made husband soon discovers that he is only as good as his most recent success and that fulfillment lies in making a self-made self, not in occupying one. He may feel the impulse to re-enact the struggle from youthful obscurity and may look for a new "my own self" to inspire him. His achieved position now becomes an obstruction; and if his wife continues to seek vicarious fulfillment in it, she is wedded to a reputation that seems a death trap for him.

These commonplace difficulties of middle-class married life may be more or less severe, of course, and they may be surmounted. The domestic ideal in its early formation, however, scarcely provided even the means of recognizing them. The sharp segregation of home from world and the idealization of wifely self-sacrifice cooperated to sustain a utopian illusion that counteracted awareness of such problems or made them appear unthinkably terrible when they broke through the veil of bliss.

After Nathaniel had finished *The House of the Seven Gables,* Ellery Channing visited the "little Red House" at Lenox and wrote to his wife how much the Hawthornes had changed for the worse since their newlywed days at the Old Manse. His description is unfriendly and was doubtless sharpened by envy; yet it evokes the marital politics that prompted Hawthorne to say

that the house "looks like the Scarlet Letter." Channing observed that
Hawthorne's "having written nine books [has] made him a lion," but that
he is more reclusive than ever. "He has lived here . . . a year & a half I
believe, & I suppose he has hardly seen a face beyond that of his wife and
children."³ What strikes Channing's eye is a scene of domestic disenchant-
ment:

> I would think Sophia could not realize his ideal of beauty at all. She is by no means
> prepossessing and has not added to her beauty by time. And she has none of the
> means whereby elegance and refinement may be shed over the humblest apartment.
> The children brought up in the worst way for visitors, by themselves, never having
> been to school, have of course nothing but bad manners. They break in when not
> required & are not in fact either handsome or attractive. But how could the parents
> help this. I have formed a very different opinion of the [Hawthornes] this visit from
> any I have ever had before, and [Hawthorne] has greatly altered.

In *The House of the Seven Gables,* Hawthorne had brooded over the
"thousand-fold" morbid influences that infiltrate the domestic hearthside
and impel a family to roam unrestfully from one place to another. Now
Channing reports that Hawthorne "thinks a good deal of coming to Concord
and possibly to buy a place"; but Channing "would not encourage" such a
plan. "Assuredly he would get tired of his purchase, and then he would be
obliged all his days to think of selling or again to go to work moving. He
always I believe finds fault with the people among whom he settles." When
the Hawthornes moved to the Wayside in Concord in 1852, it was the eighth
home they had occupied in ten years of marriage; at least eleven more would
follow in the next eight years, during the family's European sojourn, as one
place after another dissatisfied one or both of them.⁴ "I do not know what
sort of character it will form in the children," Hawthorne remarked on one
of their English moves, "this unsettled, shifting, vagrant life, with no central
home to turn to, except what we carry in ourselves" (*English,* 425).

Hawthorne's emergence from obscurity and severe financial hardship had
been remarkably swift: less than four years had elapsed between his ejection
from the Custom House at Salem and Pierce's election to the presidency.
The years of steady work in Liverpool brought a measure of wealth, and his
writings consolidated his international fame. In 1858 he was able to treat the
family to a stay in Rome and even thought of living there permanently. But
this luxurious prospect turned into a nightmare, throwing the family "soul-
system" into crisis, and breaking through Hawthorne's adamant altogether.

PART FOUR

Roman Fever

CHAPTER THIRTEEN

City of the Soul

"Oh *why not live in Rome,*" Sophia wrote to her sister Elizabeth, nearly a decade before she married Nathaniel Hawthorne. "Pack up—Betty—& let us be off—& live in Rome—the eternal—imperial 'Mother of dead empires'—the city of the soul" (CE 14:905–906). Sophia was inspired by a romantic vision of Rome that filled a substantial literature in the early nineteenth century, and Elizabeth doubtless recognized "the city of the soul" as an allusion to *Childe Harold's Pilgrimage.* But Lord Byron joined a chorus in which there were many women's voices, including Anna Jameson's in *Diary of an Ennuyée,* which Elizabeth and Sophia read together; and Sophia added her own voice when she published her *Notes in England and Italy.* This tradition of womanly response had been inaugurated by Germaine de Staël's *Corinne; or, Italy,* long before English romantic poets began their journeys of heartsick yearning to the mother of dead empires.

Sophia had devoured *Corinne* at age fifteen. It became an organizing force in her moral and aesthetic consciousness and a medium of communion with her sisters, including spiritual sisters like Sarah Clarke and Connie Hall (CE 14:906). Margaret Fuller was admired and taunted as "a Yankee Corinna" because her rapturous poetic utterance followed the example of de Staël's heroine (Chevigny, 88, 214). Fuller declared that a whole generation of American women had been touched by the liberating power of de Staël's intellect: "Its beams make the obscurest schoolhouse in New England warmer and lighter to the little rugged girls who are gathered together on its wooden benches" (Gutwirth, 308).

De Staël's depiction of Rome is governed by a feminist vision of thwarted potentiality. The remains of two empires, one dead and the other moribund, reveal a native genius that is now fettered. Rome is a great Mother who has become sterile, an imperial power rendered powerless. Italian statuary, palaces, and museums offer images of this complex plight, and the odd-sounding relation of the title *Corinne* to the subtitle *or Italy* makes sense in these terms. To know Italy is to know Corinne, and so it happens that the doomed love affair at the heart of the narrative is inaugurated when Corinne leads an English visitor, Lord Nelvil, on a series of guided tours. As Corinne explains Italian life and culture, the insistent note of feminist anguish becomes clearly audible: "Rome, so long an asylum of the exile, is she not herself dethroned? Her aspect consoles sovereigns despoiled like her" (53).

At the outset of the narrative Corinne's artistic powers are not frustrated: she is famous as a poet who rivals Petrarch and Tasso and takes part in public occasions as an *improvisatrice,* pouring forth extemporaneous odes and chants. Nelvil first sees her at the Capitol, being crowned for her achievements to the tune of citywide bell ringing and the firing of cannon, an accolade she receives, however, with a "timid air . . . [that] seemed to ask pardon for her triumph." To Nelvil she seems "born to fulfil the usual duties of life with perfect simplicity" (18), and he soon learns that she considers her fame empty because it has not brought true love. Nelvil's view of womanhood seems vindicated by Corinne's dilemma, as de Staël explains: "There can be nothing more hostile to the habits and opinions of an Englishman than any great publicity given to the career of a woman" (16). Corinne is eventually destroyed by the conflict between her public creativity and the yearning for domestic fulfillment.

De Staël moves her characters across a geography of gender in which Italy and England are poles that define a landscape of intricate conflict. Corinne's father was British, we learn, so that the happy freedom of her Italian girlhood was overlaid by the strict schooling in womanly self-effacement that she received in England, where her father took her after her Italian mother's death. Corinne rebels against this indoctrination and returns to Italy at the first opportunity; but she has internalized English ideals and finds in Nelvil a style of manhood lamentably absent in the "effeminate" Italian males by whom she is now surrounded.

De Staël's culture of origin in revolutionary France gave her a vantage from which to transform the historical actualities of England and Italy into gender allegory. Protestant, democratic, industrializing society generated an internal romantic rebellion, which found in Rome an endlessly provocative set of templates on which to formulate the contradictions inherent in the culture not of Italy but of England, and even more starkly of America, where the social order produced by industrialization was not moderated by ancient hierarchies of inherited rank.

Yet Italy was not merely a blank screen on which Anglo-American obsessions were projected; Roman Catholic gender arrangements challenged Protestant ideals. The Church did not picture family life as a haven in a heartless world but as a principal site of worldly contamination. Men and women seeking a holy life renounced the home, and the celibate males revered as "fathers" typically wore long gowns instead of trousers. Women saints and the women who headed religious houses were venerated for a spiritual fulfillment they had achieved without being wives and mothers; and the consummate Catholic goddess, the Virgin Mother of God, attained her pre-eminence though a communion with Godhead unmediated by her hapless, bewildered, and obedient husband.

When Sophia Hawthorne at last realized her ambition of living in Italy, she got a taste of the public admiration Italians were prepared to bestow on women of artistic gifts. On one of their journeys the Hawthornes stopped in Bolsena, a town of "infinite abominations," where a "stream of horror" flowed a yard or two broad down the main street, as countless hogs sprawled about and rooted through the garbage and the shit. Yet Sophia finds here a long-denied gratification:

> After lunch we went out to sketch. I was soon surrounded with most interested spectators. Boys, girls, women and men and babies in arms, all looking over my paper. They were all more nasty than I can by any means tell. . . . I could hardly breathe such an atmosphere as they created. Armies of fleas attacked me without stint besides. [But] this beggarly crowd of Italians made an impression of refinement and civilization. . . . Their splendid black eyes (which are clean) shone with delight at every new line I drew. . . . Whenever any one stood between me and my prospect the rest commanded him to move from the Signora's eye—and they kept a vista for me most jealously all the time. I showed them a few other sketches in my book. They exclaimed at the Camp Tower of Siena—O bellissima! bellissima! but always in subdued tones. . . . As I bade them Addio, they smiled and bowed and waved their hands like so many princes. It was wonderful.
>
> (Italy, 14 October 1858)

Sophia found in Italy a measure of the fulfillment promised by de Staël's geography of gender, but not without suffering the attendant miseries.

Abiding dilemmas of her life and of her marriage to Nathaniel now came to the surface; and Nathaniel too was swamped by long-standing unresolved conflicts called forth in the city of the soul.

A structural crisis gripped the Hawthorne family in Rome, centered on Una's special position within it. "I do not know how any mortal mixture can be to us what Una is," Sophia had once remarked, and the emerging family pattern bore out her intuition.[1] Julian and Rose stand apart from the intensely interinvolved trio of parents and firstborn, not as unloved or unimportant but as disengaged (blessedly disengaged) from the triangulation of forces that trapped Una. The childlike purity for which Una was named became intolerable for her during the Roman sojourn, and she suffered a psychic collapse in which the sacred marital collusion of Nathaniel and Sophia was disrupted.

That Una suffered "Roman fever," a local term for malaria, serves to connect the Hawthornes' private torment with the romantic import of "Rome"; this crisis engaged the larger community in practical terms as well. The Hawthornes' affluence and public position involved them as never before with persons not blood kin, who became in one way or another part of the household. Important parts are played in the Roman crisis by Ada Shepard, the governess who aided Sophia in nursing Una, and by Dr. Franco, who provided medical treatment. The drama also involved Louisa Lander, an American sculptor living in Rome, and the Hawthornes' deceased friend Margaret Fuller, who had come to Rome a decade earlier and whose memory now filled the Hawthornes with disgust.

These figures play out a congregation of stories at whose core is an intense hush, that of Una's sickroom, a place that remains silent because the crisis disables the language by which "the family"—both the Hawthorne family and the middle-class family—understood itself. The episodes concerning Shepard, Franco, Lander, Fuller (and others) range outward to implicate broad issues of the cultural construction of the domestic ideal, including the elaborated significance that was given to "Una" as the century unfolded. But the stories do not merge into a single narrative marching order; they interrupt one another and intersect as they circulate about a silence that encroaches on them all.

At the conclusion of *Corinne,* de Staël's heroine disappears into seclusion, where she dies, the energies of her ambiguous torment now invested in the

Italian landscape through which she had passed. The relation of Una's illness to *The Marble Faun* reverses this process. Una does not embody the alluring and contaminating antitheses of the domestic ideal but the absoluteness of its defining purity. Her collapse is everywhere present in the dispersed narrative and descriptive fragments of Hawthorne's Roman romance, most poignantly in that work's resolute yet unavailing determination to celebrate domestic innocence.

Yet this is to run ahead of our stories, which should begin where they will end, with Nathaniel and Sophia themselves, to whom Rome provided material for a dissonant marital duet. Sophia was delighted from the outset of their stay, while Nathaniel was filled with languor and peevish restlessness. "The climate is most detestable; it is full of poison. I feel no energy or enterprise, and should really be glad to lie in bed every day, and all day long, if the fleas did not make me so very uncomfortable there. Mrs. Hawthorne, on the contrary, is full of life and enterprise, and has already made acquaintance with almost every temple and church" (CE 18:138).

Nathaniel struggles "to get down upon paper the dreariness and ugliness, nastiness, discomfort, shabbiness," and finally concocts a term for the whole mess: "un-home-likeness." The great palaces, where wealthy Romans made their households, merely enlarge on the pervading worldly squalor. "There was never any idea of domestic comfort—or of what we include in the name of home—at all implicated in such structures; they being generally built by wifeless and childless churchmen for the display of pictures and statuary in galleries and long suites of rooms" (CE 14:58–59). Far from exhibiting greatness of soul, Roman splendor appears a cold and showy surrogate for domestic felicity, indulged in by the "fathers" of a corrupt church who lack the "sweet household ties connecting them with wife and daughter" (CE 4:411).

A central icon of the Anglo-American fascination with Roman un-home-likeness was a picture hanging in the vast urban palazzo of the Barberinis, before which every Romantic pilgrim paid homage: "Guido's Beatrice Cenci." It is not Guido Reni's work and not a portrait of Beatrice, yet the Hawthornes were among those who found it endlessly absorbing as an exemplum of Italian familial perversion: it evoked the evil of *il Papa* himself, united with the savage cruelty of a Roman paterfamilias and bearing down on a girl just Una's age.

"And now we sat down before Beatrice Cenci!" Sophia rejoiced. "This is a masterpiece which baffles words. No copy engraved, or in oils, gives the remotest idea of this most wonderful face." Sophia was familiar with the face, and with the general organization of the picture (Fig. 6), having seen copies before she came to Rome and having her anticipation further sharpened by the local industry in images of Beatrice, which was booming in 1858. "It is all over Rome," she observed, "in every picture dealer's, of every size, and engraved as well" (Italy, 20 February).

According to contemporary fantasy the picture captured Beatrice's appearance at the moment she emerged from prison to be beheaded for the murder of her father, Francesco Cenci, who had imprisoned her at his country estate, lashed her mercilessly with a "bull's pizzle," and raped her (Ricci, 1:122). Looking at the picture, Sophia cultivates ambiguous emotions that are evoked by these lurid particulars but not explained by them. "Never from any human countenance looked out such ruin of hope, joy and life, but there is unconsciousness still, as if she did not comprehend how or why she is crushed and lost. The white polished brow is a throne of infantine, angelic purity, without a visible cloud or furrow of pain—yet a wild endless despair hovers over it" (Italy, 20 February).

The Cenci legend was a subject of conflicting interpretations from the time of the actual events in the late sixteenth century; yet there was never any dispute concerning Francesco's horrible domestic tyranny, or any doubt that other members of the household hated him too and took a larger role in the assassination than Beatrice did. Beatrice may indeed have been entirely innocent, since she steadfastly denied any involvement in the killing until tortured by the judicial authorities (Ricci, 2:130). A prominent version of the legend held that she was executed at the behest of Pope Clement VIII, so that he could wipe out Francesco's heirs and take possession of the Cencis' vast holdings in land and treasure.

Sophia Hawthorne, like other participants in the romantic Cenci-mania, lost herself in mazes of brooding over meanings she does not clearly articulate. Beatrice's innocence, instead of providing a firm standard against which to measure the depravity of her father and of her judicial murder, is the central feature of a paradoxical inward anguish. Beatrice's purity is perfect, but it is also tainted; all innocently, it seems, she has lost her innocence. Sophia takes these contradictions as the sign of a fathomless import. "The mouth is unspeakably affecting," she muses. "The rosebud lips, sweet and tender, are parted slightly, yet with no cry or power to utter a word. . . . Night is gathering in her eyes—and the perfect face is turning to stone with

Fig. 6. "Guido's Beatrice Cenci"

the weight of voiceless woe. She is a spotless lily of Eden, trailed over by a serpent, and unable to understand the desecration, yet struck with the blight to the heart" (Italy, 20 February).

Beatrice's portrait provided a focal point for questions of incest and patricide inherent in middle-class family relations and very much alive in the Hawthorne household. Among the meanings of Beatrice's "innocence" is the claim that killing her father was justified, that she was right to assert her sexual integrity against his assaults. This view contradicts the assumption that a woman's sexuality is a vessel of male virtue, initially her father's virtue, which he transfers at marriage to her husband.

This patriarchal conception of female virtue is explicitly asserted in George Savile's *Advice to a Daughter,* which ran through many editions in eighteenth-century America. Savile informs his daughter that women deserve a heavier penalty for adultery than men because "the *Honour* of *Families* is in your keeping" (Cott, *Root,* 79). Although such dynastic imperatives have relaxed, the role of women as vehicles of male honor has not been obliterated by the domestic ideal or by subsequent enhancements of the status of women. Patriarchal folkways at the close of the twentieth century still maintain the rule in certain American jurisdictions that a husband cannot rape his wife, that is, that she has no legally recognized sexual volition independent of his. And women continue to acquire this understanding of their derivative moral status in the way George Savile's daughter acquired it, from their fathers: paternal incest as overt sexual intercourse, Linda Gordon observes, "merely exaggerates the situation of femaleness itself."[2]

The drama of Beatrice's victimization acquired a special fascination in the nineteenth century because democratic doctrines of individual dignity had strengthened the assertion of womanly autonomy and heightened the attendant conflicts. The routine exercise of patriarchal prerogatives was now implicitly recast as sexual crime, yet the rapist father could not be slain without guilt. The dilemmas inherent in this new cultural situation regularly erupted at the threshold between girlhood and womanhood where Beatrice, like Una Hawthorne, was trapped.

Tocqueville explains that the transition to adulthood was complicated for American women because girlhood was a locale at which democratic doctrines of individual autonomy were extended beyond white males. The "emancipation" of an American girl begins long before she reaches marriageable age: "She has scarcely ceased to be a child when she already thinks for herself, speaks with freedom, and acts on her own impulse" (2:198). Yet this womanly independence "is irrecoverably lost in the bonds of matrimony." Tocqueville does not shrink from underscoring the contradiction that is traversed when a young woman becomes a wife. "The former makes her father's house an abode of freedom and of pleasure; the latter lives in the home of her husband as if it were a cloister" (2:201).

Tocqueville claims that an American girl grasps the necessity of self-effacement the moment she becomes a grown woman, employing her powers of independent judgment to examine the social circumstances she confronts. She then sees that her moral virtue, and "even her social existence," have reality in the minds of male beholders, to be denied her if she "depart[s] for an instant from the established usages." Summoning "the virile habits which her education has given her" (2:201), the young woman makes her last gesture of masculine autonomy, namely its relinquishment.

This fantasy of instantaneous voluntary choice shields Tocqueville from realizing that the father's household, for all its "freedom and pleasure," is a school of submission in which a daughter learns the effacement of her sexuality that will be required in adulthood, the "constant sacrifice of her pleasures to her duties" (2:201). A growing girl learns from her father that the pleasures of women are properly at the disposal of men, such that girlish independence must be restricted as sexual appetite burgeons with the onset of puberty.

When Una Hawthorne was five years old, as we have seen, she was given repeated indications of her father's revulsion at her taking pleasure in her own body, especially when this aroused him sexually. Like middle-class girls generally, Una received a schooling in self-abnegation that set her at odds with her own desire. When she sought her own pleasure or displayed her genitals to him, Nathaniel responded as though she were a monster, and she internalized his response as an index of her own moral reality. Such a socialization proceeds without contradiction so long as adult women are seen as morally derivative beings, whose sexuality is experienced as normal only when it is pleasing to males. But as women begin to know themselves as centers of moral autonomy, such early training in "innocence" is felt to violate sexual selfhood. The invasion of a young girl's sexuality by the "earthy monster" of her father's sexual disgust then becomes tantamount to rape.

To impose this patriarchal sexuality on one's daughter is incest; the act of fighting back—as Una fought back—is patricide: it radically challenges the fatherhood being asserted. Lord Capulet felt no qualms at threatening Juliet with starvation if she refused to marry the man he had chosen, and Nathaniel likewise displayed his spontaneous fatherly conscience when he squirmed with loathing at Una's pleasure in sexually titillating fun. This paternal character could not survive the emergence of sexual autonomy in women or its cultivation in little girls. Such fatherhood had to be killed in actual fathers if independent womanhood was to be born in actual women. The incest and patricide featured together in the story of Beatrice Cenci have an interlocking relationship in the life of the Hawthorne household.

The family's Roman ordeal played out multiple ambiguous meanings of childlike innocence, including Nathaniel's innocence. Una's collapse on the threshold separating childhood and womanhood accompanied the collapse of her father's inward inviolacy and the consequent decay of his creative power. When the crisis had passed and the family was preparing to leave Rome, Nathaniel returned to the Barberini palace to take a farewell look at Beatrice Cenci. She seemed to him "unhumanized by some terrible fate, and gazing at me out of a remote and inaccessible region, where she was frightened to be alone, but where no sympathy could reach her" (CE 14:520). Nathaniel saw in her the guiltless guilt that blighted his own life.

CHAPTER FOURTEEN

Repudiations and Inward War

Hawthorne's purity was brought into question by way of a friendship he formed at Rome with a young American woman named Louisa Lander, and his effort to defend himself set the stage for Una's collapse. This strange concatenation took place because complex psychic forces interlocked feminine innocence with his own.

Observe Hawthorne's response to the satyrs in the Villa Borghese's collection of classical statuary:

> I like these strange, sweet, playful, rustic creatures, almost entirely human as they are, yet linked so prettily, without monstrosity, to the lower tribes by the long, furry ears, or by a modest tail; indicating a strain of honest wildness in them. . . . In my mind, they connect themselves with that ugly, bearded woman, who was lately exhibited in England, and by some supposed to have been engendered betwixt a human mother and an orang-outang; but she was a wretched monster—the faun, a natural and delightful link betwixt human and brute life, and with something of a divine character intermingled.
>
> (CE 14:173–174)

The masculine innocence Hawthorne visualizes here is attended by a loathing that is gendered female. To him, the satyrs are an exact obverse of the bearded woman; instead of hideous anomalies, they are innocent males who possess alluring feminine traits. This is particularly true of Praxiteles' Resting Satyr (Fig. 7), which Hawthorne eventually placed at the center of his meditations, renaming it "the marble faun," so as to remove the implication of brutish lust. His original notebook description conveys the figure's sexual appeal:

> His only garment falls half way down his back, but leaves his whole front, and all the rest of his person, exposed, displaying a very beautiful form, but clad in more flesh, with more full and rounded outlines, and less development of muscle, than the old sculptors were wont to assign to masculine beauty. . . . [The face has] beautiful and most agreeable features, but rounded, especially about the throat and chin; a nose almost straight, yet very slightly curving inward, a voluptuous mouth, that seems almost (not quite) to smile outright;—in short, the whole person conveys the idea of an amiable and sensual nature, easy, mirthful, apt for jollity.
>
> (CE 14:191–192)

Hawthorne's famous postmortem denigration of Margaret Fuller, written just two weeks before he encountered the Praxiteles statue, elaborates the same fusion of sensuality, animality, and androgyny, now in their demonic female version. Margaret becomes the orangutan's monster offspring, whose qualities invert the innocence of the faun.

The Hawthornes had known for years that Margaret had fallen in love with Giovanni Angelo Ossoli during her stay in Italy, had a child by him, and subsequently married him. As Nathaniel returns to this story he takes note of Ossoli's extraordinary good looks and his lack of intellect, concluding that Margaret had fallen victim to lust. "I do not understand what feeling there could have been, except it were purely sensual," he observes, and her acting on this impulse Hawthorne takes as evidence of a "strong, heavy, unpliable, and, in many respects, defective and evil nature" (CE 14:155–156). Margaret's effort to refine her native coarseness only compounded the anomaly, Hawthorne declares. She sought

> to make herself the greatest, wisest, best woman of the age. . . . She took credit to herself for having been her own Redeemer, if not her own Creator; and, indeed, she was far more a work of art than any of Mr. Mozier's statues. But she was not working on an inanimate substance, like marble or clay; there was something within her that she could not possibly come at, to re-create and refine it; and, by and by, this rude old potency bestirred itself, and undid all her labor in the twinkling of an eye.
>
> (156–157)

The correlation between Margaret and the faun is signaled by the incomplete self-transformation Hawthorne finds in each, through which "animal" impulses are subjected to an imperfect discipline. He points out that the faun "might be refined through his feelings, so that the coarser, animal part of his nature would be thrown into the back ground, though liable to assert itself

MUNIFICENTIA·SS·D·N·BENEDICTI
PP·XIV·A·D·MDCCLIII

Fig. 7.   Praxiteles' Resting Satyr

at any time" (CE 14:192). But the animality of the faun is a form of "honest wildness," ensuring that he cannot be subjugated by the oppressive conventions of society, even as his feelings are refined. Margaret's animal nature, by contrast, is a "rude old potency" capable of precipitating the sudden collapse of her manlike self-making.

Hawthorne's attack on Margaret is especially cruel because it betrays their early friendship; by the same token it testifies to the conflicts about "innocence" that divided his mind. The woman who had celebrated Hawthorne's divine feminine creativeness—his freedom from conventional gender definitions—is now condemned for a kindred independence. Hawthorne's voluptuous flow of venom ends in gloating over Margaret's failure on exactly this point: "On the whole, I do not know but I like her the better for it;—the better, because she proved herself a very woman, after all, and fell as the weakest of her sisters might" (CE 14:157). Her evil and defective nature was a shadow-form of his impulsive childlike purity.

Hawthorne's repudiation of Margaret is re-enacted in the radical volte-face that took place in his relation to Louisa Lander, who was trying to make a career in Rome as a sculptor. As Nathaniel got to know her, she struck him as wonderfully successful in asserting her freedom from the enthrallments of society. She was, at first glance, a female version of the faun.

Nathaniel and Sophia had probably known that Lander was in Rome before they arrived, since she was from a prominent Salem family; and Louisa was certainly well acquainted with Hawthorne's reputation. She was alert to the family's arrival in late January 1858 and paid a call at their lodgings only five days later. There swiftly developed an unprecedented family friendship between Lander and the Hawthornes; they exchanged frequent visits, and they made excursions together in the company of Una and the other youngsters. Louisa's knowledge of Rome was very helpful, in large ways and small, as on March 1 when she called in the morning to tell Sophia that the Vatican would be closed that day, just in time to prevent her wasting a journey (Italy, 1 March).

To celebrate Una's fourteenth birthday on March 3, the group made a tour of the catacombs, carrying candles to light the dank passageways. The "baby," Rose, kept a tight hold on her mamma's dress in the eerie darkness, but Una herself, not the least bit frightened, said "it was the best time she ever had in her life." That evening after dinner Louisa "turned into an old New England dame for baby's amusement—with admirable truth—in muslin cap and spectacles, old brown cloak and black gown and a cane. She looked an hundred years old, and was not Miss Lander at all. We laughed beyond all comfort and propriety" (Italy, 3 March). A thrill of liberation can be detected in this round of laughter, as Lander made fun of the harsh puritanical womanhood Sophia herself had repudiated, by way of her extraordinary self-education, her transcendental journey of the soul, and her passionate love of art. Louisa's burlesque of outdated proprieties had meaning for Una as well as she entered her fifteenth year. Louisa's independent life in Rome offered Una an image of the person she wanted to become.

Within two weeks of her first visit to the Hawthornes, Louisa asked to do a bust of Nathaniel; he readily agreed, and there followed more than a dozen sittings. Sophia at times accompanied him to Louisa's studio, but for the most part he went by himself. "She is living here quite alone, in delightful freedom," Nathaniel commented, and he found himself intrigued with her way of life, enough to "take a similar freedom with her moral likeness to that which she was taking with my physical one" (CE 14:78).

Lander was, like Sophia herself, a spiritual daughter of de Staël's Corinne. She was among the women Henry James sardonically described as "that strange sisterhood of American 'lady sculptors' who at one time settled upon the seven hills in a white, marmorean flock" (*Story,* 257), of whom the most prominent was Harriet Hosmer. Yet at the heart of Louisa's freedom, it seems to Hawthorne, is her obedience to the domestic ideal: "a young woman, living in almost perfect independence, thousands of miles from her New England home, going fearlessly about these mysterious streets, by night as well as by day, with no household ties, no rule or law but that within her; yet acting with quietness and simplicity, and keeping, after all, within a homely line of right" (CE 14:78). Recasting these issues in *The Marble Faun,* Hawthorne speaks of Hilda as "an example of the freedom of life which it is possible for a female artist to enjoy at Rome," where the "conventional rules" may be relaxed because "purity of heart and life are allowed to assert themselves, and to be their own proof and security, to a degree unknown in the society of other cities" (CE 4:54–55).

When the clay version of the bust was completed, Hawthorne, altogether delighted with it, immediately dispatched a letter to William Ticknor conveying his enthusiasm. "Miss Lander, a lady from my native town, has made an excellent bust of me, of which I will enclose a photograph, if I can get one. Even Mrs. Hawthorne is delighted with it, and, as a work of art, it has received the highest praise from all the sculptors here." Hawthorne frankly requests Ticknor's aid in advancing Lander's career: "I tell you this in the hope that you and Fields will do what may be in your power to bring Miss Lander's name favorably before the public; for she is coming back to America, (for the summer only) and might be greatly benefitted by receiving commissions for busts &c. &c." (CE 18:140–141).

Although a principal object of Louisa's trip to the United States was to seek such commissions, she also brought word of Hawthorne's personal affairs to his friends and relations. Unique in the story of the Hawthorne family, she had been taken up as an intimate. Apart from the fourteen times he had visited her studio for sittings, Hawthorne's pocket diary makes note of seventeen excursions and evening visits between late January and mid-April, including a visit on April 13, the day he made a payment for her work, when she came to Hawthorne's lodgings in the evening "after all but me had gone to bed" (CE 14:579–592). "She is a very nice person," Hawthorne explained to Ticknor, "and I like her exceedingly" (CE 18:141).

It seems plausible that Nathaniel saw in Louisa a "delightful freedom" that he himself yearned to regain, the innocent impulsiveness he had cherished with Sophia in their paradise at the Old Manse. His fame and fortune were secure after the harsh years of successful struggle as a "man among men"; and his consular duties were at an end. He now confronted a chronic male dilemma: once self-making is completed, he must settle for what he has become, and he no longer possesses a meaningful future unless the drama of self-creation can be re-enacted. What is now recognized as the crisis of "mid-life" has origins in the culture of masculine self-making, and it includes an impulse to start again at the beginning and a search for sources of spiritual regeneration. In their premarital marriage Nathaniel had adopted Sophia as the repository of his self-in-the-making and a guarantor of the innocence that entitled him to cut the unconventional path that had led to his triumphs. Did his friendship with Louisa Lander offer an extension of this sponsorship, a renewed contact with his own "feminine" creativeness? If the relationship had intimate meanings for Nathaniel as an implicit communion of souls, it was still entirely beyond reproach. The purity that authorized Louisa's independent life in the mysterious Roman streets likewise permitted Nathaniel the freedom that he enjoyed in knowing and seeing her. Yet the underlying ambivalence was likewise primed to erupt.

While Louisa was making her journey to America, the Hawthornes went for the summer to Florence, and the day after their return to Rome, in October 1858, Cephas Thompson showed up with a damaging story to tell about Louisa. Nathaniel's pocket diary records the visit, but not the story, and comments: "What a pity!" (CE 14:615).

Lander's cousin John Rogers, who came to Rome within the year, wrote home that Louisa "has the reputation of having lived on uncommonly good terms with some man here. She is very vain of her figure, and a number of respectable people affirm that she has exposed herself as a model before them in a way that would astonish all modest Yankees. I suppose there is not much doubt of that part of the story, and it probably forms the foundation of all the rest."[1] The American artists in Rome took a grave interest in this matter, and William Wetmore Story headed up an unofficial "court of inquiry," composed of several sculptors, to look into it (Craven, 332). If Lander's success with Hawthorne had aroused animosity among the male artists at Rome, this occasion certainly gave them a chance to make things difficult for her. Cephas Thompson, who showed up so promptly on Hawthorne's doorstep, had good reason for jealousy: in 1850 he had received a commission to paint the portrait marking Hawthorne's entrance into international fame, just two months after *The Scarlet Letter* was published (Gollin, *Portraits*, 29–30).

Louisa refused to respond to the "inquiry," on the ground that to do so was beneath her dignity and was inconsistent with her knowledge of her own innocence. The rumors were not halted by her stand; on the contrary, it appears that they became accepted as commonplace matters of fact, to which Louisa responded likewise with defiance. Lander "snaps her fingers at all Rome," John Rogers remarked.

The friendship between Nathaniel and Louisa now lost its protective aura of unquestionable innocence. If Hawthorne had imagined that Louisa's "purity," like Sophia's, included an exclusive mothering devotion to his own childlike nature, he now made the unwelcome discovery that she was interested in other men. Yet any such resentment would have been mingled with guilty alarm. Nathaniel's intimacy with Louisa now assumed a potentially lurid meaning, which cast light back on the story of their many hours alone together. Whether their relation was "impure" was an issue even before Nathaniel and Sophia went to see the finished bust, now carved in marble, and confronted its remarkable sensuality—the beautifully rounded throat and chin, full lips, and broad, smooth expanse of naked shoulders and chest (Fig. 8).

The Hawthornes had been startled by the nudity of the pictures and statues they viewed in Italy, and their minds insistently formed a judgment concerning the sexual interaction between artist and model. "Who can trust the religious sentiment of Raphael," Hawthorne asks, "after seeing . . . the Fornarina of the Barberini palace, and feeling how sensual the artist must have been, to paint such a brazen trollop of his own accord, and lovingly!"[2]

Fig. 8.   Louisa Lander's bust of Hawthorne

Brought to bear on Lander's Hawthorne, this convention of response would lead straight to the conclusion that she had found him sexually exciting. The imagined scene of his sitting as a model potentially took on a thick atmosphere of illicit sensuality. Together with the rumors of her undressing for "respectable" viewers, the modeling sessions with Hawthorne could make plausible any number of stories, no matter how false, of their being "on uncommonly good terms." Did Louisa take off her clothes for Nathaniel? Did he take off his clothes for her? Did they have sex? Once their relation appeared to be "impure," such speculations could not be silenced or decisively answered.

The Hawthornes promptly took action to disown the bust, an effort embarrassed, needless to say, by their earlier enthusiasm for both Louisa and the clay model. One way of covering that difficulty was to claim that Louisa's design had not been incorporated into the marble, especially in the offending parts. Julian Hawthorne's family biography states that "an American and a person of culture," who "happened to be in Rome at the time the marble work was proceeding," intervened in the marble cutting and ordered "certain alterations, for which he accepted the responsibility" (*NHW* 2:183). The ostensible purpose of this interference was to correct "some errors in the modelling of the lower part of the face," but the result—Julian affirms—was to destroy the likeness altogether. Whether Julian concocted this story himself or not, it is almost certainly false. It is sustained by none of Hawthorne's own remarks at the time and conflicts with his summary judgment, when he arranged for a final payment (through an intermediary) to Louisa: "The bust, my friends tell me, is not worth sixpence; but she did her best with it" (CE 18:230).³

Hawthorne had heard the rumors and seen the bust before Louisa got back from America, when she immediately came to see the family, full of information about Salem relatives and American friends. "In the evening, Miss Lander & her sister (just from America) called, and were not admitted," Hawthorne noted in his pocket calendar. When she called the next day, and again on Friday, the instructions to the servants were the same: she would not be seen, although the letters she had brought from Longfellow and others could be received (CE 14:619). On Saturday Hawthorne stated his views by letter:

> Mr Hawthorne begs to thank the Misses Lander for the letters which they have kindly forwarded. . . . Mr Hawthorne is glad to be informed that some (he hopes many) of Miss Louisa Lander's friends are convinced of the purity of her life and character. He is himself open to conviction on that subject; but as guardian of the sanctity of his domestic circle, he is compelled to be more cautious than if he were acting merely for himself. Before calling at Mr Hawthorne's residence, Miss Louisa Lander had been made fully aware that reports were in circulation, most detrimental to her character; and he cannot but think that any attempt at social intercourse with her former friends, (especially where young people and children are included in the number) should have been preceded by a full explanation and refutation of these reports.
>
> (CE 18:158)

Without giving her a hearing, Hawthorne has concluded that the charges against Louisa are true. "If Mr Hawthorne were one of those friends who have faith in Miss Lander's innocence, his first and last advice to her would be to sift those charges thoroughly, to meet them fully, and to throw her life open to the world. This should be done at once, and nothing short of this will enable Miss Lander to retain her position. Should Miss Lander decide to take this course, no one will be more rejoiced at the triumphant vindication of her character than the present writer" (CE 18:158).

This icy repudiation protects Nathaniel's innocence by contributing to the destruction of Louisa's. Far from asserting a stance from which to defend her, Hawthorne nervously sought to fortify his own compromised position. In this light his concluding remarks are bitterly amusing: "In any case Miss Lander may be assured of Mr Hawthorne's silence on this painful subject. He has no wish to say a word that may injure her, and would most gladly be enabled again to think and speak as highly of her as he has done hitherto" (CE 18:158–159).

At the inquest we ourselves are holding into this affair, Louisa Lander remains silent. No word from her survives concerning it, except what the bust itself may have to say and her defiance of the accusations brought against her. The affair blighted her career; after struggling on without commissions for a short while, she departed from Rome and lived thereafter in Washington, D.C., where she died in 1923 at the age of ninety-seven.

The ejection of Louisa Lander involved conflicts that bore differently on different members of the family. Louisa was living a life Sophia had dreamed of since girlhood, pursuing directly an artistic ambition that she had sought to fulfill vicariously through her marriage to Nathaniel. Sophia had ample grounds for jealous resentment, especially if Nathaniel—at age fifty-three— had become infatuated with the thirty-three-year-old woman, projecting into her some of the childlike inwardness Sophia had sacrificed so much to indulge. If Nathaniel had sought to renew his own creative capacities through friendship with the young artist, he risked losing part of himself when he joined in banishing her. Louisa had also held up before Una a vision of the womanly fulfillment available in Rome, deepening Una's passionate love for the city, which Hawthorne had already found "alarming" (CE 14:230). Was the living icon of the Hawthornes' divine marital union to follow the example Louisa had set? Nathaniel emphasized that he must act toward Louisa as the "guardian of the sanctity of his domestic circle," and Sophia vehemently agreed. His letter of dismissal survives because Sophia copied it out and kept it.

Una fell sick amid the poisonous chill that now descended on the Hawthornes, which Nathaniel projected into the Roman weather. "It is extremely spirit-crushing, this remorseless grey, with its icy heart; and the more to depress the whole family, Una has taken what seems to be the Roman fever by sitting down to sketch in the Coliseum. It is not a severe attack, yet attended with fits of exceeding discomfort, occasional comatoseness, and even delirium to the extent of making the poor child talk in rhythmical measure, like a tragic heroine—as if the fever lifted her feet off the earth."[4] Una's delirium was diagnosed as a "nervous fever," meaning that the malaria was accompanied by a psychological disturbance.

On the day Hawthorne drafted his letter of expulsion, Una wrote to her cousins, Richard and Rebecca Manning, about her desire for an independent life, like that Louisa was leading. "My ideal of existence would be to live in Italy, in a house built and furnished after my own taste, often paying long visits to England, and sometimes to America, & pursue my studies and other occupations unmolested by mankind in general. But people seldom, if ever, realize their ideal of life, and I fancy I shall never see the fulfillment of mine." She concedes that she "may be brought back to the ways of righteousness" when she returns to America, "tho it is my private opinion my feelings will be still more confirmed."[5]

Una's ideal life would be sustained by the treasures of art that America lacks, she explains to Rebecca: "I could not help smiling when you spoke of enjoying the pictures in the Athenaeum. If you had seen what I have seen I don't believe you would ever go within a hundred yards of the finest picture there." Trapped between the "ways of righteousness" and her passion for Rome, Una finds that great art provides images of her own desperate internal storm. "In a picture or a statue into which the artist has thus put his whole soul you can read his life, the hopes that bouyed him up on the tempestuous sea of life, the despair that made him sink beneath its waves, the faint & glimmering returning hope that made him raise his eyes to heaven & . . . then perhaps he moulded the statue or painted the picture that was to make the sympathizing mortals of a future age know what his sufferings were."[6]

Speaking of the artists's torment allowed Una to bring herself somewhat under control. Yet she becomes anxiously aware that her rhapsody has become compulsive, that the limits of her self-possession have been reached, and she tries to explain herself to Rebecca in a final rush of words. "I stopped as soon as I could for whenever I begin to talk of Art in which my whole heart is interested I am borne on by an irresistible impulse & if what I have written can give you any idea of how deeply I am absorbed in this subject, let it also assure you of how little it shows you the depths of my feelings."[7] Beyond what Una had said, there beckoned emotions to which she could not give utterance.

Una's native aggression played a major role in the psychological conflict that now consumed her. Her pleasure in command, evident from early childhood, led her to take up horseback riding when she was twelve, and to boast of her mastery: "I have learned how to manage the horse tolerably well, & have had several trials of my skill on spirited horses. I am perfectly fearless & I don't believe a horse *could* through [*sic*] me off."[8] This proficiency had symbolic force as a sexually charged gender anomaly, especially because a rider sitting sidesaddle cannot control a challenging animal; the horse must be grasped between the rider's legs. Harriet Hosmer's skill at riding was an object of restive attention in the community of American artists at Rome, like her male garb and the strength with which she wielded hammer and chisel. On the journey to Florence, Hawthorne noted his own uneasiness: "Nothing struck me so much, in the forenoon, as the spectacle of a peasant-woman riding on horseback astride" (CE 14:233).

Yet Una's assertiveness chronically took an involuted form: she adopted the desires of her parents as though they were her own. Sophia hid her subservience to Nathaniel by claiming that his commands were identical to her own unprompted will; it is evident that Una had internalized this stratagem. She could hardly have been pleased when Nathaniel, Julian, and Sophia took off on a three-week tour of England, leaving her to look after baby Rose, yet she declares that she had chosen this arrangement herself, so as to "study hard."[9] When the same trio made a journey to York Minster, to attend Easter services, Una admitted that she "should like to be there very much," but her responsibilities prevented it. "In the first place it would not do to have the house without either Mamma, Papa or me, and I should not like to leave Baby."[10]

Una could assert herself against her parents when she found a commanding position on the available moral terrain. Sophia noticed that a "nice sense of *propriety*" had appeared in Una's character at age two, as when she addressed her father at table: "A little water, if oo please, papa,—& be tareful & not spill, because it is not proper to spill the water on the tloth, papa."[11] This avenue toward autonomy led Una to cultivate a fastidious critical eye, and she drew a sharp line between what she approved and what was unendurable. Her lavish and protracted celebration of great art is punctuated by expressions of contempt for the less than great. Pictures that are not "pervaded with a holy interest," she declared "so glaring & insipid to me that I cannot bear to look at them."[12] Una's disgust at Titian's Venuses, Sophia noted, was even more violent than her own (Fig. 9). "They were positively disagreeable and excessively indecent

Fig. 9.   Titian's Venus

to my eye. The marvellous flesh hues alone held the attention for a moment. They are not Goddesses, not Womanhood, not Maternity, not Maidenhood but naked female figures. Una could not look at them at all" (Italy, 9 June).

With powerful impulses uneasily balanced between revulsion and haughty ecstasies of delight, Una was chronically somewhat withdrawn. Sophia commented that Una's emotional life "is sometimes veiled from our eyes with reserved lids" (Italy, 3 March); and she noticed the inward disturbance this aloofness contained. "The least dissonance, jar, disturbance clouds and dims her whole aspect and alters her tones. She is acutely sensitive under a calm and serene exterior. . . . She would suffer incredibly with no outward sign."[13] Una's way of carrying her body likewise suggested a heavy armor of self-possession encasing the erratic and ungraceful impulses that had jerked her about since early childhood. Sophia now celebrated Una's "majestic way of holding herself and moving. . . . She plants her foot evenly and firmly and carries her head with a dignity very unchildlike. . . . She has a great impatience of temperament to contend with, so that sometimes her patience is quite sublime."[14]

As Una's fierce standard of propriety was turned against itself, the warfare of self-assertion and self-abnegation reached overpowering intensity, and her psychic withdrawal and stillness resembled a coma. As the months of illness passed, Sophia noted a recurrent inward perishing.

> All her powers of body seemed to sink and wane, as if she were going out like an exhausted light. I suffered her death a thousand times instead of once—because the phases of her state were so alarming—she so constantly seemed about to die. . . . She looked at me once with particularly wide open eyes . . . and said in a natural voice—'I am going to die now. There is no use in living. Goodbye, dear.' . . . Sometimes she would lie on her back and stretch out her feet and lay her arms by her side, and with unwinking glassy eyes look straight at the bed's foot with no speculation and as if already cold and lifeless.[15]

The conflict between Una's passion for Rome and her internalized "ways of righteousness" was only one version of a deep-running dilemma that assailed her as she passed from girlhood, with its presumptive angelic innocence, into womanhood. She sustained an internal conflict like that Hawthorne depicts in *The Marble Faun* as taking place between Hilda and Miriam. The two young women had been intimate friends, yet Hilda's constitutional fidelity to exalted moral principle causes her to greet Miriam's wrongdoing with an automatic and uncontrollable recoil. Yearning for comfort in her torment of guilt, Miriam reaches out to Hilda, only to be spurned "with an involuntary repellent gesture, so expressive, that Miriam at once felt a great chasm opening itself between them. . . . It was as if Hilda or Miriam were dead, and could no longer hold intercourse without violating a spiritual law" (CE 4:207). Assailed by her own purity of soul, Una was now dead to herself; or rather she suffered continuously the inward repellent gesture that was at once like killing and being killed.

Yet "death" could also be a blessed escape. "Una was delirious during the greater part of the night," wrote Ada Shepard, her American governess and tutor:

> It was a very gentle and peaceful wandering of the mind. She spoke as if she were in the most blissful state, most of the time. She seemed to fancy herself translated to another state of being, and spoke of herself in the third person. "She is happy; she is at rest," etc. She seemed to be two distinct persons, one spiritual and the other physical. Her spirit hovered over her body, as it were, and looked pityingly on the suffering form. She described beautiful dreams in which she saw beings "too dazzling to behold," but, at the same time said: "I need earthly water."[16]

Contributing to the onset of Una's crisis was the burgeoning of sexual desire, as suggested by the imagery of surging waters with which she describes the struggle of the artist's soul, with "despair" making him "sink beneath its waves," and "hope" making him "raise his eyes to heaven & pray

. . . to rise once more." Una had internalized a feminine ideal that was defined by "Womanhood . . . Maternity . . . Maidenhood," the moral essences so spectacularly lacking in Titian's Venuses. Instead of these Titian offered "naked female figures," from which Una had recoiled in abhorrence. She now correspondingly withdrew from her own pitiful suffering body, seeking an escape into perfect spirituality.

Still, Una was aware that she needed "earthly water" to quench her earthly appetites, and there were plenty of sights in the city of Rome to arouse them, not least Praxiteles' satyr with its ambiguous playful smile and its pelvis rolled easily forward—that presumptive figure of innocent natural manliness. Did she know that Louisa Lander was now a figure of womanly filth, whose guilt had threatened to besmirch her divinely innocent father? Or was she left, with only hinted explanations, to figure out for herself why the beautiful, spirited, and talented young American woman, long accepted as worthy of friendship and emulation, had suddenly been excluded from the family? While Una's illness was in progress, an erotic drama took place within the household that elaborates further such enigmas of purity, secrecy, and desire and their relation to the "Roman fever" that engulfed her and her family together.

CHAPTER FIFTEEN

The Lions of Lust

During Una's illness, Ada Shepard fought off a campaign of sexual conquest that was undertaken by the Italian physician Dr. Franco, to whom the Hawthornes turned for medical care. Ada was a notably talented graduate of Antioch College, where Horace Mann was president, and she was engaged to marry her classmate Clay Badger, now an instructor at Antioch, to whom she wrote letters almost daily during the period of her service with the Hawthornes.

Even before she began to contend with Dr. Franco, Ada was troubled by the ambiguities of feminine purity. She broods over the tainted reputation of a college friend named Mary, who had traveled to Antioch in the company of a Mr. Keith. When their coach stopped for dinner at a hotel, Keith went off to find a place where they could rest, whereupon Mary was "shocked" to discover he had engaged only one room. Even though she refused to allow the "familiarity" of sharing the room, Mary was blamed at Antioch for an indiscretion. Ada finds this grotesquely unjust. "The whole world, excepting you, my beloved!" she tells Clay Badger, "might unite in accusing her of the slightest impurity of conduct and my faith in her would be as unshaken as a rock. I cannot say that I think her perceptions are the most delicate possible, and I know well certain faults in her; but I am as sure of her perfect purity as I am of that of my beautiful Una who writes beside me."[1]

Yet Ada knows that once "the slightest impurity" has been imputed, the

issues become murky. Is a young woman perfectly pure when her perceptions are not "the most delicate possible"? Why must Ada commend Clay
as an unerring judge of purity while defying the world at large? Why is a
reputation for purity blurred into its moral reality?

The work of articulating and stabilizing the meaning of purity in Victorian
America mobilized diverse cultural resources, among which was "Una" and
the system of literary associations the Hawthornes had invoked when they
chose this name for their daughter. Edmund Spenser's story of Una and the
lion forms only a small segment of the maiden's adventures in the first book
of *The Faerie Queene;* yet in the nineteenth century "Una" was known by the
meaning this episode came to possess.[2] When Shepard proposed "my beautiful Una" as a standard of perfect purity, she invoked a symbolic narrative
that defined the virtue she sought to defend against Dr. Franco; and she
connects Franco's conduct with Spenser's story. "With that terrible passion
in his eyes and his whole manner," Shepard says of his first onslaught, "of
which I have read in books, but of which I never had a conception before,
he poured forth such a storm of consuming and raging passion . . . that I
felt sick and dizzy. . . . This man seems to me like a raging lion" (18
December 1858). In coming to terms with Franco's erotic siege, Shepard
makes her way across a Spenserian landscape.

Spenser's Una was not a figure of Victorian purity, nor was his lion a
figure of Victorian lust. The lion bursts out of the woods looking, not for
sexual quarry, but for something to eat; and his "bloody rage" is mastered,
not by Una's purity, but by her "beautie" and "simple truth." His attack
halted by awestruck veneration, the lion becomes Una's companion and
protector in a brief series of adventures that ends when he is slain by Sansloy,
the pagan knight who forthwith attempts to seduce Una and then to rape her
(*Faerie Queene* I.iii.6).

John Bell's statue of Una and the lion, displayed at the Crystal Palace in
1851, evokes the nineteenth-century refocusing of this story. Entitled *Purity,*
it portrays a configuration of erotic experience in which purity is seen as
innate to womanhood and is credited with a momentous transformative
power that sublimates beastly lust into worship. In the statue an innocently
naked Una is seated in sidesaddle posture on the lion's back. There is,
however, no saddle; the lion submits to being ridden without external
compulsion, reduced to obedience—so the allusion to Spenser confirms—
by the spiritual force of his rider. Nor does Bell's lion assume the stance of
Una's protector; his meek submission amply testifies that feminine purity can
safeguard itself.

Observe Spenser's contrasting treatment. When Sansloy kills the lion, Una becomes vulnerable to sexual attack without becoming any less a figure of moral perfection. "Who now is left to keepe the forlorne maid/ From raging spoil of lawless victor's will?" Spenser plaintively inquires (*Faerie Queene* I.iii.43). When Sansloy assails Una, moreover, he strips away her veil and takes the force of her radiant heavenly beauty full in his face; instead of being mastered and transformed by this vision, Sansloy attempts to rape her. Nowhere does Spenser suggest that Sansloy's lustful response casts doubt on Una's virtue, as though her virtue should be able to quell him unassisted.

Yet the ideal of purity that informed Ada Shepard's consciousness carried this explicit criterion: true purity permits no glimmer of erotic solicitation to arouse base masculine desire but translates the lustful beastly male to a plane of consciousness where his imagination is disinfected by the white radiance of her moral perfection. What troubles Shepard, accordingly, is that Franco's conduct has already compromised her, already raised a suspicion that her virtue is imperfect. After writing Franco a letter intended to halt his approach, she remains uneasy about her own moral powers: "Every virtuous woman *can* protect herself by her own virtue, I think, in almost any circumstance I can imagine. I am not in the least *afraid* of this pursuing man, but I am excessively troubled to think that I should be the object of such a persecution. . . . I hope you will not be in the least anxious about my having further trouble," she tells her fiancé, "for I think I have effectually silenced him" (18 December 1858).

Shepard is humiliated, accordingly, when she discovers that Franco has become more daring than ever. "Shall I tell you," she tells Clay Badger, "that he even dared to force upon my cheek and lips his hateful, unholy kisses?" (22 December 1858). Accusing herself for having "all unconsciously awakened such a passion," Shepard determines that she cannot appeal to the Hawthornes for protection since they would surely blame her for Dr. Franco's conduct.

The silencing of Shepard's protest enabled Dr. Franco to proceed, whereupon Shepard was all the more humiliated and confounded to discover she was sexually aroused by him. She finds in him a "magnetic force" that seems to operate independent of her will; his fiery eyes mesmerize her with a "snake-like power"; she wonders whether he is giving her aphrodisiacs. Shepard concludes that her own excitement surpasses what can be explained on such self-excusing theories, and she is crushed with guilt for "looking at this man without horror and allowing him to kiss my hand without wishing to bury myself in the earth" (26 March and 16 April 1859).

Isolating her from the Hawthornes' protection, and plunging her into acute self-loathing, the ideal of womanly purity accentuated Shepard's victimization. Yet that ideal also placed Shepard in circumstances she found amenable to her own desire for moral autonomy and assured her that she was entitled to exercise such autonomy. The New York Moral Reform Society was the foremother of the women's voluntary associations that grew up in the middle years of the century; and, as Carroll Smith-Rosenberg has demonstrated, the society embraced the ideal of purity to express women's determination to take the defense of their sexual integrity into their own hands rather than entrust it to male "protectors" (109–128).

The title of the earliest feminist periodical published in America, *The Una,* likewise asserted this direct link between the transformative purity presumed native to womanly character and a broad program of social action. Spenser's heroine, the editor explains, is not a figure of cloistered virtue. She "traverses the deserts of the world, abiding with a constant patience the wrongs encountered at every step from the objects . . . of her divine mission, ever intent upon her task and hopeful of its achievement." She deploys a spirituality that wholly transcends the "unreflective savage force" symbolized by the lion.[3]

Shepard's adventure in the moral desert of Rome was likewise empowered by this womanly ideal, and it is consummated as she deliberately challenges her brutish adversary. Shortly before she left Rome, Shepard visited Franco alone in his chambers, and the outcome vindicated her claim to the moral power that conquers the lion of lust. "I *am* pure," she wrote to Badger in summing up this triumph, "perfectly pure, as we have always thought" (8 May 1859). Shepard takes the occasion to describe purity in action: Franco

> entreated me to give him one moment of happiness before I went away forever, by allowing him to embrace and kiss me. . . . Seeing me as obdurate as ever, he grew desperate, and attempted by force his embrace upon me. . . . But I prevented him. . . . He raved for a little while, calling me "stupid" and "a stone" and "a person with no heart. . . . I see that I have wasted my affection. And I loved you so!" And so he went on, until at last his passion spent itself. I reminded him of the injustice and impropriety of his words (when he was calm enough to hear me) and of my never wavering refusal to listen to a word of love from him, and my constant avoidance of him whenever it was possible.
>
> (8 May 1859)

Shepard's inflexible self-possession at length brings Franco to his senses: "And then I asked him to reply truly to a question. . . . I wished to know whether he had ever understood from me that I could give him the slightest encouragement to hope I might return his passion. 'Oh no!' said he. 'I only hoped because I loved. . . . But I knew you were indifferent' " (8 May 1859). So the lion of lust himself testifies to her purity, confessing that his assaults were prompted altogether by his own deluded passion.

Nancy Cott observes that "purity" may have afforded woman a claim to moral autonomy, but only if she sacrificed her capacity for sexual pleasure and her sexual power: "A world view in which woman's sexual nature was shadowed behind her moral and spiritual endowment eclipsed her primitive and original power over men, the power of her sexuality" ("Passionlessness," 168). Shepard's story, however, allows us to see this eclipsed sexuality at work—and not only as "power over men."

Franco's attempted sexual conquest brought Shepard a great deal of misery, but it also permitted her to explore the inward complexities of the womanhood she embodied. Shepard condemned her own desire, yet she also gave it play and searched out such gratifications as the ethos of purity afforded her. I have spoken of Shepard as "silenced" by Franco's attacks; but her story survives because she wrote it up for Clay Badger, to whom she speaks with extraordinary freedom.

Shepard clearly intends for her fiancé to be caught up in the drama she recounts so passionately. She enacts transformative purity by making herself the heroine of a pornographic romance, complete with aphrodisiacs, snake-like power, hateful kisses, and fiery Italian eyes. Shepard actively solicits the passion that she sublimates, as the ethos of purity encouraged her to do, since a woman can hardly appear transcendently pure to a man not sexually aroused by her. Una cannot work her transforming magic if there is no manly lust to be subdued, and Shepard's letters are meant, covertly yet insistently, to bring out the lion in Mr. Badger.

The triumphant victim was but one member in a proliferating family of psychic oxymorons intrinsic to Victorian sexuality. Becoming Una, the exemplum of purity, Ada Shepard makes audible the leonine growl of her own erotic yearning and demand. The middle-class ethos discouraged bodily pleasures, but it also sponsored—as Peter Gay and Michel Foucault have shown—a remarkable multiplication of the imaginable varieties of sexual experience.

Ada's lust seeks gratification through expiatory suffering; she hungers for painful inward thrustings that climax when imagined knives enter her body. She tells Badger that she feels "it would be a good thing for me to suffer physical pain," which her ensuing delirium provided. "I had such terrible dartings of pain that I fancied people stabbing me in various places. I thought I was sailing in a gondola in Venice, and people in other gondolas, passing me, reached forward and stabbed me. I kept covering my head with the bed-clothes, thinking to escape them, but vainly." The paradoxes of purity thus take a startling and sinister turn: Ada experiences her desire as phallic violation, a collective male assault from which she has no power to deliver herself. After her delirium subsided, Sophia told her that "once, only once . . . I cried out: 'Oh! Clay!' in a tone that expressed such perfect confidence that you would protect me, if I could only summon you" (15 January 1859).

The male protector for whom Ada cries out is not, or not only, one who can rescue her but also one who can answer her desire. Ada tells Clay of dreams in which "my whole frame tingled and trembled with the consciousness of your nearness" and in which "I was quivering and trembling in every fibre" (18 January 1859); and she attempts to replicate their caresses. "I raised my hand to my lips and kissed it, trying to imagine that it was the pressure of your dear lips that I felt. But there was no thrill of ecstasy such as your kiss always awakened, and the poor hand fell, nerveless, by my side" (20 January 1859). She awakens one morning "ecstatically happy" because she had dreamed of Badger's arousal, envisioned as a sick headache that she cures with her caresses, which leads to intimacies that satisfy her desire. "I magnetized you with my hands, passing them over your brow until you seemed quite well again, and then we had one of our old, happy communions" (30 January 1859).

Ada's erotic ambition also avails itself of the rhetoric of purity in her relation to Dr. Franco. The risks of having sexual intercourse with him were too great to allow the direct satisfaction of her desire, yet she uses him to keep it alive. Her description of snake-like power, daring kissing, and fiery eyes project her own sexual excitement and serve as aphrodisiacs that she eagerly consumes. Wrestling with Franco offered her pleasure, albeit truncated, and she prolonged the match until her departure from Rome was imminent. Although Ada decided that she could not tell the Hawthornes about Franco's conduct, in their climactic final encounter she makes exactly this threat—"to appeal to Mr. Hawthorne to defend me" (8 May 1859)—which precipitates Franco's outburst of frustration and terminates the struggle.

The involuted gratifications of purity, both relinquished and asserted here, take part in an elaborate scenario of sexual combat. Ada cultivates and thwarts the desires of both Badger and Franco, a teasing that deepens the erotic satisfaction she obtained from them, indirect and covert as it was. One of the ugliest privileges of patriarchal oppression lies in the common belief that the male's discovery of such womanly sexual aggression justifies his resort to violence, as though Franco would have been entitled to rape Shepard had she given overt evidence of seeking sexual pleasure or of spurring his desire. Her fantasy of being stabbed bears an ominous analogy to this perverted rationale; displacing her own desire on anonymous male attackers who punish her for wanting sex, she articulates the involuted logic that drives the victim to blame the victim. Although toward Badger she allows herself to tingle, the lust she feels for Franco is not only silenced but compelled to speak against itself.

Sophia complained that Ada spent too much time writing letters to Clay when she should have been attending to her household duties. But neither Sophia nor Nathaniel knew of the erotic struggle taking place in Una's sickroom and the adjoining parlor.

Ada had ample reason to fear a banishment in disgrace like Louisa Lander's for sliding across the gap that separated "pure" young women from the "contaminated." The life of upright social relations in the household, now focused so anxiously on Una, occupied a domain separate from that in which Ada conducted her erotic struggle with Franco. Sublimating desire into worship, the ideal of purity established a hysterical social reality, whose essence was the not-knowing of what is known.

Freud's classic description of hysteria features an individual patient whose thoughts and feelings are visible only through the symptom that masks them—as hero worship is a symptom of hatred and dread. The repression that enforces the masking is activated by the forbidden impulse when its presence is felt. A hysterical person thus does not know and feel what he knows and feels; the contours of his conscious awareness bespeak an inward knowing of which he is ignorant.[4] The Hawthornes' ignorance may be taken as a sign of their participation in a collective version of a hysterical reality of the high Victorian sort that supported Freud's belief that repressed sexuality lay at the root of all civilized and coherent mental life.

Yet Nathaniel and Sophia represent distinct versions of this normative hysteria. Their responses to the burgeoning of womanly sexuality in Una, framed in the language of purity, were accentuated differently. Sophia felt disgust at Titian's portrayal of "naked female flesh," yet the ideal of innocent maidenhood absent in Titian permitted Sophia to celebrate womanly desire. Una's breasts had begun to develop two years before, and Sophia's response emphasized her daughter's maiden purity. But she also welcomed the passion and pleasure that adulthood would bring. "Una is at the turning tide now," Sophia wrote, "& she is budding into womanhood with the loveliest forms you can imagine. I think if there is any thing in nature enchanting & touchingly beautiful, it is the gently budding bosom of a pure young girl. When one thinks how it may one day heave with emotion, with wifely love & maternal tenderness—how it may also swell with sorrow, it seems the chief scene of tender humanity, so quiet now & so innocent! henceforth possibly so tumultuous & disturbed."[5]

Within her resolute certainty that Una was an embodiment of moral perfection Sophia found it possible to celebrate the aggression, the independence of spirit, and also the sexual capacity that had set off an involuntary loathing in Nathaniel when Una was a little girl. How Nathaniel responded to Una's sexuality as it was flooded with the energies of adolescence is not made clear in any of his surviving comments about her. Yet a contrast with Sophia's response remains evident: she was able to sustain the crisis of Una's breakdown by asserting her daughter's perfect purity, while Hawthorne was overwhelmed by psychic torment and confusion.

CHAPTER SIXTEEN

Spiritual Laws

Sophia made of Una's illness a heroic drama, richly illuminated by its Roman setting, in which the final meanings of womanhood were tested. Even before Una fell ill, Sophia had concluded that "Roman fever" exemplifies the divine law at work in the fatal history of the imperial city and in her own career of maternal self-sacrifice.

Sophia recalled girlhood fantasies of Rome that project her own valiant disposition. "The Roman legions with whom I always fought, seemed to me the *sole rightful* victors—so fascinating to the imagination is success. I devoutly believed that a Roman was a cunning composition of perfect honor, bravery and virtue." Sophia's crowning image of Roman power has a womanly cast, featuring not phallic invasions, but a copious and hungry center. Rome's "power of appropriation doubtless exceeded that of any other known state": the city "builded with the world's best architects. . . . adorned itself with the world's best masterpieces. . . . Genius, Beauty, Efficiency, wherever the Imperial Eagle could see them, were pounced upon & swooped up into the service and possession of this absorbing Domination" (Italy, 18 October 1858).

Yet Sophia now recognizes the savage cruelty of Roman rule, how the city "brought captive to her throne hundreds of thousands of peoples—gentle as well as simple, to accomplish her will" (Italy, 24 May). "The six thousand crucified of Crassus—all in agony at the same moment would forever put into black eclipse my flashing Empire, were there no other of the countless crimes to be brought into the account which make the earth groan and shudder to contemplate." Sophia finds these horrors oddly thrilling because they belong to an understanding of the city's greatness that replaced the naive fancies of her youth. The "sin and shame" of Roman history affront her on every side, yet "strange to say, here I am also magnetized with the Power that hovers irresistibly in this air" (18 October).

The collapse of Rome displays, for Sophia, a spiritual force as inexorable as the imperial armies; and her vision of this "Power" is invested in a panorama she described on the family's return from Florence, when she ordered the driver of their carriage to pause at the rim of a volcanic crater, so she could see the city across the Campagna. This broad plain had once been dotted with cities like Carioli and Veii that had been erased "by the terrible and desolating hand of Rome." Yet the Romans had been unable to occupy the Campagna in the wake of conquest because God had cursed it with malaria: Roman fever as a penalty for Roman crime. "We paused and gazed from the edge of the Crater in a profound silence, upon the silvery vision of Sovereign Rome, standing alone in the midst of the vast desolation it has made, and for slain millions, receiving for poetically just guerdon the fatal breath of the malaria" (Italy, 18 October). As a target of divine vengeance, Rome retained a spiritual dominion that continues, so Sophia believed, amid the collapse of her worldly empire.

Sophia knew that England was now the pre-eminent world power, though it "has begun its downward course," and that "when America has fulfilled its destiny," she too might "also bow her beaming forehead to the mire" (Italy, 14 September). Yet Rome still rules the world, Sophia believed, through an idealist fusion of artistic and moral force: "Not all the monstrous sin and crime can smother the right royal and etherial pre-eminence of the Queen of Nations. . . . No longer ruling people externally, now she still rules them through the intellect and imagination." The remorseless spiritual power that punished Roman sin also sublimates—as womanly purity sublimates—the filth of an evil world into a vision of supernal perfection. The "etherial pre-eminence" of Rome is not a matter of "earthly" force but consists in the transformative power by which a squalid material order becomes the stainless emblem of divine law. "The yellow waters of the Tiber look as if the sins of Heliogabulus had dissolved in them when he was thrown into it, and yet the Tiber is the imagination's dearest River, and flows through the mind as pure as a mountain torrent, lucid as air" (15 October).

Una's illness brought these issues straight into Sophia's experience.

"Must Una die because the Roman Emperors outraged the patience of God and all human decencies?" she cried out, keeping vigil over her suffering child. "It is not natural that the young should die," especially "the fairest, purest of the young." Yet Sophia realized that the Roman fever routinely struck down the innocent and that life itself is "one great holocaust of innocence sacrificed for the guilty." In this recurrent catastrophe, Sophia found "GOD's high appeal to the royal soul," and she was more than ready to demonstrate her own royalty.[1]

Una's illness offered Sophia a heroic Armageddon of Motherhood, whose lineaments she had traced with fascination in Italian pictures of the Virgin Mother of God, grieving over her crucified child. In this "most heart-smiting irresistible pathos" Sophia finds majesty: a womanly grandeur born of communion with God through his dreadful judgments. Mary is "noble and grand, both the figure and the face. . . . God only can minister to her vast dismay—which clothes her with heroic dignity" (Italy, 27 May). Viewing a Perugino Pietà at Florence (Fig. 10), Sophia had seen clearly the connection between this noble agony and universal Motherhood: "What can I say of Mary Adolorata? The grief of all the mothers since Eve is concentrated in hers. . . . She asks for no sympathy. She wishes to hear no word. . . . This Mother's sorrow no plummet can sound, and no one can comfort her. She is grand and majestic from the single unapproachableness of emotion" (17 June).

Sophia took center stage in the drama of her daughter's illness. Now as before, she cannibalizes Una's emotional life in dramatizing her own struggle with the dilemmas of womanhood. The core problem in Una's "nervous fever" was the question how a woman could survive a socialization requiring her both to assert and to efface an autonomous selfhood; Sophia had solved that problem by managing the effacement so as to devour the inwardness of those for whom self-sacrifice was required. She had, as she later remarked, a "fearful power of being another."[2] On this occasion she was certain that Una wanted her constantly at hand because of the perfect union of their souls. "No one shared my nursing, because she wanted my touch and my voice and she was not obliged to tell me what she wanted. For days she only opened her eyes long enough to see I was there."[3]

As Sophia mobilized her response to the crisis, she invoked her child as a model of the exalted selflessness she herself must now display. "The baby

Fig. 10.   Mary Adolorata, from Perugino's Pietà

purity of her soul hardly has place in the murk of earth," so that she "has no fear of the accident of Death. It is only the wicket gate of the Celestial city, which she would open and pass through without surprise." Sophia recalled that from earliest infancy Una had scornfully rejected material rewards and punishments, embracing the imperative to "Do right because it is right! . . . No present, no privilege, no payment for goodness, ever sullied the pure idea of duty and rectitude in her young soul." Sophia is accordingly prepared to banish her this-worldly desire to keep Una alive. "I always held her like a precious, wondrous gift that I must be ready to resign at any moment. . . . Why should I be so rich? Has not God already led me into His counsels by the hand of this child?"[4]

Sophia traced the vicissitudes of Una's illness with obsessive fascination, seeing in them mysteries at the core of moral reality. "It was an insidious sapping of the issues of life that required the most penetrative and ceaseless care—the silver cord was repeatedly loosed, and the golden bowl often seemed to break at the fountain—Such a fine and delicate balance it was, that it took my breath away to watch it." Sophia's absorption in the psychic vagaries of her increasingly emaciated daughter forms one side of a morbid intercourse, in which Una joined. She would from time to time announce that she was dying and lie uncannily still, whereupon Sophia "also sat perfectly still, watching if the short breath would raise her shoulders—but my head was dizzy and I could not see nor stir. I thought perhaps she had gone from me then. When I could move, I would not, for then I might lose a last word or look."

Ada Shepard noticed the strange gratification Sophia received in this communion with a daughter "so dependent on her mamma in her sickness." It dawns on Ada that "there is a pure and high kind of pleasure in thus watching those so ill, so *dangerously* ill, that almost compensates for the anguish of it." She realizes that her love for Clay Badger might provide wifely pleasures comparably pure and high. "I pictured your beloved form emaciated by disease and extended upon a couch over which I constantly tended; and it was not all *pain* which I felt at the thought."[5] Sophia, for her part, was struck by the extraordinary resources of inner strength that her ordeal called forth. "GOD tempers the wind to the shorn lamb—and I endure and look very well most of the time—and indeed I believe I am a kind of a lion instead of a lamb."[6]

Una's illness persisted from October to late March, with spells of chills and fever separated by periods when she was well enough to leave the house for an excursion. But in early April she developed a cough, and Dr. Franco diagnosed galloping consumption—now known as miliary tuberculosis—a virtual sentence of death. Sophia's drama came accordingly to a climax: "All Rome was in a state of the most vivid interest and commotion about Una—Carriages were constantly drawing to the door with enquiries. Cards were brought up with enquiries. People were always coming—Even dear Mrs. Browning, who never goes upstairs, came the moment she heard Dr. Franco's diagnosis. She was like an angel—I saw her but a moment, but the clasp of her hand was electric and her voice penetrated my heart."

Rome, persuaded that Dr. Franco's diagnosis was incorrect, pressed Sophia to seek another opinion, which she was quite reluctant to do. Finally she learned "that Rome would mob Dr. Franco if he did not have a consultation. Mr Story was wild about a consultation—Mrs Story came three times in one day to talk about it. To save Dr. Franco's life and to appease Rome, we had a consultation," and the consulting physician determined that Franco was mistaken.

Yet Sophia's faith was unshaken: "Dr. Franco is vivid, impulsive, transparent, frank, thinking aloud," she declared. "People blamed him for nearly killing me, but he had no idea of killing me—His only thought was of Una's danger. . . . I cannot bear to have him blamed." Dr. Franco supplied "conscientious, devoted, tender, ceaseless care. I owe Una's life to him twice over and her health wholly, so wise, so judicious was his conduct."

Dr. Franco thrilled Sophia by his commanding manner, which gave her authority to take an imperious tone in her dealings with Rome, particularly regarding Una's diet. "Rome desired to provide her dainty fare—but Dr. Franco would accept no one's dishes—He wanted everything done exactly after his prescriptions—the wisest, the best I ever knew. . . . 'Whose broth is this?' he asked scornfully one day. 'This is Mrs. Browning's.' 'Then tell Mrs Browning to write her poesies and not meddle with my broths for my patients!' 'Whose jelly is this?' 'Mrs Story's' 'I wish Mrs Story would help her husband model his statutes and not try to feed Miss Una. Tell her so for me.' " Sophia was also excited when Franco took a masterful hand with her:

> One day when I asked him if [Una] might knit a little on her large needles he burst upon me with thunder and lightning—from voice and eyes "What now," he exclaimed. "But a few days and she was near to die, and you ask me for her to knit! Will you kill her then? NO! She shall do *nothing*. Do you hear, Miss Una? You shall not knit, you shall not read, you shall not talk. All you shall do is to sleep and eat." This in tones tremendous—then suddenly changing he bent tenderly over her "You see I am very strong—but I want you to recover—and so I speak hard."

Sophia was drawn to Franco as an intimate ally and companion at this crisis; she was stirred by him sexually and transferred to him the ardent hero worship her husband had earlier inspired. Like Nathaniel's attachment to Louisa Lander, Sophia's passionate loyalty was accentuated by the sexual deprivation that had become routine in the Hawthornes' married life since the birth of Rose. Ada had written to Clay Badger that Mr. Hawthorne "has a great many powerful attractions," yet she found him wanting "in the power or the will to show his love. He is the most undemonstrative person I ever knew, without any exception. It is quite impossible for me to imagine his bestowing the slightest caress upon Mrs. Hawthorne." Ada marveled at the contrast between Nathaniel's reserve and Sophia's hungry effusiveness, "her overflowing heart and her fondness for manifesting her affection even to friends, even to me, by kisses and embraces" (12 December 1858). Sophia's subsequent intimacy with Annie Fields likewise blended fervent adoration with erotic yearning; she remarked to Annie that Nathaniel "hates to be touched more than any one I ever knew."[7]

Sophia's emotional starvation also found a promise of relief in General Ethan Allen Hitchcock, whom she met in August 1862 when Nathaniel was away from home on a vacation trip, just two years before his death. Sophia cherished Hitchcock's kind words as "my plum cake of solace" after this first meeting and began a correspondence that lasted until Hitchcock's marriage in 1868.[8] "I am sure that for all eternity I hold your hand, and that wherever you are I can never lose you," Sophia wrote. "You are my St. Peter and hold the key. . . . You hold the magic wand that puts everything in its place."[9] Sophia's infatuation with Dr. Franco was more tumultuous and immediate, fusing sexual desire with surges of tenderness and frantic desperation, which likewise revived the passion that had vanished from her relationship to Nathaniel.

Sophia describes the climax of Una's illness as a fervent encounter with Franco, in which she nearly faints from excitement.

He listened long & carefully to her lungs, putting his ear to every part of her chest. He said nothing, and so unprepared was I, that I followed him into the drawing room saying "Do you think we had better take Miss Una to Albano?" He turned upon me with a terrible face which I shall never forget. "To Albano you say! But we have here a dreadful disease! With this he seemed to be tearing the hair off his forehead as he flung himself upon the sofa. He looked at me with such eyes that my senses seemed leaving me and I felt a cold line round my mouth as if I were going very white and about to faint. He called me back by saying "We have here florid phythis—quick consumption—In twelve hours it may be all over with that dear child. . . ." These words seemed written with fire all over the room. I said nothing at all. I only tried to be quiet and not to faint. I could not be spared from Una to faint or even to weep—But tears were not for me then. Her father was gone out—Ada Shepard was in school—Una wanted me—I went back to her—and striving in the bitter agony to clutch something I recalled other words of Dr. Franco . . . —that he said it was not impossible for her youth and constitution to overcome [a consuming infection of her lungs]. Either he said it or GOD said it to me—But the heavy iron was in my soul—In twelve hours—he even said *five!* When she coughed as he sat there, he started as if he were stung—"Dio mio" he exclaimed. I even thought of comforting him.

Sexual desire here pervades a rapture in which other strong emotions are prominently in play. Sophia was horribly afraid that Una would die, Franco was strongly responsive to the drama of the moment, and Sophia was badly in need of companionship in her terror and confusion. Compare the atmosphere of depression and inward collapse when she reports the terrible news to Nathaniel: "I dreaded my husband's return—for in his low state in Rome he could scarcely bear daily life—I must tell him. I was anxious to tell him carefully—to drop the thunderbolt gently at his feet. I told him—He said not one word, but passed his hand through his hair, and his features sunk."

Sophia's blind virtue was an intense distillation of the purity ascribed to women by the domestic ideal, of which Una herself was an emblem, and which defined the communion of souls between Nathaniel and Sophia. Sophia's purity rendered unthinkable her yearning for Dr. Franco, just as the erotic sentiment passing between Nathaniel and Louisa Lander had been obscured until circumstances broke through the wall of denial. If Ada Shepard had accused Franco of molesting her, he might never have put his ear to every part of Una's chest to hear the fatal infection that wasn't there; and Sophia might never have heard the words that tightened the rims of her mouth and put the heavy iron in her soul. Yet Sophia's faith might possibly have triumphed even here, nullifying Ada's accusation or throwing the blame for it on Ada herself.

CHAPTER SEVENTEEN

The Poet as Patriarch

"Mr. Hawthorne said that he had given up all hope," Ada Shepard observed during the crisis of Una's illness, "and wished no-one to try to inspire any in him. It is almost the worst trial in all this to see his face."[1] Sophia knew her husband could not supply companionship and emotional help but was desperately in need of it himself; she was grateful that Franklin Pierce was at hand. "I think I owe him almost my husband's life—and sanity. He was divinely tender, sweet, sympathizing and helpful. He took Mr. Hawthorne to walk and wrapped him round with the most soothing cares."[2]

"I had wonderful hours, dear Elizabeth," Sophia informed her sister, "—unshared—for I could not have my husband. I was fearfully anxious about him—He never knew what suffering was before. He was thoroughly baptized with it then. Mrs. Ward said his face surpassed any face she ever looked upon for infinite expression of sorrow too deep for tears—beautiful in endless woe—as if looking always on death." The prospect of Una's death not only produced Nathaniel's distress, Sophia explains, but also allayed it. His worst torment was aroused when he allowed himself to hope she might survive: "Alternations he could not bear of hope and fear and he sunk into fear alone."

Sophia knew that her husband had sustained earlier periods of suffering—poverty at the Old Manse, his mother's death—but now he was baptized into a new order of experience. Sophia observed that he "expected every morning to find his hair turned to snow upon his head." Una's transition from girlhood to womanhood was linked to a similarly tormented transition in Nathaniel's life. Yet Sophia did not pretend to share his feelings. During their courtship there had been moments when Hawthorne had insisted on silence, and a corresponding silence descended now upon their alienation. "We could not dare to talk together," Sophia confessed to her sister. "Words are hurricanes at such moments and would have driven us into deserts of dismay."

The bizarre paradox of Hawthorne taking refuge in despair, counting on Una's death as a talisman against unendurable inward pain, arises from conflicts buried deep in his mental life. It is true enough that Hawthorne's "fear" expresses the unconscious hope that Una would die, an evidence of the hostility toward her that had been part of his response from the beginning, when he resented giving up the undivided solicitude he had received from Sophia. Yet this crisis called forth a disturbance lying beneath his addiction to maternal care. His failure of fatherly steadfastness resulted from conflicts that had been instilled by the loss of his own father, an issue we must ourselves again take up.

Grief is a psychic furor in which powerful emotions act in response to each other and are experienced simultaneously in knotted redoublings of loss. Rage at being abandoned finds gratification in the lost one's death, which provokes guilt, so that the loss is experienced as a punishment. In the usual course of recovery, such apparently timeless syndromes of torment are resolved; the paradoxical components are sorted out and lose their uncanny power. But if not resolved, grief must be repressed, becoming an unconscious turmoil that may go out of control in subsequent personal crises and bring on disabling psychic chaos. Victims of unresolved grief yearn not only for the lost loved one but also for freedom from chronic inner misery, for an innocence and peace of which they have mysteriously been deprived.[3]

Nathaniel lacked a mature identity in which to digest this furor at age four, when his father's death inaugurated it, and he had no choice but to join in his mother's effort to perpetuate the "Hathorne" identity through him. Now, fifty years later, Hawthorne's grieving was built into the familiar pattern of his psychic life: an "outward" self recurrently obscures and makes visible his burden of occult pain. This scheme appears in his professional character as a civil servant who leads inwardly the delicate life of a poet, who in turn gestures chronically toward an incommunicable "inmost me." His most intimate relationship—the sacred "oneness" of his union with Sophia—devoted to containing his inner trouble, lay at the heart of the family system. Yet the development of this life structure, and the successes Hawthorne had enjoyed within it, did not resolve the grief and guilt inherent in its construction. He recurrently expressed disgust at being unable to put the torment behind him: the city of Rome now fills him with loathing, because it "lies like the dead corpse of a giant, decaying for centuries, with no survivor mighty enough even to bury it" (CE 4:110). Una's illness had the effect of stirring up this inward torture, as had his decision to marry Sophia and his mother's death. But in the crisis at Rome the resurgence took on a new form and acquired devastating force.

Because his life was dominated by an inward unburied father, who disabled him from participating in the "world of men," Hawthorne was exceptionally responsive to feminist rage. By the time he reached Rome, however, his achievements had made him a target for his own anti-patriarchal impulses: he was now a prominent public figure, both as a civil servant and as a "classic" American writer. He also headed a well-to-do household and was the "defender"—as he reminded Louisa Lander—of its domestic sanctity. But the grave exterior Hawthorne presented to the public world concealed an inner identity of opposite character. The anti-patriarchal vein in Hawthorne's temperament was matched by his passionate devotion to a childlike inwardness; both impulses were rooted in his grief. Cherishing an unspoiled boyishness bid defiance to his rancorous inward sorrow, which he blamed on evil "fathers."

In February 1859 Una's illness lifted somewhat, and Hawthorne took her to the carnival, with its exuberant reversals of gender identities and status hierarchies. His description sketches the analogy between his inward paradox, a reveling youngster hiding in a fifty-five-year-old man, and Una's impatience with her feminine lot. "Una kept wishing that she were a boy, and could plunge into the fun and uproar as Julian would; and for my own part (though I pretended to take no interest in the matter) I could have bandied confetti and nosegays as readily and as riotously as any urchin there. But my black hat and grave Talma would have been too good a mark for the combatants; nor was Una in fitting trim; so, much against her will, we went home before a shot was fired" (CE 14:497). Hawthorne and Una are alike prohibited from behaving like the boys they inwardly feel themselves to be, and Hawthorne's awareness that his somber clothing would draw fire from the exuberant urchins suggests how sharply the two sides of his character were potentially at odds.

Una's illness did not devastate Hawthorne's spirit because it undermined his fatherly authority; what gets disrupted, on the contrary, is the tightly interlocked scheme of psychic impulses that made up his boyishness. This was his ultimate line of defense against unendurable conflict, which he had shored up by way of his union with the comparably "childlike" soul of Sophia. Inherent in the psychic structure of their marriage was Nathaniel's fierce desire to maintain an inward entitlement, the right to see himself as Sophia saw him, as an Adam untainted by the world. The threat of death now hanging over the "symbol of the one true union in the world, and of our love in Paradise" contaminated that inward purity by unleashing the conflicts that its seeming integrity had masked.

When Una fell sick, Hawthorne adopted his characteristic recourse in the face of acute psychic stress: he started writing. The day immediately following the first onset of her fever he set to work in earnest on his romance about the Praxiteles satyr.[4] There he traces out the relation of his own boyishness to the emotional dilemmas of angry women.

The leading embodiment of corrupt patriarchy in *The Marble Faun* is the Model, a haunting figure of guilty grief who undergoes "unaccountable changes and interminglings of identity, which so often occur among the personages of a dream" (CE 4:188–189). His career as an artist's model extends back to Roman antiquity, so that he appears repeatedly in works of art across the centuries; he is also a "Man-Demon" who haunts the catacombs, coming forth in age after age to renew some "forgotten and long-buried evil" (33). In his last avatar as the dead Capuchin, the Model perfectly embodies Hawthorne's horror at the slain "father" who is kept alive by uncanny psychic energies, a trickle of blood sliding from the corpse's nostril when his murderers approach. The Model bespeaks Hawthorne's filial anguish, yet he enters the story by way of Miriam's torment over the loss of her maidenly purity.

Miriam is a young painter whose life the Model has blighted through the familiar entanglements of "purity" and imputed sin. No definite information is given about what Miriam has done, or how the Model was mixed up in it; but Hawthorne tells us that the story would ruin her reputation if it became generally known. This "past" has left Miriam doubting her own virtue, yet her grief and guilt are joined with feminist rage. Complementing the pictures in her studio that celebrate domestic purity, she has painted portraits of Jael and Judith that exalt womanly vengeance against male oppression. She gains revenge for her own victimization by spurring her

beloved Donatello to kill the Model by throwing him off the Tarpeian Rock.
Donatello is the junior male in this anti-patriarchal drama. He is the
marble faun in real life, a young Italian nobleman who exactly resembles
Praxiteles' statue and embodies its boyish purity of soul. Donatello also hates
the Model; yet he is not supplied with a complex history of betrayal and
inward consternation. He simply flies into a murderous fury against the
noxious old man by reason of natural impulse, "a tiger-like fury gleaming
from his wild eyes" that is the counterpart of his puppy-like affection for
Miriam (CE 4:148). Donatello's "wild paternity"—the fusion of animal and
human in his family line—produced his marvelous capacity for innocent
pleasure, Hawthorne later explains, but also made him "capable of savage
fierceness" (233).

A male version of Beatrice Cenci, Donatello is a creature of perfect
innocence tripped into deadly sin by Miriam's solicitations. Donatello
struggles, like Beatrice, with the dawning awareness of an evil that was
incomprehensible to him when his crime was committed. Hawthorne places
him on exactly the threshold where Una was stricken, a state of blameless
purity shadowed by an evil not of his own making, yet for which he is
doomed to suffer. In evoking the first shuddering onset of Donatello's
guiltless guilt, Hawthorne likens it to Una's disease. " 'Donatello,' said
Miriam anxiously . . . 'what can I do for you, my beloved friend? You are
shaking as with the cold fit of the Roman fever!' " (CE 4:196).

The logic Hawthorne articulates in portraying Miriam and Donatello is
that of his own buried emotions, but he reverses their direction. Miriam's
sexual contamination and patricidal guilt are not the opposite of Donatello's
innocent boyishness but its hidden meaning. Hawthorne's murderous lovers
dramatize an interactive psychic complex in which grief, guilt, and rage are
held at bay through a vehemently asserted innocence. Although this formation was sharply accentuated in Hawthorne's character by the circumstances
of his early childhood, it was typical of middle-class males generally. The
allocation of genders in this drama of masculine distress—the self-loathing
and anti-patriarchal fury of men being projected into morally compromised
women—was not a private trick of Hawthorne's imagination; it is inherent
in the Cenci myth itself, where the dilemmas of womanly innocence image
dilemmas newly developing among males in middle-class society. The story
of Beatrice, that is, concerns the lost purity of boys.

Patricide was intrinsic to the attainment of manly independence in the new democratic and industrial order. In the vanishing patrimonial family arrangement young men had been provided a situation in life by their elders, and the trusting affection of childhood was retained in the deference felt for social superiors generally. But to rise in the world without the help of elder kinsmen, as Robin Molineux discovered, it was necessary to act in defiance of such childlike sentiments, to assume an anti-patriarchal disposition all the more strenuous for being guilt-stricken. In ordaining that women remain childlike, domesticity served a nostalgia for the innocence men felt themselves to have lost, the one remaining oasis of purity in a wasteland of contaminating strife between males.

That male torment is expressed in the nineteenth-century preoccupation with Beatrice is indicated by the androgyny of the popular image, the "Guido's Beatrice Cenci" that Nathaniel and Sophia pored over so intently. The figure might as easily be an adolescent boy, mournfully looking back toward an unrecoverable innocence, with head, shoulder, and chest concealed in heavy folds of white cloth, and a few strands of unkempt hair framing the countenance. As males projected their own lost purity into girls and domestic angels, so the horror of womanly contamination arose from their own buried sense of corruption, the dead body of the slain father adrift in the soul of the self-made man.

The sexual victimization of Beatrice likewise shadows forth masculine distresses that became normative in the emerging competitive order. As networks of mutual trust and support among males gave way to individualist self-reliance, a prohibition was placed on physical intimacies between men that had earlier been accepted without qualm. As Carroll Smith-Rosenberg has observed, a "world" of same-sex love was available to women in the nineteenth century, affording them emotional support and mutual caring for which there existed no counterpart in the relations of men with men (53–76). To embrace and kiss on greeting, a male custom long established in Gallic (and Italian) society, became a focal point of anxiety for male Victorians, part of a "French" identity deemed effeminate, like the superseded Anglo-American custom of wearing lace and wigs.[5] Hawthorne notices this alienation in *The Marble Faun:* "Between man and man, there is always an insuperable gulf. They can never quite grasp each other's hands; and therefore man never derives any intimate help, any heart-sustenance, from his brother man, but from woman—his mother, his sister, or his wife" (CE 4:285).

The Victorian polarization of masculine erotic sentiment set "homosexual" pleasures sharply at odds with "heterosexual" and designated a wide range of masculine intimacies as tantamount to perversion. "Buggery" and "sodomy" were of course condemned prior to the emergence of the domestic ideal; yet the blame attaching to such conduct was now generalized into an anxiety that pervaded male-male pleasures and consolations, transforming them all into potential emblems of a corrupt identity.[6]

Such homophobic vigilance strongly characterized Hawthorne's temperament. When he visited a Shaker community in the company of Herman Melville, Hawthorne learned that the men slept two to a bed, in "particularly narrow beds," and promptly concluded that the Shakers "must needs be a filthy set" because of "their utter and systematic lack of privacy; their close junction of man with man. . . . It is hateful and disgusting to think of" (CE 8:465). Hawthorne's vehemence on this occasion may have been sharpened by the presence of Melville, with whom he shared a male friendship offering satisfactions that were anathematized in the emerging organization of male sexualities.[7]

When he visited the home of Robert Burns, Hawthorne was revolted by the pre-Victorian sleeping arrangements. Beds were crammed into a downstairs "parlor" and into storage spaces in the attic, and the place had a "frowzy smell, and also a dunghill smell. . . . No virgin can keep a holy awe about her, stowed higgledy-piggledy into this narrowness and filth; it must make beasts of men and women" (*English,* 504). Here again the purity of women is a screen upon which Hawthorne projects his anxieties about the virginity that males should retain in relation to other males, which was menaced by a lack of privacy as nasty as the smell.

The Manning household of Hawthorne's boyhood retained the pattern of intimate contact that was stigmatized in the new culture of self-contained and fastidious masculinity. Nathaniel slept with his uncle Robert into his fifteenth year, and his disgust toward the Shakers and the Burns household echoes his lifelong loathing for this uncle, who sought to become the father Nathaniel had lost.

It is possible that Uncle Robert sexually assaulted Nathaniel or seduced him, as James Mellow speculates, and that this trauma accounts for the peculiar blend of loathing and self-loathing with which Hawthorne depicts overbearing and corrupt father figures. Yet Gloria Erlich rightly observes that an overt offense would have permitted Hawthorne to repudiate his uncle decisively, either in boyhood or later, and would have removed the sexual guilt that chronically attends the anti-patriarchal impulses in his writing (Mellow, 610; Erlich, 118–119). The ambivalences that surround

Hawthorne's hatred of Robert Manning arise in part from the phobia that descended on male intimacies as middle-class norms took hold, yet they are given special intensity by the complex of yearning and rage that the boy Nathaniel brought to those intimacies. His "Hathorne" aloofness led him to scorn the affections of an alternative father; yet that aloofness and scorn were part of his effort to contain a desperate yearning for male nurture. Did Nathaniel guiltily seek physical comfort from Uncle Robert as they slept together? Did he feel trapped by the allure of a defiling solace?

The threat of homosexual rape did not have to be actual; it was inherent in the emotional situation. Robert Manning was an enterprising and successful man and a forceful leader within the extended family; Nathaniel's psychic needs, however, assigned Robert a substantial further power. If the mere presence of Uncle Robert was experienced as an invasive force, Nathaniel might well have concluded that the reasons lay within himself, that he was himself somehow to blame, particularly as he became conscious of his own physical beauty, his exceptional capacity to provoke desire.

The dichotomized gender system that portrayed women as passive recipients of male initiative structured the accompanying polarization of "heterosexual" and "homosexual" desire in men. To be the male object of womanly desire was to take a passive role in the sexual interaction, the part "unnatural" for a man. Yet Hawthorne's beauty made him pleasurable for women and men to look at ("handsomer than Lord Byron!" Elizabeth Peabody pronounced him), and his compulsive shyness may well have had roots in the impulse to shield himself from the "impure" warmth of appreciative gazes (Pearson, 264). His consternation at Louisa Lander's pleasure in his bodily loveliness is one evidence of his anxiety on this issue; and he was able to accept Sophia's worship because she hailed him as Adam, innocence incarnate, like Donatello before his fall.

Yet Sophia, implicitly recognizing the masculine erotics that her husband projected into Praxiteles' "Faun," compared it to a statue of Antinous, the Emperor Hadrian's boy lover, in which she saw a portrayal of the "northern" youth just giving way to Roman lubricity. Antinous's "perfect figure resists still a little—but the head with its clustering curls yields to the weight of artificial perfume that fills the Imperial halls. The northern flower faints in the southern hothouse." The Faun's "sunny smile" offered a joyful version of this melancholy sensuality; Sophia notes "his thorough joy and content, his air of complete though reposing power . . . his self-relying ease by the musing sadness of the Antinous at his side. No Eolian strain breathes through the faun, but songs of birds and gay rush of waterfalls" (Italy, 21 October 1858).

Sophia was able to relish the loveliness of a male sexual slave because she was not so anxious about male purity as her husband, for whom these questions were shot through with virtually unmanageable tensions. Innocent boyishness was the keystone of a defensive psychic structure that shielded him from an evil he projected into disgusting avatars of Hadrian, tyrants (like Chillingworth, Jaffrey Pyncheon, and Westervelt) who possess an erotic energy that threatens to enlist languid and sensuous younger men (Dimmesdale, Clifford, Coverdale) as catamites.

Hawthorne surrounds Donatello with associations drawn from the scenes in Hawthorne's own life where innocence was best realized. Donatello embodies "all the pleasantness of sylvan life" (CE 14:192) that Nathaniel had enjoyed at Raymond before Uncle Robert made him return to Salem, the paradise he renewed after his marriage to Sophia and sought once again at Florence. "I find him again as in the first summer in Concord at the old Manse" Sophia noted.[8] Yet Nathaniel was not fully contented until he had moved the family into the Villa Montauto in the hills of Bellosguardo outside the city wall. "I like my present residence immensely," he writes to Fields. "Here in Florence and in the summer time, and in this secluded villa, I have escaped out of all my old tracks, and am really remote" (CE 18:150). Recasting the Villa Montauto as Donatello's ancestral residence, Hawthorne marks it as a successor to Raymond and the Manse, a fortress in which a measure of childlike happiness and innocence can be protected against an encroaching dreary world of male relations. "The entire system of Man's affairs," he observes, "is built up purposely to exclude the careless and happy soul" (CE 4:239).

Hawthorne resented his children's part in spoiling this careless freedom. Just after Rose was born, for example, he reflected bitterly that "it is probably our duty to sacrifice all the green margin of our lives to these children, whom we have seen fit to bring into the world" (CE 16:440). He does not leave undeveloped the cold implications of his statement that "duty"—rather than paternal affection—prompts him to forgo pleasures for his children. "I think I never have had any natural partiality for my children. I love them according to their deserts; they have to prove their claim to all the affection they get; and I believe I could love other people's children better than mine, if I felt that they deserved it more" (441). During the European sojourn, Hawthorne complained that "a man with children in charge cannot enjoy travelling; he must content himself to be happy with them, for they allow him no separate and selfish possibility of being happy" (*English*, 184–185). "When a man has taken upon himself to beget children," he remarks a month later, "he has no longer any right to a life of his own" (210).

Sophia eliminated these passages from the version of Hawthorne's notebooks that she published; yet when she sought to construe his compulsive narcissism as communion with absolute principle, her resentment is clearly audible. "He transcends in indifference to persons," she writes to her sister, "being wholly ideal in thought and action always, really the most impersonal person I ever knew or heard of—free of every tie to anything except that of independent principle and disinterested worth."[9]

Yet Sophia intuitively recognized that a working axiom of Nathaniel's imaginative life was his conviction of an exceptional entitlement, grounded in his presumption of an inviolate boyish innocence. The crisis centered on Una's illness crippled Hawthorne's creative intelligence; as her childlike purity disintegrated at the transition to womanhood, so the contradictions within her father's innocence also erupted, and he was deprived of the inward center from which to manage his lifelong conflicts.

Hawthorne had explored the anti-patriarchal rage and guilt that had haunted his own life by projecting them into rebellious women, who are shown a measure of sympathy and then condemned. The characters of Hester and Zenobia, and now of Miriam, elaborated his inner conflicts at a safe distance and worked out the terms of his own stealthy indictment against corrupt "fathers." This long imaginative labor, for all its self-protective character, opened up an avenue through which Una's agony struck home to his unmanageable inward torments.

Hawthorne had sought to make of Una's presumptive childlike purity yet another fortification, the emblem of his childlike union with Sophia. But as Una was stricken on the threshold of womanhood, Hawthorne could no longer pretend that he was a boy in relation to her, rivaling her for her mother's affection. He was, on the contrary, her father; and as the anti-patriarchal meanings of her torment called his to life, they found their target in him. His place in relation to her suffering was that of Jaffrey Pyncheon, even of Francesco Cenci. The figures of virtue and vice that he had created to stabilize his conflicts now revealed their interdependent character. His own purity, like the womanly purity whose meanings Ada Shepard had explored, was symbiotically intertwined with the defilement that seemed its absolute opposite.

In defense of his purity, and the "sanctity of his domestic circle," Hawthorne had repudiated Louisa Lander without giving her a hearing; and he had simultaneously sought to repudiate the happy hours he had spent in her company by maintaining that the image of him she had formed during those hours, with its alluring sensuality, was a very poor resemblance "not worth sixpence." Yet Louisa had been an intimate of the household, leading the life that Una had embraced as her "ideal of living" just as the illness struck her down. Louisa had also served briefly as the angel of an innocent creativity Hawthorne sought to renew within himself, but the attraction he had felt for her now looked corrupt.

The embodiment of feminine purity in *The Marble Faun* is the stainless Hilda, an American painter who befriends Miriam and Donatello, and who nearly goes mad with moral pain when she witnesses their crime. Hawthorne remarks that evil "never becomes a portion of our practical belief until it takes substance and reality from the sin of some guide, whom we have deeply trusted and revered, or some friend whom we have dearly loved" (CE 4:328). It is tempting to suppose that behind this language there lies an interpretation of Una's distress, her horror at discovering that Louisa Lander had been spurned as corrupt and that her father was somehow implicated in her friend's moral defilement. Hilda's sinless moral torment, Hawthorne observes, caused her to resemble Beatrice Cenci when Francesco's wickedness was borne in on her. "It was the intimate consciousness of her father's sin," Hawthorne comments, "that threw its shadow over her" (205).

None of this softens the fact that in fixing his mind on the certainty Una would die, he shows that he wanted her dead. That realization was part of the torment now aroused to hurricane force as the seawall of his lifelong defense was broken through and his boyish inwardness was drowned. Hawthorne portrays in Donatello the emotional deadening that took place as he fought to keep his unsustainable feelings locked up. The faun's gnawing grief and guilt compel him to acquire a new "power of dealing with his own emotions, and, after a struggle more or less fierce, thrusting them down into the prison-cells where he usually kept them confined." Hawthorne sadly observes "the mask of dull composure which he succeeded in clasping over his still beautiful, and once faun-like face" (CE 4:250).

As his boyish innocence perished, Hawthorne found himself awash in psychic sickness and pollution. Having protracted his "youth" far beyond the customary time of its departure, he found himself on a dividing line beyond which lay, not maturity, but a corrupt and debilitated old age. At the Bowdoin semi-centennial he had described his classmates as "a set of dismal old fellows, whose heads looked as if they had been out in a pretty copious shower of snow." Hawthorne had been startled by the impression that they had "undergone this miserable transformation in the course of a single night—especially as I myself felt just about as young as when I graduated" (CE 16:607). Now he too felt a sudden decline. "One grows old in Italy twice or three times as fast as in other countries," Hawthorne wrote in September 1858. "I have three grey hairs now, for one that I brought from England" (CE 18:152). In the following March, after an illness that put him at the mercy of a physician for "the first time since my childhood" (CE 14:642), Hawthorne wrote to Ticknor, "I never knew that I had either bowels or lungs, till I came to Rome; but I have found it out now, to my cost" (CE 18:163).

Hawthorne's moral protest against the overt eroticism of Italian pictures is burdened with exhaustion and disgust. Titian's "coarse and sensual" Magdalen (Fig. 11) leads him to imagine Titian instructing her to "press the rich locks about her, and so carefully let those two voluptuous breasts be seen." Hawthorne finds this a dreary opposite of faunlike youthful spirits or even of fiery lust: "Titian must have been a very good-for-nothing old man" (CE 14:334).

This image of decaying lechery is an aspect of his relation to Louisa Lander, one of several he projects into *The Marble Faun*. Hawthorne describes Hilda's innocence, as noted, by repeating his early response to Louisa, and Donatello embodies the spontaneous male innocence he correspondingly cherished in himself. As Miriam's ruined reputation evokes the ensuing scandal, so the Model represents Hawthorne's vision of himself as Louisa's model: a contaminated and contaminating old man, implicated in the doom of a woman proud of her sexual appeal, who was responsive— before her "fall"—to his own. The middle-class culture of purity produced a male counterpart to the angel/whore: the innocent boy/dirty old man.

Hawthorne felt himself on the verge of death in multiple senses: the collapse of his customary defense against patricidal guilt and grief threatened a spiritual death brought on by the unburied corpse in himself that was still weirdly alive. Spiritual death was also threatened by his own sensuality, now no longer an expression of innocent boyishness but contaminated, like what he had projected into fallen women. His own living death was all too similar to what Una suffered, comatose and delirious on the threshold separating youth from adulthood. Nathaniel's horror of suddenly growing old is the inner meaning of Sophia's remark that he expected every morning to find the hair on his head turned to white. Sophia also recognized the analogy between Una's affliction and that of her husband, both rooted somehow in

Fig. 11.   Titian's Mary Magdalen

the poison of Rome. They both need a "change of scene and diet and circumstances," she wrote to her sister Elizabeth. "Mr. Hawthorne needs it almost as much as Una. He says he should die if he should . . . [remain in] Rome another winter. The malaria certainly disturbs him, though it is undeveloped."[10]

The character in *The Marble Faun* who represents Hawthorne's position as author is the American sculptor Kenyon, a close friend of Hilda, Miriam, and Donatello, who turn to him for solace and advice. His view of their troubles is granted a measure of authority; but he never learns what brought on the engulfing melancholy. He follows Donatello to his ancestral villa for long conversations about his distress, yet the two never mention Miriam. He seeks to mollify Hilda's bitter pain, but without learning that she witnessed the murder of the Model. In fact, Kenyon never actually finds out what happened between Miriam, Donatello, Hilda, and the Model, even though he speaks on occasion as though he knew the whole story (CE 4:384).

Hawthorne's incapacity to come to terms with the crisis of innocence in his own life is embodied in Kenyon's odd busybody role; he pokes tirelessly into the anguished predicament without ever grasping its substance. As Hilda, Miriam, Donatello, and the Model variously denote aspects of Hawthorne's internal torment, so Kenyon's detachment represents his inability to penetrate the center of that torment, to generate a narrative order giving it meaning. *The Marble Faun* thus possesses a very peculiar structure, in which the narrative consciousness is embodied in a character who is specifically designated as incapable of comprehending the narrative: the figure who emerges with final authority is not Kenyon, but Hilda.

Hilda embodies the purity at the heart of the domestic ideal, whose interior workings are dramatized throughout the Hawthornes' Roman torment. These paradoxes were active in the repudiation of Margaret Fuller and Louisa Lander and in Ada Shepard's erotic ordeal; they lay at the center of Una's illness and of Hawthorne's own psychic collapse. Only Sophia found it possible to retain her faith in the triumph of spiritual law and the unsullied ideal of perfect rectitude. Such innocence, as we have seen, depends for its moral force on the denial of its own psychic anatomy; its luminous authority is positively generated by the perceptions and impulses that are repressed within it. The high tower from which Hilda looks out over the dark streets of Rome is an emblem for her relation to the narrative, in which Hawthorne pursues with obsessive interest the ceaseless tumult of ambition, rage, grief, guilt, and desire that are "beneath" her. Yet Hilda cannot conceive her loftiness as symbiotically united with the low: she believes that there is "only one right and one wrong," and that they are "mortal foes" (CE 4:384). As though acknowledging Sophia's capacity to sustain the crisis that had crushed him, Hawthorne insists that Hilda's innocence is capable of meeting all the moral ambiguities that the story of Miriam, Donatello, and the Model has elaborated.[11]

Kenyon relinquishes his authority when he finally puts forward the sug-

gestion so obsessively intimated in the narrative at large, that the sin and
sorrow of Miriam and Donatello might be elements of a "human education,"
leading to a truer moral awareness than one who remains innocent can
possibly attain. But Hilda decisively rebukes him. " 'Oh, hush!' . . . Do not
you perceive what a mockery your creed makes, not only of all religious
sentiment, but of moral law? . . . You have shocked me beyond words!" (CE
4:460).

To this Kenyon replies with an acknowledgment of her celestial perfection, which is simultaneously a plea for her hand in marriage: "Were you my
guide, my counsellor, my inmost friend, with that white wisdom which
clothes you as with a celestial garment, all would go well. Oh, Hilda, guide
me home" (CE 4:460–461). The couple soon determine to leave behind the
moral morass of Rome, their erstwhile friend Miriam now standing apart
from them, "on the other side of a fathomless abyss." Kenyon and Hilda
look forward to establishing an ideal middle-class home, at whose moral
center will be the purity of the wife and mother, who was "to be herself
enshrined and worshipped as a household Saint, in the light of her husband's
fireside" (461).

The Hawthornes' tacit marital interplay took a new form after the crisis
at Rome. When James T. Fields requested that Sophia publish excerpts from
her notebooks, Nathaniel remarked that "she positively refuses to be famous, and contents herself with being the best wife and mother in the
world" (CE 18:204). This familiar gesture, however, has now taken on new
bearings. Their sacred oneness had been dedicated to sustaining his identity,
as the artist of divine pre-eminence in whom Sophia was able vicariously to
realize her own ambitions. But Hawthorne's creative selfhood had now been
disrupted, and what remained to him, as a talisman of the self he had once
inhabited, was her belief in him.

Sophia's vision of Nathaniel now reached beyond their intimate bond. It
was gathered into the middle-class assertion of cultural supremacy in America, which included recruiting literary champions as exemplars of its sacred
ideals and canonizing them as embodiments of a literary excellence as lofty
and unapproachable as Hilda's tower. James T. Fields was a leader of the
movement, Richard Brodhead has shown, that fashioned and emplanted the
conception of "classic" American writers. As Fields's prime exemplar, Hawthorne increasingly busied himself in promotional activities that would keep

him before the public in his canonical posture: signing autographs, sitting for portraits, interviewing awestruck younger writers, and aiding biographers. The collapse of Hawthorne's literary powers, which took place as he accepted this role, is already visible in *The Marble Faun,* where the characters move inconclusively about in an environment choked with classic masterpieces (*School,* 67–80).

Hawthorne no longer possessed the creative capacity by which to define the meaning of his life or his work, and his efforts to write another romance foundered amid obsessive rehearsals of his self-disgust.[12] The public identity he now accepted was that ascribed to him by the best wife and mother in the world: he was the priestly celebrant of the domestic sanctity he saw in her. As James Fields and Sophia Hawthorne became co-producers of the figure known as "Hawthorne," so Nathaniel's relation to the public that cherished and consumed this figure became continuous with his relation to his wife, which had become his relation to himself.

In reply to John Lothrop Motley's praise for *The Marble Faun* Hawthorne hailed him as "that Gentle Reader for whom all my books were exclusively written." Only Sophia is better able, Hawthorne explains, to "take the book precisely as I meant it," because Sophia "speaks so near me that I cannot tell her voice from my own" (CE 18:256). Sophia took part in revising the manuscript of *The Marble Faun,* marking questionable passages for discussion with Nathaniel; and she removed impurities without asking him when she knew what his exquisite taste would require. In this way "appetite" becomes "fancy," "breeds" of men become "races," and pigeons no longer "squatted" but "huddled" (CE 4:lxx). In refusing Fields's offer to publish her notebooks, Sophia conveys the same eerie message, that her husband had become her worship of him: "You forget that Mr Hawthorne is the Belleslettres portion of my being" (CE 18:202).

From the outset of their courtship, and recurrently through their lives together, Nathaniel referred to Sophia as "my own true self"; these words now received new meaning. The civil death that Sophia accepted in marrying Nathaniel is oddly matched by the spiritual death that now befell him within their union. No one had spoken more eloquently of their soul-marriage than had Sophia at the Old Manse; she was certainly as ready as Nathaniel to defy convention for the sake of a living creative communion. That the prototype of Hester Prynne had now become the fabled gorgon of propriety was in keeping with the decadence to which Nathaniel had likewise given way. Sophia had dedicated her strength and talent to seeking fulfillment in him, and in him she found her sad victory.

Deeply shaken—though not broken—by the calamity at Rome, Sophia determined she would require a year of rest and recovery in England while Nathaniel continued to work on his tribute to her victorious sainthood. Domestic spirituality worked to erect an intrafamilial matriarchy that enjoyed real power, having a purchase on the emotional liabilities of males. Even as such liabilities overwhelmed Hawthorne at Rome, however, his pocket note-books keep track of his visits to the bank, where Sophia had no power to make deposits or withdrawals; and it was finally his decision, not hers, that the family should return to America.

Epilogue

When the Hawthornes arrived as newlyweds at the Old Manse, they were greeted by Sarah, the housekeeper. She was the first in a procession of laboring-class women over the years who cleaned house, cooked, and cared for the children at Sophia's direction. Sarah's last name is not known, nor is that of Margaret, who also helped out in the early months. The "Mary" who took their place was variously "O'Brien" and "Bryan"; the "Ellen" and "Mary" who worked at the Wayside and accompanied the family to Liverpool were "Herne," "Hearne," and "Ahern."[1]

Sophia felt entitled to the social privilege that erases the last names of household help, but her dominance over these lower-class companions did not prevent a cherished intimacy from taking form. She developed a sisterly affection for Mary Bryan/O'Brien, teaching her to read and write during the long months of solitude at the Old Manse; and her hope that Mary's "little heart will not break in this lonliness," responds to a misery that Sophia shared.[2] When she discovered that Mary—skilled in the stratagems of the oppressed—had sought a countervailing power through "cajolery" and "deceit," Sophia's ruling-class disdain blazed out. She would prefer a "blackey" to another "Irisher," she declared, and after obtaining the services of Mary Pray, she rejoiced in "the luxury of having an *American* and a *Protestant* maid," with "a conscience untouched by Jesuits and priests." Still, behind Sophia's rage at Bryan/O'Brien lay feelings of personal betrayal. "How much

I cared for the little siren," she protested, sounding very much like a jilted male lover.[3]

The complicated mix of domination and affection in Sophia's relation to her maids seemed natural enough, since it echoed the politics of her marriage to Nathaniel; and there were times when Sophia and the household help suffered together under her husband's exercise of patriarchal control. Ellen Herne/Hearne/Ahern became "arrogant, hateful & bitter" in a quarrel that arose after the Hawthornes had taken her to England, whereupon Nathaniel intervened and fired the woman, much to Sophia's grief. She had always thought of Ellen as a sister, Sophia wrote home to her father, and had hoped the storm of painful emotions would blow over (Hull, *English*, 49). Sophia was haunted lifelong, as we have seen, by memories of a "little beggar girl" she had encountered in her early years, a figure of her own subjugation.

Among Sophia's dearest friends was Dora Golden, an Irish immigrant, who joined the household when Nathaniel was working at the Salem Custom House. Hawthorne's journals record that Dora cooperated fully in providing care for Una and Julian, a clear sign how deeply Sophia trusted her. Their shared household labors formed the basis of an intimate mutual reliance, which made them eager to stay in touch after the period of employment ended. Nathaniel too was very fond of Dora; he called her Golden Dora and portrayed her by name in "The Snow Image." As *The Scarlet Letter* achieved its immense early success, he declared that Dora had "brought good luck into the family." Dora Golden's descendants treasure today a table she was given by Sophia, at which Nathaniel's masterwork was written and which he cut with a jackknife while he labored over the manuscript.[4]

A telling emblem of this friendship is a photograph of Sophia that she presented to Dora in 1861. Sophia generally avoided being photographed and once turned her face away when a group picture was being taken. Of the four photos that are known to survive, this one preserves the clearest image (Fig. 12).[5] Sophia emphatically reasserted her dread of being photographed in writing to her friend Annie (Mrs. James T.) Fields about the picture and made it clear that Annie would not receive a copy. It seems likely Sophia felt secure giving Dora the picture because she knew it would remain private with her and would not be circulated in the genteel society of the Fieldses, to say nothing of being published. Sophia also gave Dora pictures of Nathaniel and the children on this occasion, and all taken together form the only "family photograph" of the Hawthornes known to exist (Figs. 13, 14).[6]

Sophia pronounced the image of herself "frightful," and it indeed contrasts violently with the appurtenances of respectable feminine delicacy around her: the book on the marble-top table, the embroidered chair, and the locket clasped beneath her breast. Sophia's body surges up from the huge shapeless black skirt, filling the bodice with powerful shoulders and forearms. Her hands are heavy and thick, like the flat breadth of her jaw and brow. It is an image of resolute endurance, the punished face bluntly refusing submission even as her eyes are cast down and inward.

The images of Una, Julian, and Rose are suspended over the same patterned rug, Una with the absent expression that had begun to trouble her parents when she was five or six, when Dora was a member of the household. Julian is placed uncomfortably in the manly station at the center, his collar a bit too large. Rose stands slightly apart from the others, looking in a direction of her own. Nathaniel is as always the most beautiful, even here under the shadow of death, with hollow cheek and exhausted eyes, his fingers barely touching the broad-brimmed pudgy hat in his lap, which looks as though it had grown there like a pale fungus.

There is truth in the family legend that says Nathaniel came to his untimely death, in May 1864, because he could not overcome the torment aroused in him by Una's Roman illness. Soon after the Hawthorne's return to the Wayside, Una's physician declared she would have another attack of "brain fever" unless she could get away from her family. "Though I appear, & am, perfectly well while I do as I please," she wrote to her cousin Richard, "there is a certain little group of events & sights & minds that in a minute by a most wonderful magic make me faint & sick & all over shooting pains."[7] Una became deranged and violent within the month and had to be tied down, whereupon the Hawthornes turned in desperation to a practicioner of electrotherapeutics, an early form of shock therapy. They were impressed by the results. "All the violent symptoms were allayed," Hawthorne wrote, "by the first application of electricity, and within two days she was in such a condition as to require no further restraint" (CE 18:327).[8] Hoping that his own strange malady might likewise be cured, Nathaniel submitted to a course of electrical treatments himself.

The horrors of the Roman ordeal also reappeared in the spells of sick despondency that increasingly beset him. "I was quite alarmed when I returned that evening to find Mr. Hawthorne very ill," Sophia wrote to Annie Fields in 1862. "It was a Roman cold, with fever and utter restlessness, and it has hardly left him yet. . . . Alas the Roman days were melancholy days for him, and he thinks he shall never recover from them. Even when he looks at his Rose of Sharon so firm and strong now, I think he feels uncertain that

Fig. 12.   Sophia Hawthorne, 1861

she still lives and blooms, so deeply scored into his soul was the expectation of her death. It was his first acquaintance with suffering, and it seemed to rend him asunder."[9]

In the slow progress of the disease that took his life, Nathaniel sought to cure his melancholy by taking trips away from Concord to refresh his spirits. He steadfastly refused to see a medical doctor, perhaps because he did not want to take up the role that Una had played as "patient" in Sophia's heroic drama of womanly self-sacrifice. "A chief difficulty about him," Julian later remarked, "was that he was extremely reluctant to be thought ill, and to receive the care which illness requires" (NHW 2:332).

In April 1864 William Ticknor accompanied Hawthorne on a journey south, which ended abruptly when Ticknor died in Philadelphia. Hawthorne was left to communicate the news to Ticknor's family, sat up with the body until the undertakers came for it, and then made his way back to Concord

Fig. 13.   Nathaniel Hawthorne, 1861

Fig. 14.   Una, Julian, and Rose Hawthorne, 1861

and the Wayside, where Sophia was startled by his condition: "so haggard, so white, so deeply scored with pain and fatigue was the face, so much more ill than I ever saw him before" (Fields, 118–119). Sophia was particularly horrified by the misfortune that had befallen Ticknor's wife. "What an inscrutable Providence that her husband should die away from her," she lamented to Annie Fields. "It is well that we have no right to question the Providence of GOD, but know that it must be best for all and each. Otherwise—what despair and madness!" Nathaniel himself was appalled, she was certain, by "his sense of the drear death in a hotel—away from his wife and children."[10]

Yet Hawthorne preferred to avail himself of Franklin Pierce's company when it became evident his own death was near, and Sophia pronounced herself entirely satisfied. "General Pierce has been a most tender constant nurse for many years, and knows how to take care, and his love for Mr. Hawthorne is the strongest passion of his soul, now his wife is departed."[11] Sophia expected that her husband would return from this journey refreshed and restored; yet behind the wall of denial lay her perception he would not. This was evident to Rose, now aged twelve, who was present at the scene. "I could hardly bear to let my eyes rest upon her shrunken, suffering form on this day of farewell. My father certainly knew, what she vaguely felt, that he would never return." He bore himself erect, Rose recalled, with "military self-command," as Sophia walked beside him sobbing to the carriage (R. H. Lathrop, 480).

As Sophia kept vigil over her husband's body, she wrote an incantatory prose poem declaring that her husband had been as remote from her as from the world at large. She saw that their marital union protected an inner sanctuary he himself could hardly enter.

> In the most retired privacy it was the same as in the presence of men.
>
> The sacred veil of his eyelids he scarcely lifted to himself. Such an unviolated sanctuary as was his nature, I his inmost wife never conceived nor knew. . . .
>
> To me—himself—even to me that was himself in unity—He was to the last the holy of holies behind the cherubim. . . .
>
> A tenderness so infinite—so embracing—that God's alone could surpass it.
>
> It folded the loathsome leper in as soft a caress as the child of his home affections.[12]

This song of grief again demonstrates Sophia's uncanny intuition of the inner life she claims never to have known: "the loathsome leper" was an image of her husband's abiding pain.

On a visit to an English almshouse Hawthorne, shown the section in which young children were kept, was appalled when one of these "very unlovely and unwholesome little imps" became attached to him. "This little sickly, humor-eaten fright prowled around me, taking hold of my skirts, following at my heels; and at last held up its hands, smiled in my face, and standing directly before me, insisted on my taking it up. . . . I held my undesirable burthen a little while; and after setting the child down, it still followed me, holding two of my fingers (luckily the glove was on) and playing with them, just as if (God save us!) it were a child of my own" (*English,* 275). Hawthorne makes no effort to conceal his fierce disgust toward the child, and toward all the filthy and diseased youngsters that are kept at the almshouse. "It would be a blessing to the world," he declares, "if every one of them could be drowned to-night, instead of being put to bed" (277).

When his tour returned to the children's ward, "there was this same child, waiting for me, with a sickly smile about its scabby mouth and in its dim, red eyes. If it were within the limits of possibility . . . I should certainly have set down its affection to the score of blood recognition; and I cannot conceive of any greater remorse than a parent must feel, if he could see such a result of his illegitimate embraces" (*English,* 276).

Sophia was right to identify this moment as central to her husband's spirituality and to celebrate the compassion he displayed. Within the holy of holies behind the cherubim was Nathaniel's sense of himself as contaminated at birth and abandoned. His own parents had married following the conception of their first child, and his father had left him and his sisters destitute. The Manning family then served as an almshouse, performing the traditional function being transferred increasingly from households to public institutions. Nathaniel's own existence was plausibly a consequence of the illegitimate embraces that had produced his older sister, and this whispered awareness was present amid the family charity that had enclosed and sustained him.

This experience haunted Nathaniel all his life and underlies an irrational obsession that seized him amid the mental disintegration at its end. He dreaded being consigned to the almshouse in Concord, and dying there.[13] The merciless power of his insight was anchored here too, however. His "catlike faculty of seeing in the dark" was sharpened by knowing what a "blessing" it would have been if he and his sisters had been drowned like kittens rather than being put to bed in Castle Dismal. Seeing a figure of his primordial desperation in the English almshouse, Hawthorne is able momentarily to take it up in his arms.

This incident has resonances that reach forward into his children's lives. Despite the favor Julian enjoyed as the male child, he was haunted by the impression that he was a foundling, not really a member of the family. There recurs in his fiction the figure of a changeling child, who is burdened by a false identity he must escape to find his real existence. Known lifelong as "Hawthorne's son," Julian brought disgrace on himself in his early sixties by playing out a drama that exploited this role as well as repudiating it. Trading on his famous name, he wrote letters on yellow stationery soliciting investments in Canadian mines, which he misrepresented as rich in silver, gold, copper, and cobalt. When the fraud was exposed, a newspaper said it was a shame he had written so many yellow letters, instead of one *Scarlet Letter,* and he served a sentence at the federal penitentiary in Atlanta, Georgia. Julian spent the remaining twenty years of his life in California, in exile from his family and inherited traditions (Bassan, *Hawthorne's Son,* 213–220).

Rose Hawthorne also grew up feeling out of place in the family, like "a stranger who had come too late," and she eventually mastered the ambiguities of her own existence by creating a saintly vocation, modeled on her father's Christlike compassion. But this consummation was reached only after years of family discord.

Her marriage to George Parsons Lathrop infuriated Julian, and when Lathrop published *A Study of Hawthorne* in 1876, Julian responded as though the familial holy of holies had been despoiled. He claimed that Lathrop had illicitly obtained "peculiarly private and delicate" family papers through Rose, declaring in the *New York Tribune* that the book was "composed and published in violation of a trust." Such a work, he declared, "no member of Mr. Hawthorne's own family would have ventured to undertake" (Bassan, *Hawthorne's Son,* 116–117). Rose was pregnant when Julian launched this attack, and when her son, Francis, was born, she became "raving mad." Far from lifting the "curse" under which Rose was fated to live, Elizabeth Peabody observed, the birth renewed the "mental agonies" resulting from her brother's conduct, so they came "rushing back upon her" (Peabody, *Letters,* 378–379).

Rose, Julian, and George found themselves intractably at odds because none of them could secure a standpoint outside the complex of family tensions bequeathed by Nathaniel and Sophia, though each struggled to do so. Elizabeth Peabody stated that Rose and George had deliberately sought to "commence a new life entirely separate from the family blood of Hawthorne" (Peabody, *Letters,* 379). Yet in saying this she reveals her own entanglement in the struggle, repeating the Peabodys' self-serving theory that there was "hereditary madness" in the Hawthorne "family blood." Hawthorne biography was a battleground even as the principals lived out their lives, and the warfare was intensified when it was carried over into print. There is no reason to suppose this will cease to be so, given the family's role in the fashioning of middle-class selfhood at large. We have all become, for better or worse, members of the family.

Rose made her way through this strife for the next two decades, in the course of which Julian published his two-volume *Nathaniel Hawthorne and His Wife* and George published a substantial "Biographical Sketch" for the Riverside edition of Hawthorne's works. Rose's saintly vocation took form slowly, following her treatment for insanity, the death of Francis, her conversion with George to Roman Catholicism, the termination of her married life with him, and his death.

When Rose published *Memories of Hawthorne* in 1897, she devoted the proceeds to her work among impoverished victims of cancer, who were shunned because of the social stigma they bore. It was not then possible to forestall or correct the shocking disfigurement cancer often produced, and the disease was superstitiously considered infectious, especially amid the filth of poverty. Rose singled out these pariahs for a ministry of compassion and founded a still vital Dominican order that offers bed care to persons who are destitute and fatally ill. Rose re-created the almshouse as a place of sacred motherhood and re-created herself as Mother Alphonsa without a husband to obey.

A founding metaphor of this extraordinary spiritual and institutional achievement was Nathaniel's compassion toward "the loathsome leper." Looking back on her life, Rose wrote that her patients "are of the class to which belonged the child whom my father found in an English hospital. . . . His words in regard to this little child, whose flesh reeked with parental desecration, made a deep impression upon me when I read them as a girl; and I was glad to have the latter years of my life devoted to the field of diseased poverty" (Valenti, *To Myself,* 134–135).

The firstborn of Nathaniel and Sophia lived a contained and quiet life that was interrupted by attacks of severe mental disorder. Yet far from appearing emotionally crippled, Una created an impression of extraordinary self-possession and personal force: "Tall beyond the average height of women, absolutely erect," wrote Thomas Wentworth Higginson, "bearing her fine head upon the body of a gymnast, she herself kept no account of the eyes resting upon her, or of the heads that were turned to watch her as she swept by. It was this nobleness of carriage which first arrested attention, and her

superb Titianesque coloring which afterwards held it,—the abundant hair of
reddish auburn and the large grey eyes" (Hull, "Una," 101). Una had
periods of vigor and relative equilibrium in the ensuing years, yet she was
never freed from the danger of mental collapse, especially when circumstances arose bespeaking her constitutional dilemma. When Rose married
George Lathrop in September 1871, Una responded as though the event
signaled her own failure to achieve this presumptive *sine qua non* of womanly
fulfillment. Word soon reached Dora Golden that Una "became dangerously
insane, spent great sums of money, nearly took the lives of three persons, and
is confined in an asylum."[14]

Una was twice engaged to be married, both times to notably unlikely
prospects, as she both obeyed and disobeyed the imperative to take up the
roles of wife and mother that Sophia had enacted so triumphantly. The first
engagement was to Storrow Higginson (a nephew of Thomas Wentworth
Higginson), who professed himself not to believe in marriage and in the
event displayed the courage of this conviction; the second was to Albert
Webster, a tubercular poet of modest means, who set off for the Sandwich
Islands to regain his health and died on the voyage (Hull, "Una," 101–
108).[15] Julian describes Una's response to the news of Webster's death:
" 'Ah—yes!' she said, slowly, with a slight sigh. She made no complaint, nor
gave way to any passion of grief, but she seemed to become spiritualized,—
to relinquish the world, along with her hopes of happiness in it" (*NHW*
2:373).

Una was then engaged in Anglican volunteer service and had become
associated with a sisterhood at Clewer, where she acted as a "district visitor."
She had been confirmed in the Church of England in 1869, after a period
of religious struggle, and in the early 1870s had devoted her energies to
assisting in an orphans' home. She solicited public support by printing
appeals in the newspapers that invoked her father's name, the method Rose
was later to adopt in sustaining the Servants of Relief for Incurable Cancer
(Hull, "Una," 117; Marks, 18). Unlike Rose, Una did not succeed in creating
a coherent existence from her religious service, and within six months of
learning Webster was dead, Una herself died at the Clewer convent, aged
thirty-three.

Una never doubted that she was fully a member of the family, since she
was aware that her parents' divine union was the substance of her own inner
life. "I have more than ever realized what their love was since reading lately
some of their exquisite letters to each other," she wrote to Rebecca Manning
after Sophia's death. "I never could have known without the proof, that I

do indeed love them better than myself—and that being the case is a continual encouragement to bear the cost bravely. And I do feel as if they lived in my deepest heart and pervaded my life more fully than they ever did before."[16] Una had cared for her mother with zealous solicitude during her lengthy terminal illness, held her hand as she died, assisted in preparing the body for burial, and then kept watch. "Her face looked more and more like an angel's," Una wrote. "A delicate color stayed upon the cheeks, a lovely smile upon the slightly parted lips; her beautiful white hair was brushed a little back from her face, under a pretty cap, and her waxen hands lay softly folded against each other upon her breast" (NHW 2:371). On the last day of this vigil Una removed the wedding ring from her mother's finger and placed it on her own.

Acknowledgments

When I started this project a decade ago I expected it would take four years, maybe five. That was before I realized how extensively the traditional understanding of Hawthorne's family would have to be revised and began to encounter the interpretive problems that arose once the conventional picture was set aside. I have acquired many debts along the way.

Evan Carton, Stephen Greenblatt, Mary Kelley, David Leverenz, Megan Marshall, and Warwick Wadlington read large quantities of early draft and provided invaluable commentary. I am also indebted for friendly assistance and generous professional support to John Elliott, Gloria Erlich, Stephanie Fay, Rita Gollin, Karen Halttunen, Alex Hill, Joy Kasson, Doris Kretschmer, Edwin Haviland Miller, Fabrizio Barbolani di Montauto, Jan Ramirez, Larry Reynolds, Patricia Valenti, and Joseph Wakefield.

I am especially grateful to the Ohio State University Center for Textual Studies, under the direction of Thomas Woodson, and to Neal Smith, for making available photocopies of their annotated typescripts of Hawthorne letters before they were published. The Center's Centenary Edition of the Works of Nathaniel Hawthorne is a major achievement of contemporary scholarship and will sustain future generations of interpretive study.

My work has also been aided by several fine biographical studies that have appeared since I began work. I am indebted in countless ways to Gloria Erlich's *Family Themes and Hawthorne's Fiction,* Rita Gollin's *Portraits of Nathaniel Hawthorne: An Iconography,* Raymona Hull's *Nathaniel Hawthorne: The English Experience, 1853–1864,* James Mellow's *Nathaniel Hawthorne in His Times,* and Arlin Turner's *Nathaniel Hawthorne, A Biography.* Edwin Miller's *Salem Is My Dwelling Place* appeared as this book was in the last stages of preparation and provided welcome assistance at several points. I am particularly grateful to Megan Marshall for sharing information with me that will appear in her forthcoming biography of the Peabody sisters.

It is a pleasure to thank the research libraries that have given me access to unpublished materials pertinent to the story of the Hawthorne family and have given me permission to publish photographs and manuscript text: Hawthorne Family Papers, The Bancroft Library, University of California, Berkeley; Henry W. and Albert Berg Collection, The New York Public Library, Astor, Lenox and Tilden Foundations; Department of Rare Books and Manuscripts, Boston Public Library; Concord Free Public Library, Concord, Mass.; Hawthorne-Manning Collection, Essex Institute, Salem, Mass.; Massachusetts Historical Society, Boston; Pierpont Morgan Library; Rogers Collection, New-York Historical Society; Beinecke Rare Book and Manuscript Library, Yale University; Archivi Musei Capitolini, Rome. Special thanks are due to Alice Perry for permission to publish excerpts from Margaret Fuller's Commonplace Book for 1844, and to Barbara Bacheler for permission to publish the photographs of Nathaniel, Sophia, and the children taken in 1860.

This project was begun with the support of a Guggenheim Fellowship for 1981 and has been sustained by the research assistance provided by Southwestern University. I have also received valuable help from the interdisciplinary Writers' Group at Southwestern, especially Winston Davis, Jan Dawson, Dan Hilliard, Ed Kain, Gwen Neville, and Ken Roberts. The students in my advanced seminars over the years have possessed a remarkable knack for locating real issues.

A semester as Mrs. William Beckman Professor at Berkeley gave me an invaluable opportunity to advance this work, as did invitations to read and discuss papers at several other research institutions: the University of California at Santa Barbara, the University of Florida, the University of North Carolina at Chapel Hill, Texas A&M University, and the University of Texas at Austin.

My wife has been throughout an incomparable loving companion. While

I've been working on this project, she has established a thriving solo law practice, specializing in family law, and has served as the president of the Williamson County Bar Association. We have seen our son and daughter through high school and college. How our lives are intertwined and touch upon the issues of this book would make another book, but not for me to write.

Notes

Abbreviations for archival sources are given in the first section of Works Cited. Hawthorne's works are cited in the notes by full title.

INTRODUCTION

1. According to Julian Hawthorne, Sophia also cut out and destroyed eleven pages and five partial pages from the earlier of the original manuscript volumes. See *The American Notebooks*, 703.

2. Twentieth-century students have embraced the tranquil Hawthorne so ardently that Frederick Crews was compelled to argue against a critical consensus in 1966, pointing to Hawthorne's persistent fascination with familial conflict as described in the work of Freud. But Crews reclaimed Hawthorne's "dark" imagination only in his literary work, where Hillard had observed it a century before. In the biographies of Arlin Turner and James Mellow, the story of Hawthorne's incongruously placid home still runs on much as before. More recent biographical work is more perceptive. Gloria Erlich, in *Family Themes and Hawthorne's Fiction*, finds sources in Hawthorne's early life for the troubled preoccupations of his writing, though she does not relate them to his intimate relationships in adulthood. Edwin Miller's *Salem Is My Dwelling Place* makes extensive use of Sophia's letters and journals and provides a sensitive treatment of the Hawthorne marriage, including certain of the tensions within it. Yet such conflicts remain a private matter in Miller's study, rather than illuminating the dilemmas intrinsic to the domestic ideal and the social energies of Hawthorne's art.

Feminism—in Hawthorne's time as in our own—demystifies the matrimonial ideal that the Hawthornes exemplified; yet the vision of their home life as uniformly blissful has found acceptance with pioneers of contemporary feminist criticism, as it did with Margaret Fuller. Annette Kolodney, in her introduction to *The Blithedale Romance*, refers to the "happy and ordered domesticity" of the Hawthornes at the Old Manse and speaks of Nathaniel's "enjoying unblemished domestic happiness until his death" (ix, xxxviii). Nina Baym, in the course of a penetrating discussion of Hawthorne's relationship to his mother, speaks of Sophia's "limpid, unsophisticated imagination," and of the "simple sincerity" by which she took Hawthorne's deceptions at face value ("Nathaniel Hawthorne and His Mother," 5). Joyce Warren provides a richer portrait of Sophia (*The American Narcissus*, 189–208), yet her appreciation of Sophia's independence does not lead her to suspect marital combat.

3. For an understanding of the symbolic processes at work here see Claude Lévi-Strauss, "The Sorcerer and His Magic" and "The Effectiveness of Symbols," in *Symbolic Anthropology*, 167–205. Also see Victor Turner, *The Ritual Process*, 47; and "Passages, Margins, and Poverty," in *Dramas, Fields, and Metaphors*, 231–271. Turner tellingly describes the contradictions at the heart of symbolic systems and the sacred monsters active in the rituals that maintain normality.

4. Hawthorne's continuing power to assert the gender arrangements typical of the domestic ideal and to disarm opposition is witnessed by efforts to claim this champion of male dominance as an ally of feminism. For a discussion of this impulse in Hawthorne criticism by a writer who does not share it, see Louise DeSalvo, *Nathaniel Hawthorne*, 23–38. Also see below, Chapter 9, n. 8.

CHAPTER ONE: INDICES OF A PROBLEM

1. For a discussion of such conflicts see Daniel J. Levinson, *The Seasons of a Man's Life*.

2. The entries Sophia made in the Family Notebook (Journal Dated 1842–1854 [Morgan]) while Nathaniel was absent from the Wayside are in the second manuscript volume and cover the dates from 30 August to 16 September 1852. Except where otherwise noted, quotations of Sophia Hawthorne in this chapter are from this section of the journal and are noted by date.

3. For a discussion of Fields's promotional campaign and its impact on the cultural formation of the "literary" see Richard H. Brodhead, *The School of Hawthorne*.

4. Gloria Erlich observes that this pairing had an early origin in Hawthorne's relation to his two sisters, whose temperaments counterpointed hauteur and meekness. Erlich also argues that the male counterparts—anguished poets recoiling before thick-skinned men of affairs—recapitulate Hawthorne's boyhood relationship to his uncle Robert Manning, who sought to take charge of Hawthorne's life and became the object of acute resentment (Erlich, *Family Themes and Hawthorne's Fiction*, 8–9, 94–95, 133–38).

5. See Joel Schwartz, *The Sexual Politics of Jean-Jacques Rousseau*, 34–35, 41–42. For a discussion of the American reception of this debate see Linda K. Kerber, *Women of the Republic*, 222–226.

6. In setting apart a "sphere" where women had special authority, domesticity supported an enlargement of women's power within the home; a sector of the public

domain also became accessible to women's leadership: churches, schools, benevolent societies, and the literary marketplace. See Norma Basch, *In the Eyes of the Law;* Kathryn Kish Sklar, *Catharine Beecher;* and Mary Kelley, *Private Woman, Public Stage.*

7. See, for example, the comments from the *Westminster Review* for October 1852 in Donald J. Crowley, *Hawthorne: The Critical Heritage,* 262–263.

8. For an excellent presentation of Fuller's life and work, see Bell Gale Chevigny, *The Woman and the Myth: Margaret Fuller's Life and Writings.*

9. Margaret Fuller's Commonplace Book, 1844, now at the Massachusetts Historical Society, is quoted by permission of Alice Perry. It indicates that Fuller was in Concord from July 9 to August 8. She complains of headaches before, during, and after this visit and in an entry for 6 September explicitly connects them with her work on "the pamphlet," suggesting that they may foretell "a prophet birth." Sophia's comment appears in the entry for 31 July.

10. See Jane Tompkins, *Sensational Designs,* 122–146.

11. In Susan Warner's *Wide, Wide World,* a popular work that appeared at mid-century, the "terrible punishment" (72) accepted by Jesus is proposed as a biblical type for the sufferings of selfless motherhood.

12. For a detailed study of this disciplinary strategy see Richard H. Brodhead, "Sparing the Rod."

13. The term "romantic religion" is usually invoked to separate transcendentalism and literary romanticism from evangelical Christianity. Yet as Sophia's example makes evident, and as Richard Brantley, *Locke, Wesley, and the Method of English Romanticism,* has shown in detail, there were strong continuities between the "romantic" formation of spiritual experience and that of the surrounding culture.

CHAPTER TWO: ZENOBIA'S GHOST

1. Unless otherwise noted, subsequent quotations from Sophia Hawthorne in this chapter are from entries for 1852 in the second manuscript volume of the Family Notebook (Journal Dated 1842–1854 [Morgan]) and are cited in the text by date.

2. Several lines of evidence sustain the conclusion that the Hawthornes refrained from intercourse after the birth of Rose; some of these will accumulate in the course of the following chapters as I discuss their sexual relation more fully. A summary of the key issues should begin with Elizabeth Peabody's remarks: "[Sophia] also told me, in the last part of her life, that he so respected the delicacy of [her] constitution . . . that he proposed they should have but three children, and that there should be two and a half years between the first two, and five years between the second and third. And this was what happened, for, as she added, 'Mr. Hawthorne's passions were under his feet' " (Norman Holmes Pearson, "Elizabeth Peabody on Hawthorne," 276).

The Hawthornes did not control the spacing of children so precisely as Sophia asserts, yet her general claim that they limited the number through abstinence from intercourse deserves to be believed. Four methods of birth control were available to the Hawthornes: contraception, coitus interruptus, rhythm, and marital continence. Contraception is ruled out by Sophia's statement, and coitus interruptus is virtually so. Saying that Nathaniel's desires were "under his feet" implies a degree of self-denial inconsistent with penetration followed by withdrawal before orgasm. John and Robin Haller (*The Physician and Sexual-*

ity in Victorian America, 113–131) demonstrate that rhythm was notoriously unreliable during the Hawthornes' childbearing years, because there was "complete confusion within medical circles concerning the fertile and infertile periods of the woman's monthly cycle" (119). The Hallers show that marital continence was a routine method, and indeed the most approved way, of limiting fertility in the early nineteenth century. Edwin H. Miller, in *Salem is My Dwelling Place,* does not bring these issues of medical history to bear and states that the Hawthornes might have used contraceptives earlier in their marriage (344). But he concludes that Nathaniel "apparently pledged himself to chastity" (397) at the time of Rose's birth.

The Hawthornes clearly took pleasure in sexual intercourse during the early years of their marriage, when they were trying to conceive their firstborn, and subsequently when they conceived Julian. Yet their enjoyment of intercourse does not mean it was free of severe anxieties, in particular those arising from the new middle-class imperative to limit the number of children. For a fuller discussion of these issues see below, Chapters 9, 13, and 14.

3. For a discussion of weeping as orgasmic where the psychic routines of domesticity reveal the erotics of submission, see Jane Tompkins, Afterword to *The Wide, Wide World,* 599–600.

4. Hawthorne refers to Reichenbach in *Blithedale* when he notes that the authority claimed for such dissociated states was just then shifting from spiritual to scientific grounds, with discussions of a "universally pervasive fluid" tricked out in "terms of art, as if it were a matter of chemical discovery" (200). Reichenbach's *Physico-Physiological Researches* announced his discovery of the "Od" in just these terms, as a *"natural force extending over the universe"* (175) to which clairvoyance and mesmerism were to be attributed. Electrical, magnetic, chemical, and thermal energies—which he renamed *elod, magnetod, chymod, thermod*—were as well suited to empirical study as psychically registered versions of the odic force. Hawthorne denounces both sets of claims in *Blithedale:* if mesmeric consciousness has a physical basis, it represents a "cold and dead materialism"; if spiritual, it indicates that "the soul of man is descending to a lower point than it has ever before reached" (199–200). Yet Sophia stubbornly maintained her interest in spiritualism and mesmerism because they articulated her recognition of contradictory emotional states while affording her a selfless role as the passive recipient of forces beyond herself.

5. Sophia Peabody to Nathaniel Hawthorne, 30 May 1841 (quoted in Chapter 8, at n. 6), and 12 May 1841 (Berg). See also letter of 31 December 1839, quoted in Julian Hawthorne, *Nathaniel Hawthorne and His Wife,* 1:208, and letter of 6–8 December 1838, quoted in Edwin H. Miller, *Salem is My Dwelling Place,* 164.

PART TWO: NUMINOUS MATES

1. This transformation had multiple dimensions across a span of American history broader than Hawthorne's lifetime. See the works of Bernard Bailyn, Richard L. Bushman, Dixon Ryan Fox, Karen Halttunen, James A. Henretta, Paul E. Johnson, Jackson Turner Main, Anne C. Rose, Mary Ryan, Robert H. Wiebe, and Gordon Wood listed in the Works Cited.

2. For comparable expressions of this sentiment see Thoreau, *Walden,* 2; and Horace Mann, *A Few Thoughts for a Young Man,* 60.

CHAPTER 3: THE QUEEN OF ALL SHE SURVEYS

1. See the discussions of "neurasthenic" illness as disclosing the predicament of women in works by Elaine Showalter, Jean Strouse, Ruth Bernard Yeazell, and Kathryn Kish Sklar listed in Works Cited.

2. Sophia Peabody to her sister Elizabeth Palmer Peabody, journal-letter of 24 April–1 June 1838 (Bancroft). Entry for "27th Friday Morning."

3. I am indebted to Megan Marshall for information that corrects Louise Hall Tharp. Here, for example, Tharp identifies the invalid daughter of General Palmer as Elizabeth. Although Marshall's forthcoming biography of the Peabody sisters will shed new light on their character and relationships, Tharp's interpretation of the impulses at work within the family remains plausible in general outline, in keeping with the social transformation taking place during this period. For an illuminating recent discussion see Bruce Ronda, Introduction to *Letters of Elizabeth Palmer Peabody.*

4. For a fine discussion of Mrs. Peabody's youthful struggle to express her remarkable talents see Megan Marshall, "Two Early Poems by Mrs. Elizabeth Palmer Peabody." During her adulthood as in her youth Mrs. Peabody's contemporaries noted disapprovingly her "determination to be independent and self-supporting." See Ronda, Introduction to *Letters of Elizabeth Palmer Peabody,* p. 9.

5. See Burton J. Bledstein, *The Culture of Professionalism,* on the "career" as a creation of middle-class culture.

6. Sophia Peabody Hawthorne, "Remembrance of a visit to her grandmother, written in story form" (Berg). Julian's use of the narrative confirms its autobiographical character (*Nathaniel Hawthorne and His Wife,* 1:51).

7. Lydia Sigourney offers a parable of such womanly desperation in *Letters to Mothers* (215–216): she relates the experience of a "young girl, brought up in comparative affluence," who becomes impoverished after the death of her father and perishes soon after, when ill-paid and degrading work destroys her health.

8. Sophia Peabody [Hawthorne] Journal, Boston, 1 April–8 August 1829, with entries for 1831 (Berg). Entry for 19 March 1831.

9. Sophia cites this dream at the time of her husband's death, in a letter to Annie Fields, 30 May 1864, that indicates she had told Annie about the dream earlier, when their intimate friendship was taking form. See Letters to Annie Fields, (Boston).

10. Hilda, in *The Marble Faun,* is similarly a copyist. Her divine selflessness permits her to comprehend paintings of male masters from their point of view (56–57).

11. Sophia Peabody [Hawthorne] Journal, Boston, January–18 February 1832 (Berg). Entry for 10 January.

12. Sophia Peabody [Hawthorne] Journal, Boston, 1 April–8 August 1829, with entries for 1831 (Berg). Entry for "Monday 28th."

13. See Patricia Valenti, "Sophia Peabody Hawthorne's Continuation to 'Christabel,' " 14–15.

14. Sophia Peabody [Hawthorne], Holograph Notebook, January–June 1835 (Berg).

15. Sophia Peabody [Hawthorne], Holograph Notebook, January–June 1835 (Berg).

16. Sophia Peabody to her sister Elizabeth Palmer Peabody, journal-letter of 24 April–1 June 1838 (Bancroft). "Entry for April 24th."

17. Sophia Peabody [Hawthorne] Commonplace Book, 1835 (Berg).

18. Sophia Peabody to her sister Elizabeth Palmer Peabody, 26 April–1 May 1838 (Berg).

19. Sophia Peabody to Mary W. Foote, 19 June 1842 (Berg).

CHAPTER FOUR:
PORTRAIT OF THE ARTIST
AS A SELF-MADE MAN

1. See David Leverenz, *Manhood and the American Renaissance*, chap. 3, "The Politics of Emerson's Man-Making Words."

2. Priscilla Manning to Richard and Robert Manning, 29 August 1814 (Essex). In this letter Manning urges Nathaniel's uncles to require that he attend to his studies.

3. Elizabeth Manning Hawthorne to Una Hawthorne, 23 November 1865, ms. copy (Bancroft). See James R. Mellow, *Nathaniel Hawthorne in His Times*, 18–19.

4. Elizabeth Manning Hawthorne to Una Hawthorne, 23 November 1865, ms. copy (Bancroft). See Stewart, "Recollections of Hawthorne by His Sister Elizabeth," 320.

5. See in particular Gloria C. Erlich, *Family Themes and Hawthorne's Fiction*.

6. See Erlich, 35–36.

7. See James A. Henretta, *The Evolution of American Society, 1700–1815*, for a discussion of the high level of premarital pregnancy in the period 1775–1800, as marriages preserving property arrangements gave way to marriages based on the choice of the marrying couple.

8. For discussions of the long-term personal consequences of unresolved mourning and its nineteenth-century cultural meaning see Neal Tolchin, *Mourning, Gender, and Creativity in the Art of Herman Melville*.

9. "Some Facts about Hawthorne," [Rebecca B. Manning] (Essex).

10. For a discussion of the consequences of a grieving child's role as "linking object" see Tolchin, 19–20. On Elizabeth, see Richard Manning to Robert Manning, 10 November 1816 (Essex). According to Julian Hawthorne, Elizabeth refused all her life to keep house (*Nathaniel Hawthorne and His Wife*, 1:353).

11. Ebe related this incident in letters to Una Hawthorne (12 November 1865 [Bancroft]) and to James T. Fields (12 December 1870 [Boston]). See Stewart, "Recollections," 320.

12. Vernon Loggins, *The Hawthornes*, 213–215, recounts this incident in a telling discussion of class relations in Salem during Hawthorne's boyhood.

13. See Paul E. Johnson, *A Shopkeeper's Millennium*, 55–61, on the role of drinking in the shift from patriarchal to middle-class household organization.

14. Stewart, "Recollections," 321. George Parsons Lathrop recounts a version of this refrain that explicitly identifies young Nathaniel's imagined destiny with his father's: "Before he had passed from his mother's care to that of the schoolmaster, it is known that he would break out from the midst of childish broodings and exclaim, 'There, mother! I is going away to sea, some time . . . and I'll never come back again!' " (*A Study of Hawthorne*, 63–64).

15. Hawthorne's incestuous relation with his mother and sisters is ably discussed by Gloria Erlich, 90–99, as a source of sexual contamination that Hawthorne explores in his

fiction. But incest is not only, and not mainly, a matter of private sexual contact. It has a social meaning that is pertinent to the whole shape of Hawthorne's life.

The prohibition against incest simultaneously requires exogamy. Anthropological studies have shown that the circulation of persons through the social system beyond the family virtually constitutes that system and is necessary to its maintenance. With social change and correspondingly broadened mobility, the demand for out-marrying threatens elites, as the supply of suitable high-status mates is sharply decreased. The problems in Hawthorne's immediate family thus intensified the pressures on descendants of the colonial seaboard gentry; such pressures have become chronic in American family life amid what Hawthorne terms "the fluctuating waves of our social life" (*House of the Seven Gables*, 38). It was said of Henry James that he was "a citizen of the James family and knew no other country," a phrase that captures the defensive anxieties of many another notable clan.

Such larger meanings of incest are beginning to make themselves felt in Hawthorne criticism, as in Teresa Goddu's "Circulation of Women in *The House of the Seven Gables*." Frank Whigham's "Sexual and Social Mobility in *The Duchess of Malfi*" provides a good brief introduction to the pertinent social theory.

16. Nina Baym, in discussing Hawthorne's relationship to his mother, rightly observes that the myth of Castle Dismal contained implications that were simply untrue, most notably that Mrs. Hathorne was a victim of morbidity who imprisoned her son in her own gloom. It is likewise true, as Baym observes, that Hawthorne presented this myth to Elizabeth and Sophia Peabody to invite them to play the role of savior. Yet the myth was not a creation *ex nihilo*. Hawthorne was psychologically trapped by attitudes he had internalized, so that blaming his mother did not allow him to pursue an alternative mode of life without severe conflict. What held him in the magic circle was not merely his mother's morbidity or her warmth and charm but the psychic forces inherent in their shared bereavement as they cultivated an identity that made the outward world seem alien and threatening. The psychic stagnation betokened by the term *dismal* was an experience Hawthorne truly had reason to dread.

17. Other family members criticized Mary Manning's characteristic bad spelling enough to draw a spirited rejoinder from her. See Hawthorne, *Letters, 1813–1843*, 145.

18. See Myra Jehlen, *American Incarnation*, 76–92; Amy Schrager Lang, *Prophetic Woman*, 107–136; David Leverenz, *Manhood and the American Renaissance;* and Howard Horwitz, "The Standard Oil Trust as Emersonian Hero."

CHAPTER FIVE: SUBSERVIENT ANGEL

1. Nancy Cott presents the "sphere" of womanhood as an invention of the male-dominated culture of the early nineteenth century to imprison women, a major component in the system of "bonds" that kept women together as it kept them down (*The Bonds of Womanhood*, 1–2). Mary Ryan has observed, however, that women themselves took part in defining domesticity, so that its eventual character testifies to their resourcefulness and strength (*The Empire of the Mother*, 1–18). These views support the discussion that follows, in which "woman's sphere" is recognized as a creation of the male imagination, a new version of patriarchal domination that foreclosed some of the limited avenues to power women had had earlier even as it opened up new avenues, also limited. The

numinous authority ascribed to women by the domestic ideology was essential to both their new servitude and their new opportunities.

CHAPTER SIX: DEMOCRATIC MYTHMAKING IN *THE HOUSE OF THE SEVEN GABLES*

1. The colonial struggles over these issues reached into the life of the early republic and came to a spectacular climax in the anti-rent agitations in New York State during the 1840s. In the face of the anti-renters, the Whigs themselves had to yield their traditional claim that an aristocratic class served the public good (Dixon Ryan Fox, *The Decline of Aristocracy in the Politics of New York,* 435–439; Arthur M. Schlesinger, *The Age of Jackson,* 375–380). The new democratic ethos made the term *aristocrat* the deadliest of political epithets; wealth might still proclaim high status, but only if it "was theoretically accessible to all who had the industry and enterprise to gain it" (Fox, 437).

2. Mary Ryan, in *The Empire of the Mother,* observes that the emergence of the "domestic" household organization, as against patriarchal forms, was a lengthy process, beginning before 1800 and extending beyond 1900 in certain regions of the United States. This historical shift must be distinguished from the relatively swift ideological change in which, from 1830 to 1860, the domestic ideal came to dominate fiction and the advice literature of the urban Northeast.

3. Gillian Brown treats Phoebe's exemption from "toil" in the midst of her labors as the incorporation of aristocratic status into domesticity and provides convincing evidence from contemporary advice literature that "true women" were "ladies." Hawthorne's denial of this claim marks Phoebe as a guarantor of religious reality, upon whom the transfer of legitimacy from the gentry to the middle class can be authenticated. See "Women's Work and Ladies' Leisure," in *Domestic Individualism.*

4. Ann Douglas's argument, in *The Feminization of American Culture,* that women were "disestablished" as they moved from their role in the patriarchal household to the "sphere" of the middle-class home has been corrected by Mary Beth Norton, "The Evolution of White Women's Experience in Early America." Norton shows that there was no colonial "golden age," since the labor women provided in the household economy gave them no significant leverage against male prerogatives. Advice manuals addressed to "true women" in the early nineteenth century dinned into them the need for habits of industry and good management. Douglas's assessment of the new wifely role as "euphemistic" remains compelling nonetheless, inasmuch as the toil of the "true woman" was rendered invisible through a systematic denial of its economic function. This self-contradictory situation was, Douglas writes, "itself an obfuscation of a culturally vital kind" (65), whose meaning the current discussion seeks to understand.

5. In *Domestic Individualism* Gillian Brown provides a fine discussion of the cultural situation at stake in this thematic pattern, in which domesticity is constituted simultaneously as a refuge from "the world" of possessive individualism and as a place where that world is produced and situated.

6. Brook Thomas confirms the root identity of Holgrave and Judge Pyncheon in observing that both characters reflect features of the career of the prominent Salemite Judge Joseph Story (*Cross-Examinations of Law and Literature,* 56–70). Thomas notes, in particular, that Story's first wife was a descendant of the Pynchon family, which was grievously offended by Hawthorne's adaptation of the name (64).

PART THREE: MARITAL POLITICS

1. Sophia Hawthorne to her mother, Elizabeth Palmer Peabody, 23–25 June 1850 (Berg).

2. Sophia Hawthorne to her mother, Elizabeth Palmer Peabody, 29 September 1850 (Berg).

3. Sophia Hawthorne to her mother, Elizabeth Palmer Peabody, 23–25 June 1850 (Berg).

4. Sophia Hawthorne to her mother, Elizabeth Palmer Peabody, 12 February 1851 (Berg).

5. Sophia Hawthorne to her mother, Elizabeth Palmer Peabody, 23–25 June 1850 (Berg).

CHAPTER SEVEN: INWARD AND ETERNAL UNION

1. Sophia Peabody to Mary W. Foote, 19 June 1842 (Berg).

2. Mary Ryan, *The Empire of the Mother,* 87.

3. Sophia Hawthorne to her mother, Elizabeth Palmer Peabody, 6 April 1845 (Berg).

4. See Norma Basch, *In the Eyes of the Law,* especially chap. 6.

5. For the conventional association see John Mack Faragher, *Women and Men on the Overland Trail,* 121; and John Haller and Robin Haller, *The Physician and Sexuality in Victorian America,* 101.

CHAPTER EIGHT: TRANSPLANTING THE GARDEN OF EDEN

1. See Hawthorne, *Letters, 1813–1843,* 352, 422, 513, 560, 562, 592, 635.

2. Nina Baym, in "Nathaniel Hawthorne and His Mother," discusses the anxious attachment to his mother that is hidden behind Hawthorne's myth of "Castle Dismal." See Chapter 4, n. 16.

3. No record survives of the terms under which Osgood painted this picture, but it seems likely that Hawthorne commissioned it as a gift to his mother and sisters. Because the daughter of Robert Manning owned it until her death in 1933, Manning Hawthorne proposed that Robert Manning might have commissioned it. But it is doubtful that he would have done so, as Manning Hawthorne conceded, without commissioning pictures of his own children (Rita K. Gollin, *Portraits of Nathaniel Hawthorne,* 19–20). It is hardly likely, moreover, that Nathaniel would have permitted such a commission to be carried out, considering his resentment against his uncle Robert.

Louisa Hawthorne's comment on receiving the picture gives no hint it was on loan and confirms that it was a consolation for Nathaniel's absence. "The portrait came home a fortnight ago," she writes, "and gives great delight. Mother says it is perfect. . . . But good as it is, it does not by any means supply the place of the original, and you are not to think that you can stay away any longer than before we had it. . . . It is a comfort to look at the picture, to be sure; but I am tempted to speak to it sometimes . . . and when mother looks at it, she takes up a lamentation because you stay away so long and work so hard" (Julian Hawthorne, *Nathaniel Hawthorne and his Wife* 1:229–231).

4. For "absurdly obedient" see undated fragment in copies of letters to Una Hawthorne from Elizabeth Manning Hawthorne 9 December 1861–2 January 1870 (Bancroft). For Elizabeth's choosing books see Elizabeth Manning Hawthorne to James T.

Fields, 26 December 1870 (Boston). For his fears of her ridicule see Julian Hawthorne, *Nathaniel Hawthorne and His Wife,* 1:5.

5. See Hawthorne, *Letters, 1813–1843,* 19, 62, 63, 699.

6. Sophia Peabody to Nathaniel Hawthorne, 30 May 1841 (Berg).

7. My discussion of the Hawthornes' relationship has been aided throughout by Jurg Willi's description of "narcissistic collusion" (*Couples in Collusion,* 60–81).

8. "Some Facts about Hawthorne," [Rebecca B. Manning] (Essex). This document, though it does not appear to have been written by Elizabeth Manning Hawthorne, records her opinions, together with those of other offended Mannings and Hawthornes, who jointly condemn the effusive Peabodys as emotionally dishonest.

9. Nina Baym observes that Nathaniel's delay in telling his mother expressed an unconscious desire to "kill" her, partly to annihilate her as a presence in his inward life so as to make a place for Sophia, and partly out of vengeance for the years he had spent at the Herbert Street house while the "world of adult sexual relationships passed him by" ("Nathaniel Hawthorne and His Mother," 17).

10. Elizabeth Manning Hawthorne to Sophia Peabody, 23 May 1842 (Berg).

11. This psychic strategy has led some critics to conclude there must actually have been a "secret," which once known would explain the mystery Hawthorne gathered about himself (Philip Young, *Hawthorne's Secret,* 3–8).

CHAPTER NINE: ANDROGYNOUS PARADISE LOST

1. Sophia Hawthorne to her mother, Elizabeth Palmer Peabody, 30 August–4 September 1842 (Berg). Unless otherwise indicated, all the quotations of Sophia Hawthorne in this chapter are from letters to her mother, in the Berg Collection at the New York Public Library. They are cited in the text by date.

2. This entry in the Family Notebook (Journal Dated 1842–1854 [Morgan]) is undated and precedes the first dated entry, by Nathaniel Hawthorne, for 5 August 1842.

3. For a good discussion of the emergence of this sexual ideal see John D'Emilio and Estelle B. Freedman, *Intimate Matters,* 55–84. See also Peter Gardella, *Innocent Ecstasy.*

4. See Hawthorne, *Letters, 1843–1853,* 226, 241. The *OED* lists the earliest uses of *intercourse* bearing a sexual meaning in 1798 and 1804. A telling precursor of the companionate view that became dominant in nineteenth-century America is John Milton's ideal of marriage, described in "The Doctrine and Discipline of Divorce" as "a meet and happy conversation" without which "corporall delight will soon become unsavoury and contemptible" (*The Prose of John Milton,* 148).

5. See Peter Gay, *The Education of the Senses,* pp. 109–168; and Michel Foucault, *The History of Sexuality,* pp. 3–35. Although Gay's Freudian premises lead him to treat sexuality as a psychic universal independent of social context, his recounting of the voluminous nineteenth-century record frequently carries him beyond these assumptions. Foucault's notion of the "power" shaping sexuality likewise grants it a seemingly trans-historical status, with autonomous operations, deployments, and circulatory routines; yet it is clear that he believes "power" operates differently in different epochs.

6. Sophia Peabody [Hawthorne], *The Cuba Journal, 1833–1835,* xx–xxi, 266–267, 356, 387, 453, 467, 513–516, 522–523, 526–527, 535–536, 546; and Louisa Hall Tharp, *The Peabody Sisters of Salem,* 8, 73–74, 80–84.

7. Henry Rose, *An Inaugural Dissertation on the Effects of the Passions upon the Body,* 15–16. See also Charles Rosenberg, "Sexuality, Class, and Role in Nineteenth-Century America," 145–146. At times effeminacy was identified not as the result of sexual desire itself but of "spermatorrhea," the "excessive" loss of sperm that takes place when sexual activity passes beyond voluntary control, especially in masturbation. See George P. Calhoun, *Report of the Counselling Surgeon on Spermatorrhea,* 14.

8. *The Letters of Margaret Fuller,* 3:66. The pathbreaking work of Nina Baym developed this thesis, and Leland Person, in *Aesthetic Headaches,* has elaborated it to good effect. Yet confusions have arisen from an ambiguity regarding the term *woman* in Fuller's thought because of the patriarchal gender definitions she and the Hawthornes accepted. Both Baym and Person assume correctly that for Hawthorne *woman* often refers to what Jung later termed the anima, which is intrinsic to male personality. It "stands for a set of qualities which the male denies within himself and rejects in others. She represents warmth, imagination, intuition, and love; identified with nature and the heart, she also implies the nonrational complexities of the self" (Baym, "Hawthorne's Women," 258; see also "Thwarted Nature," 62). This "inner woman" is a man's creativity, just as the conventional nineteenth-century responses to Hawthorne repeatedly indicate, and is linked with other qualities that the nineteenth century identified as "feminine."

Yet male and female qualities in this understanding of androgyny retain their patriarchal cast, so that confusions may easily arise when the "feminine" aspect of a man's personality is identified with actual women. As Baym observes, Hawthorne eloquently articulated his feminine identity by projecting it into strong women like Hester Prynne; and this has produced feminist celebrations like that of Carolyn Heilbrun, who observes that "America has not produced a novel whose androgynous implications match those of *The Scarlet Letter*" (*Toward a Recognition of Androgyny,* 63). How could Hawthorne's most powerful and famous character be so inspiring to feminists while he himself remains a persistent and emphatic advocate of male dominance in his family, in his judgment of social issues, and in his work?

Women are in fact distinct from the "inner women" of men, however. As we shall see, Hawthorne was struggling to subject his own "feminine" impulses to an inward "male" authority at the time he wrote *The Scarlet Letter,* and it is correspondingly Hester's destiny in the novel to submit to Dimmesdale's will.

Leland Person takes this dilemma by the horns in replying to feminist critics who object to male "pseudo-feminocentrism." He claims, for example, that in taking Sophia as "my own self," Hawthorne identified his creative power "not with a feminized, narcissistic self-image, but with an autonomous female other. Sophia would not inspire creativity but be creative, inscribing herself, so to speak, in and through his imagination or 'heart' " (*Aesthetic Headaches,* 103). Person thus endorses the impossible concept at the heart of the confusion: Sophia's autonomy cannot be Nathaniel's creative power. It is noteworthy that Person's most recent work has described Hawthorne's effort to assert an "autogenetic" creativity in "The Old Manse," from which every trace of Sophia's influence is erased ("Hawthorne's Bliss of Paternity," 47).

I have sought to keep these issues clear by maintaining a degree of distance from the terms *woman* and *man* as applied to aspects of the Hawthornes' inner lives. It is possible to say that Nathaniel and Sophia's narcissitic marital collusion involved his projecting an "inner" woman on her and her projecting an "inner" man on him; but this mutual projection should not imply an "equality" that cancels awareness of the fundamental difference in social power between them and Hawthorne's interest in preserving that difference.

9. The role of feminine purity in bolstering "self-made" manhood has not been treated as fully as it deserves, although the issue has been identified. Mary Ryan observes that advice to young women urged them to use their "allure as marital and sexual partners" to inspire young men to "morality and middle-class competence," transferring the disciplinary effect upon male passion from the mother to the wife. Ryan does not observe, however, that the sexual allure in question works through being sublimated, in such a way as to reinforce sexual self-control and other forms of self-mastery needed for middle-class success. See *Cradle of the Middle Class*, 180. Nancy F. Cott, "Passionlessness," 173-174, also notices this issue in the course of discussing a presumptive absence of womanly passion—not the transformative power it attained in the form of "purity." For an excellent general discussion of reproductive control see D'Emilio and Freedman, 57-62.

10. John Humphrey Noyes, *Male Continence*, 12. Stephen Nissenbaum, in *Sex, Diet, and Debility in Jacksonian America*, 165-166, discusses Noyes in relation to the culture of male purity that took form in the 1830s, centering on the quasi-medical issues of health and "hygiene." See Ryan, *Cradle of the Middle Class*, 155-157, for an excellent statement of the economic motives for sexual self-control within marriage. See also Linda Gordon, *Woman's Body, Woman's Right;* and Daniel Scott Smith, "Family Limitation, Sexual Control, and Domestic Feminism in Victorian America." G. J. Barker-Benfield, *The Horrors of the Half-Known Life*, 3-60, provides a richly suggestive treatment of the obsessive masculine quest for sexual self-mastery.

11. *Hawthorne's Lost Notebook, 1835-1841*, 7, 25.

12. Samuel Woodward, in *Hints for the Young*, 32, particularly recommends a "sea bath," of the sort Hawthorne found unavailable now that he lived in Concord.

13. Nina Baym stresses the essential recognition that the issues of womanly "impurity" have their origin not in the real nature of women but in the way men imagine women to be. See "Thwarted Nature," 63-66. Frederick Crews also discusses sexual dread and the desire of Hawthorne's protagonists to escape it (*Sins of the Fathers*, 98-111, 116-135).

14. R. T. Trall's *Sexual Physiology and Hygiene* (1866) offers conventional advice in which this inherent precariousness is visible: intercourse should take place only "when there is mental harmony and congeniality between the parties" so there is "no sense of discord, no feeling of repugnance." Otherwise it is "cruelty" (quoted in Degler, *At Odds*, p. 278). Eliza P. Duffy similarly declares, in *What Women Should Know*, that "a pure marriage, in which affection is the ruling power and passion is curbed and held in control—in which the thought of self is kept secondary—is a true sacrament—blessing its participants. A marriage in which passion, unguided by reason, degenerates into lust, is a sacrament desecrated, a blessing turned into a curse" (quoted in Peter Gay, *The Tender Passion*, 289).

15. See Carroll Smith-Rosenberg, *Disorderly Conduct*, pp. 109-128. Daniel Scott Smith, in "Family Limitation," gives the term "domestic feminism" to this increase of women's power within the home. See also Cott, "Passionlessness."

16. This fragment, tentatively dated March 1844 in the Berg Collection catalogue, clearly belongs to the correspondence regarding Sophia's miscarriage, of which Sophia took steps to obscure the documentary record. See James R. Mellow, *Nathaniel Hawthorne in His Times*, 624. For another use of "Sophiechen" see the letter of 5 August 1842 (Berg).

17. Sophia Hawthorne, "A Sophia Hawthorne Journal, 1843–1844," 3.

18. See Nathaniel Hawthorne to Sophia Hawthorne, 27 May 1844, in *Letters, 1843–1853*, 37.

19. See Hawthorne, *Letters, 1813–1843*, 644, 658, 677–680, 681–683.

20. Sophia Hawthorne to her mother-in-law, Elizabeth Clarke Manning Hathorne, 22 March 1844 (Berg).

21. Margaret Fuller, Commonplace Book, 1844, entry for 18 July (Massachusetts Historical Society). Quoted by permission of Alice Perry.

22. See Hawthorne, *Letters, 1843–1853*, 41, 94, 140, 142.

23. The Hawthornes moved into a house on Chestnut Street in Salem in early August 1846, but they found it inadequate. Repaying the expenses of Sophia's life in Boston and insufficient fees from the Custom House, however, prevented them from securing a better situation. Only in September 1847 did they occupy the dwelling on Mall Street that accommodated Nathaniel's mother and sisters as well as his wife and children. See Mellow, *Nathaniel Hawthorne in His Times*, 274–275, 283.

CHAPTER TEN: SOUL-SYSTEM IN SALEM

1. Julian Hawthorne concludes that "Main Street," "The Snow Image," and "Ethan Brand" were written during his father's service at the Custom House (*Nathaniel Hawthorne and His Wife*, 1:330). It is possible that "The Great Stone Face" and "Feathertop" were also written during this period, since they were published subsequently. See Hawthorne, *The Snow Image*, 488.

2. See Mary Kelley, *Private Woman, Public Stage;* Michael T. Gilmore, *American Romanticism and the Marketplace;* Ann Douglas, *The Feminization of American Culture;* and Hawthorne, *Letters, 1853–1856*, 304.

3. Rita Gollin, *Portraits of Nathaniel Hawthorne*, 27. See Gollin 26–29 for a detailed discussion of this picture.

4. See Julian Hawthorne, *Nathaniel Hawthorne and his Wife*, 1:354–355; and Hawthorne, *Letters, 1843–1853*, 310.

5. I am following the account of this exchange published in George Parsons Lathrop, "Biographical Sketch," 496–497. See also Julian Hawthorne, *Nathaniel Hawthorne and his Wife*, 1:340, and "The Making of 'The Scarlet Letter.' " Gary Scharnhorst, in " 'Now You Can Write Your Book,' " argues that this story became "a family tradition" only when George Parsons Lathrop (the husband of Rose Hawthorne) published it in 1883 and Julian recounted it the following year. He observes that the earliest printed versions of this story may be traced to the close friendship between Sophia and William Henry Channing, on whose word Moncure Daniel Conway and George William Curtis relied in publishing the story in 1871, the year of Sophia's death. Yet it hardly seems likely that Sophia would have told this story to Channing but not to her children.

The accounts published by Conway and Curtis, in any event, contain the details critical to my interpretation: that Nathaniel was surprised to learn that Sophia saved money from the household budget to support the family while he wrote and that she supplemented the family income during this period by painting lampshades to sell.

6. See, for example, Hawthorne, *Letters, 1813–1843,* 692, 697, and *Letters, 1843–1853,* 21.

7. Sophia Hawthorne to her mother, Elizabeth Palmer Peabody, 1 August 1849 (Berg). Unless otherwise indicated, all the quotations of Sophia in this chapter are from letters to her mother in the Berg Collection at the New York Public Library. They are cited in the text by date.

8. In "The Making of 'The Scarlet Letter,' " Julian Hawthorne discusses Una as a model for Pearl with particular reference to the "torture" (404) Hawthorne experienced because of Una's fascination with the physical details of Mrs. Hawthorne's illness, and the children's playacting the scene.

9. The view that children form selves as they internalize the roles made available to them in early life has been elaborated in a variety of ways in the work of Nancy Chodorow, Kenneth Kaye, Heinz Kohut, Jacques Lacan, Margaret S. Mahler, and D. W. Winnicott; see Works Cited. Certain forms of mental disorder, possibly including the condition that blighted Una's life, have a genetic origin. In that case the search for causes within the family system is vain, though the system constructs the meaning of what is taking place, both for the afflicted person and the family as a whole. This is abundantly illustrated by the Hawthorne household, whatever the etiology of Una's disorder may have been: the family's response reveals discordant psychosocial themes, even if they were not the cause of her problems.

The nineteenth century recognized the genetic explanation as "hereditary madness," which the Hawthorne side of the family was suspected of possessing. Writing to Una in later years, Aunt Ebe rejects this suspicion, asserting that she "never heard of any insanity in the family" (Julian Hawthorne, *Nathaniel Hawthorne and His Wife,* 1:9). My discussion assumes that Aunt Ebe was right, though the surviving information is hardly complete.

10. "She always . . . to me" quotes a letter from Elizabeth Manning Hawthorne to "My dear cousin," 23 February, no year. Transcript by Marylou Birchmore, p. 32 (Essex); "and then. . . . to her" is from Elizabeth Manning Hawthorne to "My dear Cousins," 18 February 1867. Transcript by Marylou Birchmore, p. 162 (Essex).

11. These remarks, which stand in contrast to the view Mann customarily expressed, may allude to Una Hawthorne. Exponents of the domestic ideal frequently stressed the importance of the mother's providing exclusive care, especially during a child's "first sacred year." "Trust not your treasure too much to the charge of hirelings," Lydia Sigourney commanded. "Have it under your superintendence, both night and day" (*Letters to Mothers,* 31). I am indebted to Megan Marshall for the information that Mary Mann endorsed this view in "The Care of Little Children" (1868) and likewise refused to hire anyone to care for her children. When Mann declares, "I have seen the victims of private education perpetuate family faults" because of a "too exclusive and oppressive" home influence, she is departing from the conventional advice to concede a striking counter-example. Mann produced a draft of *The Moral Culture of Infancy* in 1841, before Una was born, but did not publish until 1864, after Una's psychological difficulties became manifest.

12. Sophia Hawthorne to Nathaniel Hawthorne, July 1847 (Berg).

13. See Sandra M. Gilbert and Susan Gubar, *The Madwoman in the Attic,* 30, for a discussion of Duessa as a presence in nineteenth-century women's consciousness.

CHAPTER ELEVEN:
DOUBLE MARRIAGE, DOUBLE ADULTERY

1. See Charles Ryskamp, "The New England Sources of *The Scarlet Letter.*"

Recent studies of *The Scarlet Letter* have treated Hawthorne's social and historical concerns without taking up the issues of gender and family examined here. Michael Colacurcio's "Footsteps of Anne Hutchinson: The Context of *The Scarlet Letter*" and his " 'Woman's Own Choice': Sex, Metaphor, and the Puritan 'Sources' of *The Scarlet Letter*" offer illuminating discussions of Hawthorne's rewritings of Puritan texts. Amy Schrager Lang's *Prophetic Woman* shows that the legend of Anne Hutchinson merged gender anxieties into an argument against antinomianism that extended from Puritan times into the nineteenth century.

A number of studies addressing *The Scarlet Letter* as a response to nineteenth-century historical conditions have focused on antebellum political disputes and the formation of a national ideology. Larry J. Reynolds's *European Revolutions and the American Literary Renaissance* discusses the imagery Hawthorne draws from contemporary American responses to the revolutions of 1848. In "The Politics of *The Scarlet Letter,*" Jonathan Arac finds that American debates about slavery set the terms for Hawthorne's treatment of social issues. Jean Fagan Yellin, in *Women and Sisters,* demonstrates that Hawthorne uses specific icons and motifs of antislavery discourse so as to undermine their authority. In *The Office of the Scarlet Letter,* Sacvan Bercovitch holds that Hawthorne promoted gradualist solutions to potentially radical conflicts, in keeping with the progressivist dialectics of American liberalism, which Hester's letter is meant to articulate and enforce. Lauren Berlant, in *The Anatomy of National Fantasy,* by contrast, finds that Hawthorne resists the idea of America as Utopian consensus even as he explores it.

Gillian Brown's "Hawthorne, Inheritance, and Women's Property" aptly observes that such studies identify Hester's A with everything except adultery (with antinomianism, abolition, anarchy, and America). Yet Brown finds that Hawthorne's own usage anticipates the direction of recent criticism in dismissing adultery as a "vestige of the past" rather than treating the new meanings it had acquired in the nineteenth century. Brown's discussion ably develops Hawthorne's interest in the role of women as transmitters of property, both in *The Scarlet Letter* and in *The House of the Seven Gables.*

Carol Bensick, in "His Folly, Her Weakness," discusses the "generic affinities" connecting *The Scarlet Letter* with the nineteenth-century "novel of adultery" and holds that Hawthorne transfers the issue of adultery from the sphere of moral mystery to that of marital sociology. My discussion proposes, by contrast, that Hawthorne takes part in a historical transformation in which one marital sociology superseded another. The fashioning of gender is also central to Robert K. Martin's "Hester Prynne, *C'est Moi,*" which discusses the nineteenth-century polarization of homosexuality and heterosexuality.

2. See Michel Foucault, *Discipline and Punish.* Richard Brodhead, "Sparing the Rod," discusses the new forms of criminal penalty, as well as domestic practices, in relation to *The Scarlet Letter.*

3. When Hester and Roger converse, she becomes "thou that wast my wife" (*The Scarlet Letter*, 76), and Roger is "him whom thou didst call thy husband" (73).

4. See Norma Basch, *In the Eyes of the Law*, 162–199.

5. See also John D'Emilio and Estelle B. Freedman, *Intimate Matters*, 73.

6. Sophia Hawthorne to her mother, Elizabeth Palmer Peabody, 6 June 1843 (Berg).

7. The literature of sexual hygiene contains works on female masturbation that typically stress "the unnatural and precocious or excessive development of the sexual instinct" as violating the "passionless" delicacy considered innate to womanly character and foretelling "furious, noisy and filthy" forms of idiocy, such as "nymphomania." Masturbating women presented the "melancholy spectacle of human misery, without mind, without delicacy or modesty, constantly harassed by the most ungovernable passion." Masturbation in women was dreaded, thus, as a sign of monstrously enlarged sexual energy, not as a collapse of the purposeful self-sufficiency suited to worldly strife. See Samuel Gregory, M.D., *Facts and Important Information for Young Women on the Subject of Masturbation*, 16–17, 19–20.

8. For further discussion of this issue see Howard Gadlin, "Private Lives and Public Order"; and Charles Rosenberg, "Sexuality, Class, and Role in Nineteenth-Century America."

9. The "tenth edition" offers 32 pages of text and 143 pages of letters and replies. I have not been able to locate any earlier editions and thus have not determined whether this epistolary form grew up as described or was invented *de novo*.

10. See Ann Douglas, *The Feminization of American Culture*, 17–49, 143–196. See also Barbara Welter, "The Feminization of American Religion," in *Dimity Convictions*, 83–102; and Nancy F. Cott, *The Bonds of Womanhood*, 126–159.

11. David Reynolds, *Beneath the American Renaissance*, treats in detail the tradition of "dark reform" that supplied themes and characters to Hawthorne's work and documents the period's fascination with tales of fallen ministers (118–134, 249–268). But he identifies Hawthorne's literary power with the "almost mathematical care" with which he creates a "unified artistic structure" in *The Scarlet Letter* as in other works (268).

12. See Peter Gay, *The Education of the Senses*, 294–318, for the sadistic theme in the medical response to masturbation.

CHAPTER TWELVE: DOMESTICITY AS REDEMPTION

1. Sophia Hawthorne to her sister Elizabeth Palmer Peabody, 21 May 1850 (Berg). Cited in Edwin H. Miller, *Salem Is My Dwelling Place*, 302. As Miller observes, Sophia likewise informed Elizabeth it was "funny" (336) readers should associate Holgrave and Phoebe with Nathaniel and herself.

2. See Leland Person, "Hawthorne's Bliss of Paternity."

3. Ellery Channing to Ellen Channing, 30 October 1851. Channing Family Papers (Massachusetts Historical Society).

4. Hawthorne refers to the first eight residences in a letter to G. P. Putnam (CE 16:530). These were the Old Manse, his mother's Salem home, a house on Carver Street in Boston, the Chestnut Street house in Salem, the Mall Street house in Salem, the Red House in Lenox, the Mann home in West Newton, and the Wayside. During their stay

in Europe at least the following count as residences, as opposed to lodgings occupied for less than six weeks, in what Hawthorne termed their "strange, vagabond, gypsy sort of life" (*The English Notebooks,* 424): In England: Rock Ferry, Southport, Manchester (during this period, moreover, Sophia spent several months in Lisbon with Una and Rose, while Nathaniel stayed with Julian in Liverpool); at Rome, the Palazzo Laranzani; at Florence, the Casa del Bello and Villa Montauto; at Rome again, an apartment in the Piazza Poli; and in England again, Redcar (in Yorkshire), Leamington, and Bath.

CHAPTER THIRTEEN: CITY OF THE SOUL

1. Sophia Hawthorne to her mother, Elizabeth Palmer Peabody, 8–9 August 1846 (Berg).

2. See Linda Gordon, *Heroes of Their Own Lives,* 227. This ethos also attributes pollution to the victim of rape, a further contemporary analogue of the guiltless guilt that fascinated nineteenth-century viewers of the Cenci portrait. See Gordon, 216.

CHAPTER FOURTEEN: REPUDIATIONS AND INWARD WAR

1. John Rogers, Jr., to Henry Rogers, 13 February 1859. The Rogers Collection. Quoted by courtesy of the New-York Historical Society.

2. *The Marble Faun,* 337. For analogous responses to Raphael and Titian see Hawthorne, *The French and Italian Notebooks,* 93, 334.

3. Julian's account also conflicts with John Rogers's description of the finished bust as "very good" (Wayne Craven, *Sculpture in America,* 332). Jan Ramirez, curator of paintings and sculpture, Museum of the City of New York, states that such unauthorized meddling as Julian alleges would have been a scandal in itself, particularly if Nathaniel was in consequence displeased by the finished bust, and that Lander herself might well have protested in the art periodicals of the day, as it appears she did not. John Idol and Sterling Eisiminger, in "Hawthorne Sits for a Bust by Maria Louisa Lander," raise cogent doubts about Julian's story, even though Hawthorne's 13 November letter of dismissal to Louisa was not available to them.

4. Hawthorne drafted this comment on 2 November 1858, Una having developed symptoms on 24 October while sketching with Ada Shepard in the Palace of the Caesars (*The French and Italian Notebooks,* 455, 852). The family had returned from Florence on 16 October; on the seventeenth Thompson told them the story about Louisa Lander; and on the twenty-first Nathaniel and Sophia went to see the bust (*The French and Italian Notebooks,* 615). I am indebted to Dr. Stephen Benold, a specialist in internal medicine, for the information that the incubation period of the malarial spirochete is a week at minimum, possibly several weeks, and that psychological stress could reduce resistance and permit a long-standing infection to become clinically apparent. The disease was poorly understood in the 1850s and was blamed on the "bad air" from which it takes its name. Neither Dr. Franco nor the Hawthornes were in a position to realize that Una did not contract the infection on 24 October, when it became apparent, but at some earlier time.

5. Una Hawthorne to Richard Manning, 13 November 1858 (Essex).

6. Una Hawthorne to Rebecca Manning, 13 November 1858 (Essex).

7. Una Hawthorne to Rebecca Manning, 13 November 1858 (Essex).

8. Una Hawthorne to Rebecca Manning, 10 September 1856 (Essex).

9. Una Hawthorne to Richard Manning, 9 March 1857 (Essex).

10. Una Hawthorne to Rebecca Manning, 25 March 1857 (Essex).

11. Sophia Hawthorne to her mother, Elizabeth Palmer Peabody, 22 March 1846 (Berg).

12. Una Hawthorne to Rebecca Manning, 13 November 1858 (Essex).

13. Sophia Hawthorne to Mary Mann, 8 April 1859 (Berg).

14. Sophia Hawthorne to Mary Mann, 16 May 1858 (Berg).

15. Sophia Hawthorne to her sister Elizabeth Palmer Peabody, 3 July 1858 (Berg).

16. Letter of 31 October 1858. Letters of Ada Shepard to Clay Badger (Bienecke).

CHAPTER FIFTEEN: THE LIONS OF LUST

1. Letter of 16 October 1858. Letters of Ada Shepard to Clay Badger (Bienecke). Subsequent references to Shepard's letters will appear in the text by date.

2. When Una Hawthorne was a newborn, George Prescott gave her a stuffed lion (Hawthorne, *Letters, 1843–1853,* 37) and Louis O'Sullivan gave her a puppy named Leo (entry for 8 May 1844, Journal Dated 1842–1854 [Morgan]). Sophia casually invoked this conventional association in 1856, stating that everyone said "How like *a Una* she is!" and that Julian had a "great mighty nature . . . like a lion" (letter to Mary Mann, 12 August 1856 [Berg]).

3. In the inaugural issue the editor invokes the "mystical name of Una" as a banner under which discussions of the legal disabilities of women, women's inequality in marriage, women's suffrage, and reports on recent women's rights conventions subsequently take place. See "Prospectus" and "The Myth of Una."

4. Freud's early essay "On the Psychical Mechanism of Hysterical Phenomena" is particularly telling in tracing hysteria to "reminiscences" that are "completely absent from . . . [the patient's] memory" (40–41).

5. Sophia Hawthorne to Mary Mann, 13–22 April 1856 (Berg).

CHAPTER SIXTEEN: SPIRITUAL LAWS

1. Sophia Hawthorne to Mary Mann, 8 April 1859 (Berg).

2. Sophia Hawthorne to Annie Fields, 20 February 1863 (Boston).

3. Sophia Hawthorne to her sister Elizabeth Palmer Peabody, 3 July 1859 (Berg). Unless otherwise noted, all subsequent quotations of Sophia Hawthorne in this chapter are from this letter.

4. Sophia Hawthorne to Mary Mann, 8 April 1859 (Berg).

5. Letter of 11 April 1859. Letters of Ada Shepard to Clay Badger (Beinecke). Cited hereafter in the text by date.

6. Sophia Hawthorne to her sister Elizabeth Palmer Peabody, 24 April 1859 (Berg).

7. Sophia Hawthorne to Annie Fields, 1 January 1862 (Boston).

8. Sophia Hawthorne to Julian Hawthorne, 18 August 1862. Quoted in Edwin H. Miller, *Salem Is My Dwelling Place,* 478.

9. Sophia Hawthorne to Ethan Allen Hitchcock, 30 November 1862. Quoted in Miller, *Salem Is My Dwelling Place,* 479.

CHAPTER SEVENTEEN: THE POET AS PATRIARCH

1. Letter of 3 April 1859. Letters of Ada Shepard to Clay Badger (Beinecke).

2. Sophia Hawthorne to her sister Elizabeth Palmer Peabody, 3 July 1859 (Berg). Unless otherwise indicated, subsequent quotations from Sophia in this chapter are from this letter. Hawthorne himself recognized Pierce's critical role: "Never having had any trouble, before that pierced into my very vitals, I did not know what comfort there might be in the manly sympathy of a friend" (*The French and Italian Notebooks,* 518–519).

3. See Neal Tolchin, *Mourning, Gender, and Creativity in the Art of Herman Melville,* 5–7, for a summary of current studies of mourning. As Tolchin observes, healthy grieving takes place over a long period of time, during which there are periods when the initial suffering is renewed. Mitchell Breitwieser, *Despite Best Intentions,* discusses mourning in Lacanian terms eloquently describing the destruction of the aggrieved person's subject world and the uncertain processes by which it may be rebuilt.

Of special pertinence to Hawthorne is Vamik Volkan's conclusion that particularly severe and enduring conflicts are instilled in a child who becomes a "linking object" through which a grieving parent attempts to retain contact with a lost spouse, so that the image of the lost spouse becomes fused with the child's identity. See Tolchin, p. 19.

4. Though he had been sketching ideas for it earlier, Hawthorne's 1858 pocket diary shows that he "began to write a Romance" on 25 October, in the midst of the stresses the family encountered on their return from Florence on the sixteenth. On the seventeenth Thompson had given him the rumor about Louisa Lander; and on the twenty-first he went to see the bust (*The French and Italian Notebooks,* 614–616). Una was thought to have contracted malaria while sketching with Ada Shepard in the Palace of the Caesars on 24 October; she was seriously ill on the twenty-seventh, and on 1 November Dr. Franco determined that she had Roman fever (*The French and Italian Notebooks,* 852, 616, 617).

5. David Greenberg, in *The Construction of Homosexuality,* reports that the aversion to male-male embraces developed earlier in England than in America, as did competitive capitalism. It would follow that in the United States homophobia would emerge sooner in urban industrial and financial centers than elsewhere. Greenberg cites a study claiming that as late as the 1880s it was still possible for heterosexual male friends in America to lie embracing in bed without "any suggestion of eroticism." He observes, however, that this state of affairs was "probably not common" (359), and it hardly seems likely that it was possible for middle-class businessmen and professionals. Hawthorne clearly did not contemplate such intimacies without disgust, and his aversion bespeaks the stresses of a masculine character structure that emerged earliest in the urban Northeast.

6. See Eve Kosofsky Sedgwick, *Between Men,* 1–15, 83–96. David Greenberg enlarges this discussion instructively to include a treatment of the economic and social anxieties that entered the formation of homophobia, which, like masturbation phobia, was experienced predominantly by males (see 356–368, 386–390).

7. In *Melville,* Edwin H. Miller provides a searching discussion of this friendship, which he develops further from Hawthorne's point of view in *Salem Is My Dwelling Place,* 313–314, 351, 353–363. As themes in Melville's writing these issues have been instructively pursued by Robert K. Martin, in *Hero, Captain, and Stranger.* Martin's "Hester Prynne, *C'est Moi"* offers an illuminating treatment of the fascination and loathing with

which Hawthorne treats male-male desire, especially in the relation between Coverdale and Westervelt in *The Blithedale Romance.*

8. Sophia Hawthorne to Mary Mann, 16 May–7 June 1858 (Berg).

9. Sophia Hawthorne to her sister Elizabeth Palmer Peabody [1859?] (Berg).

10. Sophia Hawthorne to her sister Elizabeth Palmer Peabody, 24 April 1859 (Berg).

11. I have discussed Hilda's authority more fully in "The Erotics of Purity."

12. "Literary biography has few more ghastly tales than that of Hawthorne's enfeeblement," Richard Brodhead remarks, noting the image of "hideous incontinence" with which Hawthorne invoked his flounderings (*The School of Hawthorne,* 68–69, 197). An image of Hawthorne's inward loathing and horror in the late manuscripts is Dr. Portsoaken's monstrous pet spider, bloated with poison, which, occupying a huge flabby web, on signal let "himself down by a cord, which he extemporized out of his own bowels, and came dangling his huge bulk down before his master's face" (*The Elixir of Life Manuscripts,* 138).

EPILOGUE

1. Regarding Sarah, see Hawthorne, *Letters, 1813–1843,* 660. Sophia mentions Margaret in her letter to her mother, 9 November 1842 (Berg). For Ellen and Mary see Raymona Hull, *Nathaniel Hawthorne: The English Experience,* 6; and Hawthorne, *Letters 1853–1856,* 102n, 357.

2. Sophia Hawthorne to her mother, Elizabeth Palmer Peabody, 9 November 1842 (Berg).

3. Sophia Hawthorne to her mother, Elizabeth Palmer Peabody, 19–20 August 1844 and 13–14 January 1845 (Berg).

4. See Rita Gollin, "The Hawthorne's 'Golden Dora,' " 393, 398.

5. The Bancroft Library Portrait Collection has a dim retouched image dated 1855, also in the Essex Institute. The two others are the group picture in which Sophia spoiled her image and a photograph of her and Nathaniel in front of the Wayside, as remodeled in 1860, in which the figures are so small as to be unrecognizable.

6. See Rita Gollin, *Portraits of Nathaniel Hawthorne,* 43–45, 80–90. Sophia wrote to Annie Fields that she had the pictures of herself and the children made "for a very dear elderly lady, who is on her death-bed, but with love for her beloved so vivid still, that she is collecting them all into her beautiful clasped volume to hold in her hand and look at until her eyes close on mortal life. No other circumstances could have persuaded me to be photographed" (quoted in Gollin, *Portraits,* 89). Dora Golden was then thirty-six years old and lived until 1903, so she is not the expiring "elderly lady" Sophia invokes. Whether or not the pictures were made to complement the deathbed scene Sophia paints, her letter has the force of telling Annie she will not receive copies.

7. Una Hawthorne to Richard Manning, 25 July 1860 (Essex).

8. For a more complete discussion see my "Nathaniel Hawthorne, Una Hawthorne, and *The Scarlet Letter.*"

9. Sophia Hawthorne to Annie Fields, 14 December 1862 (Boston).

10. Sophia Hawthorne to Annie Fields, 13 and 18 April 1864 (Boston).

11. Sophia Hawthorne to Annie Fields, 29 April 1864 (Boston).

12. Sophia Hawthorne to Annie Fields, 20 May 1964 (Boston). Noted by Annie Fields as having been written "by Mrs. Nathaniel Hawthorne while her husband lay dead."

13. Edwin H. Miller discusses this lifelong dread in *Salem Is My Dwelling Place*, 19, 27, 515.

14. Nathaniel C. Peabody to Mrs. James (Dora Golden) Inwood, 11 October 1871. This letter is owned by Mrs. Barbara Bacheler, and is quoted with her permission.

15. On Storrow Higginson's view of marriage see the letter written by Nathaniel's sister Elizabeth Manning Hawthorne to "My dear Maria [Manning?]" on 20 February 1868, transcript by Marylou Birchmore, pp. 30–31 (Essex).

16. Una Hawthorne to Rebecca Manning, 16 April 1871 (Essex).

Works Cited

ARCHIVAL SOURCES

Bancroft   Bancroft Library, University of California, Berkeley. Hawthorne Family Papers (72/236 z)
       Hawthorne, Elizabeth Manning. Letters, manuscript copies.
       [Hawthorne,] Sophia Peabody. Letter in journal form to Miss Elizabeth Peabody, April–May 1838.

Beinecke   Beinecke Rare Book and Manuscript Library, Yale University. Norman Holmes Pearson Collection, Collection of American Literature
       Shepard, Ada. Letters to Clay Badger.

Boston   Boston Public Library, Department of Rare Books and Manuscripts
       Hawthorne, Elizabeth Manning. Letters.
       Hawthorne, Sophia Peabody. Letters to Annie Fields.

Essex   Essex Institute, Salem, Massachusetts. Hawthorne-Manning Collection
       Hawthorne, Elizabeth Manning. Letters. Transcribed by Marylou Birchmore, 1976.
       Hawthorne, Una. Letters.
       "Some Facts about Hawthorne." [Rebecca M. Manning.]
       Manning, Richard. Letters.

Massachusetts Historical Society. Channing Family Papers
       Channing, William Ellery. Letters.
       Fuller, Margaret. Commonplace Book, 1844.

New-York Historical Society. The Rogers Collection
       Rogers, John, Jr. Letters.

Berg   New York Public Library, Astor, Lenox and Tilden Foundations. Henry W.
            and Albert A. Berg Collection
                 Hawthorne, Elizabeth Manning. Letters.
                 [Hawthorne,] Sophia Peabody. Commonplace Book, 1835.
                 ———. Letters.
                 ———. Holograph Notebook, January–June 1835.
                 ———. Journal, Boston, 1 April–8 August 1829, with entries for 1831;
                 January–18 February 1832.
                 Hawthorne, Sophia Peabody. Journal, Rome, 14 February–15 March
                 1858.
                 ———. Journals, Italy. 5 vols, 17 March–21 October 1858.
                 ———. Letters.
                 ———. Remembrance of a visit to her grandmother, written in story
                 form.
                 Hawthorne, Una. Holograph Notebook, January–June 1835.
Morgan   Pierpont Morgan Library
                 Hawthorne, Nathaniel, and Sophia Peabody Hawthorne. Journal Dated
                 1842–1854. 2 vols. MA 569 and MA 580.

WORKS BY NATHANIEL HAWTHORNE

The American Claimant Manuscripts. Ed. Edward H. Davidson, Claude M. Simpson, and
    L. Neal Smith. Vol. 12, Centenary Edition, 1976.
The American Notebooks. Ed. Claude M. Simpson. Vol. 8, Centenary Edition, 1972.
The Blithedale Romance and Fanshawe. Ed. Fredson Bowers, Matthew J. Bruccoli, and
    L. Neal Smith. Vol. 3, Centenary Edition, 1964.
The Elixir of Life Manuscripts. Ed. Edward H. Davidson, Claude M. Simpson, and L. Neal
    Smith. Vol. 13, Centenary Edition, 1977.
The English Notebooks. Ed. Randall Stewart. New York: Russell & Russell, 1962.
The French and Italian Notebooks. Ed. Thomas Woodson. Vol. 14, Centenary Edition,
    1984.
Hawthorne's Lost Notebook, 1835–1841. Ed. Barbara S. Mouffe, intro. Hyatt Waggoner.
    University Park: Pennsylvania State University Press, 1978.
The House of the Seven Gables. Ed. Fredson Bowers, Matthew J. Bruccoli, and L. Neal
    Smith. Vol. 2, Centenary Edition, 1965.
The Letters, 1813–1843. Ed. Thomas Woodson, L. Neal Smith, and Norman Holmes
    Pearson. Vol. 15, Centenary Edition, 1984.
The Letters, 1843–1853. Ed. Thomas Woodson, L. Neal Smith, and Norman Holmes
    Pearson. Vol. 16, Centenary Edition, 1985.
The Letters, 1853–1856. Ed. Thomas Woodson, L. Neal Smith, James A. Rubino, and
    Norman Holmes Pearson. Vol. 17, Centenary Edition, 1987.
The Letters, 1857–1864. Ed. Thomas Woodson, James A. Rubino, L. Neal Smith, and
    Norman Holmes Pearson. Vol. 18, Centenary Edition, 1987.
The Marble Faun; or, the Romance of Monte Beni. Ed. Matthew J. Bruccoli and L. Neal
    Smith. Vol. 4, Centenary Edition, 1968.

Mosses from an Old Manse. Ed. Fredson Bowers, L. Neal Smith, John Manning, and J. Donald Crowley. Vol. 10, Centenary Edition, 1974.

"Mrs. Hutchinson." In *Fanshawe and Other Pieces.* Boston: Houghton Mifflin, 1876.

The Scarlet Letter. Ed. Fredson Bowers and Matthew J. Bruccoli. Vol. 1, Centenary Edition, 1962.

The Snow Image and Uncollected Tales. Ed. Fredson Bowers, L. Neal Smith, John Manning, and J. Donald Crowley. Vol. 11, Centenary Edition, 1974.

True Stories from History and Biography. Ed. Fredson Bowers, L. Neal Smith, and John Manning. Vol. 6, Centenary Edition, 1972.

A Wonder Book and Tanglewood Tales. Ed. Fredson Bowers, L. Neal Smith, and John Manning. Vol. 7, Centenary Edition 1972.

OTHER SOURCES

Ahlstrom, Sydney E. *A Religious History of the American People.* New Haven: Yale University Press, 1972.

Alcott, A. Bronson [and Elizabeth Palmer Peabody]. *Conversations with Children on the Gospels.* Boston: James Monroe, 1836.

Arac, Jonathan. "The Politics of *The Scarlet Letter.*" In *Ideology and Classic American Literature,* edited by Sacvan Bercovitch and Myra Jehlen, 247–266. Cambridge: Cambridge University Press, 1986.

Bailyn, Bernard. *The New England Merchants in the Seventeenth Century.* Cambridge: Harvard University Press, 1955.

Barker-Benfield, G. J. *The Horrors of the Half-Known Life.* New York: Harper and Row, 1976.

Basch, Norma. *In the Eyes of the Law: Women, Marriage, and Property in Nineteenth-Century New York.* Ithaca, N.Y.: Cornell University Press, 1982.

Bassan, Maurice. *Hawthorne's Son: The Life and Literary Career of Julian Hawthorne.* Columbus: Ohio State University Press, 1970.

———. "Julian Hawthorne Edits Aunt Ebe." *Essex Institute Historical Collections* 100(1964): 274–275.

Baym, Nina. "Hawthorne's Women: The Tyranny of Social Myths." *Centennial Review* 15(1971): 250–272.

———. "Nathaniel Hawthorne and His Mother: A Biographical Speculation." *American Literature* 54(1982): 2–27.

———. *The Shape of Hawthorne's Career.* Ithaca, N.Y.: Cornell University Press, 1976.

———. "Thwarted Nature: Nathaniel Hawthorne as Feminist." In *American Novelists Revisited: Essays in Feminist Criticism,* edited by Fritz Fleischmann, 58–77. Boston: G. K. Hall, 1982.

Bellah, Robert N., Richard Masden, William M. Sullivan, Ann Swidler, and Steven M. Tipton. *Habits of the Heart: Individualism and Commitment in American Life.* Berkeley and Los Angeles: University of California Press, 1985.

Bensick, Carol. "His Folly, Her Weakness: Demystified Adultery in *The Scarlet Letter.*" In *New Essays on The Scarlet Letter,* edited by Michael J. Colacurcio, 137–159. Cambridge: Cambridge University Press, 1985.

Bercovitch, Sacvan. *The Office of the Scarlet Letter.* Baltimore: Johns Hopkins University Press, 1991.

Berlant, Lauren. *The Anatomy of National Fantasy: Hawthorne, Utopia, and National Fantasy.* Chicago: University of Chicago Press, 1991.

Bledstein, Burton J. *The Culture of Professionalism: The Middle Class and the Development of Higher Education in America.* New York: Norton, 1978.

Boyer, Paul, and Stephen Nissenbaum. *Salem Possessed: The Social Origins of Witchcraft.* Cambridge: Harvard University Press, 1974.

Brantley, Richard. *Locke, Wesley, and the Method of English Romanticism.* Gainesville: University of Florida Press, 1984.

Breitwieser, Mitchell. *Despite Best Intentions: Religion, Mourning, and Ethnology in Mary Rowlandson's Captivity Narrative.* Cambridge: Cambridge University Press, 1990.

Bridge, Horatio. *Personal Recollections of Nathaniel Hawthorne.* New York: Harper, 1893.

Brisbane, Albert. *Social Destiny of Man; or, Association and Reorganization of Industry.* Philadelphia: Stollmeyer, 1840.

Brodhead, Richard H. *The School of Hawthorne.* New York: Oxford University Press, 1986.

―――. "Sparing the Rod: Discipline and Fiction in Antebellum America." *Representations* 21(1988): 67–96.

Brown, Gillian. *Domestic Individualism: Imagining Self in Nineteenth-Century America.* Berkeley: University of California Press, 1990.

―――. "Hawthorne, Inheritance, and Women's Property." *Studies in the Novel* 23(1991): 107–118.

Bushman, Richard L. *From Puritan to Yankee: Character and Social Order in Connecticut, 1690–1765.* Cambridge: Harvard University Press, 1967.

Calhoun, George P. *Report of the Counselling Surgeon on Spermatorrhea.* Philadelphia: Howard Association, 1858. Reprinted in Rosenberg and Smith-Rosenberg, *The Secret Vice Exposed!*

Carton, Evan. " 'A Daughter of the Puritans' and Her Old Master: Hawthorne, Una, and the Sexuality of Romance." In *Daughters and Fathers,* edited by Linda Boose and Betty Sue Flowers, 87–109. Baltimore: Johns Hopkins University Press, 1989.

Chevigny, Bell Gale. *The Woman and the Myth: Margaret Fuller's Life and Writings.* New York: Feminist Press, 1976.

Chodorow, Nancy. *The Reproduction of Mothering: Psychoanalysis and the Sociology of Gender.* Berkeley: University of California Press, 1985.

Colacurcio, Michael J. "Footsteps of Ann Hutchinson: The Context of *The Scarlet Letter.*" *English Literary History* 39(1972): 466–489.

―――. *The Province of Piety.* Cambridge: Harvard University Press, 1984.

―――. " 'The Woman's Own Choice': Sex, Metaphor, and the Puritan 'Sources' of *The Scarlet Letter.*" In *New Essays on The Scarlet Letter,* edited by Michael J. Colacurcio, 101–135. Cambridge: Cambridge University Press, 1985.

Cott, Nancy F. *The Bonds of Womanhood: "Woman's Sphere" in New England, 1780–1835.* New Haven, Conn.: Yale University Press, 1977.

―――. "Passionlessness: An Interpretation of Victorian Sexual Ideology, 1790–1850." In *A Heritage of Her Own: Toward a New Social History of American Women,* edited by Nancy F. Cott and Elizabeth H. Pleck, 162–181. New York: Simon and Schuster, 1979.

———, ed. *Root of Bitterness: Documents of the Social History of American Women.* New York: Dutton, 1972.

Craven, Wayne. *Sculpture in America.* Newark: University of Delaware Press, 1984.

Crews, Frederick. *The Sins of the Fathers: Hawthorne's Psychological Themes.* New York: Oxford University Press, 1966.

Crowley, J. Donald, ed. *Hawthorne: The Critical Heritage.* London: Routledge, 1970.

Csikszentmihalyi, Mihaly, and Eugene Rochberg-Halton. *The Meaning of Things: Domestic Symbols and the Self.* Cambridge: Cambridge University Press, 1981.

Degler, Carl N. *At Odds: Women and the Family in America from the Revolution to the Present.* New York: Oxford University Press, 1980.

D'Emilio, John, and Estelle B. Freedman. *Intimate Matters: A History of Sexuality in America.* New York: Harper and Row, 1988.

Demos, John. *A Little Commonwealth: Family Life in Plymouth Colony.* New York: Oxford University Press, 1970.

DeSalvo, Louise. *Nathaniel Hawthorne.* Atlantic Highlands, N.J.: Humanities Press International, 1987.

Deslandes, Leopold. *Manhood; the Causes of Its Premature Decline, with Directions for Its Perfect Restoration; Addressed to Those Suffering from the Destructive Effects of Excessive Indulgence, Solitary Habits, etc.* Boston, 1843.

Douglas, Ann. *The Feminization of American Culture.* New York: Avon Books, 1978.

Emerson, Ralph Waldo. *Selections from Ralph Waldo Emerson: An Organic Anthology.* Ed. Stephen E. Whicher. Boston: Houghton Mifflin, 1957.

Erlich, Gloria C. *Family Themes and Hawthorne's Fiction: The Tenacious Web.* New Brunswick, N.J.: Rutgers University Press, 1984.

Faragher, John Mack. *Women and Men on the Overland Trail.* New Haven, Conn.: Yale University Press, 1979.

Fields, James T. *Yesterdays with Authors.* Boston: James R. Osgood, 1872.

Fisher, Philip. Introduction to *The New American Studies: Essays from Representations.* Berkeley and Los Angeles: University of California Press, 1991.

Fliegelman, Jay. *Prodigals and Pilgrims: The American Revolution against Patriarchal Authority, 1750–1800.* Cambridge: Cambridge University Press, 1982.

Forgie, George. *Patricide in the House Divided: A Psychological Interpretation of Lincoln and His Age.* New York: Norton, 1979.

Foucault, Michel. *Discipline and Punish: The Birth of the Prison.* Trans. Allen Sheridan. New York: Vintage Books, 1977.

———. *The History of Sexuality, Vol. 1: An Introduction.* Trans. Robert Hurley. New York: Vintage Books, 1980.

Fox, Dixon Ryan. *The Decline of Aristocracy in the Politics of New York.* New York: Longmans Green, 1919.

Freud, Sigmund. "On the Psychical Mechanism of Hysterical Phenomena." In *Early Psychoanalytic Writings,* 35–50. Trans. Philip Rieff. New York: Collier, 1963.

Fuller, Margaret. *The Letters of Margaret Fuller.* Ed. Robert N. Hudspeth. 3 vols. to date. Ithaca, N.Y.: Cornell University Press, 1983–.

————. *Woman in the Nineteenth Century.* Intro. Bernard Rosenthal. New York: Norton, 1971.

Gadlin, Howard. "Private Lives and Public Order: A Critical View of the History of Intimate Relations in the U.S." *Massachusetts Review* 17(1976): 304–330.

Gardella, Peter. *Innocent Ecstasy: How Christianity Gave America an Ethic of Sexual Pleasure.* New York: Oxford University Press, 1985.

Gay, Peter. *The Education of the Senses.* Vol. 1 of *The Bourgeois Experience: Victoria to Freud.* New York: Oxford University Press, 1984.

————. *The Tender Passion.* Vol. 2 of *The Bourgeois Experience: Victoria to Freud.* New York: Oxford University Press, 1986.

Gilbert, Sandra M., and Susan Gubar. *The Madwoman in the Attic: The Woman Writer and the Nineteenth-Century Literary Imagination.* New Haven, Conn.: Yale University Press, 1979.

Gilman, Charlotte Perkins. *Women and Economics: A Study of the Economic Factor between Men and Women as a Factor in Social Evolution.* Ed. Carl Degler. New York: Harper Torchbooks, 1966.

————. "The Yellow Wallpaper." In *The Norton Anthology of Literature by Women,* edited by Sandra M. Gilbert and Susan Gubar, 1148–1161. New York: Norton, 1985.

Gilmore, Michael T. *American Romanticism and the Marketplace.* Chicago: University of Chicago Press, 1985.

Goddu, Teresa. "The Circulation of Women in *The House of the Seven Gables.*" *Studies in the Novel* 23(1991): 119–127.

Godwin, Parke. *A Popular View of the Doctrines of Charles Fourier.* New York: Redfield, 1844.

Gollin, Rita K. "The Hawthornes' 'Golden Dora.' " *Studies in the American Renaissance, 1981,* 393–401.

————. *Portraits of Nathaniel Hawthorne: An Iconography.* DeKalb: Northern Illinois University Press, 1983.

Gordon, Linda. *Heroes of Their Own Lives: The Politics and History of Family Violence, Boston, 1880–1960.* New York: Viking Press, 1988.

————. *Woman's Body, Woman's Right.* New York: Grossman, 1976.

Greenberg, David F. *The Construction of Homosexuality.* Chicago: University of Chicago Press, 1988.

Gregory, Samuel. *Facts and Important Information for Young Women on the Subject of Masturbation; with Its Causes, Prevention, and Cure.* Boston: George Gregory, 1845. Reprinted in Rosenberg and Smith-Rosenberg, *The Secret Vice Exposed!*

Greven, Philip. *The Protestant Temperament: Patterns of Child-Rearing, Religious Experience, and the Self in Early America.* New York: Knopf, 1977.

Gutwirth, Madelyn. *Madame de Staël, Novelist: The Emergence of the Woman as Artist.* Urbana: University of Illinois Press, 1978.

Haller, John and Robin Haller. *The Physician and Sexuality in Victorian America.* Urbana: University of Illinois Press, 1974.

Halttunen, Karen. *Confidence Men and Painted Women: A Study of Middle-Class Culture in America, 1830–1870.* New Haven, Conn.: Yale University Press, 1982.

Hawthorne, Julian. "The Making of 'The Scarlet Letter.'" *The Bookman* 74(1931): 401–411.

———. *Nathaniel Hawthorne and His Wife: A Biography.* 2 vols. Boston: Houghton Mifflin, 1884.

Hawthorne, Manning. "Hawthorne and 'The Man of God.'" *The Colophon* 2(1937): 262–278.

Hawthorne, Sophia Peabody. *The Cuba Journal, 1833–1835.* Ed. Claire Badaracco. 1981. Facsimile, Ann Arbor, Mich.: University Microfilms, 1985.

———. "A Sophia Hawthorne Journal, 1843–1844." Ed. John J. McDonald. *Nathaniel Hawthorne Journal* 4(1974): 1–30.

Heilbrun, Carolyn G. *Toward a Recognition of Androgyny.* New York: Knopf, 1973.

Henretta, James A. *The Evolution of American Society, 1700–1815: An Interdisciplinary Analysis.* Lexington, Mass.: Heath, 1973.

Herbert, T. Walter, Jr. "Doing Cultural Work: 'My Kinsman Major Molineux' and the Construction of the Self-Made Man." *Studies in the Novel* 23(1991): 20–27.

———. "The Erotics of Purity: *The Marble Faun* and the Victorian Construction of Sexuality." *Representations* 36(1991): 114–132.

———. "Nathaniel Hawthorne, Una Hawthorne, and *The Scarlet Letter:* Interactive Selfhoods and the Cultural Construction of Gender." *PMLA* 103(1988): 285–297.

Horwitz, Howard. "The Standard Oil Trust as Emersonian Hero." *Raritan* 6(1987): 97–119.

Hull, Raymona E. *Nathaniel Hawthorne: The English Experience, 1853–1864.* Pittsburgh: University of Pittsburgh Press, 1980.

———. "Una Hawthorne: A Biographical Sketch." *Nathaniel Hawthorne Journal* 6(1976): 87–119.

Idol, John L., Jr, and Sterling Eisiminger. "Hawthorne Sits for a Bust by Maria Louisa Lander." *Essex Institute Historical Collections* 114(1978): 207–212.

James, Henry. "Hawthorne." 1879. Reprinted in *The Shock of Recognition.* Ed. Edmund Wilson. New York: Modern Library, 1943, 425–565.

———. *William Wetmore Story and His Friends.* New York: Da Capo Press, 1969.

Jameson, Frederic. *The Political Unconscious: Narrative as a Socially Symbolic Act.* Ithaca, N.Y.: Cornell University Press, 1981.

Jehlen, Myra. *American Incarnation: The Individual, the Nation, and the Continent.* Cambridge: Harvard University Press, 1986.

———. "Introduction: Beyond Transcendence." In *Ideology and Classic American Literature,* edited by Sacvan Bercovitch and Myra Jehlen. Cambridge: Cambridge University Press, 1986.

Johnson, Paul E. *A Shopkeeper's Millennium: Society and Revivals in Rochester, New York, 1815–1837.* New York: Hill and Wang, 1978.

Kasson, Joy S. *Marble Queens and Captives: Women in Nineteenth-Century American Sculpture.* New Haven, Conn.: Yale University Press, 1990.

Kaye, Kenneth. *The Mental and Social Life of Babies: How Parents Create Persons.* Chicago: University of Chicago Press, 1982.

Kelley, Mary. *Private Woman, Public Stage: Literary Domesticity in Nineteenth-Century America.* New York: Oxford University Press, 1984.

Kerber, Linda K. *Women of the Republic: Intellect and Ideology in Revolutionary America.* Chapel Hill: University of North Carolina Press, 1980.

Kesterson, David B. *Critical Essays on Hawthorne's "The Scarlet Letter."* Boston: G. K. Hall, 1988.

Kohut, Heinz. *The Analysis of the Self: A Systematic Approach to the Psychoanalytic Treatment of Narcissistic Personality Disorders.* New York: International Universities Press, 1971.

Kolodney, Annette. Introduction to Nathaniel Hawthorne, *The Blithedale Romance.* New York: Penguin Books, 1983.

Kraditor, Aileen S. *Up from the Pedestal: Selected Writings in the History of American Feminism.* Chicago: Quadrangle Books, 1968.   .

Lacan, Jacques. *The Language of the Self: The Function of Language in Psychoanalysis.* Trans. Anthony Wilden. Baltimore: Johns Hopkins University Press, 1968.

Lang, Amy Schrager. *Prophetic Woman: Anne Hutchinson and the Problem of Dissent in the Literature of New England.* Berkeley and Los Angeles: University of California Press, 1987.

Lathrop, George Parsons. "Biographical Sketch." In Nathaniel Hawthorne, *Tales, Sketches, and Other Papers.* 1883. Reprint. Freeport, N.Y.: Books for Libraries Press, 1972.

———. *A Study of Hawthorne.* Boston: James R. Osgood, 1876.

Lathrop, Rose Hawthorne. *Memories of Hawthorne.* Boston: Houghton Mifflin, 1897.

Lebsock, Suzanne. *The Free Women of Petersburg: Status and Culture in a Southern Town, 1784–1860.* New York: Norton, 1984.

Leinwand, Theodore B. "Negotiation and New Historicism." *PMLA* 105(1990): 477–490.

Lerner, Gerda. *The Female Experience: An American Documentary.* Indianapolis, Ind.: Bobbs-Merrill, 1977.

Leverenz, David. *Manhood and the American Renaissance.* Ithaca, N.Y.: Cornell University Press, 1989.

Levinson, Daniel J. *The Seasons of a Man's Life.* New York: Ballantine Books, 1978.

Lévi-Strauss, Claude. *Symbolic Anthropology.* Trans. Claire Jacobson and Brooke Grundfest Schoepf. New York: Basic Books, 1963.

Lofland, Lyn. *A World of Strangers: Order and Action in Urban Public Space.* New York: Basic Books, 1973.

Loggins, Vernon. *The Hawthornes.* 1951. Reprint. New York: Greenwood, 1968.

Luedtke, Luther S. *Nathaniel Hawthorne and the Romance of the Orient.* Bloomington: Indiana University Press, 1989.

Mahler, Margaret S. *On Human Symbiosis and the Vicissitudes of Individuation.* New York: International Universities Press, 1968.

Mahler, Margaret S., Fred Paine, and Anni Bergman. *The Psychological Birth of the Human Infant: Symbiosis and Individuation.* New York: Basic Books, 1975.

Main, Jackson Turner. *The Social Structure of Revolutionary America.* Princeton, N.J.: Princeton University Press, 1965.

Mann, Horace. *A Few Thoughts for a Young Man: A Lecture Delivered before the Boston Mercantile Library Association, on Its Twenty-ninth Anniversary.* Boston: Ticknor, Reed and Fields, 1850.

Mann, Mrs. Horace [Mary Peabody]. "The Care of Little Children." *Herald of Health and Journal of Physical Culture* 11(1868): 241–246.

Mann, Mrs. Horace [Mary Peabody], and Elizabeth Palmer Peabody. *The Moral Culture of Infancy, and Kindergarten Guide.* Boston: Burnham, 1864.

Marks, Patricia. "Una Hawthorne's 'House for Orphans Tiny.' " *Emerson Society Quarterly* 25(1979): 3–22.

Marshall, Megan. "Two Early Poems by Mrs. Elizabeth Palmer Peabody." *Massachusetts Historical Society Proceedings* 100(1988): 40–59.

Martin, Robert K. *Hero, Captain, and Stranger: Male Friendship, Social Critique, and Literary Form in the Sea Novels of Herman Melville.* Chapel Hill: University of North Carolina Press, 1986.

———. "Hester Prynne, *C'est Moi:* Nathaniel Hawthorne and the Anxieties of Gender." In *Engendering Men: The Question of Male Feminist Criticism,* edited by Joseph A. Boone and Michael Cadden, 122–139. New York: Routledge, 1990.

Martineau, Harriet. "Marriage." *Harbinger* 4(December 1846): n.p.

Mason, John. *Self Knowledge: A Treatise Shewing the Nature and Benefit of That Important Science and the Way to Attain It.* 1744. Reprint. Boston: I. Thomas and E. T. Andrews, 1800.

Mellow, James R. *Nathaniel Hawthorne in His Times.* Boston: Houghton Mifflin, 1980.

Meyers, Marvin. *The Jacksonian Persuasion: Politics and Belief.* Stanford, Calif.: Stanford University Press, 1960.

Miller, Edwin Haviland. *Melville.* New York: Braziller, 1975.

———. *Salem Is My Dwelling Place: A Life of Nathaniel Hawthorne.* Iowa City: Iowa University Press, 1991.

Milton, John. "The Doctrine and Discipline of Divorce." In *The Prose of John Milton.* Ed. J. Max Patrick. Garden City, N.Y.: Doubleday, 1967.

Myerson, Joel. "Margaret Fuller's 1842 Journal: At Concord with the Emersons." *Harvard Library Bulletin* 21(1973): 320–340.

"The Myth of Una," *The Una* 2(1854): 212.

Nissenbaum, Stephen. "The Firing of Nathaniel Hawthorne." *Essex Institute Historical Collections* 114(1978): 57–86.

———. *Sex, Diet, and Debility in Jacksonian America: Sylvester Graham and Health Reform.* Westport, Conn.: Greenwood, 1980.

Norton, Mary Beth. "The Evolution of White Women's Experience in Early America." *The American Historical Review* 89(1984): 593–619.

Noyes, John Humphrey. *Male Continence.* Oneida, N.Y.: Office of the Oneida Circular, 1872. Reprinted in *Sexual Indulgence and Denial: Variations of Continence.* Ed. Charles Rosenberg and Carroll Smith-Rosenberg. New York: Arno Press, 1974.

Onania; or, the Heinous Sin of Self-Pollution. London, 1724. Reprinted in Rosenberg and Smith-Rosenberg, *The Secret Vice Exposed!*

Osborne, Martha Lee, ed. *Woman in Western Thought.* New York: Random House, 1979.

Peabody, Elizabeth Palmer. *Letters of Elizabeth Palmer Peabody: American Renaissance Woman.* Ed. Bruce A. Ronda. Middletown, Conn.: Wesleyan University Press, 1984.

[Peabody, Elizabeth Palmer, and] A. Bronson Alcott. *Conversations with Children on the Gospels.* Boston: James Monroe, 1836.

[Peabody, Mrs. Elizabeth Palmer]. *Holiness; or, the Legend of St. George: A Tale from Spenser's Faerie Queene, by a Mother.* Boston: E. R. Broaders, 1836.

Pearson, Norman Holmes. "Elizabeth Peabody on Hawthorne." *Essex Institute Historical Collections* 94(1958): 256–276.

Person, Leland S., Jr. *Aesthetic Headaches: Women and Masculine Poetics in Poe, Melville, and Hawthorne.* Athens: University of Georgia Press, 1988.

———. "Hawthorne's Bliss of Paternity: Sophia's Absence from 'The Old Manse.' " *Studies in the Novel* 23(1991): 46–59.

Porter, Carolyn. "Are We Being Historical Yet?" *South Atlantic Quarterly* 87(1988): 743–786.

"Prospectus." *The Una,* 1(1853): 1.

Reynolds, David. *Beneath the American Renaissance: The Subversive Imagination in the Age of Emerson and Melville.* New York: Knopf, 1988.

Reynolds, Larry J. *European Revolutions and the American Literary Renaissance.* New Haven: Yale University Press, 1988.

Ricci, Corrado. *Beatrice Cenci.* Trans. Morris Bishop and Henry Longan Stuart. 2 vols. New York: Boni and Liveright, 1925.

Rogin, Michael Paul. *Fathers and Children: Andrew Jackson and the Subjugation of the American Indian.* New York: Knopf, 1975.

———. *Subversive Genealogy: The Politics and Art of Herman Melville.* New York: Knopf, 1983.

Root of Bitterness: Documents of the Social History of American Women. Ed. Nancy Cott. New York: Dutton, 1972.

Rose, Anne C. *Transcendentalism as a Social Movement, 1830–1850.* New Haven, Conn.: Yale University Press, 1981.

Rose, Henry. *An Inaugural Dissertation on the Effects of the Passions upon the Body.* Philadelphia, 1794.

Rosenberg, Charles. "Sexuality, Class, and Role in Nineteenth-Century America," *American Quarterly* 25(1973): 131–153.

Rosenberg, Charles, and Carroll Smith-Rosenberg, eds. *The Secret Vice Exposed! Some Arguments against Masturbation.* New York: Arno Press, 1974.

Rothman, Ellen K. *Hands and Hearts: A History of Courtship in America.* New York: Basic Books, 1984.

Ryan, Mary. *Cradle of the Middle Class: The Family in Oneida County, New York, 1790–1865.* Cambridge: Cambridge University Press, 1981.

———. *The Empire of the Mother: American Writing about Domesticity, 1830–1860.* New York: Haworth Press, 1982.

Ryskamp, Charles. "The New England Sources of *The Scarlet Letter.*" In *Twentieth Century Interpretations of The Scarlet Letter,* edited by John C. Gerber, 19–34. Englewood Cliffs, N.J.: Prentice-Hall, 1968.

Scharnhorst, Gary. " 'Now You Can Write Your Book': Two Myths in Hawthorne Biography." *Nathaniel Hawthorne Review* 15(1989): 6–9.

Schlesinger, Arthur M. *The Age of Jackson.* Boston: Little, Brown, 1950.

Schneider, David. *American Kinship: A Cultural Account.* 2d ed. Chicago: University of Chicago Press, 1980.

Schumpeter, Joseph A. *Capitalism, Socialism, and Democracy.* 3d ed. New York: Harper Torchbooks, 1962.

Schwartz, Joel. *The Sexual Politics of Jean-Jacques Rousseau.* Chicago: University of Chicago Press, 1984.

The Secret Vice Exposed! Some Arguments against Masturbation. Ed. Charles Rosenberg and Carroll Smith-Rosenberg. New York: Arno Press, 1974.

Sedgwick, Eve Kosofsky. *Between Men: English Literature and Male Homosocial Desire.* New York: Columbia University Press, 1985.

Showalter, Elaine. *Women, Madness, and English Culture, 1830–1980.* New York: Pantheon Books, 1985.

Sigourney, Lydia H. *Letters to Mothers.* New York: Harper and Brothers, 1845.

Sklar, Kathryn Kish. *Catharine Beecher: A Study in American Domesticity.* New Haven, Conn.: Yale University Press, 1973.

Smith, Daniel Scott. "Family Limitation, Sexual Control, and Domestic Feminism in Victorian America." In *A Heritage of Her Own: Toward a New Social History of American Women,* edited by Nancy F. Cott and Elizabeth H. Pleck, 222–245. New York: Simon and Schuster, 1979.

Smith-Rosenberg, Carroll. *Disorderly Conduct: Visions of Gender in Victorian America.* New York: Knopf, 1985.

Spenser, Edmund. *The Faerie Queene.* Intro. J. W. Hales. 2 vols. London: J. M. Dent, 1955.

Staël, Madame [Germaine] de. *Corinne; or, Italy.* Trans. Isabel Hill. Philadelphia: David McKay, n.d.

Stewart, Randall. "Recollections of Hawthorne by His Sister Elizabeth." *American Literature* 16(1945): 316–331.

Stoehr, Taylor. *Hawthorne's Mad Scientists: Pseudoscience and Social Science in Nineteenth-Century Life and Letters.* Hamden, Conn.: Archon Books, 1978.

Stone, Lawrence. *The Family, Sex, and Marriage in England, 1500–1800.* Abridged ed. New York: Harper Colophon, 1975.

Strouse, Jean. *Alice James: A Biography.* Boston: Houghton Mifflin, 1980.

Sundquist, Eric. *Home as Found: Authority and Genealogy in Nineteenth-Century American Literature.* Baltimore: Johns Hopkins University Press, 1979.

Tharp, Louisa Hall. *The Peabody Sisters of Salem.* Boston: Little, Brown, 1950.

Thomas, Brook. *Cross-Examinations of Law and Literature: Cooper, Hawthorne, Stowe, and Melville.* Cambridge: Cambridge University Press, 1987.

Thoreau, Henry David. *Walden and Civil Disobedience.* Ed. Sherman Paul. Boston: Houghton Mifflin, 1957.

Tissot, Samuel A. A. D. *A Discourse on Onanism.* New York, 1832. Reprinted in Rosenberg and Smith-Rosenberg, *The Secret Vice Exposed!*

Tocqueville, Alexis de. *Democracy in America.* 2 vols. Trans. Henry Reeve. Revised by Francis Bowen. Ed. Phillips Bradley. New York: Knopf, 1976.

Tolchin, Neal. *Mourning, Gender, and Creativity in the Art of Herman Melville.* New Haven, Conn.: Yale University Press, 1988.

Tompkins, Jane. Afterword to Susan Warner, *The Wide, Wide World.* New York: Feminist Press, 1987.

————. *Sensational Designs: The Cultural Work of American Fiction, 1790–1860.* New York: Oxford University Press, 1985.

The Transcendentalists. Ed. Perry Miller. Cambridge: Harvard University Press, 1950.

Turner, Arlin. *Nathaniel Hawthorne: A Biography.* New York: Oxford University Press, 1980.

Turner, Victor. *Dramas, Fields, and Metaphors: Symbolic Action in Human Society.* Ithaca, N.Y.: Cornell University Press, 1974.

————. *The Ritual Process: Structure and Anti-Structure.* Chicago: Aldine, 1969.

Valenti, Patricia. "Sophia Peabody Hawthorne's Continuation to 'Christabel.' " *Nathaniel Hawthorne Review* 13(1987): 14–16.

————. *To Myself a Stranger: A Biography of Rose Hawthorne Lathrop.* Baton Rouge: Louisiana State University Press, 1991.

Wadlington, Warwick. *Reading Faulknerian Tragedy.* Ithaca, N.Y.: Cornell University Press, 1987.

Wagenknecht, Edward. *Nathaniel Hawthorne: Man and Writer.* New York: Oxford University Press, 1961.

Walker, Williston. *A History of the Christian Church.* Revised by Cyril C. Richardson, Wilhelm Pauck, and Robert L. Handy. New York: Scribner, 1959.

Warner, Susan. *The Wide, Wide World.* Afterword by Jane Tompkins. New York: Feminist Press, 1987.

Warren, Joyce W. *The American Narcissus: Individualism and Women in Nineteenth-Century American Fiction.* New Brunswick, N.J.: Rutgers University Press, 1984.

Welter, Barbara. *Dimity Convictions: The American Woman in the Nineteenth Century.* Athens: Ohio University Press, 1976.

Whicher, Stephen E., ed. *Selections from Ralph Waldo Emerson: An Organic Anthology.* Boston: Houghton Mifflin, 1957.

Whigham, Frank. "Sexual and Social Mobility in *The Duchess of Malfi.*" *PMLA* 100(1985): 167–186.

Wiebe, Robert H. *The Opening of American Society: From the Adoption of the Constitution to the Eve of Disunion.* New York: Vintage Books, 1984.

Willi, Jurg. *Couples in Collusion.* New York: Aronson, 1982.

Winnicott, D. W. *The Family and Individual Development.* London. Tavistock, 1965.

Wollstonecraft, Mary. *A Vindication of the Rights of Woman [1792].* New York: Norton, 1975.

Wood, Gordon, *The Creation of the American Republic, 1776–1787.* New York: Norton, 1969.

Woodward, Samuel Bayard. *Hints for the Young in Relation to the Health of Body and Mind.* Boston: G. W. Light, 1856. Reprinted in Rosenberg and Smith-Rosenberg, *The Secret Vice Exposed!*

Wyllie, Irvin G. *The Self-Made Man in America: The Myth of Rags to Riches.* New Brunswick, N.J.: Rutgers University Press, 1954.

Yeazell, Ruth Bernard, ed. *The Death and Letters of Alice James.* Berkeley and Los Angeles: University of California Press, 1981.

Yellin, Jean Fagan. *Women and Sisters: The Antislavery Feminists in American Culture.* New Haven, Conn.: Yale University Press, 1989.

Young, Philip. *Hawthorne's Secret: An Un-told Tale.* Boston: Godine, 1984.

Index

Designer: Barbara Jellow
Compositor: ComCom, Inc., Division of Haddon Craftsmen
Text: Garamond Simonici
Display: Garamond Simonici
Printer: Haddon Craftsmen
Binder: Haddon Craftsmen